WHAT HAPPENED
IN OHIO?

WHAT HAPPENED IN OHIO?

A DOCUMENTARY RECORD OF THEFT AND FRAUD IN THE 2004 ELECTION

Robert J. Fitrakis
Steven Rosenfeld
Harvey Wasserman

THE NEW PRESS

NEW YORK
LONDON

Requests for permission to reproduce selections from this book should be mailed to:
Permissions Department, The New Press, 38 Greene Street, New York, NY 10013.

Published in the United States by The New Press, New York, 2006
Distributed by W. W. Norton & Company, Inc., New York

ISBN-13: 978-1-59558-069-6 (pbk.)
ISBN-10: 1-59558-069-7 (pbk.)
CIP data available.

The New Press was established in 1990 as a not-for-profit alternative to the large, commercial publishing houses currently dominating the book publishing industry. The New Press operates in the public interest rather than for private gain, and is committed to publishing, in innovative ways, works of educational, cultural, and community value that are often deemed insufficiently profitable.

www.thenewpress.com

Composition by Westchester Book Group
This book was set in Janson

Printed in the United States of America

2 4 6 8 10 9 7 5 3 1

Contents

I can tell you right now that if we hadn't had the preparation that we did have, it would have been a catastrophe.
—Ohio Secretary of State, Republican J. Kenneth Blackwell, testifying before the House Committee on Administration, field hearing in Columbus, Ohio, March 21, 2005

Acknowledgments

This book is the end-product of a long road that began well before Election Day 2004.

Bob Fitrakis would like to thank Rady Ananda for both her research assistance and analysis. Dr. Victoria Lovegren's data on Cleveland voter purges proved invaluable, as well as her insights on election activities in Cuyahoga County. Dr. Ron Baiman offered many useful insights on exit polling as well as detailed investigative reports on election irregularities in southwest Ohio. Cliff Arnebeck provided key analytical perspectives and consistent encouragement. Dorri Steinhoff spent many hours pouring over data from Lucas County and relaying her findings to me and other editors. My wife, Suzanne Patzer, as usual, bailed out the project through her tireless efforts when all looked lost. The individual who bore the brunt of the responsibility for scanning the documents in this book was the indefatigable Byron Bird-Conliff. I also need to thank my co-authors on this book: Steven Rosenfeld, who willed the book to completion through long hours of toil and Harvey Wasserman, my longtime comrade and co-conspirator. I would also like to thank Joel Ariaratnam and Diane Wachtell of The New Press, who refused to give up on this project even when it was long overdue. Finally, I must acknowledge that the genesis of this project, particularly the collecting of documents, came as the result of an idea and a generous grant from John Irwin, who also provided funds for us to keep our doors open at the *Free Press*.

Steven Rosenfeld would like to thank everyone in Ohio, starting with Cliff Arnebeck, Bob Fitrakis, Amy Kaplan, and Jonathan Meier, for allowing a national radio producer to put what happened in Ohio on the air as the major media turned the page after November 2, 2004. The initial tip came from Bill Stetson, who said to call Miles Gerety, a Connecticut public defender who was in Columbus. Air America hosts Laura Flanders and Randi Rhodes helped by raising money for an election challenge lawsuit. Ronnie Dugger's Alliance for Democracy helped us get going. Ted Kalo in Rep. John Conyers office invited us to brief congressional Democrats, and then a collaborative process began with Bob Fitrakis and Harvey Wasserman, leading to numerous FreePress.org reports, and ultimately, to this book. That would not have happened without Suzanne Patzer.

The evidence in this volume would not have been possible without the research of many people working with the Columbus Institute of Contemporary Journalism, most notably Richard Hayes Phillips, and others such as Ron Baiman. The clarity of this book owes much to The New Press's Diane Wachtell, who embraced this project from day one and is one of the best editors I've known, and The New Press's Joel Ariaratnam. I'd also like to thank John and Bill Moyers for their enduring encouragement, and my family and colleagues for their support of a long and exacting process.

Harvey Wasserman thanks his wife Susan for the love and support that make it possible for him to do this work, and our wonderful daughters Rachel, Annie, Abbie, Julie, and Shoshanna, our grandchildren and grand-niece, and the rest of our extended family for constantly reminding us why democracy must be preserved.

Bob Fitrakis and Suzanne Patzer are the quintessential collaborators, keeping the Free Press and Freepress.org alive as the only outlet that would initially carry this story. Were it not for the Internet (and our mystery webmaster) the mainstream media would have rendered this a total non-story. Bev Harris and Greg Palast set the informational foundation with their work on Florida 2000, and MotherJones.com carried the first Ohio story when we saw it coming in the spring of 2004, long before the actual election.

Diane Wachtell has done more than just superbly edit this book, she has made history. Our co-author Steven Rosenfeld labored long and hard with her to get this done, along with Joel Ariaratnam and the rest of The New Press team. Lori Grace and Avi Peterson have been crucially and brilliantly supportive. Robert F. Kennedy, Jr., and the editors of *Rolling Stone* had the wisdom and courage to finally take this story into the mainstream. The Rev. Jesse Jackson and Rep. John Conyers have been essential from the start. Rep. Stephanie Tubbs Jones and Sen. Barbara Boxer made possible the first challenge to a state's Electoral College delegation. Rep. Lynn Woolsey allowed Bob and I to brief the Congressional Progressive Caucus.

Also essential have been Mark C. Miller, Rady Ananda, Ron Baiman, Steve Freeman, Brad Friedman, Nancy Tobi and family, Victoria Lovegren, Victoria Parks, Bob Koehler, Andy Ostroy, Danny Schechter, Rene Krause, Rory O'Connor, Peter B. Collins, Dorothy Fadiman, Jim and Mary Beth Heddle from EON, Christopher Hitchens, Keith Olbermann, Cliff and Sibley Arnebeck, Richard Hayes Philips, Dorri Steinhoff, Ilene Proctor, Kat L'Estrange, Cindy Sheehan, Mary Ellen Starr, Medea Benjamin, Thea and Adam Paneth, Laurie Bratz, the Urda family, the Rocky Mountain Peace and Justice Center, the World Fellowship Center, the Mainstream Media Project, the Waterkeepers, Commondreams.org, Counterpunch.org, and so many others.

Howard Zinn showed his usual integrity and genius in immediately grasping the importance of this story. To Paul and Sheila Wellstone, for all they were and might have done to prevent this from happening again. And to the people of Ukraine, Mexico and everywhere else stolen elections are effectively resisted. May our own nation finally join them.

List of Documents

Chapter 1

Chapter 5

WHAT HAPPENED
IN OHIO?

Introduction

Can presidential elections be stolen in twenty-first-century America?

The answer is yes—but it is not a simple yes, with a simple explanation, because elections are not simple affairs. Stealing a contemporary American election—and having the theft go largely unnoticed by the major media—requires a systematic targeting of every stage of the election process, starting many months, if not years, before Election Day. It requires some luck, such as a national political landscape that ends in a final swing state where partisans control the electoral process and have been planning and working for months. And it requires an opposition political party that wages no effective counter-campaign on behalf of its voters and ticket.

In America's 2004 presidential election, these factors all came into play in Ohio. This book tells the story of what happened in Ohio, where perhaps the nation's most partisan secretary of state, Republican J. Kenneth Blackwell, systematically steered his state's election laws and voting machinery to benefit Republicans and to reelect President George W. Bush. These efforts harmed not just the Democratic Party, its voters, and nominee John Kerry, but the democratic process itself.

Ohio in 2004 was not a replay of Florida in 2000, although there are some echoes. Both states had secretaries of state who also co-chaired Republican presidential campaigns. And both states saw deliberate targeting of minority voters, such as Florida's pre-2000 election voter roll purges of African American voters wrongly identified as felons. But Ohio in 2004 was a far more concerted effort, where Republicans intentionally targeted every stage of the election process in a steady, cumulative effort intended to suppress Democratic turnout, disqualify or reject their votes, and stuff ballots in Republican strongholds. The minority voters who waited for hours in the rain in Ohio's largely democratic cities on November 2, 2004, were only the most visible consequence of this effort. This book shows how it was done.

Our motivation is not to vindicate John Kerry's 2004 campaign. The stakes are larger. The vote is the basis for all other democratic rights. Without meaningful elections, our system of checks and balances unwinds. American elections have never been pristine affairs, but our history has shown a steady progress toward greater participation and accountability. What makes Ohio's 2004 election so disturbing is that Republicans effectively *turned back the clock*, reviving playbooks from the Jim Crow era—when blacks and minorities were targeted with impunity—and also from the Boss Tweed heyday of ballot stuffing and fraudulent vote counts, to "win" in an election that was neither free, fair, nor honestly counted.

While book authors are often dismissive of work on their topic by others, the authors of this book are heartened by the recent appearance of other books and articles making the case that the 2004 election was stolen. Indeed, the authors of this book have tried, largely without success, in the two years since the election, to engage the country's major media in uncovering and reporting on the problems that plagued the election process in Ohio. One exception was Air America Radio hosts Laura Flanders and Randi Rhodes, whose advocacy helped raise $120,000 to fund an election challenge lawsuit filed at Ohio's Supreme Court and to pay for much of the investigation first reported on FreePress.org and in this book. This book's authors have also provided primary source material to authors of other works on this topic in an effort to help ensure the arguments they make are fair and substantiated.

Beginning with the excellent account "Preserving Democracy: What Went Wrong in Ohio," the January 2005 report by the House Judiciary Committee Democratic staff; and going on to include *Fooled Again: How the Right Stole the 2004 Election and Why They'll Steal the Next One Too (Unless We Stop Them)*, by Mark Crispin Miller; *Was the 2004 Presidential Election Stolen?: Exit Polls, Election Fraud, and the*

Official Count, by Steven F. Freeman and Joel Bleifus; *Armed Madhouse*, by Greg Palast; and a June 2006 article in *Rolling Stone* titled "Was the 2004 Election Stolen?" by Robert F. Kennedy Jr.; an increasing number of analysts are reaching the same conclusions: the 2004 presidential election was stolen.

What this book adds to the available analysis is the primary source documentation on which these analyses are based. The documents in this book—many of which are made available here to the general public for the first time—include statements taken under oath, provided by poll workers and frustrated voters; screen shots of exit poll results on election night; precinct-by-precinct vote tallies; official directives and memos from Secretary Blackwell to the heads of Ohio boards of election (BOEs) outlining (and then changing) procedures for counting votes; congressional testimony by BOE officials saying how they were threatened and intimidated by Blackwell; letters and postcards from Republican ("Grand Old Party," or GOP) partisans telling citizens their vote would be challenged or voided, and misinformation about when and where to vote on Election Day; affidavits from BOE whistleblowers who were fired for complaining about the fact that private GOP-connected firms had access to key vote-counting machinery; and copies of actual ballots themselves that point to several varieties of vote-count fraud.

The full versions of documents that are excerpted here have been posted at www.openelections.org. By reading this primary data in conjunction with the analysis provided here and elsewhere, readers can arrive at their own, informed opinions of what happened in Ohio. Is there sufficient, on-the-ground evidence to show that enough votes were taken from the Democrats and shifted to the GOP in 2004 Ohio to change the outcome of the election? In an election decided by 118,775 votes counted out of nearly 5.7 million cast, the documents and explanations presented in this book show that the answer is yes.

Sworn, first-person statements and public testimony show the tremendous problems that deprived thousands of registered Democrats of their right to vote. Though public calls were issued for comparable statements from Bush supporters, no such complaints arose from Republican precincts or individual voters. Various studies, figuring conservatively, conclude that at least 2 percent of the electorate— 113,000 voters—did not vote because of long lines created by shortages of voting machines, ballot problems, and other discouragements, deliberate and otherwise.

Public records, sworn statements, and precinct-by-precinct analysis of voting results show how Kerry lost 39,500 votes from a variety of voter suppression tactics in just three cities: Columbus, Cleveland, and Toledo, where pro-Kerry margins in many of the precincts in which those votes would have been cast were as high as 90 percent. Under the direction of Secretary of State Blackwell, election administrators went further and disqualified or did not count 129,000 ballots, which conservatively cost Democrats an estimated 26,000 or more votes from the 82,806 regular paper ballots alone (the balance are rejected electronic votes and provisional ballots). This came after selectively purging 196,000 people from voter rolls in two counties, which cost Kerry more than 4,700 votes.

Additionally, sworn testimonials and precinct-by-precinct analyses reveal how new electronic voting machines failed or—more plausibly—were manipulated in various ways. In Youngstown, dozens of machines registered Bush votes even when Kerry's name was selected. Those machines were kept in use all day, costing Democrats 2,250 votes in that city alone. Another 18,615 votes were mysteriously added to totals in Miami County after 100 percent of the precincts had reported, increasing Bush's margin by 6,000 votes. More than 3,300 provisional ballots were rejected in the Democratic strongholds of Cleveland and Cincinnati because people turned them in at the correct building, but wrong table. These are but a few examples of election anomalies that had the effect of tilting the field in George W. Bush's favor. (No such anomalies have been documented favoring Kerry, another reason to conclude the problems were deliberate.)

Finally, we show how reported results from Republican strongholds can be explained only by election fraud. Perhaps the most glaring example of vote count fraud are 10,500 voters from three counties in southwest Ohio's Bible Belt, whose ballots were read to register votes both *for* gay marriage (by opposing a proposed statewide constitutional amendment banning it) and for George W. Bush. In one of those southwest counties, Warren County, a "level 10" homeland security alert was declared on Election Night. Ballots were taken to a warehouse and counted out of the view of the public and press. When that county reported its results—the last in Ohio to do so—it gave the president a 14,000-vote boost. When the authors of this book were allowed to examine ballots from a dozen Warren County precincts in spring 2006, we saw how a simple swap of ballots between precincts during the vote count, while the media and observers were barred from the counting arena, could produce such far-fetched results.

In these three critical southwestern Ohio counties, similar anomalies surround the vote count for the Democratic candidate for chief justice of the Ohio Supreme Court, C. Ellen Connally, a retired African American judge from Cleveland. Certified results showed Connally with 5,000 more votes than Kerry, in a race for chief justice that statewide drew 1.2 million fewer votes than the presidential contest. Such an outcome is a virtual statistical impossibility, and indicates a very significant shaving of votes from the Democratic presidential tally. In fact, with their stunning range of irregularities and anomalies, these three counties alone provided Bush with his entire margin of victory in Ohio.

Our analysis of the results in 9,300 of Ohio's 11,300 precincts found Bush's total was probably inflated by nearly 53,000 votes in Republican strongholds. If the certified results are to be believed, Ohio's GOP-majority counties or locales saw unprecedented, near-perfect turnouts in the 95-plus percent range, while Democratic urban strongholds, using the same voting machines and vote-counting technologies, had turnouts hovering around 50 percent. Needless to say, no other areas of the country experienced this kind of disparity.

The November 2 exit poll by the major national television networks (ABC, CBS, CNN, Fox, NBC) and the Associated Press indicated that Bush's totals in Ohio would be far lower than the certified results, a further suggestion of vote count fraud. Until shortly after midnight on November 3, 2004, the National Election Pool exit poll—the most sophisticated in American politics—projected a Kerry victory nationally and in Ohio. The networks and their two polling firms still have not released all of their 2004 data, instead offering the explanation that more Kerry than Bush voters spoke to pollsters, thereby skewing the results. This book includes data refuting that claim along with statistical analysis showing why the numbers in the certified vote, not the exit polls, are suspect.

Our overall methodology was simple and conservative. We did what no national news organization did after the election: examine the available statewide record to determine who voted and who was not accommodated. And then we asked why. The voter turnout statistics begin to tell that story. We looked at conditions in neighboring precincts, within the same cities, and saw big disparities between how many voting machines per capita were deployed to Democratic versus Republican strongholds. We saw similar disparities with voter purges, ballot rejection rates, and use of provisional ballots; all were far higher in historically Democratic regions. Then we did the math, projecting how many additional Democratic votes would have been cast if voters in the same locales had been treated equally.

This approach is fundamentally conservative because there were a handful of Democratic strongholds in Ohio cities where conditions *were* similar to nearby Republican precincts. Indeed, there were locales where Democrats had ample voting machines or did not face undue administrative or partisan challenges. As a result, the turnout, voter accommodation rates, ballot rejection rates, and other indices were on par with nearby GOP strongholds.

In chronicling the range of problems, we tried to maintain a sense of scale. Voter purges have a much bigger impact than threatening phone calls to ex-felons, for example. Most election accounts lack this sense of magnitude and proportionality. Where possible, we also try to explain votes that do not add up or make political sense. In some cases, however, we do not precisely know—not because the evidence does not or did not exist, but rather because Ohio's Republican secretary of state and attorney general aggressively shut down the evidence trail in the weeks after the 2004 election. One of this book's co-authors, Robert Fitrakis, was one of four lawyers who, in December 2004, filed an election challenge lawsuit of Ohio's presidential results. Some documentation in this book derives from litigation, where evidence standards are higher than those used by the media. The balance of our evidence comes from public election records, campaign materials, or analyses of official results.

Our reporting ended in July 2006, when some local prosecutors were still fighting our requests to view ballots and election records. Ohio's secretary of state told countywide election boards to forward public record requests to local law enforcement, another intimidation tactic and indication of the ongoing partisan administration of elections in the state. In a handful of other Republican-majority counties—Warren, Delaware, and Miami Counties—access to the ballots themselves confirmed our conclusions in the precinct-by-precinct analyses, and suggested explanations for vote-count fraud.

It is important to comment on the role computer hacking played in the 2004 vote count. Although no one has proven election software was tampered with, employees of private voting-machine companies had access to the computers just before the election. But there has been no independent audit of the machines, no questioning of these private employees under oath, and these computers have been used in subsequent elections, thwarting further inquiry. Though computer hacking cannot be proven based on the available public record, it is one theory to explain results that defy political logic.

But there is a larger point: what happened in Ohio was primarily the result of old-school, Jim Crow– and Boss Tweed–era election thuggery. In the 2004 cycle, most of Ohio voted using paper punch-card and optical-scan ballots. The big-picture story of Ohio's 2004 election is how Republicans targeted every stage of the election process in a determined, cumulative effort to undermine Democrat votes through a thousand points of deceit and fraud.

This book is organized into chapters following the election's timeline. In each chapter, an initial narrative is followed by documentation or source material and related analysis. The documents are preceded by editor's notes explaining their significance.

Chapter 1 documents the targeting of the voter registration process, voter intimidation tactics, organization of precincts, and implementation of new ballot-rejection rules before Election Day. Chapter 2 recounts the chaos of Election Day, when many thousands of Ohioans, nearly all Democrats, expected to vote but were not accommodated. Chapter 3 reviews the discrepancy between the network television exit poll and the official reported results and explains why the gap is a statistical impossibility. Chapter 4 estimates the impact of the various partisan tactics on the vote count: repressing the Democratic numbers and inflating Bush's totals. Chapter 5 describes a flawed and incomplete recount that occurred after Ohio's Republican Electoral College members had already met and voted to reelect the president.

This book catalogs Republican abuses of the election process, and a corresponding disengagement from this part of the political process by Democrats. Our research, though still an incomplete accounting, offers more than a cautionary tale. The pain and anguish that tens of thousands of Democratic voters in Ohio experienced on Election Day 2004 was very real. But ultimately, it is the documents and analysis, not our opinions, that speak the loudest. We have attempted to compile the most complete record of the essential evidence from Ohio's 2004 election. As befits a healthy democracy, it is for you, the reader, to draw your own conclusions from the available (and to date unavailable) evidence. If American democracy is to withstand the test of time, there can be no other way.

1

Suppressing the Vote

The story of what happened in Ohio in the 2004 presidential election does not start on Election Day. It begins many months before with an explanation of how Ohio Secretary of State J. Kenneth Blackwell, a partisan Republican and the co-chairman of the Bush-Cheney 2004 Ohio campaign, selectively used his power and authority as Ohio's chief election administrator to suppress and disenfranchise mostly Democratic voters.

Ohio's secretary of state has constitutional authority to issue directives on election procedures: from the voter registration process; to how votes are counted or disqualified on Election Day; to any recount that might ensue. He also has the authority to decide how federal election funds can be spent, whether for public education campaigns or replacing old voting machines. And he can decide how and when to update and make public the state's voter registration, precinct, and poll records.

At the time of the 2004 election, Blackwell was in his sixth year as Ohio's chief election officer and was overseeing his second presidential election, having served as a Bush election advisor in Florida in the aftermath of the 2000 presidential election. The documents in this chapter will show that Blackwell used his constitutional authority—as Ohio secretary of state—to create a cascading series of conditions that would suppress Democratic voter registration, thwart likely Democratic voters from casting ballots, keep "alternative" or provisional ballots from being counted, and skew the 2004 presidential vote in favor of Republicans.

Critical to understanding what happened in the lead-up to the 2004 election is the story of the network of eighty-eight county boards of election (BOEs), whose members, with equal membership from both political parties, serve at Secretary of State Blackwell's pleasure. One of the big myths of what happened in Ohio in 2004 is that these boards, particularly in the counties with the state's biggest cities, were bipartisan, and as such, an effective counter or balance on the secretary's administrative powers. The political reality is both more nuanced and harsher.

While representatives of both parties do sit on the BOEs, Ohio's secretary of state can dismiss board of election officials for not following his administrative orders and directives, a situation that effectively renders the term "bipartisan" meaningless. As several of the following documents show—from Blackwell's letters to top county election officers to statements by BOE officials at congressional hearings about Blackwell's firing powers and threats—he freely wielded his constitutional authority in the 2004 election, threatening, for example, to fire the entire Cuyahoga County (Cleveland) Board of Elections if it did not do his bidding. (Of course, Blackwell did not work alone; he was assisted by many GOP partisans in election administration positions across Ohio and a corresponding lack of Democratic political will to counter these efforts.)

Another series of documents deals with a range of efforts to make it more difficult and discouraging for certain segments of the population—ex-felons, African Americans, college students, and Democrats in general—to vote. It is well known by those who study elections that anything that complicates voting rules discourages political participation, beginning with the registration process.

During the summer of 2004, even as he talked about increasing voter turnout, Blackwell took a number of steps to make registration difficult or confusing, especially in heavily Democratic areas. For instance, he issued an order requiring new voter registrations to be printed on 80-pound paper stock; registration forms printed on any other stock would be rejected. This order came in September, after the state's largest daily newspaper had already printed and distributed voter registration forms on lighter-weight paper. It ensured that many voter registration efforts, particularly by national groups focusing their efforts in Ohio's cities, the Democratic strongholds, would be hampered. After three controversy-filled weeks, Blackwell issued a modifying directive telling county BOEs to process all registrations, but ordering them to contact new voters, advising them to resubmit their registrations on the proper paper-weight application. Those who did not do so risked being turned away at the polls. It is impossible to know how many thousands of voters were disenfranchised by this confusion and the ensuing backlogs, but newly registered Ohio voters numbered over 800,000 by early fall 2004, and many Ohio newspapers and other political observers said the paper-weight controversy prevented thousands of additional voter registrations from being validated.

The secretary, in concert with Republican-dominated county election boards in twenty of Ohio's eighty-eight counties, also conducted voter roll purges. In Cuyahoga County, where the state's biggest city and Democratic stronghold, Cleveland, is located, BOE records obtained in spring 2006 reveal that 168,000 voters, or nearly one-fifth of the county's voters, were taken off voter rolls between 2000 and 2004 under a little-used National Voting Rights Act clause allowing purges of voters who had not voted in two previous federal elections. Another 10,000 voter registrations were lost by county workers in the spring and summer of 2004, according to the Greater Cleveland Voter Registration Coalition, when Cuyahoga County transitioned to a new, computerized voting system. Voter purges are not required by law, and there is no evidence they were similarly conducted in Republican-majority counties.

In GOP-controlled Hamilton County, where largely Democratic Cincinnati is surrounded by Republican suburbs, BOE records show that 105,000 voters were moved from active to inactive status between 2000 and 2004 under the same Voting Rights Act clause. During that time, the county's population fell by 3 percent, but voter rolls shrank by 12 percent. People listed as inactive in voter rolls were required to present identification (ID) such as a utility bill, to poll workers. If the ID was accepted as valid, the voter received a regular ballot. If their identification was rejected, they would receive a provisional ballot. In Hamilton County in 2004, most of the inactive voters and 95 percent of the provisional ballots were from Cincinnati.

While election officials have the option of removing voters who have been inactive, they are not required to do so under Ohio law, and enforcing such a purge seems contrary to the spirit of the Help America Vote Act (HAVA), and Blackwell's own pro-turnout rhetoric. Indeed, the purged voters in Cleveland could have been reclassified as inactive voters, still allowing the possibility of voting come November. A similar purge was conducted in Lucas County (Toledo) in the summer of 2004, where some 28,000 voters were removed from the largely Democratic Toledo rolls, just months before Election Day.

Other significant voting blocks of likely Democratic voters were also targeted before Election Day. Disenfranchising ex-felons is illegal under Ohio law, as ex-felons have a right to vote in the state unless they are currently incarcerated. Yet in various counties, Republican-controlled BOEs either revoked the right of ex-felons to vote or gave out misleading information about their voting rights.

The sample letter (at the end of this chapter) from Matt Damschroder, the Franklin County election director and former GOP chairman, includes a first paragraph stating that Franklin County election records show that "you have been convicted of a felony." The second paragraph states "your voter registration status has been cancelled. . . ." This letter, revoking the recipient's right to vote, was sent to a person who was not a convicted felon, but rather a person who was accused but never convicted. The effect of sending such letters is inevitably to discourage voting individuals who are both qualified and registered to vote. Indeed, this recipient had never received a letter when he lived in a Republican suburb, but received this one after moving to Columbus, a Democratic stronghold. Interviewed after the election by co-author Robert Fitrakis, Damschroder conceded that in 2004, some 3,500 registrations had been cancelled this way in the county where Columbus is located, compared to 200–300 in a typical year.

Misinformation distributed by different BOEs across the state further disenfranchised ex-felons. The Cincinnati-based Prison Reform Advocacy Center issued a report in August 2004 saying, "an Ohio ex-offender's right to vote may well depend on where he or she lives," referring to other efforts akin to Damschroder's efforts in Franklin County. It conservatively estimated that 20 percent of Ohio's 34,000 ex-felons then under "community supervision," or 6,800 people, did not believe they could vote due to misinformation received from their local BOE. Ex-felons were told, for example, they had to get a judge's permission to vote, which is not the case. In fact, it is often the policy of probation officers to *require* ex-offenders to register as part of their rehabilitation. In Cincinnati, for instance, a survey by the Prison Reform Advocacy Center indicated that 40 percent of ex-offenders believed they could not vote.

Ex-felons were targeted in other smaller but patently dishonest ways. In Columbus, days before the vote, for example, Republican "volunteers" claiming to be members of "the Texas Strike Force" and subsidized by the Republican National Committee were overheard by workers at a downtown Holiday Inn behind Ohio GOP headquarters using pay phones to call former felons and threaten them with arrest if they tried to vote. The statements in a sworn affidavit by Jim Branscome, who was one of two hotel workers who reported the threatening phone calls to the police, have never been denied or refuted by the Ohio GOP.

And there were other forms of targeted disenfranchisement by Ohio Republicans. A post-election report by House Judiciary Committee Democratic staff described so-called caging tactics, whereby the state GOP "sent registered letters to newly registered voters in minority and urban areas, and then sought to challenge at the polls 35,000 individuals who refused to sign for the letters or the mail otherwise came back as undeliverable." While poll challengers—individuals assigned by Republicans to issue on-the-spot challenges to individual voters' eligibility, based largely on response to these letters—were initially blocked in court, their right to be at polling places was reinstated on Election Eve. The decision to allow their presence at the polls reflected a broader GOP mind-set intent on limiting rather than maximizing the vote, a stance fully embraced by Ohio's Republican election administrators.

The secretary of state and county BOEs knew 2004 would be a nearly record turnout. Registration forms indicated that there would be close to 1 million new voters, and Blackwell's office was predicting a statewide turnout of 72.7 percent (a forecast that is important to keep in mind in later chapters, when comparing the turnouts in Democratic- and Republican-majority districts). For now, the importance of a projected record turnout is the context it provides for viewing the remaining Blackwell initiatives documented in this chapter. As the documents make clear, the secretary of state created a set of conditions guaranteed to create chaos in Democratic districts, suppressing both the number of votes cast and the number of votes counted.

The most egregious initiative concerned provisional ballots—a voting option affirmed by the Help America Vote Act (HAVA), passed by Congress in 2002 to expand voting rights. The idea behind provisional ballots is to give voters the benefit of the doubt in situations where their name does not appear on a voter roll, but where they feel they should be allowed to vote. By offering a "provisional" ballot, poll workers do not have to make an on-the-spot determination about eligibility, but can record an individual's voting preferences on a ballot whose legitimacy can be determined later, by cross-referencing it with registration lists and voter rolls. In the summer and fall of 2004, Blackwell created new rules both on who would be given provisional ballots and on when and how these ballots would be tallied.

Most significantly, the secretary of state decreed that voters had to cast a provisional ballot in their own precinct or it would not be counted. In prior elections, *including the 2004 primaries*, voters could cast provisional ballots anywhere in their county. However, Blackwell, explaining that decree at the time and after the election, said he was clarifying what election "jurisdiction" meant. Despite a subsequent federal court ruling affirming HAVA's intent to guarantee the right to vote, the secretary would insist his new precinct-specific standard be rigorously followed. Republican Governor Robert Taft told reporters the decision could disenfranchise 100,000 voters. Still, Blackwell maintained that his new "correct precinct only" rules were a legitimate state's rights exercise, and he again defended that decision in congressional field hearings after Election Day in March 2005.

Blackwell's insistence on the proper precinct rule takes on huge partisan significance in light of the enormous confusion over Democratic precincts created by Blackwell's own office in the months prior to Election Day. In several of the state's pro-Kerry cities, the secretary of state effectively engendered a classic "catch-22" situation: as BOEs changed long-standing Democratic precinct locations shortly before the elections, Blackwell simultaneously disseminated out-of-date voter rolls to county officials, ensuring that many new voters would not be on precinct lists given to poll workers. Then, to people who were confused as a result and did not end up at the correct precinct, he offered provisional ballots, but subsequently refused to count provisional ballots cast in the wrong precinct—which was often simply the wrong table in the correct building and room. He also instructed vote counters to disqualify provisional ballots submitted without properly labeled voter identification envelopes, after issuing conflicting directives about labeling requirements.

As affidavits in later chapters state, because of voting machine shortages, misinformation sent out by the secretary of state's office, and/or improper or no signage at the precincts, many people waited for hours in the wrong precinct line in a newly relocated precinct. Often, these people found themselves ineligible to receive a provisional ballot unless they stood again in a different line. And, as Blackwell made clear to congressional investigators after the fact, receiving and filling out a provisional ballot was no guarantee that your vote would be counted. In addition to the "correct precinct" rule, Blackwell created new standards for counting provisional ballots—which he modified after Election Day—requiring additional voter identification. Not all counties followed his directives, but in Cuyahoga County (Cleveland), which did abide by Blackwell's standards, provisional ballots were not counted unless voters wrote their birth dates on ballot envelopes. Many poll workers did not follow that rule, prompting more disqualifications.

Further, Blackwell decreed that voters who requested absentee ballots but who did not receive them before Election Day could not vote provisionally. While a federal court found that ruling was illegal, the Judiciary Committee Democratic staff report later determined that the confusion Blackwell created did indeed suppress turnout, particularly among senior citizens. The committee cited two mailings sent out by the secretary of state's office clearly saying that individuals who had requested absentee ballots, whether or not they had received them, would not be given provisional ballots on Election Day. Despite sending out a press release reversing this decree, the confusion created an impression that some voters felt they would not be eligible to vote provisionally.

Meanwhile, people seeking to vote by an absentee ballot were often met with other bureaucratic challenges or notices (often inaccurate) that their registration was not valid, along with onerous instructions to show up in person to address this. In Franklin County, the BOE issued a blanket challenge to students who were studying away from home and wanted absentee ballots. The board sent cards summoning all these absentee voters to a mass hearing, and reserved the 10,000-seat capacity Veteran's Memorial Hall, for the Thursday prior to Election Day. A court overruled this obvious attempt at caging, but the confusion lingered. Again, these tactics fell predominantly on Democratic voters because most of the affected people were in its strongholds: in cities and on campuses.

Statewide, Blackwell's office reported that 156,640 provisional ballots were cast. While the secretary later said that his state's rate of validating these ballots was among the highest in the nation at 77.9 percent, 34,617 votes cast this way were disqualified. Analyses discussed later in this book (by independent analysts, such as Richard Hayes Phillips, as well as by the Democratic National Committee) counter Blackwell's interpretation, finding that, in Ohio, provisional ballots were used at a higher rate than in bigger swing states such as Florida, fell disproportionately on first-time voters, and were cast and discarded at a rate of two-to-one by pro-Kerry supporters. Indeed, a third of the state's provisional ballots were cast in Cuyahoga County, where Democratic Cleveland is located.

Another area where Blackwell, an ostensibly disinterested public servant, consistently acted to favor the Republican ticket involves decisions about how to handle the Green Party candidates Ralph Nader and Peter Camejo. Blackwell has often taken public credit for determining that the Nader-Camejo ticket did not garner enough valid signatures in Ohio to be eligible for the ballot. In fact, however, a memo proves that it was an Ohio judge who made the determination that Green Party advocates had falsified signatures (Blackwell had independently concluded that the potentially "spoiling" Nader-Camejo ticket *did* qualify for the ballot). If Blackwell was dogmatic that his provisional ballot rules be followed, even issuing job-threatening memos to anyone defying his orders, on the Nader issue he gave the local BOEs total discretion. They could block out the names of the Green Party candidates, or they could "Post a notice in each precinct where the candidates' names remain on the ballot informing voters that any vote cast for these two candidates will not be counted, if the board determines it is not feasible to remove the two names from the ballots." Thus, just so long as there was a posted notice somewhere in the polling place that votes for Nader-Camejo would not be counted, their names could remain on the ballot, leaving as much room as possible for fruitless Nader votes to be cast. In other states, this issue is typically addressed by reprinting ballots so there is no voter confusion. In at least one southern Ohio county, the BOE dealt with this by placing paper stickers over Nader's name—stickers that also happened to cover Kerry's name as well. (This was discovered during the presidential election recount, and was cited in the House Judiciary Democrat's report and legal briefs filed during the recount by attorneys for the Green and Libertarian Parties.)

The secretary of state did more than decide which registrations would be accepted, which voters would be given provisional ballots, and whether those ballots would count or be disqualified ("They disenfranchised themselves if they didn't vote in the right precinct," was his official statement on the matter). He also oversaw a $2.5 million statewide voter education campaign that failed to inform people of a critical piece of information: voting rules allowed them to vote at their local BOE offices if their local precincts were too busy. Blackwell's response was positively defiant when he was asked about this omission from the voter education advertising campaign by U.S. Representative Stephanie Tubbs Jones, D-OH, at the March 21, 2005, congressional field hearing—the only time after the election that the secretary was held accountable by other public officials:

> MS. TUBBS JONES: In this ad you said, "Vote your precinct," but you never told them that if they couldn't vote in precinct, they could go to the Board of Elections and vote. Did you, sir?
>
> SECRETARY BLACKWELL: I sure didn't.
>
> MS. TUBBS JONES: Excuse me?
>
> SECRETARY BLACKWELL: Can't you hear? I said I sure didn't.

That omission proved extremely important on Election Day, when lines in Ohio's largely Democratic-leaning inner cities were hours long, due to insufficient numbers of voting machines—another political decision that will be discussed in later chapters.

The "Democracy at Risk" report by the Democratic National Committee concluded that on Election Day 2004, a total of between 2 and 3 percent of Ohioans who intended to vote were for one reason or another discouraged from doing so. In an election where 5.62 million votes were counted in Ohio, 2 percent 113,000 votes is almost equal to the final certified spread between George W. Bush and John Kerry, which was 118,775 votes. Had an additional 3 percent of Ohioans voted—more than 169,000 people—and had their votes been accurately counted, the state could have elected a different president.

Chapter 1 Documents: Suppressing the Vote

1.1 Letter to Robert Bennett from Ohio Secretary of State, October 5, 2004, p. 31

This letter from Ohio Secretary of State J. Kenneth Blackwell threatens to fire the entire Cuyahoga County Board of Elections (Cleveland) if it allows provisional voting in precincts other than where the voter is registered. The letter is indicative of Blackwell's heavy hand in overseeing Ohio's supposedly "bipartisan" boards of elections (BOEs). In this case, even Ohio Republican Party Chair Robert Bennett wanted to follow past precedent and allow any registered voter in his county to vote provisionally at any precinct in his or her county. Blackwell disagreed, thereby limiting participation and voting rights. Incredibly enough, Blackwell couched his disagreement in language designed to accuse Bennett of wanting to disenfranchise voters, when clearly the opposite was true. In Ohio's 2004 spring presidential primary, votes for president were counted if cast in the correct county, even if in the wrong precinct. (Blackwell used his position as secretary of state to reinterpret the meaning of "jurisdiction" to mean precinct rather than the county.)

1.2 *Congressional Record* Transcript, House Committee on Administration Field Hearing, Columbus, OH, March 21, 2005, pp. 32–33

This congressional field hearing was the only time Ohio Secretary of State J. Kenneth Blackwell was questioned and challenged in public by other elected officials about his management of the November 2004 election (109th Congress House Hearings, from the U.S. Government Printing Office via GPO Access, DOCID: f:20790 .wais).

1.2.1 The following exchange from the March 2005 House of Representatives field hearing is between U.S. Representative Stephanie Tubbs Jones, D-OH, and Ohio State Representative Kevin DeWine, R-7th district, the majority leader of the Ohio House. Here Representative Tubbs Jones explores how Ohio's BOEs are not independent and truly bipartisan, as Blackwell can threaten and dismiss members at will. Under Ohio Revised Code, section 3501.06, BOE members "shall be appointed by the secretary of state, as the secretary's representatives, to serve for the term of four years."

1.2.2 In an exchange from the same congressional field hearing, U.S. Representative Juanita Millender-McDonald, D-CA, the ranking Democrat on the House Committee on Administration, further explores the "bipartisan" nature of Ohio's Boards of Election with Michael Vu, director of the Cuyahoga County Board of Elections (Cleveland), William Anthony, chairman of the Franklin County Board of Elections (Columbus), and Keith Cunningham, president of the Ohio Association of Election Officials. These county BOE directors can have outside political roles. For instance, William Anthony heads the Franklin County Democratic Party. The significance of this exchange is that it shows how Blackwell not only *threatened* BOE directors in two of Ohio's biggest Democratic counties, Franklin and Cuyahoga Counties, but exercised that authority. Thus, in Cuyahoga County the secretary insisted the BOE follow his order, not a court ruling. And in Franklin County, Democratic Party Chair William Anthony also had to follow Blackwell's orders if he wanted to keep his civil service post as an election administrator.

1.3 Ohio Secretary of State Directive No. 2004-31 on Voter Registration Paper Stock, September 7, 2004, pp. 34–35

Section II of this order by Ohio Secretary of State J. Kenneth Blackwell states that only those voter registrations printed on 80-pound paper stock will be accepted, which has the effect of narrowing the pool of eligible newly registered voters. This directive came after many of Ohio's newspapers, such as the *Columbus Dispatch*, printed voter registration forms on newsprint for their readers. (Meanwhile, the *Dispatch* weighed registration forms issued by *Blackwell's office* and found they were 60 pound paper stock.) Many county BOEs were using 20-pound paper stock and scanning the registrations into the computer. The archaic law invoked by Blackwell dates back prior to the widespread use of scanners, when paper registrations had to be permanently retained on card stock. The first part of this order asserts Blackwell's jurisdiction in this matter (http://www.sos.state.oh.us/News/Read.aspx?ID=98).

1.4 Website Posting from Delaware County Board of Elections on Voter Registration Paper Stock, p. 36

After Blackwell's directive, the Delaware County BOE immediately notified voters on their website that they were not accepting "a copy" of the voter registration form. Prior to this, thousands of voters had downloaded voter registration forms from BOE sites and used them to register to vote. The best estimates indicate that thousands of people either had their registrations returned or failed to vote because of Blackwell's ruling. This disproportionately impacted Democratic voting blocks and Kerry supporters who constituted most of the pool of newly registered voters in 2004.

1.5 Ohio Secretary of State Advisory 2004–06 on 80-pound Voter Registration Paper Stock, September 29, 2004, p. 37

This advisory (issued in response to a ruling countermanding Blackwell) clarifies Blackwell's former demand for uniquely heavy paper for voter registration forms, saying all registrations "should be processed" but "newly registered voter should be sent and asked to return the legally prescribed form." This created more confusion among voters and administrative backlogs with qualifying new voters. While documents like this, in isolation, appear to be innocuous, the bigger picture is the ensuing confusion, which meant that many people who registered to vote would not see their forms processed—finding this out only on Election Day (http://www.sos.state.oh.us/News/Read.aspx?ID=96).

1.6 The Sentencing Project, Felon Disenfranchisement Laws in the United States, November 2005, p. 38

This nationwide chart shows that Ohio bars people convicted of felonies from voting only while they are in prison (and not all felony convictions result in prison sentences). Letters and phone calls to Ohio's ex-offenders saying they had no right to vote, as well as voter roll purges based on their criminal records, would be illegal under Ohio law, but, as subsequent documents show, that did not prevent BOEs and GOP activists from conducting purges, sending letters, and making phone calls in 2004 (http://www.sentencingproject.org/pdfs/1046.pdf).

1.7 Letter from Matthew Damschroder, Director, Franklin County Board of Elections, August 19, 2004, p. 39

This letter from Matthew Damschroder, the director of the Franklin County Board of Elections and former executive director of the Franklin County Republican Party, is an example of the voter intimidation tactics targeting ex-offenders. The individual in question had never been convicted of a felony, but is incorrectly identified as a felon by the BOE and illegally stripped of his right to vote. (He had been indicted on a felony charge several years before, but subsequently pleaded guilty to a misdemeanor.) Woodford had voted since 1998 in the Republican enclave of Westerville, Ohio, where his right to vote was not questioned. He had his voting rights cancelled only after he moved to the Democratically dominated city of Columbus and voted as a Democrat in the primary. Damschroder, in an interview with co-author Robert Fitrakis, admitted that some of the people who lost their right to vote had merely been "indicted" as a felon, a clearly illegal practice.

1.8 Prison Reform Advocacy Center Report, "The Disenfranchisement of the Re-enfranchised," August 2004, pp. 40–42

This statement accompanying an August 2004 report from the Prison Reform Advocacy Center, a Cincinnati-based group, notes how different boards of election dispensed different information on ex-offender voting rights, including twenty-one BOEs across the state that "frequently gave erroneous and misleading information to felons inquiring about their voting rights." In 2005, Ohio had 34,000 ex-offenders still under some kind of court supervision, but eligible, under Ohio law, to vote. In Cincinnati, however, nearly half of the ex-offenders surveyed did not know they were allowed to vote, a situation exacerbated by faulty information provided by BOEs.

1.9.1 Cuyahoga County Voter Purges, by Victoria Lovegren, Ph.D., p. 43

1.9.2 Cuyahoga County Voter Purges, by Richard Hayes Phillips, Ph.D., pp. 44–48

The first chart, prepared by Victoria Lovegren, Ph.D., a Cleveland voting-rights activist and mathematics instructor at Case Western University, is based on BOE data made available in early 2006. It summarizes voter registration purges in Cayuhoga County (Cleveland) after the 2000 presidential election (as of August 2004). "NCOA postcard" refers to the "no change of address" file maintained by the U.S. Postal Service. "NVRA" refers to the National Voting Rights Act, which allows election officials to place a voter on "inactive" status if he or she has not responded to an address confirmation notice. If voters have not voted in two prior federal election cycles, they can be removed from the voter roll.

A second, more detailed chart shows a precinct-by-precinct analysis of the Cayuhoga County's voter purges. It was prepared by Richard Hayes Phillips, Ph.D., who specializes in analyzing anomalous data, and is based on the BOE data released in spring 2006. Up to 30 percent of the registered voters were purged in many neighborhoods.

1.10 The Greater Cleveland Voter Registration Coalition (GCVRC) Report to the House Judiciary Committee Democratic Staff, December 7, 2004, pp. 49–55

This is the summary section of a report by the Greater Cleveland Voter Registration Coalition, a nonprofit group that works to maximize voting rights in Cuyahoga County. The report was presented by Norman Robbins, study leader, at a field hearing in Columbus, Ohio, on December 13, 2004, by the Democratic members of the House Judiciary Committee.

During the 2004 election cycle, the group followed 9,600 voter registrations through the BOE administrative process, to monitor how they were being processed and to see if people were being denied the right to vote. That study's findings are first summarized and then are detailed; documenting problems with registration, provisional ballots, and absentee ballots. Cumulatively, the study estimates up to 10,000 voters in the Cleveland area alone were disenfranchised.

1.11 Notice to Addie Smith from the Franklin County Board of Elections (Postmarked October 25, 2004), p. 56

This notice shows other bureaucratic challenges to the right to vote of likely Democratic voters, this time students. This postcard challenged Addie Smith's right to vote, and put the burden of proof on her, requiring that she appear on October 28, 2004, at Franklin County Veteran's Memorial Hall to contest that decision. (Note the postcard is postmarked October 25, eight days before the election, and offers little recourse if the assigned hearing date poses a problem for the recipient.)

1.12 Branscome Statement on the Texas Strike Force, p. 57

Jim Branscome, a downtown Holiday Inn employee and self-described conservative Republican, confronted a member of the Texas Strike Force just prior to the 2004 elections. In a videotaped interview, Branscome went into detail on why he and a co-worker called the police to report what they alleged to be illegal voter intimidation. The following affidavit was based on Branscome's statement. (It is unsigned because the anticipated legal action was never filed.) The Texas Strike Force, which has a website recruiting members (www.texasstrikeforce .com), claimed to have been part of a Republican Party operation sanctioned by Karl Rove, President Bush's top political strategist. While its impact on the vote was marginal, Branscome's allegations have never been refuted or denied, and show the lengths the Republican National Committee (RNC) were prepared to go to win in 2004.

1.13 House Judiciary Committee Democratic Staff Report Section on "Caging" and "Targeting Minority and Urban Voters for Legal Challenges," January 5, 2005, pp. 58–66

Representative John Conyers, D-MI, the highest-ranking Democrat on the House Judiciary Committee, directed his staff to report on the

2004 presidential election in Ohio. The report, "Preserving Democracy: What Went Wrong in Ohio?" includes sections on what they term "caging" and the legal challenges for newly registered minority voters. Both sections are reproduced here and describe attempts by the Ohio Republican Party to restrict the ability to vote of minorities in urban areas.

1.14 Blackwell Predicts 72 Percent Voter Turnout, Press Release, p. 67

This press release, reprinted here, is from the secretary of state's website (http://www.sos.state.oh.us/News/Read.aspx?ID=92) on the eve of the 2004 vote. It predicts a 72.68 percent turnout statewide, the highest since 1992. Blackwell and county BOEs knew that Election Day would be challenging, under the best of circumstances. Blackwell's other directives, which follow, show how he made voting a more complicated affair, thereby deterring many would-be voters.

1.15 Blackwell Defends Decree That Voters Had to Cast a Provisional Ballot in Their Precinct, p. 68

Congressional Record transcript, House Committee on Administration field hearing, Columbus, OH, March 21, 2005 (109th Congress House Hearings, from the U.S. Government Printing Office via GPO Access, DOCID: f:20790.wais).

This exchange between Blackwell and Representative Millender-McDonald, D-CA, the ranking Democrat on the House Administration Committee, is from the *Congressional Record* transcript of that panel's field hearing in Columbus on March 21, 2005. This is the best summary by the secretary of state of the thinking behind his 2004 directives on provisional ballots. Here, Blackwell is asked by Millender-McDonald to explain his assertion that he issued no orders denying people a provisional ballot if they didn't vote at their precinct. It is noteworthy how Blackwell's response—where he distinguishes between giving out ballots and *counting* them—is at odds with HAVA's intent to make every vote count. His statements, such as, "We don't run a taxicab service," show Blackwell's arrogance with respect to HAVA's intent.

1.16 Blackwell Statement on Judge Carr's Decision, Press Release, October 14, 2004, p. 69

During the fall of 2004, Blackwell's provisional ballot rulings were challenged in court. Blackwell issued this press release after Federal District Court judge James G. Carr ruled against the secretary of state in a provisional ballot case. In this statement, Blackwell reasserts that state's rights allow him to restrict the use of provisional balloting. Judge Carr's decision accused Blackwell of "failure to do his duty." Blackwell eventually prevailed when the Sixth Circuit Court of Appeals overturned Carr's decision. In Lucas County (Toledo), where Judge Carr presided, 41 percent (3,122) of the provisional ballots cast on Election Day were rejected because of Blackwell's new "proper precinct only" directive. It is hard to imagine any reason for arguing so strenuously that provisional ballots filed in the wrong precinct should not be counted except as part of an effort to suppress the vote (http://www.sos.state.oh.us/News/Read.aspx?ID=95).

1.17 Testimony that the Secretary of State's Voter Data Given to Counties in Fall 2004 Was Six Months Old, p.70

Congressional Record transcript, House Committee on Administration field hearing, Columbus, OH, March 21, 2005 (109th Congress House Hearings, from the U.S. Government Printing Office via GPO Access, DOCID: f:20790.wais).

In congressional hearings after the 2005 election, William Anthony, the chairman of the Franklin County Board of Elections, testified that voter information—names, addresses, precincts—coming from the secretary of state's office was six months old and did not match Franklin County's election records. Blackwell said this discrepancy was due to efforts to modernize this data at the secretary of state's office. However, this lack of continuity between state and county levels, going into a controversial, high-turnout election, is a formula for massive Election Day chaos and disenfranchisement. As a result, people were sent to the wrong precincts, newly registered voters found they were not on voter rolls and were given provisional ballots (many of which were later disqualified), and the ensuing confusion at the polls contributed to the long waits—at precincts with too few voting machines. Together, all these factors became a "perfect storm" that frustrated attempts to vote, as was immediately recognized by Representative Juanita Millender-McDonald, D-CA.

1.18 Blackwell Directive 2004-37, Removal of Nader/Camejo from Ohio ballot, September 29, 2004, p. 71

1.19 Blackwell Directive 2004-38, Removal of the Names of Nader and Camejo from the Ballot, September 29, 2004, p. 72

In a close election, where votes for Ralph Nader would come at Kerry's expense and benefit Bush, Blackwell allowed boards of elections discretion in dealing with Nader's name on the ballot. Although he issued his directive more than a month prior to Election Day—certainly enough time for accurate ballots to have been printed—Blackwell explicitly allowed the option of leaving Nader's name on the ballot. There was no indication by his name that Nader was not an official candidate and that votes for him would not be counted. Posting a notice elsewhere in the polling place noting that Nader votes would not be counted was deemed adequate.

1.20 Confusing Absentee Ballot Layout, Which Led Kerry Backers to Vote for Nader, pp. 73–74

Absentee ballots in Franklin County (Columbus) had a similar design to the infamous 2000 presidential "butterfly" ballots in Florida. By punching the hole next to the candidate's name, instead of by the number assigned to the candidate, it was very easy to accidentally vote for the wrong candidate. On the first page (document 1.20.1), a voter would see Kerry-Edwards third from the top. But on the second page (document 1.20.2), to vote for Kerry, the voter would have to punch the fourth hole on their punch card ballot—not the third. Punching the third hole would be a vote for Bush. An October 21, 2004, Associated Press (AP) article by Connie Mabin titled "Layout Confuses Some Ohio Absentee Voters" noted the same problem in Ohio's largest county, Cuyahoga (Cleveland): "If absentee voters cast their vote by trying to line up the arrow with the punch card, they will punch the wrong number." The vast majority of absentee ballots came from urban areas and the elderly, traditionally Democratic voting blocks. The *Cincinnati Enquirer* reported that the initial absentee ballots sent out to Hamilton County voters *completely lacked an option to vote for Kerry*. Thus, Ohio's three largest counties, with heavily Democratic absentee voters, had faulty absentee ballots, all favoring the Republican candidates.

1.21 Blackwell's Statewide Voter Education Campaign Did Not Include Key Provisional Voting Options, pp. 75–76

Congressional Record transcript, House Committee on Administration Field Hearing, Columbus, OH, March 21, 2005 (109th Congress House Hearings, from the U.S. Government Printing Office via GPO Access, DOCID: f:20790.wais).

In this contentious exchange, U.S. Representative Stephanie Tubbs Jones, D-OH, presses Secretary of State Blackwell on why he did not tell voters they could vote at county BOE offices, in addition to the precincts. That information could have alleviated long lines and lowered the number of would-be voters walking away on Election Day. Blackwell spent $2.5 million on state voter education before the election, but failed to make the option of voting at BOE offices clear. Here, again, Blackwell's defiant tone must be noted. Two months before this hearing, Representative Tubbs Jones and Senator Barbara Boxer, D-CA, challenged the certification of Ohio's Electoral College votes in Congress, a largely symbolic move that nonetheless attempted to highlight the state's problem-plagued election. Blackwell refused to testify in Washington about the 2004 election; thus, this poorly attended congressional hearing was the only time Blackwell was held to account.

1.22 "Democracy at Risk: The 2004 Election in Ohio," June 9, 2005, Cover Page and Page 2 Only, pp. 77–78

The report "Democracy at Risk: The 2004 Election in Ohio" by the Democratic National Committee (DNC) estimates that 2 percent of Ohioans who intended to vote were discouraged from doing so because of long lines. The report contends that an additional group of slightly less than 1 percent did not vote because they did not receive absentee ballots, heard about long lines, or faced registration challenges and confusing polling sites. In an election where 5.63 million votes were counted, 2 percent—113,000 votes—is almost equal to the final certified spread in Ohio between George W. Bush and John Kerry, which was 118,775 votes.

The DNC says those who left because of lines (see page 20, http://a9.g.akamai.net/7/9/8082/v001/www.democrats.org/pdfs/ohvrireport/fullreport.pdf) would have split their votes evenly between Bush and Kerry. We view that conclusion as highly questionable, because, as the testimony and evidence in Chapter 2 will show, nearly all the voting problems occurred in Democratic precincts. No evidence exists suggesting disenfranchised voters were split evenly between the two parties. In one inner-city precinct in Columbus alone, for instance, a survey done under the auspices of the Columbus Institute for Contemporary Journalism found that 20 percent of registered voters contacted said they had attempted to vote on Election Day, but left due to the waiting time of more than three hours.

Document 1.1

J Kenneth Blackwell

J. KENNETH BLACKWELL
Ohio Secretary of State

180 E. BROAD STREET / 16TH FLOOR / COLUMBUS, OH 43215
614.466.2655 / TOLL FREE: 877.767.6446 / FAX: 614.644.0649
e-mail: blackwell@sos.state.oh.us   www.state.oh.us/sos/

October 5, 2004

Robert Bennett, Chairperson
Cuyahoga County Board of Elections
2925 Euclid Avenue
Cleveland, Ohio 44115-2497

VIA FACSIMILE AND U.S. MAIL

Dear Mr. Bennett:

It has been reported to me that you are directing your election officials to give provisional ballots to persons who are not registered to vote in the precinct where they are reporting to vote. Effective immediately, you are to cease and desist this direction to your election officials.

The Board's actions are in direct violation of Ohio Revised Code 3599.12 and my Directive 2004-33 as issued on September 16, 2004. The statute specifically prohibits anyone from voting or attempting to vote in any election in a precinct in which that person is not a legally qualified elector. The "Help America Vote Act" instructs states to count provisional ballots in accordance with state law. The Directive ordered providing provisional ballots only when the elector resides in the precinct in accordance with state law. Electors not residing in the precinct are to be directed to the proper polling location, the Boards of Elections, or an assigned polling place as designated by the Board of Elections in accordance with R.C. 3503.16. As Chief Elections Officer for the State of Ohio, I am directing you to rescind the decision of the Board regarding provisional balloting and instruct your employees per the above Statutes and Directive.

The conduct of the Board and its Director is a cynical attempt to cause voter confusion by giving voters the false impression that the votes cast in the wrong precinct will be counted. Your actions would disenfranchise thousands of Ohio voters by accepting provisional ballots, which based upon Ohio law cannot be counted. The action of the Board in publicly announcing that it will not obey the law is a disingenuous practice, which serves to purposefully deceive voters. Your defiance of my Directive would have resulted in voters relying upon the ability to show up at incorrect precinct locations believing that their votes would be counted and having your election officials later disqualify those provisional ballots cast in good faith.

Be advised that your actions are not in compliance with Ohio law and further failure to comply with my lawful directives will result in official action, which may include removal of the Board and its Director. If, at some time in the future, legal action results in a definitive finding contrary to the Directive, Boards of Elections will be notified and instructed accordingly. Until such time, Directive 2004-33 stands with the full force and effect of law and is to be followed by all Boards of Elections.

Sincerely,

J Kenneth Blackwell

J. Kenneth Blackwell

cc: Members of the Cuyahoga County Board of Elections
    Michael Vu, Director, Cuyahoga County Board of Elections
    County Boards of Elections

Document 1.2.1

Part 1

Ms. Tubbs Jones. Lastly, sir, are you aware that, in fact, the Secretary of State has the ability to dismiss members of boards of elections?

Mr. DeWine. Yes, I am.

Ms. Tubbs Jones. And so the argument that it is a bipartisan system, you have one partisan who is capable of dismissing members of the Board of Elections as Kenneth Blackwell threatened to do in this past election, HAVA gives way to the real bipartisan nature of the boards. Does it not, sir?

Mr. DeWine. Mr. Chairman, to the representative, I believe that he can only remove those board members for cause and would have to replace them with a person of the same party.

Ms. Tubbs Jones. I understand but I am saying to you that he has the ability to dismiss members of the board. In fact, he threatened to do that in this election. Did he not, sir?

Mr. DeWine. I believe I heard that, yes.

Ms. Tubbs Jones. He did, in fact. You didn't just hear it. It was, in fact, all over the newspaper and television that he, in fact, did that. Correct?

Mr. DeWine. Correct.

Document 1.2.2

Part 2

Ms. Millender-McDonald. Mr. Vu, just one more question, or quick series of questions. In fact, the Cuyahoga County Board of Elections made the decision to not follow a directive of the Secretary of State with regard to the provisional ballot. Is that correct, sir?

Mr. Vu. I apologize that I need to elaborate on this. We had a forum, a road map to the 2004 election forum where we stated that there was a directive and that we were going to err on the side of the voter that if the voter, similar to what Chairman Ney (U.S. Rep. Bob Ney, R-OH) was saying, is that if the voter insisted that they were in that precinct, that we would give them that provisional ballot.

Of course, this was contrary to a directive that we had received because we had specifically stated and asked for clarification on this directive as to whether or not we could issue a provisional ballot. It was the issuing portion of it.

Ms. Millender-McDonald. Right.

Mr. Vu. Whether we could issue a provisional ballot to the voter and the answer to that was no. Of course, that went to litigation and the appeals court, 6th District Appeals Court, said it was parallel to what the Board of Elections in Cuyahoga County thought.

Ms. Millender-McDonald. In fact, the Secretary of State said to you if you don't follow his directive, he threatened every member of that Board of Elections for choosing to make that claim. Did he not?

Mr. Vu. That is correct. We received a letter from the Secretary of State's office that if we did not follow the directive that the director and its board may be dismissed.

Ms. Millender-McDonald. Thank you. I better follow up on that. Was this the only county where that threat was made by the Secretary of State or was it all of you?

Mr. Cunningham. I wasn't threatened.

Mr. Anthony. It was implied.

Ms. Millender-McDonald. I am sorry?

Mr. Anthony. It was an implied threat.

Ms. Millender-McDonald. Sir, threats are not implied. They are directed.

Mr. Anthony. Yes, ma'am.

Ms. Millender-McDonald. They are direct threats. Threats are not implied.

Document 1.3

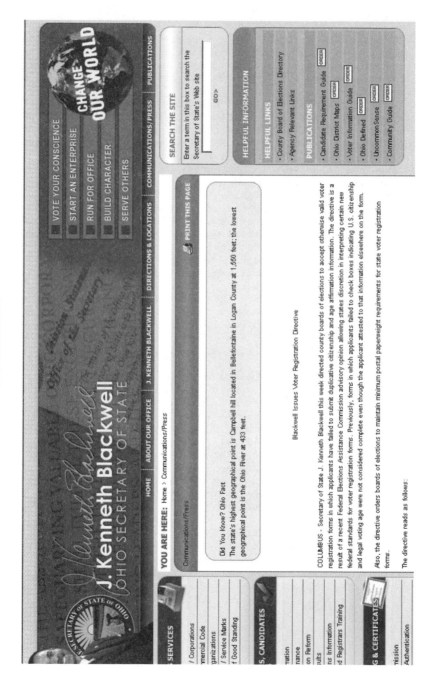

PROGRAM INITIATIVES

* Ohio Center for Own Character
* Collegiate Alliance for Character
* A Guide for New Citizens
* Xpect More
* Your Vote Counts

E-MAIL SIGN-UP

Enter your e-mail address to receive e-mail updates

TO: ALL COUNTY BOARD OF ELECTIONS
Members, Directors and Deputy Directors

I. VOTER REGISTRATION FORMS – LINE 1 AND 2

In accordance with the Help America Vote Act of 2002 (HAVA), the Ohio voter registration form was revised to meet the new federal requirements, which included adding the following questions that the applicant must answer affirmatively in order for the form to be processed:

1. Are you a U.S. citizen? Yes No
2. Will you be 18 years of age on or before the next general election? Yes No

The prescribed form also contains the following affirmation:

"I declare under penalty of election falsification I am a citizen of the United States, will have lived in this state for 30 days immediately preceding the next election, and I will be at least 18 years of age at the time of the general election."

The Elections Assistance Commission (EAC) recently issued an opinion that a state may choose to honor the affirmation of citizenship and age, even if the applicant did not check the "yes" boxes for questions 1 and 2. Therefore, I am instructing county boards of elections to accept otherwise valid voter registration applications even if the applicants did not check the "yes" boxes. Please inform all staff processing voter registrations of this important change of instructions.

II. VOTER REGISTRATION FORMS – PAPERWEIGHT

We have received numerous questions concerning the paperweight of the Ohio voter registration form. The form prescribed by the Secretary of State must be printed on white, uncoated paper of not less than 80 lb. text weight. Any Ohio form not printed on this minimum paperweight is considered to be an application for a registration form. Your board should mail the appropriate form to the person listed on the application.

However, this office cannot dictate the paperweight of the federally prescribed voter registrations forms: the on-line Federal Post Card Application (FPCA) and the "national" form prescribed by the Federal Elections Commission (FEC). Both of those forms may be printed on regular weight (e.g. 20 lb.) white paper.

If you have any questions on this directive, please call my Elections Division at 614-466-2585.

Sincerely,

J. Kenneth Blackwell

J. Kenneth Blackwell
OHIO SECRETARY OF STATE

p: 614 466 2655
tf: 877 767 6446
e-mail us

Privacy | Accessibility

Document 1.4

WANT TO REGISTER TO VOTE, CHANGE YOUR ADDRESS OR NAME? MAYBE YOU WOULD LIKE TO ABSENTEE VOTE?

Due to the new paper weight restrictions set forth by the Secretary of State, we can no longer accept a copy of the Voter Registration form. Please call us at 740-833-2080 and we will be happy to send one to you. Thank You for your cooperation.

Registration Deadline for the November 2, 2004 General Election is 4:00pm on October 2, 2004.
If you have moved with in the State of Ohio, call us and we will send you to your new polling location on Election day.

To absentee vote, go to Absentee Voting and print an absentee request, fill it out and send it to us!

The Delaware County Board of Elections
140 N. Sandusky St.
Delaware, Ohio 43015

Judicial

POLITICAL PARTIES
Republican
Democrat
Other

ELECTIONS CALENDAR

HOW TO RUN FOR OFFICE

HOMEPAGE

Document 1.5

Ohio Secretary of State J. Kenneth Blackwell
Elections Division - 180 E. Broad St., 15th Floor, Columbus, OH 43215
Tel. (614) 466-2585   Fax (614) 752-4360   e-mail: election@sos.state.oh.us

Advisory 2004-06
September 29, 2004

All County Boards of Elections

This advisory is a clarification of Directive 2004-31.

The voter registration form prescribed by the Secretary of State must be printed on white, uncoated paper of not less than 80 lb. text weight. However, any otherwise valid Ohio forms received by your Board of Elections not on 80lb. text **should be processed** and the newly registered voter should be sent and asked to return the legally prescribed form to be kept by your Board as a permanent record.

Sincerely,

J. Kenneth Blackwell

Document 1.6

Categories of Felons Disenfranchised Under State Law

STATE	PRISON	PROBATION	PAROLE	EX-FELONS All	EX-FELONS Partial
Alabama	X	X	X		X (certain offenses)
Alaska	X	X	X		
Arizona	X	X	X		X (2nd felony)
Arkansas	X	X	X		
California	X		X		
Colorado	X		X		
Connecticut	X		X		
Delaware	X	X	X		X (5 years)
District of Columbia	X				
Florida	X	X	X	X	
Georgia	X	X	X		
Hawaii	X				
Idaho	X	X	X		
Illinois	X				
Indiana	X				
Iowa *	X	X	X		
Kansas	X	X	X		
Kentucky	X	X	X	X	
Louisiana	X	X	X		
Maine					
Maryland	X	X	X		X (2nd felony, 3 years)
Massachusetts	X				
Michigan	X				
Minnesota	X	X	X		
Mississippi	X	X	X		X (certain offenses)
Missouri	X	X	X		
Montana	X				
Nebraska	X	X	X		X (2 years)
Nevada	X	X	X		X (except first-time nonviolent)
New Hampshire	X				
New Jersey	X	X	X		
New Mexico	X	X	X		
New York	X		X		
North Carolina	X	X	X		
North Dakota	X				
Ohio	X				
Oklahoma	X	X	X		
Oregon	X				
Pennsylvania	X				
Rhode Island	X	X	X		
South Carolina	X	X	X		
South Dakota	X		X		
Tennessee	X	X	X		X (post-1981)
Texas	X	X	X		
Utah	X				
Vermont					
Virginia	X	X	X	X	
Washington	X	X	X		
West Virginia	X	X	X		
Wisconsin	X	X	X		
Wyoming	X	X	X		X (5 years)
U.S. Total	49	31	36	3	9

* In July 2005, Iowa Governor Vilsack issued an executive order restoring the right to vote for all persons who have completed supervision. However, the lifetime prohibition on voting remains Iowa law.

11/05

Document 1.7

 Franklin County

Board of Elections

Director
MATTHEW DAMSCHRODER

Deputy Director
MICHAEL R. HACKETT

280 E. Broad Street, Room 100, Columbus, OH 43215-4572
www.co.franklin.oh.us/boe

(614) 462-3100
Fax: 462-3489

AUGUST 19, 2004

MARK A WOODFORD
1196 STRIEBEL RD
COLUMBUS, OH 43227

DEAR MARK A WOODFORD:

ACCORDING TO RECORDS PROVIDED TO THE FRANKLIN COUNTY BOARD OF ELECTIONS BY THE FRANKLIN COUNTY CLERK OF COURTS OR THE UNITED STATES DISTRICT COURT, YOU HAVE BEEN CONVICTED OF A FELONY.

THE PURPOSE OF THIS LETTER IS TO NOTIFY YOU THAT YOUR VOTER REGISTRATION STATUS HAS BEEN CANCELLED DUE TO YOUR CONVICTION AND INCARCERATION, PURSUANT TO SECTION 3503.21(A)(3) OF THE OHIO REVISED CODE.

UNDER OHIO LAW (§ 2961.01), YOU ARE ALLOWED TO RE-REGISTER TO VOTE ONLY AFTER YOU HAVE BEEN RELEASED FROM PRISON. YOU MAY RE-REGISTER EVEN IF YOU ARE ON JUDICIAL RELEASE (JUDICIAL RELEASE INCLUDES PROBATION, COMMUNITY BASED CORRECTIONS FACILITIES, AND RESIDENTIAL SANCTIONS SUCH AS HALFWAY HOUSES). REGISTRATION FORMS ARE AVAILABLE AT ANY PUBLIC LIBRARY, BUREAU OF MOTOR VEHICLES, ONLINE AT WWW.FRANKLINCOUNTYOHIO.GOV/BOE, OR BY CALLING THE OHIO SECRETARY OF STATE AT (614) 466-2585. THE DEADLINE TO REGISTER FOR THE NOVEMBER 2, 2004 GENERAL ELECTION IS OCTOBER 4, 2004.

IF YOU HAVE ANY QUESTIONS REGARDING YOUR VOTING STATUS OR RIGHTS, PLEASE CALL THE FRANKLIN COUNTY BOARD OF ELECTIONS AT (614) 462-5353.

SINCERELY,

MATTHEW M. DAMSCHRODER, DIRECTOR
FRANKLIN COUNTY BOARD OF ELECTIONS

Document 1.8

THE DISENFRANCHISEMENT OF THE RE-ENFRANCHISED:

How Confusion Over Felon Voter Eligibility in Ohio Keeps Qualified Ex-Offender

Voters From the Polls

A 2004 investigation by the **Prison Reform Advocacy Center** finds that many former Ohio prisoners may be disenfranchised because officials have wrongly told them they cannot vote. This disenfranchisement disproportionately affects African-Americans, who comprise 49 % of the states' prison population.

The study reveals that a significant percentage of released prisoners, including 43% of those surveyed in Hamilton County, believe they are ineligible to vote while on community supervision. An Ohio ex-offender's ability to exercise his or her lawful voting rights may well depend on where he or she lives in the state, according to the report PRAC released August 3, 2004, entitled "The Disenfranchisement of the Re-Enfranchised: How Confusion over Felon Voting Rights in Ohio Keeps Qualified Ex-offender Voters from the Polls." The report documents the problem and offers solutions to help ex-offenders exercise the right to vote in coming elections.

Approximately 22,000 Ohio prisoners are released each year to live in communities across the state. Though not eligible to vote while incarcerated, these individuals automatically become eligible to vote upon release from confinement. In Ohio, there is no requirement that released prisoners be "off papers" before they can register to vote. Thus, the more than 34,000 ex-offenders statewide who are currently under some form of community supervision, including probation, parole, and post-release control are eligible to vote in the state.

Document 1.8—Continued

Ohio law permits all former prisoners to resume voting after their release from custody, but election officials' knowledge of this law varies by region. PRAC's research found that 21 Boards of Election across the state, including Hamilton County's, frequently gave erroneous and misleading information to felons inquiring about their voting rights. Surveys of Boards of Elections across the state revealed mixed awareness of the laws. For example, representatives from the Cuyahoga County Board of Elections consistently gave accurate information regarding ex-offenders' voting rights; additionally most Cleveland ex-offenders knew they could vote. However, in Cincinnati, where nearly half of the ex-offenders PRAC surveyed did not know they were allowed to vote, information on ex-offender voter registration provided by Hamilton County Board of Elections was often inaccurate and misleading.

David Singleton, the Executive Director of The Prison Reform Advocacy Center, is troubled by the results of the study: "States like Ohio, where all former prisoners can vote as soon as they are released, should take steps to ensure that ex-offenders fully understand this important right. When former prisoners believe that they are stakeholders in their communities and that they have the power to contribute to civic life, they are more likely to succeed, which is in all of our best interests. Our democracy suffers when the voices of all eligible voters, including former prisoners, are not heard."

The report calls upon the Secretary of State, the County Boards of Elections, the Ohio Department of Rehabilitation and Correction, the Correctional Institution Inspection Committee, and other state and county agencies to act promptly on the issue. PRAC makes recommendations to increase awareness of felon voter eligibility within these agencies. Some of the suggestions include designating Adult Parole Authority offices as official voter registration locations, providing training classes for employees of the

Document 1.8—Continued

Boards of Elections about felon voting rights, and posting signs in all Ohio prisons and parole offices that inform inmates and released prisoners of their ability to vote upon release.

Although the majority of ex-offenders are aware of their voting rights, a significant percentage of felons who are eligible to register are not doing so because they lack awareness of their rights. Singleton points out, "If 20% of the 34,000 ex-offenders on community supervision in Ohio are not voting because they erroneously believe they are ineligible to do so, then 6,800 potential votes have been lost. The 2000 presidential election showed that every vote matters. We want to ensure that ex-prisoners are not being inadvertently disenfranchised on account of misinformation."

Document 1.9.1

Voters "Batch-Cancelled" in Cuyahoga County, Ohio

Date Cancelled	Cancellation Reason	Number of Voters Purged
8/26/2003	NCOA Postcard	7,118
1/5/2002	Purge at end of Inactive Period	84,876
7/6/2001	NVRA	83,420

Based on "snapshot" from Aug 2004, prior to converting to Diebold DIMS Voter Registration System
Sunday, February 19, 2006   Analyst: Victoria Lovegren, Ph.D.

Document 1.9.2

PRECINCT	Number Purged	Voters Not Purged	Before Two Purges	Percent Purged	Registered Voters 2000	Ballots Cast 2000	Percent Turnout 2000	Percent Gore 2000
BAY VILLAGE	1441	10751	12192	11.82%	12294	8441	68.66%	37.16%
BEACHWOOD	1018	7740	8758	11.62%	9071	5628	62.04%	82.52%
BEDFORD	1524	7071	8595	17.73%	8201	5319	64.86%	62.10%
BEDFORD HEIGHTS	1251	5715	6966	17.96%	6661	4418	66.33%	86.61%
BENTLEYVILLE	91	582	673	13.52%	717	470	65.55%	31.20%
BEREA	2048	9838	11886	17.23%	11961	7337	61.34%	53.86%
BRATENAHL	174	890	1064	16.35%	1052	724	68.82%	54.55%
BRECKSVILLE	1089	8639	9728	11.19%	9570	6552	68.46%	34.86%
BROADVIEW HEIGHTS	1690	9568	11258	15.01%	10277	6990	68.02%	40.64%
BROOKLYN	1196	6250	7446	16.06%	7609	4965	65.25%	61.41%
BROOKLYN HEIGHTS VIL	101	921	1022	9.88%	1159	771	66.52%	51.46%
BROOK PARK	2392	11205	13597	17.59%	13933	8301	59.58%	62.64%
CHAGRIN FALLS	629	2414	3043	20.67%	2732	1989	72.80%	36.68%
CHAGRIN FALLS TWP	25	80	105	23.81%	118	69	58.47%	27.54%
CLEVELAND 01	2850	12090	14940	19.08%	15065	9401	62.40%	97.16%
CLEVELAND 02	2559	10095	12654	20.22%	12321	7343	59.60%	94.61%
CLEVELAND 03	3496	9988	13484	25.93%	12528	7421	59.24%	97.00%
CLEVELAND 04	3383	9387	12770	26.49%	11945	7389	61.86%	92.66%
CLEVELAND 05	3694	8602	12296	30.04%	8180	4725	57.76%	96.24%
CLEVELAND 06	4569	9323	13892	32.89%	11397	6158	54.03%	88.18%
CLEVELAND 07	4133	9537	13670	30.23%	10494	5758	54.87%	94.06%
CLEVELAND 08	3491	9152	12643	27.61%	11112	6477	58.29%	95.63%
CLEVELAND 09	3456	8655	12111	28.54%	11793	7247	61.45%	94.03%

CLEVELAND 10	2595	9572	2167	21.33%	10552	6539	61.97%	95.15%
CLEVELAND 11	1884	10220	2104	15.57%	11386	6895	60.56%	75.51%
CLEVELAND 12	1876	7773	9649	19.44%	9017	4569	50.67%	70.74%
CLEVELAND 13	3566	10493	4059	25.36%	10210	4784	46.86%	73.23%
CLEVELAND 14	4352	8251	2603	34.53%	10758	4752	44.17%	72.85%
CLEVELAND 15	2934	9141	2075	24.30%	11278	6531	57.91%	64.27%
CLEVELAND 16	2912	10123	3035	22.34%	12332	7378	59.83%	58.54%
CLEVELAND 17	3524	7147	0671	33.02%	9555	4679	48.97%	71.35%
CLEVELAND 18	3533	8645	2178	29.01%	10190	5397	52.96%	69.66%
CLEVELAND 19	3158	9024	2182	25.92%	11618	6877	59.19%	68.02%
CLEVELAND 20	3021	10286	3307	22.70%	10886	6540	60.08%	64.26%
CLEVELAND 21	1893	13352	5245	12.42%	14663	9417	64.22%	55.95%
CLEVELAND TOTAL	63721	191832	255553	24.93%	237280	136277	57.43%	80.48%
CLEVELAND HEIGHTS 01	1557	3867	5424	28.71%	4779	3453	72.25%	67.78%
CLEVELAND HEIGHTS 02	1144	4960	6104	18.74%	6278	4467	71.15%	70.49%
CLEVELAND HEIGHTS 03	1115	3644	4759	23.43%	4780	3297	68.97%	80.73%
CLEVELAND HEIGHTS 04	1799	6917	8716	20.64%	8423	5874	69.74%	80.32%
CLEVELAND HEIGHTS 05	1310	5598	6908	18.95%	7001	4975	71.06%	85.23%
CLEVELAND HTS TOTAL	6925	24986	31911	21.70%	31261	22066	70.59%	77.50%
CUYAHOGA HEIGHTS	26	472	498	5.22%	525	319	60.76%	55.52%
EAST CLEVELAND	4234	10632	4866	28.43%	12896	7939	61.56%	96.53%
EUCLID 01	1250	6900	8150	15.34%	7857	5308	67.56%	58.02%
EUCLID 02	1793	6554	8347	21.43%	7440	4819	64.77%	61.45%
EUCLID 03	1306	5990	7296	17.90%	7292	4630	63.49%	69.82%

Document 1.9.2—Continued

EUCLID 04	1404	7010	8414	16.69%	7055	4806	68.12%	73.90%
EUCLID TOTAL	5753	26454	32207	17.86%	29644	19563	65.99%	65.51%
FAIRVIEW PARK	2020	10441	12461	16.21%	12566	8303	66.08%	46.32%
GARFIELD HEIGHTS	3398	14472	17870	19.02%	18844	11346	60.21%	61.23%
GATES MILLS	145	1747	1892	7.66%	1773	1344	75.80%	28.67%
GLENWILLOW	56	307	363	15.43%	277	166	59.93%	46.95%
HIGHLAND HEIGHTS	506	5019	5525	9.16%	5596	3804	67.98%	43.90%
HIGHLAND HILLS	175	512	687	25.47%	603	273	45.27%	96.95%
HUNTING VALLEY	72	408	480	15.00%	484	296	61.16%	27.89%
INDEPENDENCE	614	4592	5206	11.79%	5269	3563	67.62%	42.58%
LAKEWOOD 01	1940	6997	8937	21.71%	8288	5446	65.71%	51.79%
LAKEWOOD 02	1829	6995	8824	20.73%	8490	5665	66.73%	54.73%
LAKEWOOD 03	1841	7040	8881	20.73%	8467	5548	65.52%	55.31%
LAKEWOOD 04	2260	6956	9216	24.52%	7860	4992	63.51%	59.23%
LAKEWOOD TOTAL	7870	27988	35858	21.95%	33105	21651	65.40%	55.17%
LINNDALE	11	76	87	12.64%	92	57	61.96%	69.81%
LYNDHURST	1303	9767	11070	11.77%	11199	7560	67.51%	51.92%
MAPLE HEIGHTS	2576	13495	16071	16.03%	16032	9612	59.96%	76.52%
MAYFIELD HEIGHTS	2330	9689	12019	19.39%	11795	7459	63.24%	61.26%
MAYFIELD VILLAGE	398	2076	2474	16.09%	2427	1634	67.33%	39.74%
MIDDLEBURG HEIGHTS	1502	9172	10674	14.07%	10193	6683	65.56%	50.30%
MORELAND HILLS	379	2300	2679	14.15%	2635	1752	66.49%	46.27%
NEWBURGH HEIGHTS	154	1016	1170	13.16%	1174	737	62.78%	62.20%
NORTH OLMSTED	3306	19332	22638	14.60%	21645	14422	66.63%	47.81%

NORTH RANDALL	99	674	773	12.81%	694	344	49.57%	86.75%
NORTH ROYALTON	3076	16371	19447	15.82%	18051	12130	67.20%	41.86%
OAKWOOD VILLAGE	394	2006	2400	16.42%	2475	1446	58.42%	83.80%
OLMSTED FALLS	701	4792	5493	12.76%	5117	3539	69.16%	46.84%
OLMSTED TOWNSHIP	978	6245	7223	13.54%	6890	4547	65.99%	48.21%
ORANGE	164	2174	2338	7.01%	2259	1599	70.78%	68.12%
PARMA 01	1204	4517	5721	21.05%	5454	3388	62.12%	55.09%
PARMA 02	1017	5011	6028	16.87%	6213	3964	63.80%	55.88%
PARMA 03	863	3808	4671	18.48%	5414	3411	63.00%	58.28%
PARMA 04	974	4056	5030	19.36%	4979	3141	63.08%	58.63%
PARMA 05	732	5198	5930	12.34%	6088	4215	69.23%	49.65%
PARMA 06	794	4752	5546	14.32%	5744	3934	68.49%	52.53%
PARMA 07	965	5230	6195	15.58%	6255	4226	67.56%	50.93%
PARMA 08	1155	4898	6053	19.08%	5940	3755	63.22%	52.62%
PARMA 09	869	4581	5450	15.94%	5571	3602	64.66%	54.56%
PARMA TOTAL	8573	42051	50624	16.93%	51658	33636	65.11%	53.99%
PARMA HEIGHTS	2496	11063	13559	18.41%	13543	8361	61.74%	51.31%
PEPPER PIKE	487	4120	4607	10.57%	4625	3138	67.85%	56.14%
RICHMOND HEIGHTS	1256	5570	6826	18.40%	6413	4197	65.45%	59.51%
ROCKY RIVER	2082	12960	15042	13.84%	14652	9650	65.86%	38.64%
SEVEN HILLS	1144	7329	8473	13.50%	8763	6020	68.70%	47.21%
SHAKER HEIGHTS	4595	17430	22025	20.86%	21270	14182	66.68%	71.54%
SOLON	2569	12094	14663	17.52%	14747	9850	66.79%	51.41%
SOUTH EUCLID	2675	12127	14802	18.07%	15047	10323	68.61%	65.81%

Document 1.9.2—Continued

STRONGSVILLE 01	1094	5745	6839	16.00%	6276	4324	68.90%	43.80%
STRONGSVILLE 02	1694	8310	10004	16.93%	9461	6542	69.15%	38.31%
STRONGSVILLE 03	415	6106	6521	6.36%	6154	4306	69.97%	41.48%
STRONGSVILLE 04	367	5705	6072	6.04%	5837	4079	69.88%	41.22%
STRONGSVILLE TOTAL	3570	25866	29436	12.13%	27728	19251	69.43%	40.87%
UNIVERSITY HEIGHTS	1595	7010	8605	18.54%	9032	5961	66.00%	69.77%
VALLEY VIEW	131	1511	1642	7.98%	1718	1132	65.89%	47.97%
WALTON HILLS	191	1567	1758	10.86%	1805	1306	72.35%	49.37%
WARRENSVILLE HEIGHTS	2202	7504	9706	22.69%	8908	6059	68.02%	95.33%
WESTLAKE	3753	18415	22168	16.93%	21915	13916	63.50%	36.45%
WOODMERE VILLAGE	137	366	503	27.24%	392	273	69.64%	82.53%
REGULAR VOTERS					820372	519660	63.34%	
ABSENTEE					820372	70813	8.63%	
COUNTY TOTALS	168169	696718	864887	19.44%	820372	590473	71.98%	62.62%

Document 1.10

The Greater Cleveland Voter Registration Coalition

Summary of Testimony Prepared by Norman Robbins, Study Leader, Greater Cleveland Voter Registration Coalition, for Congressional Forum in Columbus, Ohio – December 13, 2004

DE FACTO DISENFRANCHISEMENT OF VOTERS BY THE CUYAHOGA COUNTY BOARD OF ELECTIONS

MAJOR FINDINGS

- Significant flaws in registration: Based on our studies on the fate of about 9600 applications we submitted to the Board of Elections, we warned that the votes of about 10,000 Cuyahoga County citizens could be compromised because of failures or errors in entering registrations. Response of the Board: denigration, minimization. Result: many were informed they could not vote, others had provisional ballots rejected.

- Provisional ballot rejections: Cuyahoga County had one of the highest rejection rates in the state. By computer matching, we found that at least 600 fully registered individuals had been wrongfully deleted from the polling lists and then had their provisional ballots rejected. Response of the Board: Chalk it up to "human error" and proceed with certification (Oct. 29, 2004).

- Inadequate or delayed response to constructive citizen input: On numerous occasions where the Voter Registration Coalition pointed out serious errors in registration or voting practices – e.g., the registration errors noted above, policies on correcting incomplete registrations, erroneous information on Board of Elections web site, request for vital data on provisional ballot rejections – there was either no response or defensive opposition.

- These and other flaws negatively many voters but disproportionately disenfranchise the poor, the young, and minorities – in effect, denying them equal protection.

RECOMMENDATIONS:

- Federal Voting Legislation should insist that as a condition for receiving federal funding, states MUST repair ALL election-related procedures that have been shown to produce disproportionate disenfranchisement, directly or indirectly. By the same token, all new procedures must first evaluate to ensure they do not selectively tend to disenfranchise any sector of the population.

- As a requirement for states to receive HAVA funding, a state bipartisan citizen advisory committees drawn from a fair cross-section of the population, must be established. Such committees, whose core mission should be to provide responsible citizen input, should be required to submit annual reports to the Federal government on the degree to which their advice is seriously considered and followed.

Document 1.10—Continued

The Greater Cleveland Voter Registration Coalition

RECOMMENDATIONS (continued):

- In order to avoid disenfranchisement lost or incorrect entries, voters or registration groups should receive scanned and verified receipts for registrations submitted to Boards of Election.

- No provisional ballots should be rejected without consulting the original registration form and without searching for glitches, which cause voters to be inadvertently dropped from the Boards database of registered voters. In all cases voters should be given timely notice of rejection and opportunity to contest their rejections.

Document 1.10—Continued

The Greater Cleveland Voter Registration Coalition

THE GREATER CLEVELAND VOTER REGISTRATION COALITION (GCVRC)* REPORT TO THE HOUSE JUDICIARY COMMITTEE, DEC. 7, 2004

12-13-04 UPDATE OF DOCUMENT SUBMITTED TO THE JUDICIARY COMMITTEE ON 12-7-04
ELECTION IRREGULARITIES IN CUYAHOGA COUNTY, OHIO
Submitted by: Norman Robbins, Study Leader
(Contact information: N. Robbins 216-767-1525; nxr@cwru.edu;
J. Gallo 216-391-0900, judy.gallo@ula-ohio.org)

PROBLEM ONE:

Lack of response to local studies showing that a significant number of submitted registration applications were never entered on the rolls or were entered incorrectly

The studies: The GCVRC registered approximately 10,000 voters (new registrations and changes of address), making copies of all submissions to the Board of Elections (BOE).
Two studies were done, comparing registrations submitted by the GCVRC to the Cuyahoga BOE, to those that appeared on the official rolls and on the BOE's computer database. The first study (in September) tracked 2183 and the second (late October) approximately 7400 submissions. A total of 3.5% of these applications were never entered (new registrations and address updates) or the addresses were entered incorrectly. These errors would either totally disenfranchise voters or cause their entries on the polling books to be erroneous, forcing some voters to use provisional ballot. Projecting our results from these approximately 9500 individual submissions to the 312,000 non-duplicate submissions received by the Cuyahoga County BOE, we estimate that over 10,000 voters in Cuyahoga County would be compromised because of these clerical errors.

See Attachment 1 – Table 1

Supporting data available on request: Databases of individuals suffering clerical errors found in these two studies, plus copies of original registration cards for almost all of these individuals.

Lack of BOE Response to requests for action:
(Documentation available on request)
1. Preliminary results of the first study were sent to the BOE on Sept. 17, 2004 for them to check our results. No response.
2. When we used our results to do a media campaign to warn all voters to check their registration status before the registration deadline of Oct. 4, 2004, and to re-register if necessary, BOE Director Michael Vu accused study leader, Norman Robbins, of "inciting panic".
3. BOE Director Vu was present at 2 County Commissioner's meetings where the first study results were presented, and a request was made for a search at the BOE for missing applications. Director Vu strongly objected.

Document 1.10—Continued

The Greater Cleveland Voter Registration Coalition

4. A law suit to force the BOE to correct errors pointed out by the studies and to search its files for lost registrations was denied by U.S. District Judge Matia on Oct. 27, 2004, on the basis that he was satisfied that "The procedures put in place by the Board of Elections appear to be reasonably calculated to correct any defects in the registration process". This, despite his statement at the outset of the hearing that the facts should not be the issue.

5. On Oct. 29, Director Vu received a list and documentation of 303 applications from our study with a written request that these voters be reinstated before the deadline for correction. No response received.

6. On Nov. 29, when we presented to the full BOE our findings that at least 30 of the registrations submitted had ended up voting provisional ballots which were rejected, and when we projected that nearly1,000 voters in Cuyahoga County were likely to be in the same predicament, the BOE refused to accept our plea to check all rejected provisional ballots against the original application, nor to accept as evidence for reinstatement our copies of applications that were never entered. They did not contest our findings, but rather said this was normal "human error" and was a small percent of all voters.

PROBLEM TWO:

Failure of the Cuyahoga BOE to investigate and reinstate rejected provisional ballots where our evidence showed that 463 fully registered voters were probably incorrectly classified as "not registered" or rejected for other reasons ("no signature on provisional ballot envelope") when they should not have had to vote a provisional ballot in the first place.

Using a computer cross-check search of the entire county data bases of registered voters on August 17 and on Oct. 22, and comparing these against the list of rejected provisional ballot voters, we found that:

1. 201 voters who were registered in August 17, were taken off the rolls by Oct. 22, and forced to vote provisional ballots which were then rejected because they were not found to be registered.

2. 262 fully registered voters as of the BOE list of Oct. 22 were nonetheless found on the provisional rejection list, 183 classified as "Not Registered" and 79 as "No Signature".

These data, with full documentation of names and addresses, were presented to the full Cuyahoga BOE on 11-29-04. In addition, we pointed out that our searches were incomplete because of limitations of data and time, i.e. that many more individuals were likely to be found with more additional cross-check searches, and that date of birth information would make the search results more secure. The Board did not contest our data, but said again it was just a small percentage due to human error, and then proceeded to certify the entire Cuyahoga County vote even though they thereby knowingly possibly disenfranchised 463 individuals.

(Full Data sheets of these names and addresses available; also cover sheet accompanying our presentation to the BOE on 11-29-04)

Director Vu was quoted in the Plain Dealer as saying he was willing to look into the data supplied at the Oct. 29 meeting. This was e-mailed to him on Oct. 30, but there has been no further response.

Document 1.10—Continued

The Greater Cleveland Voter Registration Coalition

We knew that our estimates of wrongfully disenfranchised voters were low, because we were not able to obtain date-of-birth and precinct information from the BOE, which would have allowed a better search and are essential for analyzing rejections due to voting in the wrong precinct. Also, we know of individuals who are not on our database but who claimed they were regular voters and yet did not find their names on the polling lists on Nov. 2, 2004.

Update: When we at last obtained date of birth information and put it in usable format, we found (Dec. 12, 2004) even a greater number of individuals affected than in the earlier searches. There were 286 provisional ballots rejected as "not registered" from individuals that had been dropped from the rolls after Aug. 17 and about 320 that were on the registration lists on Oct. 22 but not on the polling lists on November 2, or about 600 total. In addition, we were apprised of several individuals, not on our list, that claimed they had voted regularly and yet were not on the rolls. For this reason, we know that our searches are incomplete.

PROBLEM THREE:
In their printed communications with voters, the Cuyahoga BOE incorrectly told absentee voters that if they applied for an absentee ballot, thereafter they could not vote instead at their assigned polling place.

In contrast to many if not all other counties in Ohio, the Cuyahoga BOE policy was to allow absentee applicants to vote at regular polling places once the poll worker determined they had not voted already via absentee ballot. This option became necessary for absentee applicants who never received their ballots in the days before the election, or who chose for other reasons to vote at the polling place (e.g. far easier to manage punch card ballot with polling machine).

However, the "Absent Voter Booklet" sent to all absentee applicants states "Any voter who has requested an absent voter ballot will not be permitted to vote in person at a polling place on election day". Also, the "Official Voter Information Guide", sent about 1 week before the election to all registered voters in Cuyahoga County, states "Once you have requested such a {absentee}ballot, you will not be allowed to vote in person at your precinct".

When this error was pointed out to Director Vu, he issued one press release with a correction, but this was totally inadequate public communication to a county with over some 90,000 absentee applicants. Given the seriousness of the error, notification should have been sent in writing to all absentee voters who had not yet voted.

(Documentation available: Copies of Absent Voter Booklet and Voter Information Guide.

Document 1.10—Continued

PROBLEM FOUR:

Failure of the Cuyahoga County Board to provide the public with readily usable and timely election data:

When the provisional ballot acceptance/rejection information was first made available on Oct. 22, 2004, as a printed document listing only cities and wards, GCVRC asked for data on the names and addresses of accepted and rejected provisional voters. On Oct. 23, the BOE supplied only a pdf file, saying it could not supply the information in database format. In response to a subsequent request on Oct. 23 or 24, Director Vu promised Dan Kozminski, GCVRC volunteer, that he would make a database format file available in 2-3 days and that it would include ward, precinct, and date of birth. Despite 3 follow-up calls, there was no response as of 18 days later (Dec. 6, 2004). While date of birth information in pdf format was obtained in the week of Dec. 6, it took intervention by Congresswoman Tubbs-Jones to get a promise of access to ward and precinct information (Result remains to be seen, as of this date).

PROBLEM FIVE:

Lack of response of the BOE Director to public input on correction of registrations

As of Oct. 14, the Cuyahoga County Board of Elections listed almost 10,000 voters as "fatal pending" – meaning that if errors in their registration were not corrected by Oct. 29, they would lose their vote. Another 3,500 voters are on the same list, pending further Board investigation. In the studies cited above, we predicted that 10,000 individuals might be affected because of clerical errors. Unfortunately, Michael Vu, Board of Elections Director, effectively delayed correction of these errors for 11 of the 19 workdays between the end of registration and the deadline for changes. Further, despite requests, Mr. Vu has issued no formal policy, and different voters calling the BOE got different stories on how to correct registration errors from the BOE phone operators.

The Board has complete authority in setting the rules for correcting "fatal pendings". Indeed, those with omitted information (date of birth, identification, signature) were sent letters requesting correction, but those letters did not indicate any deadline for receipt, and those who registered close to the deadline were at first unable to make changes. In addition, for 8 working days of the 19 day window for correction, Vu suspended the past practice of correcting registrations, claiming he needed a legal opinion from the County Prosecutor and the Sec. of State. However, that opinion was requested only one week before Oct. 4, thus losing part of the correction time because of the late moment at which this opinion was requested.

One day after receiving the County Prosecutor's opinion that the past practices were legitimate, Director Vu still held out until he heard from the Sec. of State. The next day, Oct. 14, he suddenly reversed his decision, supposedly allowing corrections of registration. However, after telling 4 individuals what the process for correction would be, he refused to correct or sign a written summary of his statements, and Board phone operators give inconsistent responses to requests for corrections. There was not a clear-cut or written set of policies to follow, leaving voters thoroughly confused.

Document 1.10—Continued

The Greater Cleveland Voter Registration Coalition

PROBLEM SIX:

Failure of the Secretary of State to respond to responsible citizen input on election procedures. The Greater Cleveland Voter Registration Coalition sent a letter to Secretary of State Blackwell on July 29 (Attachment Two) making numerous practical suggestions to improve the upcoming elections. These suggestions were related to registration, administration of polling places, proper use of voting machines (especially punch cards), and need for voter education in specific areas where voters are typically confused. Many of these suggestions, to be effective, required early action, but no answer was received for over 1 month, and only in response to follow-up calls. No specific actions were promised. Another citizen's group (Citizens Alliance for Secure Elections) later pressed for some of the same reforms with little result. The one exception was a voter educational program on punch card voting.

Document 1.11

Addie Smith
1991 Fountainview Ct
Columbus, OH 43232

```
SMIT991*  432322009 1603  19 10/29/04
FORWARD TIME EXP  RTN TO SEND
SMITH SR
1445 E BROAD ST APT 402A
COLUMBUS OH 43205-1561
            RETURN TO SENDER
```

Received 11/2/04

IMPORTANT REMINDER

You have previously received a notice informing you that your right to vote has been challenged. This card is to remind you that you have the right to appear at a hearing before the Franklin County Board of Elections to answer that challenge. **The Board will meet on Thursday, October 28, 2004 beginning at 9:00 a.m. at Franklin County Memorial Hall, 280 East Broad Street, in downtown Columbus.** It is recommended that you bring identification documents with you that show your place of residence such as a valid Ohio Driver's license, a utility bill, a bank statement, or a government check.

Document 1.12

Affidavit

I, James Branscome, residing at 115 South 36th Street, Newark, Ohio, 43055-3682, do swear and affirm the following:

1. I am an employee of the Holiday Inn, 175 E. Town St., Columbus, Ohio 43215. I work the 3:30-12pm shift drivng people to and from the airport. I have personal knowledge of the incidents relayed below.

2. On October 27, 2004, I picked up 7-10 individuals from the airport to drive them to the Holiday Inn. I made two more runs to pick up people from the group, for a total of approximately 25 people.

3. The individuals identified themselves as the Texas Strike Force. Most of them said they were from Texas, one person was from Florida.

4. The individuals stated they had paid their own way to come to Ohio. The Holiday Inn record for payment for their hotel rooms indicated the rooms were paid for by the Ohio Republican Party.

5. Their hotel rooms were in the back of the hotel, directly overlooking the Republican Party headquarters, which was behind the Holiday Inn.

6. On November 1, I overheard one of the Texas Strike Force men talking on the pay phone in the hotel lobby. He was telling someone that he would call the FBI on them if they went out to vote. He had a big "W" on his shirt.

7. Laverne Sanders, night auditor at the hotel, called the police. When the police arrived, they did nothing. One of the female Texas Strike Force individuals told the police about Democrats at the hotel who were "speaking Arabic."

8. The phone caller from the Texas Strike Force accused the hotel personnel of violating his civil rights. He was staying in room 617 and was identified by another individual in the hotel as an attorney from California.

TO THIS I SWEAR AND AFFIRM,

_____   _____
NAME (Signature)   DATE

_____
        Notary Public

Document 1.13

Preserving Democracy: What Went Wrong in Ohio

Status Report of the
House Judiciary Committee Democratic Staff

January 5, 2005

Document 1.13—Continued

4.   Targeting New Minority Voter Registrants – *Caging*

Facts

The Ohio Republican Party attempted to engage in "caging," whereby it sent registered letters to newly registered voters in minority and urban areas, and then sought to challenge 35,000 individuals who refused to sign for the letters or the mail otherwise came back as undeliverable (this includes voters who were homeless, serving abroad, or simply did not want to sign for something concerning the Republican Party). Mark Weaver, an attorney for the Ohio Republican Party, acknowledged the Party used this technique.[167] During a hearing before the Summit County Board of Elections, a challenger admitted that she had no knowledge to substantiate her claim that the voters she was challenging were out of compliance with Ohio's election law:[168]

MS. Barbara MILLER (Republican Challenger): That was my impression that these items that I signed were for people whose mail had been undeliverable for several times, and that they did not live at the residence.

MR. Russell PRY (Member, Summit County Board of Elections): Did you personally send any mail to Ms. Herrold?

MS. MILLER: No, I did not.

MR. PRY: Have you seen any mail that was returned to Ms. Herrold?

MS. MILLER: No, I have not.

MR. PRY: Do you have any personal knowledge as we stand here today that Ms. Herrold does not live at the address at 238 30th Street Northwest?

MS. MILLER: Only that which was my impression; that their mail had not been able to be delivered.

MR. PRY: And who gave you that impression?

MS. MILLER: Attorney Jim Simon.

MR. PRY: And what did --

MS. MILLER: He's an officer of the party.

---

[167]Bill Sloat, *Judge Orders Halt to County Hearings Challenging Voters*, PLAIN DEALER, Oct. 30, 2004, at A1.

[168]Hearing of the Summit County Board of Elections, Oct. 28, 2004, partial transcripts available at http://www.mydd.com/story/2004/10/28/192844/76.

Document 1.13—Continued

MR. PRY: An officer of which party?

MS. MILLER: Republican party.

MR. PRY: Where did you complete this challenge form at?

MS. MILLER: My home.

MR. PRY: What did Mr. Simon tell you with respect to Ms. Herrold's residence?

MS. MILLER: That the mail had come back undeliverable several times from that residence.

MR. PRY: And you never saw the returned mail?

MS. MILLER: No, I did not.

MR. PRY: Now, you've indicated that you signed this based on some personal knowledge.

MR. HUTCHINSON: (Joseph F. Hutchinson, Jr. Summit County Board of Elections) No

MR. ARSHINKOFF: (Alex R. Arshinkoff, Summit County Board of Elections) Reason to believe. It says, "I have reason to believe." It says it on the form.

MR. JONES: It says, "I hereby declare under penalty of election falsification, that the statements above are true as I verily believe."

MR. ARSHINKOFF: It says here, "I have reason to believe."

MR. HUTCHINSON: It says what it says.

MR. ARSHINKOFF: You want her indicted, get her indicted.

MR. PRY: That may be where it goes next.

Among other things, the Republican Party arranged for the Sandusky County sheriff to visit the residences of 67 voters with wrong or non-existent addresses.[169]

The caging tactics were so problematic that a federal district court in New Jersey and a panel of the Third Circuit found that the Republican Party was egregiously in violation of the 1982 and 1987 decrees that barred the party from targeting minority voters for challenges at the polls.[170] They found sufficient evidence that the Ohio Republican Party and the RNC conspired

---

[169]*See id.*

[170]DNC v. RNC, No. 04-4186, slip. op. (3d Cir. 2004) (upholding DNC v. RNC, No. 81-cv-3876, slip op. (D.N.J. 2004)).

Document 1.13—Continued

to be "disruptive" in minority-majority districts and enjoined the party from using the list.[171] The Third Circuit granted a hearing en banc and therefore stayed the order and vacated the opinion.[172]

The U.S. District Court for the Southern District of Ohio found the same activities to violate the Due Process Clause of the Constitution.[173] Most importantly, notice of the Republican-intended challenge and subsequent hearing was sent to the 35,000 voters far too late to be of any use to the challengee.[174] In fact, the notice was sent so late, that many did not receive it before the election at all, and the court found that ineffective notice must have been the intent:

> The Defendants' intended timing and manner of sending notice is not reasonably calculated to apprise Plaintiff Voters of the hearing regarding the challenge to their registrations, nor to give the them opportunity to present their objections, as demonstrated by the individual situations of Plaintiffs Miller and Haddix...it seems that Defendants intend to send the notice to an address which has already been demonstrated to be faulty.[175]

The court also found that the challenge statute in general was not narrowly tailored enough justify the "severe" burden on voters.[176] While the state's interest in preventing fraudulent voting was compelling, there were other ways to do that besides allowing partisan groups to arbitrarily challenge voters.[177]

Analysis

Although the "caging" tactics targeting 35,000 new voters by the Ohio Republican Party were eventually struck down, it is likely they had a negative impact on the inclination of minorities to vote; although, it is difficult to develop a specific estimate.

---

[171]*Id.* at 5.

[172]DNC v. RNC, No. 04-4186 (3d Cir. 2004) (granting en banc hearing and staying panel's order enjoining use of caging list). While District Courts in Ohio granted preliminary injunctions to the same effect, the Sixth Circuit overturned their orders because the opinions did not rely on racial discrimination. Those cases both found constitutional violations from the presence of challengers generally. *See* Summit County Democratic Central and Executive Committee v. Blackwell, 388 F.3d 547 (6th Cir. 2004).

[173]Miller v. Blackwell, 2004 WL 2827763 (S.D. Ohio 2004).

[174]*Id.* at *4.

[175]*Id.*

[176]Spencer v. Blackwell, 2004 WL 2827758, (S.D. Ohio 2004).

[177]*Id.* at *8.

Document 1.13—Continued

The caging tactics were clearly both discriminatory and illegal. All three district court cases ruled in favor of the plaintiffs, finding the challenges to be politically and racially charged, and burdening the fundamental right to vote. As one court stated, "This Court recognizes that the right to vote is one of our most fundamental rights. Potential voter intimidation would severely burden the right to vote. Therefore, the character and magnitude of Plaintiffs' asserted injury is substantial."[178] It went on to note that the right to vote is paramount to any interest in challenging other people: "...Plaintiff's right to cast votes on election day is a fundamental right. The challengers, however, do not have a fundamental right to challenge other voters.[179] These decisions correctly overturned these caging and challenging activities because *they violated the right to equal protection, due process, and Ohioans' fundamental right to vote.*

Ralph Neas, President of the People for the American Way Foundation, emphasized the seriousness of these tactics when he testified that "the 35,000 people that were threatened with being challenged. That's not the spirit of democracy; that's the spirit of suppression. [The Republican Party] did everything to minimize the vote in the urban areas and to engage in voter suppression, and I hope the hearings really emphasize this. *I think that prosecution is something that should be considered with respect to what happened in Ohio.* "[180]

5.   Targeting Minority and Urban Voters for Legal Challenges

Facts

The Ohio Republican Party, which Secretary Blackwell helped lead as Chair of the Bush-Cheney campaign in Ohio, engaged in a massive campaign to challenge minority voters at the polls.[181] The Republican Party lined up poll challengers for 30 of Ohio's 88 counties, and the vast majority were focused in minority and urban areas.[182] In addition to intimidating minority voters, this scheme helped lead to increased delays and longer waits in voting lines in these areas. This was a particularly damaging outcome on a day of severe adverse weather in Ohio. As a federal court looking at these issues concluded:

---

[178] *Id.* at 10 (internal citations omitted).

[179] *Id.* at 12.

[180] *Preserving Democracy – What Went Wrong in Ohio: Democratic Forum Before the House Comm. on the Judiciary* (Dec. 8, 2004) (statement of Ralph Neas) (emphasis added).

[181] *See* Tim Jones, *Court OK's GOP Bid to Challenge Voters*, CHICAGO TRIB., Nov. 2, 2004, at C14.

[182] *Id.*

Document 1.13—Continued

if challenges are made with any frequency, the resultant distraction and delay could give rise to chaos and a level of voter frustration that would turn qualified electors away from the polls.[183]

Three separate courts issued opinions expressing serious concerns with Ohio's voter challenge processes. At the state level, Cuyahoga County Common Pleas Judge John O'Donnell found that Secretary Blackwell exceeded his authority in issuing a directive that let each political party have multiple challengers at each polling place.[184] While the Democratic Party registered only one challenger per polling place, the Republican Party had registered one challenger for each precinct (there are multiple precincts in many polling places).[185] Judge O'Donnell found the directive to be "unlawful, arbitrary, unreasonable and unconscionable, coming *four days after the deadline* for partisan challengers to register with their county boards of elections."[186] An attorney with the Ohio Attorney General's office, Jeffrey Hastings, admitted to Judge O'Donnell that Secretary Blackwell had changed his mind in first limiting challengers to one per polling place and then, after the October 22 challenger registration deadline, allowing multiple challengers.[187]

Two federal district court judges also found the challenge procedure to be problematic and tantamount to voter disenfranchisement.[188] In one lawsuit, the plaintiffs were Donald and Marian Spencer, an elderly African-American couple who alleged the challenge statute harkened back to Jim Crow disenfranchisement. In her opinion rejecting the GOP challenger system, U.S. District Court Judge Susan Dlott wrote that "there exists an enormous risk of chaos, delay, intimidation and pandemonium inside the polls and in the lines out the door."[189] In the other district court case, *Summit County Democratic Central and Executive Committee, et. al. v.*

---

[183]Mark Niquette, *Finally, It's Time to Vote*, COLUMBUS DISPATCH, Nov. 2, 2004, at 1A.

[184]Donna Iacoboni, *Judge Cuts Number of Challengers at Polling Stations*, PLAIN DEALER, Oct. 31, 2004, at A1.

[185]*Id.*

[186]*Id.* (emphasis added).

[187]*Id.*

[188]*See* Summit County Democratic Central and Executive Committee v. Blackwell, 2004 U.S. Dist. LEXIS 22539 (N.D. Ohio 2004); Spencer v. Blackwell, 2004 U.S. Dist. LEXIS 22062 (S.D. Ohio 2004).

[189]*Spencer*, 2004 U.S. Dist. LEXIS at *20. *See also* Mark Niquette, *Finally, It's Time to Vote*, COLUMBUS DISPATCH, Nov. 2, 2004, at 1A. In an instance of rare involvement, the Assistant Attorney General for the U.S. Department of Justice, Alex Acosta, sent Judge Susan Dlott an unsolicited letter arguing in favor of the challenge statute and against the plaintiffs. *See* Henry Weinstein, *The Race for the White House: Justice Department Joins Election Legal Fight in Ohio*, L.A. TIMES, Nov. 1, 2004, at A15.

Document 1.13—Continued

Blackwell, Judge John R. Adams noted the risk that "the integrity of the election may be irreparably harmed."[190] "If challenges are made with any frequency," he wrote, "the resultant distraction and delay could give rise to chaos and a level of voter frustration that would turn qualified electors away from the polls."[191]

Judge Dlott also noted the racial disparity inherent in challenges, citing that only 14% of new voters in white areas would face challenges while up to 97% of new voters in black areas would face them.[192] The Chair of the Hamilton County Board of Elections, Timothy Burke, was an official defendant in the lawsuit but testified the use of the challenges was unprecedented.[193] Chairman Burke stated that the Republican Party had planned for challengers at 251 of Hamilton County's 1013 precincts; 250 of the challenged precincts have significant black populations.[194]

Both federal courts blocking the use of challengers highlighted that challengers were not needed because Ohio law already safeguarded elections from voter fraud by the use of election judges.[195] In particular, Ohio law mandates that four election judges staff each polling place and provides that the presiding judge of each group can make decisions regarding voter qualifications.[196]

Although Secretary Blackwell reversed his position and issued a statement on October 29, 2004, excluding challengers from polling places, his position became less relevant when Jim Petro, Ohio's Attorney General, argued in favor of the challenges taking place and said the Secretary's new statement was unlawful.[197] Seeing the irony in these conflicting opinions, Judge

---

[190]*Summit County Democratic Central and Executive Committee*, 2004 U.S. Dist. LEXIS at *25.

[191]*Id.*

[192]*Spencer*, 2004 U.S. Dist. LEXIS at *5. *See also* Henry Weinstein, *Late Ruling Allows GOP to Challenge Ohio Voters*, L.A. TIMES, Nov. 2, 2004, at A1.

[193]Henry Weinstein, *The Race for the White House: In Ohio Courts, It's Almost Like Florida in 2000*, L.A. TIMES, Oct. 30, 2004, at A20.

[194]*Id.*

[195]*Summit County Democratic Central and Executive Committee*, 2004 U.S. Dist. LEXIS at *21.

[196]OHIO REV. CODE § 3501.22.

[197]*See* Statement of Jim Petro, Attorney General of the State of Ohio, Election Issues (Oct. 29, 2004) (press release) ("Neither the Secretary of State nor I can negotiate away the legal rights of Ohio's citizens. Thus, I cannot submit to the federal courts the Secretary's unlawful proposal to ban all challengers for all parties, candidates or issues on Election day."). *See also Spencer*, 2004 U.S. Dist. LEXIS at *25-26.

Document 1.13—Continued

Dlott asked "how can the average election official or inexperienced challenger be expected to understand the challenge process if the two top election officials cannot?"[198]

These two lower court rulings did not stand. The Sixth Circuit Court of Appeals reversed the two lower court opinions on a 2-1 vote.[199] The Supreme Court of the United States denied the applications to vacate the 6th Circuit's stays of the lower court rulings.[200] While troubled about the "undoubtedly serious" accusation of voter intimidation, Justice John Paul Stevens said the full Court could not consider the case because there was insufficient time to properly review the filings and submissions.[201]

Analysis

The decision by the Ohio Republican Party to utilize thousands of partisan challengers in the voting booths undoubtedly had an intimidating and negative impact on minority voters. While it is difficult to estimate how many voters were disenfranchised by the challenger program, *given the adverse weather conditions and the lack of trained pollworkers, the disruptions caused by challengers could easily have reduced minority turnout by tens of thousands of voters, if not more. It is noteworthy that these disruptions were predicted by Republican officials:*

> *Mark Weaver, a lawyer for the Ohio Republican Party, acknowledged, "[the challenges] won't be resolved until [Election Day], when all of these people are*

---

[198]*See* Henry Weinstein, *Late Ruling Allows GOP to Challenge Ohio Voters*, L.A. TIMES, Nov. 2, 2004, at A1.

[199]*See* Summit County Democratic Central and Executive Committee v. Heider; Spencer v. Pugh, 388 F.3d 547 (6th Cir. 2004) (the 6th Circuit granted stays of the temporary restraining orders issued by the lower courts and thus permitted the vote challengers to enter the polls at the general election).

[200]Spencer v. Pugh; *Summit County Democratic Central and Executive Committee v. Heider*, 125 S. Ct. 305 (2004) (Stevens, J.). *See also* Adam Liptak, *Justice Lets Ohio Ruling on Monitors at Polls Stand*, N.Y. TIMES, Nov. 3, 2004, at 6.

[201]*Spencer*, 2004 U.S. LEXIS at *2-3 ("The allegations of abuse made by the plaintiffs are undoubtedly serious - the threat of voter intimidation is not new to our electoral system - but on the record before me it is impossible to determine with any certainty the ultimate validity of the plaintiff's claims. Practical considerations, such as the difficulty of digesting all of the relevant filings and cases, and the challenge of properly reviewing all of the parties' submissions as a full Court in the limited timeframe available, weigh heavily against granting the extraordinary type of relief requested here."). *See also Summit County Democratic Central and Executive Committee*, 388 F.3d at 547; *see also* Tim Jones, *Court Ends Ohio GOP's Challenge of Voter Rolls*, Chicago Trib., Oct. 30, 2004.

Document 1.13—Continued

trying to vote. It can't help but create chaos, longer lines and frustration."[202]
He reiterated that "[challengers at the polls] were "bound to slow things down.
This will lead to long lines."[203]

While the program of challenging voters was ultimately upheld, after a series of back and forth decisions, clearly this is an issue which harkens back to the "Jim Crow" era. As U.S. District Court Judge John R. Adams wrote in his Summit County opinion:

> In light of these extraordinary circumstances, and the contentious nature of the imminent election, the Court cannot and must not turn a blind eye to the substantial likelihood that significant harm will result not only to voters, but also to the voting process itself, if appointed challengers are permitted at the polls on November 2. . . . The presence of appointed challengers at the polls could significantly impede the electoral process, and infringe on the rights of qualified voters."[204]

As a result, the Ohio challenger system deserves reconsideration by the legislature or further judicial appeal.

----

[202]James Dao, *GOP Bid to Contest Registrations is Blocked*, N.Y. TIMES, Oct. 28, 2004, at A25 (quoting Mark R. Weaver).

[203]Lisa Abraham, *Most Challenges Halted*, AKRON BEACON JOURNAL, Oct. 28, 2004 (quoting Mark R. Weaver).

[204]*Summit County et. al. Democratic Central and Executive Committee, et. al. v. Blackwell*, 2004 U.S. Dist. LEXIS 22539, *24 (N.D. Ohio 2004).

Document 1.14

YOU ARE HERE: Home > Communications/Press

Communications/Press

Did You Know? Ohio Fact
Ohio takes its name from the Ohio River. "Ohio" is an Iroquoian word meaning "great river."

Blackwell Predicts 72 Percent Voter Turnout

COLUMBUS – Secretary of State J. Kenneth Blackwell today announced that he anticipates approximately 72.68 percent of Ohio's 7.98 million registered voters will go to the polls on Tuesday, November 2.

"All registered voters, who haven't already voted by absentee ballot, should go to their correct precinct on Tuesday and exercise their most sacred civic right by voting for the candidates and issues of their choice," Blackwell said.

Ohio voter turnout for the General Election in 2000 was 63 percent; turnout in 1996 was 68 percent; turnout in 1992 was 77 percent. The prediction is based on information provided to the secretary of state by county boards of elections. Calculations were derived from the total number of registered voters, turnout figures of similar election years and other factors specific to individual counties, such as local races and ballot issues.

On Tuesday, polls throughout the state will be open from 6:30 a.m. until 7:30 p.m. Ohioans who have questions about the status of their voter registration or location of their assigned polling place should call their county board of elections. A directory of boards of elections is available at the secretary of state Web site by clicking here (PDF).

Click here for a county-by-county chart of registered voters (PDF File).

Document 1.15

Ms. Millender-McDonald. But are you saying----

Secretary Blackwell. So the answer to your question is in Ohio in this election, everybody got a provisional ballot that demanded one. There was a good-faith effort made to tell them that it had to be cast in the precinct in which they resided. Or, as Ohio law says, they could go down and vote at the County Board of Elections and if you happen to live in the county that was forward thinking enough and if they had provisional ballot centers, they could have voted there.

Ms. Millender-McDonald. I was going to ask you that. Why is it--so, in other words, provisional ballots are one thing but to count those that were submitted is another thing.

Secretary Blackwell. Right.

Ms. Millender-McDonald. So you still disenfranchise people for not counting these ballots when, in fact, you should have dragged them down to this provisional center where I suppose you have the setup for them to then follow through on whatever they need to for clearance.

Secretary Blackwell. They can be told that.

Ms. Millender-McDonald. I am sorry?

Secretary Blackwell. I would say in most counties they were told that. Voters have some responsibility. We don't run a taxicab service. The fact is that they were told the precinct in which they could vote and had that vote counted in accordance with Ohio law, not California law, not Massachusetts law. Well, in Massachusetts it wouldn't have counted. We, in fact, told voters that if they still insisted on a ballot, HAVA said they could get a ballot.

Ms. Millender-McDonald. That is correct.

Secretary Blackwell. And they got a ballot in Ohio. But Ohio law and the courts that upheld this said, ``We are not going to, in fact, be responsible for disenfranchising you. We will tell you where you are supposed to vote and if you don't want to do it and for whatever reason you want a provisional ballot----

Ms. Millender-McDonald. But they disenfranchised them anyway.

Secretary Blackwell. They disenfranchised themselves if they didn't vote in the right precinct.

Document 1.16

Statement by Secretary of State J. Kenneth Blackwell

Secretary of State J. Kenneth Blackwell today issued the following statement in reference to U.S. District Judge James G. Carr's provisional ballot decision:

"Judge Carr's decision today is a misinterpretation of the Help America Vote Act (HAVA). While HAVA establishes provisional voting nationally, the law specifically leaves the issuing and counting of those ballots to states in accordance with state law. On Tuesday, a federal court in Missouri reaffirmed our understanding of HAVA and contradicted Judge Carr's interpretation. In addition, the bi-partisan Federal Election Assistance Commission, in a resolution issued Tuesday, acknowledged that Ohio's provisional ballot law – which is shared by 27 other states – is in compliance with the Help America Vote Act. We continue to believe that Ohio's laws are fair, just and in compliance with all federal statutes.

"The State of Ohio will file an immediate and expedited appeal with the 6th Circuit Court of Appeals."

J. Kenneth Blackwell

Ohio Secretary of State

Document 1.17

Ms. Millender-McDonald. It was very honorable of you to 30 days out map outline differences of precincts as you outlined here where people should go to vote. It was three weeks, you say, from this information. Yet, you put out these cards to folks to let them know where they were supposed to go. Am I correct on what you said there?

Mr. Anthony. Yes, ma'am. It is two different things there. We had found out that a lot of groups had gotten the voter registration information from the Secretary of State's office. That information is probably six months old so it is not real current information. We provide the information to the Secretary of State's office. Then what happened----

Ms. Millender-McDonald. Are you saying information from the Secretary of State's office is old?

Mr. Anthony. It is six months beyond ours. We give to him and then we----

Ms. Millender-McDonald. How can that be?

Mr. Anthony. All that is getting ready to change now with the new voter registration system. During this time frame----

Ms. Millender-McDonald. That is awful.

Mr. Anthony. What happened was a lot of those groups purchased those lists from the Secretary of States and had the wrong precinct on them. That information was sent out to voters telling them where to go vote. There were phone calls out to some voters to tell them where to go vote and it was not the correct information. We took it upon ourselves that we should do that.

Ms. Millender-McDonald. So your Secretary of State was blaming you guys for this information.

Mr. Anthony. The other part of this, too, if you have got-- these guys probably know this.

Ms. Millender-McDonald. You can just answer yes or no on that.

Mr. Anthony. Yes. What happened is we are taking in voter registration forms on a daily basis so our stuff is up to date. Our information is up to date. We transmitted to the Secretary of State's office. I am not sure how that process works.

Ms. Millender-McDonald. Obviously they are not checking it or even implementing it if it is six months late for Heaven's sake.

Mr. Anthony. At any rate----

Ms. Millender-McDonald. You don't have to answer that. You have already done that by your silence.

Document 1.18

Ohio Secretary of State J. Kenneth Blackwell
Elections Division - 180 E. Broad St., 15th Floor, Columbus, OH
43215
    Tel. (614) 466-2585   Fax (614) 752-4360 e-mail:
election@sos.state.oh.us

Directive 2004-37
September 29, 2004

All County Boards of Elections

Consistent with my Order below rendered yesterday, you are to remove Nader/Camejo from the ballot immediately. You will receive more detailed instructions by the close of business today.

ORDER OF THE SECRETARY OF STATE

R.C. 3513.257 (A) provides that the nominating petitions at issue "shall be signed by no less than five thousand qualified electors." I find that the nominating petition at issue was in fact signed by no less than five thousand qualified electors, however, I accept the Recommendations as stated in the Findings of Fact and Conclusions of Law of the Hearing Examiner. Therefore, based upon the evidence presented the Nader petition will have 3,708 valid signatures, which is less than the minimum 5000 valid signatures necessary to appear on the presidential ballot in the State of Ohio. Therefore, the Boards of Elections will be ordered to remove the Nader/ Camejo joint candidacy from the presidential ballot or to otherwise notify voters that a vote cast for the Nader/Camejo candidacy will not be counted.

J. Kenneth Blackwell
Secretary of State
September 28, 2004

Sincerely,

J. Kenneth Blackwell

Document 1.19

 Ohio Secretary of State J. Kenneth Blackwell
Elections Division - 180 E. Broad St., 15th Floor, Columbus, OH 43215
Tel. (614) 466-2585 Fax (614) 752-4360   e-mail: election@sos.state.oh.us

Directive 2004-38
September 29, 2004

ALL COUNTY BOARDS OF ELECTIONS
TO: Members, Directors & Deputy Directors

REMOVAL OF NAMES OF NADER AND CAMEJO FROM THE BALLOT

This is a follow-up to Directive 2004-37 issued earlier today in which I directed you to remove the names Nader and Camejo from the ballot. Boards of elections shall remove the names of these joint candidates for president and vice president from the ballot to the extent practicable in the time remaining before the election and according to the instructions below.

A board of elections shall do one of the following:

(1) **Reprint the ballots without the names** of these joint candidates for president and vice president.

(2) **Remove these names** from existing ballots by use of stickers or other method adopted by the board as in the case of a withdrawn candidate.

(3) **Post a notice** in each precinct where the candidates' names remain on the ballot informing voters that any vote cast for these two candidates will not be counted, if the board determines it is not feasible to remove the two names from the ballots.

The board is obligated to revalidate the programming for accuracy regardless of the option chosen.

In determining which method to use, a board of elections shall consider all of the following factors:

(a)   The type of voting system used by the county;
(b)   The number of precincts and number of ballots, including absentee ballots yet to be distributed; and
(c)   The time remaining before election day.

A board of elections shall make all reasonable efforts to remove these two names from absentee ballots yet to be mailed. In the event the board determines it is not feasible to remove these two names from the absentee ballots yet to be mailed, a statement must be included with the ballot that informs the voter that any vote cast for these two candidates will not be counted. A board of elections shall not send new absentee ballots to absentee voters who have been sent an absentee ballot containing the names of these two candidates.

If you have any questions, please call the Elections Division at (614) 466-2585.

Sincerely,

J. Kenneth Blackwell

Document 1.20.1

IAL PRESIDENTIAL BALLOT
ELECTION – NOVEMBER 2, 2004
RANKLIN COUNTY, OHIO

For President:	For Vice-President:
MICHAEL BADNARIK	RICHARD V. and CAMPAGNA
other-party candidate	

For President:	For Vice-President:
GEORGE W. BUSH	DICK and CHENEY
Republican	

For President:	For Vice-President:
JOHN F. KERRY	JOHN and EDWARDS
Democrat	

For President:	For Vice-President:
RALPH NADER	PETER MIGUEL and CAMEJO

For President:	For Vice-President:
MICHAEL ANTHONY PEROUTKA	CHUCK and BALDWIN
other-party candidate	

OFFICIAL OFFICE TYPE BALLOT
GENERAL ELECTION – NOVEMBER 2, 2004
FRANKLIN COUNTY, OHIO

Office	Candidate	No.
For United States Senator (Vote for not more than ONE)	ERIC D. FINGERHUT Democrat	11
	GEORGE V. VOINOVICH Republican	12
For Representative to Congress (15th District) (Vote for not more than ONE)	MARK P. BROWN Democrat	14
	DEBORAH PRYCE Republican	15
For State Representative (27th District) (Vote for not more than ONE)	JOYCE BEATTY Democrat	24
For County Commissioner (Full Term Commencing 1-2-2005) (Vote for not more than ONE)	PAULA BROOKS Democrat	28
	ARLENE SHOEMAKER Republican	29
For County Commissioner (Full Term Commencing 1-3-2005) (Vote for not more than ONE)	DAVID GOODMAN Republican	31
	MARY JO KILROY Democrat	32
For Prosecuting Attorney (Vote for not more than ONE)	RON O'BRIEN Republican	34
For Clerk of Court of Common Pleas (Vote for not more than ONE)	JOHN O'GRADY Democrat	36
	AMY SALERNO Republican	37
For Sheriff (Vote for not more than ONE)	JIM KARNES Democrat	40

[handwritten:] Hhis is the Absente ballot (this page is as it opers to the voter & the second page is real!) Aaron 2 226-7076

[handwritten:] QF 3³ᵈ p Fitrakis (0)/21/04

Page 2

Page 3

Document 1.20.2

OFFICIAL PRESIDENTIAL BALLOT
GENERAL ELECTION – NOVEMBER 2, 2004
FRANKLIN COUNTY, OHIO

For President and Vice-President

To vote for President and Vice-President, punch the hole beside the number for the set of candidates of your choice. Your vote will be counted for each of the candidates for presidential elector whose names have been certified to the Secretary of State.

(Vote not more than ONCE)

For President:
MICHAEL BADNARIK
other-party candidate

For Vice-President:
RICHARD V. and **CAMPAGNA**   2

For President:
GEORGE W. BUSH
Republican

For Vice-President:
DICK and **CHENEY**   3

For President:
JOHN F. KERRY
Democrat

For Vice-President:
JOHN and **EDWARDS**   4

For President:
RALPH NADER

For Vice-President:
PETER MIGUEL and **CAMEJO**   5

For President:
MICHAEL ANTHONY PEROUTKA
other-party candidate

For Vice-President:
CHUCK and **BALDWIN**   6

OFFICIAL OFFICE T
GENERAL ELECTION – N
FRANKLIN COU

For United States Senator
(Vote for not more than ONE)

ERIC D.
Democrat

GEORGE
Republican

For Representative to Congress (15th District)
(Vote for not more than ONE)

MARK F
Democrat

DEBORA
Republican

For State Representative (27th District)
(Vote for not more than ONE)

JOYCE I
Democrat

For County Commissioner
(Full Term Commencing 1-2-2005)
(Vote for not more than ONE)

PAULA I
Democrat

ARLENE
Republican

For County Commissioner
(Full Term Commencing 1-3-2005)
(Vote for not more than ONE)

DAVID G
Republican

MARY J
Democrat

For Prosecuting Attorney
(Vote for not more than ONE)

RON O'I
Republican

For Clerk of Court of Common Pleas
(Vote for not more than ONE)

JOHN O
Democrat

AMY SA
Republican

For Sheriff
(Vote for not more than ONE)

JIM KAI
Democrat

Rot. 1   Page 2   Page 3

Document 1.21

Ms. Tubbs Jones. Now, let me also ask you, sir, I saw your TV ads giving education to people about voting. Can you tell us specifically what you told the voter with regard to voting location, sir?

Secretary Blackwell. Vote in your precinct. What we, had instructed and in accordance with Ohio law, Boards of Elections were to tell voters that they must, in fact, vote in their precinct for their vote to count.

Ms. Tubbs Jones. Did you tell them in their ad that if they couldn't vote in your precinct they could go vote at the Board of Elections?

Secretary Blackwell. No, the Boards of Elections did.

Ms. Tubbs Jones. No, but you were the one spent $2.5 million doing a TV ad for people who, in fact, have the opportunity to do punch card voting because 70 percent of the people in Ohio do punch card voting.

Secretary Blackwell. Absolutely.

Ms. Tubbs Jones. In this ad you said, ``Vote your precinct,'' but you never told them that if they couldn't vote in precinct, they could go the Board of Elections and vote. Did you, sir?

Secretary Blackwell. I sure didn't.

Ms. Tubbs Jones. Excuse me?

Secretary Blackwell. Can't you hear? I said I sure didn't.

Ms. Tubbs Jones. And you did not why?

Secretary Blackwell. Because you can only get so much information in a 30-second ad which is the most----

Ms. Tubbs Jones. That was important information because you just gave that to all of us for the world to see, sir, that either you go vote at a designated voting location, you vote in your precinct, or you go to the Board of Elections.

Secretary Blackwell. Absolutely. And that is what they were told. We made sure that those 50,000 election officials and poll workers understood that was an option for someone who was in the wrong precinct but was insisting on----

Ms. Tubbs Jones. But you did an ad statewide.

Secretary Blackwell. Just----

Ms. Tubbs Jones. You did an ad statewide that you spent $2.5 million on and you didn't tell them.

Secretary Blackwell. And it worked.

Ms. Tubbs Jones. Except----

Secretary Blackwell. It worked. It worked. It worked.

Ms. Tubbs Jones. When you get through saying ``it worked'' let me go on. How many more times are you going to say it worked?

Secretary Blackwell. It worked. It worked and I will say it worked every time you ask the question. The education program worked and if you want the details on it, you can have them, but it worked. The fact of the matter is that we have--among popular states, we had the best validation rate and that meant that those folks counted.

Ms. Tubbs Jones. But you----

Secretary Blackwell. And our campaign was----

Document 1.21—Continued

Ms. Tubbs Jones. Just let me know when you are done.

Secretary Blackwell. I sure will. Our campaign was Make Your Vote Count. The surest way to make your vote count was to vote your precinct. What I don't have in here--let me tell you what I don't have in here. We went into a million households by phone and they were essentially urban households and they were disproportionately in your district and in Cleveland. We told people there how to vote their provisional ballot. We told them to call their Board of Elections and we had a system that allowed for that. Let me tell you, as much as you want----

Ms. Tubbs Jones. Mr. Chairman, I can't let you use all my time answering the questions you have already answered.

Secretary Blackwell. As much as you want to create a third-world situation in the United States, most households, even in your district, have telephones and we, in fact, called them. We called them. I want you to know that we paid particular attention to your constituents. We called in and told them how to vote that provisional ballot to make their votes count because what I wanted was as many votes to count as humanly possible.

Ms. Tubbs Jones. Are you done, sir?

Secretary Blackwell. For right now.

Ms. Tubbs Jones. So you specifically said--you called into my district and you told people to go vote their precinct but you never told them they could go vote at the Board of Elections?

Secretary Blackwell. No, we told them----

Ms. Tubbs Jones. The answer is yes or no, sir.

Secretary Blackwell. No, it is not yes or no. We told them to call the Board of Elections so that they would, have the option of where to go.

Ms. Tubbs Jones. But you could have told them. Let us count the words. Vote in your precinct or vote at the Board of Elections. Call the Board of Elections. Same number of words. You could have said to them vote at the Board of Elections. Could you have not, sir?

Secretary Blackwell. But given that I was elected Secretary of State with a constituency much larger than yours, I chose the language for that ad.

Ms. Tubbs Jones. And in the ad you specifically excluded you could vote at the Board of Elections.

Secretary Blackwell. Right. Look, let me just say, all you had to do was go back and look at that ad. We told them where to call. We got them to our website. That information was right there so they got that information. We, in fact, made sure that coworkers understood to give them that information. I will tell you what. I refuse to sit here and be harangued by you.

Ms. Tubbs Jones. You know what, Mr. Blackwell? I am not trying to harangue you, sir. If you choose not to----

Secretary Blackwell. Hold on. Let me----

The Chairman. Time has expired.

Document 1.22

Democracy at Risk: The 2004 Election in Ohio

Section III
Voting Experience Survey

Document 1.22—Continued

Memo –Ohio Voting Experience Survey – March 2005--FINAL   Page 2
The Feldman Group, Inc. and Brilliant Corners Research & Strategies

uniform. African Americans were far more likely to have experienced voting problems,
as were voters in Franklin and Cuyahoga counties.

African Americans experienced more ballot and polling place problems than
whites, and were more likely to have felt intimidated on Election Day. The high number
of newly registered African American voters does not explain the disparity in experiences
between white voters and African American voters. In fact, registration history had little
to do with the different experiences, as African Americans registered to vote before 2004
were far more likely to have experienced problems than white voters who were registered
before 2004. The disparity is also not a function of party registration, as African
American Democrats had far more problems than white Democrats.

Voting problems also varied widely by geography. Polling place problems and
long lines were heightened in Franklin County, which used DRE voting machines, as
well as in the other counties that used this electronic voting equipment. Voters in
Cuyahoga County also experienced significant voting problems, particularly in terms of
ballot problems and intimidation.

Despite the problems on Election Day, there is no evidence from our survey that
John Kerry won the state of Ohio. Two (2) percent of voters who went to the polls on
Election Day decided to leave their polling locations due to the long lines. This resulted
in approximately 129,543 lost votes. However, these potential voters would have divided
evenly between George Bush and John Kerry. A smaller group of potential voters (0.08
percent) were not given ballots at all due to registration challenges. These approximately
4,798 voters favored Kerry, according to the poll (extreme sample size caution).

Finally, a third group of voters (equivalent to 0.83 percent of the voting
population) did not go to the polls at all because they did not receive their absentee
ballots, or had heard about long lines, registration challenges, and confusing polling sites.
We do not know the voting preferences of these approximately 47,979 voters. However,
even if they had all chosen Kerry, his overall gain of 52,777 votes would not have erased
Bush's 118,000 vote margin in the state.

Polling Place Problems

More than one-fourth (26 percent) of voters experienced polling place problems.[2]
These problems included going to more than one poll, waiting on line to vote for more
than twenty minutes, or leaving the polling place without voting. African Americans and
voters using DRE machines experienced the most polling place problems.

African Americans were twice as likely to experience polling place problems as
white voters. As Table 1 shows, nearly half (46 percent) of African Americans

---

[2] There were two subdivisions of voters in the survey: Those who voted by absentee and those who went to
the polls to vote. Most percentages cited in this memo refer voters *who went to the polls*, rather than all
voters. Exceptions include the "Ballot Problems" and "Demographic Differences" sections, which use
percentages referencing *all* voters.

2

Election Day

Election Day in Ohio was a gray, chilly day marked by blustery weather and cold rain. Bad weather usually deters voter turnout, but not in Ohio in 2004. After unprecedented voter registration efforts, nearly 1 million new voters were ready to cast their first ballots. As the day progressed, that simple hope would be frustrated for innumerable Ohioans.

Heading into Election Day, both sides were posturing and poised. On October 23, the *New York Times* reported the GOP would position 3,600 "poll challengers" across Ohio. These registered partisans are legally permitted to question voters' credentials, forcing people to document their identities and addresses prior to voting. This Jim Crow–era holdover, which targets new voters—first aimed at ex-slaves during Reconstruction—conflicts with HAVA's intent of maximizing voter participation. The *Times* report came several days after Ohio Secretary of State J. Kenneth Blackwell issued a directive that, for the first time, allowed political parties to assign partisan challengers by precinct, rather than by polling site. Blackwell's order suggested the GOP would deploy teams of challengers in Democratic strongholds, where many established polling stations were moved and consolidated by BOEs for the 2004 General Election. The prospect of new voters being challenged en masse, with the delays it would inevitably cause at the polls, raised tensions and provoked a series of challenges in federal court. There, the poll challengers were barred and then reinstated on the eve of the vote.

In response, the Kerry camp recruited 2,000 of its own poll challengers at the last minute, the *New York Times* reported. (On Election Day, the Ohio media estimated Republicans would deploy some 10,000 challengers, to be countered by 3,000 from the Democratic Party.) In addition, several thousand "Election Protection" volunteers from a large voting-rights coalition, including People for the American Way, the American Federation of Labor and Congress of Industrial Organizations (AFL-CIO), and the National Association for the Advancement of Colored People (NAACP) were assigned to polling sites in urban Democratic strongholds. Their job was to pass out voter rights information, videotape proceedings, and provide legal assistance.

The threat of poll challengers was the tip of a much larger, multipronged voter suppression iceberg targeting Ohio's minority communities and newest voters, who have historically voted Democratic. In an October 22, 2004, article, the *Columbus Dispatch*, which endorsed Bush, reported phone calls being made by people impersonating board of election workers directing registered voters to incorrect polling sites. In some cities, notices were left on front doors saying that, due to the big expected turnout, Republicans would vote on Tuesday and Democrats on Wednesday. An "Urgent Advisory" (a forgery) by the Lake County Board of Elections stated that "independent efforts by the NAACP, America Coming Together, John Kerry for President and Capri Cafaro for Congress campaigns have been illegally registering people" and warned that "you will not be able to vote until the next election."

These thuggish tactics did not deter Election Day turnout, but they set a tone and should have been seen as a warning of more trouble to come. Instead, they were brushed off as last-minute heat in a red-hot campaign. The GOP poll challengers reinstated an eleventh-hour federal court ruling and thus created an expectation, certainly among the national press, that voter challenges would be the great controversy once the voting began.

Voter challenges did indeed occur, but not en masse. This tactic was arguably one of the great feints of recent presidential elections. As election protection workers and reporters awaited this fight, what unfolded around them on Election Day largely escaped notice: a widespread breakdown of the voting process and election machinery that targeted the Democratic Party's newest and lowest-income members. In contrast, because the GOP controls most of the election process in

Ohio, voting among that party's base and core communities remained relatively unaffected.

The bulk of the documents in this chapter are first-person accounts of what happened as people attempted to vote and election protection workers tried to redress the most visible problems. These accounts were given under oath or submitted as signed, sworn affidavits at public hearings initiated by the Columbus Institute for Contemporary Journalism (CICJ) and other local voting-rights activists after the election. More than 500 people gave statements at hearings in Columbus, Cleveland, Cincinnati, Youngstown, and Toledo. National groups such as Common Cause, the League of Women Voters, People for the American Way, the NAACP, and Rainbow-Push co-sponsored the later sessions. The statements were used for, among other things, an Ohio election challenge lawsuit, *Moss v. Bush*, and for reporting for the CICJ's *Free Press* newspaper and its website, www.freepress.org. The House Judiciary Committee Democratic staff relied on these statements and other documentation gathered in Ohio to produce its own report of 2004 election irregularities. Added up, they create a massive, eyewitness catalog of the ways the election machinery broke down and prevented tens of thousands of people from voting.

The actual voting started with high hopes and anxiety on both sides. A near record turnout had been predicted. The Democrats focused their Get-Out-the-Vote efforts in Ohio's urban centers. The Republicans were similarly focused in suburban, outlying, and rural areas. When long lines formed at the polls, both parties felt that would favor their side. But as the day progressed, vast numbers of Ohioans—depending on their location, race, and economic class—were having dramatically different voting experiences.

As Robin Smith, a poll monitor in Democratic Franklin County, who herself voted in the largely Republican Columbus suburb of Upper Arlington, stated in an affidavit,

> Back home at 8:00 P.M., I watched on TV how some areas of Franklin County still had long lines of people that were going to have to wait hours to vote. This could not have been by accident. In my affluent, predominantly white community where 62 percent of the people voted for George Bush in the 2000 election, lines were not a problem.

In Ohio's Republican-leaning suburbs and rural areas, voting proceeded as most middle-class Americans expect: it was orderly; it did not take too long; there were sufficient numbers of voting machines; and there were few surprises, such as poll challenges or registration and voter roll snafus. Election protection volunteers such as Smith, who live in GOP-leaning suburbs but who went to work in the Democrat-dominated inner cities, were among the first to notice this discrepancy.

The experience in Democratic strongholds, particularly among the urban poor, could not have provided more contrast. Different things happened in different cities, but in precinct after precinct in Ohio's cities—most visibly in the state capital, Columbus—hundreds of people, tens of thousands in all, had to wait for hours to vote, often standing in the cold or rain before they could even get inside their local polling station. Once inside, they were often directed to the incorrect precinct, as multiple or dual precincts often were in the same building, and when they arrived at the front of the line, often were told they had to start in a different line all over again. Once at voter check-in tables, many people were often told that their voter registrations were incomplete or missing, and that they therefore had to use provisional ballots. Instructions from poll workers on filling these out were murky at best, owing to Blackwell's flurry of last-minute directives. In some Columbus precincts, people had to get into yet another long line to wait for provisional voting booths.

Cleveland, the state's largest city and Democratic stronghold, experienced many of the same problems as Columbus. Reports compiled from election protection workers on November 2 documented more than 200 precincts with many of these same problems—all frustrating efforts to vote. Long lines, registration snafus, poll worker confusion, voting machines breaking down in sixty-nine precincts, and improper labels for provisional ballots were among the problems cited by Election Day observers in that city's Democratic strongholds.

Many people who expected to vote were prevented from doing so completely. People who had requested an absentee ballot but had not received one in the mail were told they could not use a provisional ballot—under an order issued by Blackwell late in the campaign. At 3 P.M. on Election Day, U.S. District Court Judge David Katz reversed that directive and ordered that poll workers provide absentee ballots. The court urged the media to tell people they could return to their polls and vote provisionally.

Old or infirm people, as well as people needing language assistance to vote—who under law are entitled to such help—were told by poll workers they could not be aided, and many consequently did not vote. Some people became sick or frustrated while standing in the long lines, and left, not voting. Many people, faced with the long lines, who had to get to work, or to pick up their children after school, also left and did not vote.

Franklin County, where the state capital, Columbus, is located, displayed the breakdown of the voting process most vividly. In mid-October, Matthew Damschroder, the Franklin County BOE director, who was also the county's former GOP chair, told a local business journal that he expected voters would take three and a half minutes to vote and wouldn't have to wait for more than fifteen minutes. That scenario might have been true if the county had deployed some 5,000 voting machines that were needed, based on a 1955 Ohio court ruling requiring there to be one voting machine for every 100 voters. But the county election office deployed only 2,798 machines, and did not distribute them evenly across all neighborhoods, regardless of race, class, or party affiliation.

The result—coming in tandem with the other impediments created by Blackwell's directives—created massive lines and waits of hours, not minutes, costing Kerry many thousands of votes by preventing people from voting. In Columbus alone, a post-election analysis by Richard Hayes Phillips, an analyst with a special expertise in spotting anomalous data, found the 346 precincts won by Kerry registered a median voter turnout of 50.78 percent, compared to a 60.56 percent median voter turnout in the city's 125 precincts won by Bush. Hayes and others attribute this ostensible discrepancy directly to the difference in voting conditions, *rather* than to the Republicans' superior prowess in turning out voters. Democrats turned out plenty of voters—they simply were not permitted to vote.

Franklin County's voter turnout in 2004 (which includes towns outside Columbus) was 60.95 percent, or nearly 10 percentage points below the turnout rate in the rest of Ohio. *Thus, the voter accommodation rate in urban Columbus was fully 20 percent below the statewide average.* (This figure excludes absentee ballots, which are counted on a county-wide basis.)

There was no comparable disparity between the county's turnout and rest of the state in prior recent presidential elections. Phillips found that the precincts where Kerry won and had the highest voter turnout—which was on par with turnout levels in precincts where Bush won—had one defining feature: there were ample voting machines. Fewer people per machine means more people get to vote. While this disparity was not the only factor that suppressed Democratic votes, it suggests a way to calculate at least a portion of the votes Kerry lost to Republican voter suppression tactics.

Using a conservative calculation, if Franklin County had a 60 percent voter turnout, the average percentage everywhere there were *not* long lines or other impediments, Phillips estimates that Kerry would have picked up an additional 17,000 votes in that county.

(Indeed, Columbus's unprecedented lines suggest more than 60 percent of registered voters intended to vote. The statewide turnout was just under 72 percent.)

Other studies found that even though Kerry carried the county, the president won in most of the new precincts created after the 2000 election. Franklin County's BOE, headed by Matthew Damschroder, a former Republican county chairman, redrew precinct boundaries before the 2004 election. By consolidating many inner-city precincts into single locations, but mostly leaving suburban precincts as they were, the BOE made voting easier in Bush strongholds than in Democratic strongholds. Thus, in a year when election officials knew they would be facing record high turnout, the BOE created a massive "traffic jam" by combining Democratic precincts, while failing to provide adequate voting machines.

This pattern was not confined to Columbus. Werner Lange, an Edinboro University of Pennsylvania sociology professor, voting-rights activist, and part-time pastor from Youngstown, saw the same pattern in that city. He estimated at a post-election public hearing that "over 8,000 votes from the African American community in the City of Youngstown, alone, with its eighty-four precincts were lost due to insufficient voting machines, and that would translate to some 7,000 votes lost for John Kerry for President in Youngstown." (These analyses and estimates, which are consistent with exit poll results, will be discussed in later chapters.)

Indignities and obstacles fell disproportionately on Ohio's minority and poor citizens, communities that historically tend to vote Democratic, and on newly registered voters, who were disproportionately young people—and also overwhelmingly Democratic. But there were other problems in these same precincts on Election Day. For one thing, some voters noted the ballot layout was unclear. Moreover, inside the voting booths, there were a range of machine malfunctions. Most notably, in cities across the state, there were reports—later confirmed by county election officials—of new electronic machines failing to record votes, or registering votes for Bush after people said they voted for Kerry (and never the other way around). Voting machines with these malfunctions in Youngstown remained in service even after multiple reports of malfunctioning, election protection observers reported. Some Cleveland voters said they were given punch-card ballots that had been prepunched with votes for President Bush. This meant the ballots would be disqualified if the voter picked Kerry, as ballots with two votes were rejected by the counting machines. In Toledo, the wrong markers were distributed for filling out optical-scan ballots, which also resulted in ballots with no votes being read for president. In Franklin County, seventy-seven machines malfunctioned on Election Day, according to the BOE. Yet even as thousands of Ohioans put up with the cold and long lines to vote, the secretary of state's certified 2004 results said 92,672 ballots had been cast with no vote at all recorded for president. (Blackwell and the BOEs would not allow these ballots to be publicly inspected until Spring 2006).

Of course, Democratic voters and their election protection allies knew something was not right from the time the polls opened on Election Day. The first insight that struck voters was the shortage of voting machines. Many people noticed there were fewer machines in their precinct than had been there in the presidential primary, just that prior spring. But efforts to get poll workers and county election officials to redress that shortage were mostly unsuccessful.

Documents obtained after Election Day from the contractor who delivered Franklin County's voting machines, for example, showed that only slightly more than half of the needed 5,000 machines—2,741—were in place for the opening of polls. Fifty-seven voting machines did not arrive until later in the day, some at the close of polls, and sixty-eight machines were held back and not used at all. The three- to seven-hour wait in Columbus's inner city resulted in a federal court order directing the polls to stay open until everyone who was in line at 7:30 P.M. had voted.

While most of the press attention focused on the long lines in Columbus, there were other notable incidents and patterns, again targeting Democratic strongholds and revealing a wider pattern of voter suppression. Many of Ohio's private liberal arts colleges, including

Oberlin, Antioch, and Denison, are located in rural areas. At Kenyon College in rural Knox County, students waited in line until 4 A.M. because county officials had assigned two machines for 1,300 voters, and one was broken. Meanwhile, at the nearby Mt. Vernon Nazarene University, an evangelical Christian school in the same county, there were a half-dozen voting machines and no waits. Wilberforce University and Central State University, two historically black colleges, and several schools in the state university system experienced similar shortages and unreasonable delays.

In Lucas County, where the city of Toledo is located, pre- and post-election problems were so severe the secretary of state had to order an investigation and publish the results on his website. The Lucas County Board of Elections and Lucas County Republican Party were chaired by Bernadette Noe, wife of Bush's chief Ohio fund-raiser, Tom Noe (who was indicted in federal court in October 2005 on three campaign finance and money laundering counts related to raising money for Bush's 2004 campaign, and in May 2006 pleaded guilty to those charges). During the summer of 2004, Lucas County's BOE removed 28,000 people from voter rolls, the *Toledo Blade* reported on January 9, 2005. A month before the election, the county BOE had "20,000 unprocessed voter registration applications" and employees told the state investigators that "more resources would be needed to process them," according to Blackwell's report. Because new registrations must be processed a month before Election Day, a largely Democratic pool of voters would discover on Election Day they had been disenfranchised. On Election Night, Blackwell's report states Bernadette Noe and other GOP partisans interfered with counting votes, prompting the report to say, under "result of investigation":

Listed below, in order of importance, are areas of grave concern:

- Failure to maintain ballot security;
- Inability to implement and maintain a trackable system for voter ballot reconciliation;
- Failure to prepare and develop a plan for processing of the voluminous amount of voter registration forms received;
- Issuance and acceptance of incorrect absentee ballot forms;
- Manipulation of the process involving the 3 percent recount;
- Disjointed implementation of the Directive regarding removal of

Nader and Camejo from the ballot;
- Failure to properly issue hospital ballots in accordance with statutory requirements;
- Failure to maintain the security of poll books during the official canvas (http://www.sos.state.oh.us/sos/electionsvoter/lucas/LucasCountyInvestigationReport.pdf).

Bernadette Noe resigned from her BOE job in December 2004—and after the election, the full county BOE was forced to resign.

Ohio's eighty-seven other counties were not carbon copies of Lucas County. But elements of partisan manipulation that benefited Republicans at the expense of Democratic voters were present throughout Ohio.

Chapter 2 Documents: Election Day

2.1 Voting Misinformation Flier in Franklin County, p. 95

Fliers posted in the Ohio State University area on Election Day stated, completely erroneously, that Democrats should vote on November 3, the day after Election Day. The "Bi-Partisan Voting Authority (BPA)" cited in the fliers does not exist; it is a fabricated name intended to appear as a government agency. Calls to local radio stations, such as WVKO-AM in Columbus, the city's oldest black-owned radio station, reported hundreds of these fliers were put on car windshields, telephone poles, and doorways.

2.2 Lake County Voting Letter, October 22, 2004, p. 96

Corresponding with the arrival of the so-called Texas Strike Force (http://www.texasstrikeforce.com/), fake letters began to appear in Columbus, Cincinnati, and Cleveland informing newly registered voters that they had been "illegally registered" and could not vote in the presidential election. These fake letters carried the letterhead of county boards of elections and were specifically sent to voters likely to vote for Kerry. (These letters suggest that only Democrats erred with registering voters, not Republicans.)

2.3 Franklin County, New Voting Precincts Created Since the 2000 Election, p. 97

Although George Bush lost Franklin County with 46 percent of the vote, the following chart indicates that the vast majority of new precincts created in the county following the 2000 election voted more than 50 percent for Bush. This is because the BOE, run by former Republican party chair Matt Damschroder, created new precincts in the Republican majority suburbs, making it easier for Bush voters to cast ballots. Unlike the county's urban Democratic core, where many precincts were moved and consolidated, the new precincts in the largely Republican suburbs were conveniently located, less crowded, and had ample voting machines. This chart shows most of the new precincts supported the president's reelection. In contrast, the Franklin County BOE consolidated many longtime precincts in the heavily Democratic wards in the inner city, funneling more people to fewer voting locales, which led to numerous problems and discouraged voting on Election Day.

2.4 Cover Page and Excerpt from 2001 Board of Elections Report Warning Franklin County Would Face a Shortage of Voting Machines, p. 98

Ed Leonard, former deputy director of the Franklin County Board of Elections and a Democrat, wrote a lengthy memo following the 2000 election indicating that the county might need to purchase more machines for future elections. In this excerpted paragraph, Leonard predicts the county will need more voting machines to meet voter demand in 2001. Three years later, the county was still using the same machines.

2.5 Excerpts of Rhonda Frazier Affidavit on Ohio Secretary of State Use of Funds, December 17, 2004, pp. 99–100

Rhonda Frazier, a political appointee on Blackwell's administrative staff, performed internal audits at the secretary of state's office and was fired for questioning whether that office had fulfilled the terms of its HAVA grant agreements. She swore in this affidavit, beginning with paragraph eight, that a federal grant "worth $40 million for training, reforming, adding machines to precincts, and education of the voting population" was not used for its intended purpose. Additional machines were never purchased and existing machines were never properly inventoried per the grant requirements. Not using federal grants intended to update machinery and educate the public is consistent with Blackwell's selective and partisan administration of the election.

2.6 William Anthony, News Release, March 16, 2006, p. 101

While campaigning for governor in March 2006, Blackwell blamed William Anthony, the chairman of the Franklin County Democratic Party and also of the Franklin County BOE, for the shortage of voting machines in the county during the 2004 presidential election. In response, Anthony and the county Democratic Party issued this press release saying the fault lay with Blackwell, whose implementation of many HAVA requirements for that election was deeply flawed.

2.7 Testimony and Affidavits, pp. 102–112

What follows are excerpts from notarized affidavits from voters taken on Election Day and sworn testimony from voters, campaign volunteers, and poll workers at public hearings convened in several Ohio cities immediately after the 2004 vote, as well as other first-person accounts of what happened on November 2, 2004. Most of the Election Day affidavits are short, quickly filled out by voters or people wanting to vote. After the election, hearings were organized by the Columbus Institute of Contemporary Journalism (CICJ) and a coalition of local voting-rights activists to create a record under oath. More than 500 people gave sworn statements in Columbus, Cleveland, Cincinnati, Youngstown, and Toledo. That record is more detailed and points to the variety of obstacles facing mostly Democratic voters. We begin with two longer statements that convey a somewhat larger perspective on what happened on November 2.

2.8 Election Incident Reports, pp. 113–115

Another indicator of what went wrong in Ohio were election incident reports called in to Election Protection hotlines (1-866-OUR-VOTE) throughout the day. This log of calls is not under oath but echoes the same complaints heard in the sworn testimonies and written affidavits. We have included the first thirty-three out of 378 total reported incidents that comprise the Ohio report.

2.9 Ohio County by Voting Machine Vendor and Election Incident Report, pp. 116–124

Working with the Columbus Institute of Contemporary Journalism and voting-rights groups in Ohio, researcher Rady Ananda compiled a chart of election incident reports by Ohio county and noted the private voting machine vendor involved. The significance of this chart, of which four pages are reproduced here, is that it notes problems associated with the different types of voting machines. More than 92,000 Ohio ballots in 2004 did not record a vote for president. This chart breaks that down, referring to "undervotes" on punch-card machines (which produced Florida's infamous hanging chads in 2000), and also identifies new electronic voting machines and the counties where people intended to vote for Kerry, but saw the vote "switch" or register as a Bush vote.

2.10 Franklin County Voting Machine Allocation Chart
by Precinct on Election Day, pp. 125–128

These are the first two pages from a spreadsheet showing the voter registration and allocation of voting machines in 2000 and 2004 in Franklin County's 793 precincts. They clearly demonstrate that while voter registration increased, the city did not provide ample voting machines. They also show the city disproportionately lost more machines than the suburbs. The document's final page also notes that the Franklin County Board of Elections delivered 2,741 machines at the start of Election Day and also notes that, even by "Close of Polls," only 2,798 were in use. The chart also shows that it is almost impossible to have more than 180–200 people vote at any one machine during allocated voting hours, which is to be contrasted to numerous reports from precincts where several hundred people were expected to use each machine.

Franklin County and the state of Ohio traditionally use a formula of one machine per 100 voters with machine usage allowable up to 125 votes per machine. The rationale for the formula is as follows. Polls are open thirteen hours. The assumption is it will take each voter five minutes to vote. That means twelve people can vote in an hour and 120 people can vote in ten hours. The remaining three hours are spent signing people in and moving them to and from voting machines. In Democratic Columbus, thirty-nine voting machines had more than 200 votes per machine and an additional forty-two registered more than 190 votes per machine. This means 17 percent of Columbus machines were operating at between 90 and 100 percent over capacity. In the Republican enclave of Upper Arlington, no voting machines recorded more than 200 votes per machine in the city's thirty-four precincts. Only one, Ward 6F, had over 190 votes, at 194. In Columbus, 139 of the 472 precincts had at least one and as many as five fewer machines than in the 2000 presidential election. By contrast, only two of Upper Arlington precincts had one fewer machine than in 2000. Of those two precincts, one had a 25 percent decline in voter registration, the other only a 1 percent gain. Compare this to Columbus Ward 1B, where voter registration increased 27 percent but two fewer machines were supplied than in the 2000 election. Ward 23B had a 22 percent increase in voter registration; the polling site likewise had two fewer machines.

Overall, Columbus saw an increase of 25 percent in voter registration, but 29 percent of its precincts had fewer machines, leading to three- to seven-hour waiting lines.

2.11 Franklin County Voting Machine Allocation Chart with Blacked-out Machines, pp. 129–130

These two pages, from a sixty-three-page chart showing voting machine precinct assignments in Franklin County, document that seventy-six machines were held back after being assigned to polling sites in the city's Democratic neighborhoods. The machines were assigned by serial numbers to each precinct. Then seventy-six machines were withdrawn and crossed off the list. The *Free Press* obtained a copy of the report from the Franklin County Board of Elections. This chart was the basis of a freepress.org article that was designated the third most censored story in the world by Project Censored in 2005. Statistician Richard Hayes Phillips calculated the non-random odds of all the broken or undelivered machines being from Columbus rather than the suburbs of Franklin County at 72,500,000,000,000,000 to 1.

2.12 Franklin County Bill of Lading, p. 131

The invoice from the trucking company that delivered the voting machines for Franklin County, E.E. Ward Moving & Storage Company, also indicates that only 2,741 voting machines were delivered to polling sites for Election Day. By the close of polls, the Board of Elections claimed it had put out 2,798 machines. Some eyewitnesses testified at public hearings after Election Day that voting machines were being rolled in as the polls were closing. The effect of these machines being placed so late allowed them to be averaged into Columbus precincts, thus distorting the overwhelming number of voters per machine in African American wards. For example, if a black ward had 600 voters and two machines, bringing in a third machine by the close of polls allows the county to claim that there were 200 voters per machine rather than 300. The document also shows that the trucking company picked up only 2,787 machines, twelve fewer than the

Franklin County Board of Elections claims to have put out by the close of polls.

2.13 Video Frame Grabs of Long Lines, pp. 132–133

The wait to vote was between three and seven hours long on Election Day in Columbus's inner city, predominantly African American wards. These frame grabs were taken from video shot on Election Day by videographers working with Election Protection.

2.14 Secretary of State Report on Problems of the Lucas County Board of Elections, pp. 134–136

In heavily Democratic Lucas County (Toledo), the BOE's preparation for the 2004 election, the actual vote on November 2, and the ensuing recount were so chaotic that Secretary of State Blackwell was forced to ask the entire board of elections to resign. The CICJ conducted a hearing in Lucas County, which revealed problems with the Diebold Opti-scan machines malfunctioning, failure to set precinct boundaries, and incorrect ballot marking devices in use, causing higher than normal ballot rejection rates. The pre- and post-election problems were so severe that Blackwell had to order an investigation and post the results on his website, the first two pages of which are reproduced here.

2.15 "Stealing Votes in Columbus" by Richard Hayes Phillips, Ph.D., pp. 137–146

This is a precinct-by-precinct analysis by statistician Richard Hayes Phillips that looks at the turnout disparities in precincts won by Bush versus precincts won by Kerry in the city of Columbus, as well as the allocation of voting machines between the known Democratic and Republican strongholds. As the analysis makes clear, voter turnout disparity may be directly attributed to Republican voter suppression tactics. The heart of Phillips's analysis is explained on page 8, starting with, "It is important to understand what these numbers mean." The analysis is printed in full to show the conservative methodology used. Phillips concludes if the turnout in Kerry-majority precincts were equal to that in the precincts that Bush won (as it was in Democratic

precincts where long lines and other forms of suppression were not issues), Kerry would have picked up 17,000 votes in Franklin County.

Phillips has done further analysis to show that voting machines
were consistently (and Phillips contends intentionally) misallocated,
with enough extra machines in Republican suburbs to ensure the voter
accommodation rates would be significantly higher than in the Democratic inner city. "All this mattered a lot," he concluded in another paper on urban-suburban differences in Franklin County. "The median
ward with fewer than 300 registered voters per voting machine registered a 62.33 percent turnout. The median ward with 300 or more
registered voters per voting machine registered a 51.99 percent
turnout." Merely shifting fifty machines from the Republican suburbs
to Columbus's core would have led to a far more acceptable voter/ma-
chine ratio, Phillips states, and accommodated many more voters.

2.16 Ohio Secretary of State's *Washington Times* Piece
on the Success of the Elections in Ohio, November 17,
2004, p. 147

On November 17, 2004, the *Washington Times* published this op-ed by
Ohio Secretary of State J. Kenneth Blackwell. Blackwell characterized
Ohio's Election Day as "tremendously successful." Several people at
the November 13 hearing in Columbus said they would like to hear
Mr. Blackwell testify under oath. That would not come until the following March, when the House Committee on Administration held its
first-ever field hearing on election reform in Columbus.

Document 2.1

Due to record numbers of registered voters
this year the Bi-partisan Voting Authority
(BPA) has implemented a slight change in
election day policy as follows:

The voting process will now have
specific attendance dates, instead of
being able to cast your vote
Nov. 2nd or Nov. 3rd ————————

- Those voters registered as
REPUBLICAN or UNDECIDED
should cast their ballot on **Nov. 2nd**

- Those voters registered as
DEMOCRAT or UNDECIDED
Should cast their ballot on **Nov. 3rd**

The BPA would also like to remind you that
YOUR VOTE COUNTS!
So make a point to show up to the polls on

YOUR DESIGNATED VOTING DAY

Document 2.2

LAKE COUNTY BOARD OF ELECTIONS
105 Main Street PO Box 490, Painesville, Ohio 44077-0490

URGENT ADVISORY

October 22, 2004

Dear Newly Registered Voter,

The voter registration deadline passed on October 4, 2004 and we registered a record number of new voters. The demand on our office has been great and we appreciate your cooperation. Unfortunately independent efforts by the NAACP, America Coming Together, John Kerry for President and the Capri Cafaro for Congress campaigns have been illegally registering people to vote and apply for absentee ballots. This is a terrible occurrence that will undermine the process of democracy. If you have been registered by any of these entities then you may run the risk of being illegally registered to vote. Please be advised that if you were registered in this capacity that you will not be able to vote until the next election. We apologize for these problems and we will pursue these entities to the fullest extent. Please notify the Lake County Sheriff's office if you have any questions.

Document 2.3

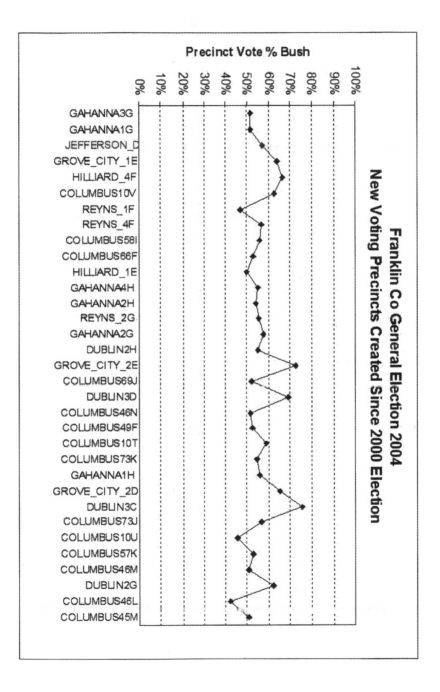

Franklin Co General Election 2004
New Voting Precincts Created Since 2000 Election

Precinct Vote % Bush

0% 10% 20% 30% 40% 50% 60% 70% 80% 90% 100%

GAHANNA3G
GAHANNA1G
JEFFERSON_D
GROVE_CITY_1E
HILLIARD_4F
COLUMBUS10V
REYNS_1F
REYNS_4F
COLUMBUS58I
COLUMBUS66F
HILLIARD_1E
GAHANNA4H
GAHANNA2H
REYNS_2G
GAHANNA2G
DUBLIN2H
GROVE_CITY_2E
COLUMBUS69J
DUBLIN3D
COLUMBUS46N
COLUMBUS49F
COLUMBUS10T
COLUMBUS73K
GAHANNA1H
GROVE_CITY_2D
DUBLIN3C
COLUMBUS73J
COLUMBUS10U
COLUMBUS57K
COLUMBUS46M
DUBLIN2G
COLUMBUS46L
COLUMBUS45M

Document 2.4

MEMORANDUM

TO: Guy L. Reece, II, Director
           Chris Wilson, IT Administrator
           Mike Sexton, Administrative Division Manager
           Mike Hackett, Absentee Department Supervisor

FROM: Ed Leonard

DATE: February 20, 2001

SUBJ: Pending Issues and Parting Thoughts

These issues and thoughts are in no particular order. If I come up with any additional issues, I will be sure to put them to paper for your consideration.

New Danaher Machines

Before the Board makes any commitments to buy new machines from Danaher, I would strongly suggest that the BOE find out where the legislature is on the "no-fault" or open absentee legislation. If it has any chance of passing this year, the Board may want to hold off on the purchase of some or all of the new Danaher machines. The money could then be used for a new ballot on demand system to use in a regional absentee office configuration. Although the growth in the number of precincts in 2001 could possibly be handled by a redistribution of existing machines, a purchase of some machines will likely be needed in 2001. The Board should limit the purchase to only the machines needed.

Document 2.5

EXCERPTED AFFIDAVIT OF RHONDA J. FRAZIER (EXCERPTS)

I, Rhonda J. Frazier, declare all the foregoing to be true and correct to the best of my knowledge, information and belief under penalty of perjury under the laws of all applicable state laws, including the laws of Ohio and all Federal Laws. I further state that I am over the age of 18 and am competent and willing to testify to all the information stated herein in any court of competent jurisdiction.

1. I am an African American female, I am 36 years old.

2. I started working in December of 2002 at the Secretary of State J. Kenneth Blackwell's office under Blackwell reporting to the Secretary of State's Director of Finance Dilip Metha. I was on Blackwell's Administrative Staff as a political appointee in his office. My functions entailed expenditure review, all acquisitions and auditing manager. My job was to perform the inner audits in the office with regard to all the Ohio Secretary of State office expenditures in the entire Secretary of State office for all Divisions in each location. I studied Non Profit management and finance and have worked in finance for 11 years in both State government and for private firms.

* * *

8. There was a grant given to the Secretary of State for them to administer the "Voting Reform." It was called in the office "The Voting Reform Grant." The grant was awarded by the Federal government and is based on per capita population of the State. Every 88 counties in Ohio were supposed to have certain things done by certain dates or they were to lose or repay the grant money. We had to put together a "Pre-Budget" detailed business and strategic plan where we got price quotes for voting machines that went into a report that had to be submitted to the Federal government in order to qualify for the grant funding.

9. Before they got the grant there was a detailed protocol required to be fulfilled in order to get the grant. The grant was worth 40 Million dollars for training, reforming, adding machines to precincts, and education of the voting population. This was the first grant that the Secretary of State ever received and it required that they have additional staffing to engage the process.

* * *

12. I learned that the grant funds were given. At the time that I left, we had assessed which precincts needed more machines and we priced additional machines. I knew that the new machines had not been ordered for any precincts that were short on machines. From what I learned after leaving the office I don't believe they were ever ordered at any time before the November 2 general election.

* * *

15. After complaining about the office's repeated practices of violation of grants and contracts I was fired. There were other personal reasons that I left. I was very vocal about what I perceived to be untruthfulness in the contracting practices and the lack of financial accountability and integrity I observed.

Document 2.5—Continued

16. They retained all of my office files after I was fired. I was not allowed to retrieve any files or print any emails.

EXECUTED THIS __17th__ day of __December__ 2004 in the City of __Columbus__

State of __Ohio__   _Rhonda Frazier_

RHONDA J. FRAZIER

NOTARY ~~seal~~ _Susan Giller_

My Commission never expires

Document 2.6

FRANKLIN COUNTY DEMOCRATIC PARTY

FOR IMMEDIATE RELEASE

March 16, 2006

BLACKWELL BREAKS THE TEN COMMANDMENTS

COLUMBUS The Franklin County Democratic Chair issued a stinging rebuttal to counter Ken Blackwell's slanderous accusation against him. Ken Blackwell is not telling the truth. He should be ashamed of himself for misrepresenting facts and impugning my integrity in order to deflect criticism away from his questionable activities as Secretary of State, said William A. Anthony Jr.

Anthony was responding to a Cleveland Plain Dealer article reporting on Blackwell's luncheon with members of the United Pastors Mission held at Cleveland's Antioch Baptist Church.

According to the article, Blackwell told the group that Anthony was to blame for unconscionably long lines at polling locations during the 2004 presidential election.

"I wish Mr. Blackwell had the honor and decency to tell the truth while appearing before a group of church leaders. Unfortunately, he is unwilling to confess his own sins and would rather cast unwarranted blame onto others."

Anthony concluded, "I'm outraged that Mr. Blackwell thinks he can get away with this deceitful misdirection. Franklin County and many other counties throughout the state did not have nearly enough voting machines because Ken Blackwell mismanaged the HAVA-implementation process from the start. The only HAVA funds spent in Franklin County during 2004 was Gene Pierce's no-bid contract. No HAVA money was spent on voting machines."

A copy of Anthony's letter to Blackwell is attached.

Contact: William A. Anthony or Mark Rutkus at (614) 224-1193 or franklin@ohiodems.org

Document 2.7

2.8 Testimony, Affidavits, Personal Statements

(Ray Beckerman is an attorney from Jamaica, NY, who was an observer at Ohio Democratic Party headquarters in Columbus. He published the election blog: www.fairnessbybeckerman.blogspot.com and wrote this account, which was posted there and on www.FreePress.org just after Election Day.)

I worked for 3 days, including Election Day, on the statewide voter protection hotline run by the Ohio Democratic Party in Columbus, Ohio.

I am writing this because the media is inexplicably whitewashing what happened in Ohio, and Kerry's concession was likewise inexplicable.

Hundreds of thousands of people were disenfranchised in Ohio. People waited on line for as long as 10 hours. It appears to have only happened in Democratic-leaning precincts, principally (a) precincts where many African Americans lived, and (b) precincts near colleges.

I spoke to a young man who got on line at 11:30 am and voted at 7 pm. When he left at 7 pm, the line was about 150 voters longer than when he'd arrived, which meant those people were going to wait even longer. In fact they waited for as much as 10 hours, and their voting was concluded at about 3 am. The reason this occurred was that they had 1 voting station per 1000 voters, while the adjacent precinct had 1 voting station per 184. Both precincts were within the same county, and managed by the same county board of elections. The difference between them is that the privileged polling place was in a rural, solidly Republican, area, while the one with long lines was in the college town of Gambier, OH.

Lines of 4 and 5 hours were the order of the day in many African-American neighborhoods.

Touch screen voting machines in Youngstown OH were registering "George W. Bush" when people pressed "John F. Kerry" ALL DAY LONG. This was reported immediately after the polls opened, and reported over and over again throughout the day, and yet the bogus machines were inexplicably kept in use THROUGHOUT THE DAY.

Countless other frauds occurred, such as postcards advising people of incorrect polling places, registered Democrats not receiving absentee ballots, duly registered young voters being forced to file provisional ballots even though their names and signatures appeared in the voting rolls, longtime active voting registered voters being told they weren't registered, bad faith challenges by Republican "challengers" in Democratic precincts, and on and on and on.

I was very proud of the way so many Ohioans fought so valiantly for their right to vote, and would not be turned away. Many, however, could not spend the entire day and were afraid of losing their jobs, due to the severe economic depression hitting Ohio.

(Carolyn Sherman was a poll worker in Columbus and wrote a vivid account of the day and her struggle to ensure every voter had a chance to cast their ballot. Her story is typical of what campaign workers felt as they saw their efforts collapse, starting with a shortage of voting machines.

It was 8:30 pm, and the polls had closed an hour ago. The basement of the Centenary United Methodist Church just outside Columbus was steamy and dank, filled with a line of voters that snaked through several hallways. There were so many loops that the beginning and the end of the line were indistinguishable, but no one fought about it. Several hundred people stood or sat on the floor or on stools they had brought, waiting. At the rate the line was moving, it would take hours more for them all to finish. They had already been waiting for up to eight hours, and they were ready to wait hours more. To vote.

Ten minutes and a world away, TV sets at the America Coming Together Victory Party blared, "It's all coming down to Ohio." Those of us volunteers who had gone out in vans in the pouring rain to help at the polls watched it slip away. In this church basement, like so many polling places in predominantly poor, Democratic precincts, our little outpost of hope and grit stood solid, and I watched it refuse to flinch, and I watched it lose.

There were three voting booths for all those hundreds of people. Most of the voters were black, with some whites and Hispanics mixed in the endless lines. It was a poor neighborhood, but there was a dignity in their calmness that moved me to both respect and tremendous sadness. It was hot and steamy, they were hungry, they were tired, and they were determined to keep on waiting.

Why were there so few machines for so many people? Why in the richer districts was the wait only about an hour? Why was Ohio's Secretary of State Blackwell telling the press the election was going so smoothly? Why was the press buying it? Precincts just like Centenary were being reported on all over the state, but no one who could change things was listening. I was enraged and incredulous.

How can we help, we asked. We brought pizza and cokes and chips and Twizzlers, we brought encouragement, and we brought the press. We called Channel 4 and Channel 10, telling them that the real story wasn't the challengers brought out by the Republicans. The real story was the determination of so many people to vote, no matter how long they had to

Document 2.7—Continued

wait. The real story was that even now, decades after the Civil Rights movement, justice is so far away. The real story was that this could happen, and no one did anything.

Channel 4 appeared with its TV truck, and the voters were elated. Dozens of children, remarkably well behaved considering the hour and the circumstances, ran out onto the sidewalks, delighted at the prospect of being on TV. The Channel 4 reporter was a heroine. The crowd began to stir, and anyone who might have been thinking about leaving was now determined to stay and vote. Reporter Teresa Garza spoke out for the waiting voters, interviewing a jovial man who had waited over six hours but had no intention of going home without casting his vote.

Back at ACT headquarters later, we watched the reporter's story, lost in the hubbub of the night, the point and the people in the Centenary Church a blip soon forgotten. The next day, Matt Lauer did a quick piece on a cute blond co-ed from Kent State (another Democratic precinct, surprise) who waited for hours to vote and even had to miss hockey practice! The little girls at Centenary whose mother lost a full day's pay to vote, who missed lunch and dinner both, the toothless, gentle man who had come directly from working the night shift at a bakery and quietly stood in line in the pouring rain the whole next day - they were now gone from everyone's TV and radar screen. Bush had won, and that was that. Vague talk about long lines, then on to some other topic.

How many hundreds and thousands of voters were essentially denied their right to vote that day? How accurate were the election results? Why wasn't the press talking about this?

Where is the outrage? Why were the voting machines so unevenly distributed? Our experience was anecdotal. Yet the entire day we heard constant first-person accounts of incredible lines in the poorer Democratic precincts, and much shorter ones in the Republican precincts. People told of polling places where in the last election people voted in the gym, but who this year voted in a tiny room where the lines let out into the outdoors and the merciless rain.

(Christopher Hicks was an election protection poll worker in Columbus on Election Day. He monitored six precincts in African-American neighborhoods, starting at the Linden Library. What's notable in this excerpt of his account is the determination of people to endure the voting problems and vote.)

"A funny thing happened in Columbus, Ohio. People stayed in line and voted anyway. And not just a couple of people. Thousands of people. All day long they braved the rain and voted, determined to have their voices heard. There were hundreds of first-time voters. Hundreds of young voters, and many voters you thought you would never see in line to cast a ballot. I had one young man come up and ask me if he could vote even though he had an outstanding arrest warrant. I told him he could. Perhaps the most rewarding moment came when I saw a visibly upset man in his late 60s storming out of the polling place. I followed him and asked him what was wrong. He told me they would not let him vote because they said he was not registered. He assured me he was registered and had voted at the same location for 30 years. I asked him to come back to the polling place. We marched into the precinct and I asked the officials why he had been denied the right to vote. They told me that he wasn't on the register list. I informed them that under federal law he was entitled to a provisional ballot. They agreed and gave him one.

Document 2.7—Continued

(The following are statements from one-page affidavits collected on Election Day, Nov. 2, 2004. They were statements to poll watchers and election protection observers from precincts and cities that comprise Ohio's Democratic strongholds. They underscore the human impact of barriers that prevented people from voting.)

Luther Greene, Columbus, affidavit, 11/2/04,
I reside... in Columbus, OH. My race is black. I am, or believe I am, a registered voter in Columbus, OH. I have been registered for 40 years. On Nov. 2, 2004, I arrived at the polls at 9:45 AM. I left at 1:15 PM. There were only three voting booths. I had to wait 3 ½ hours to vote.

Christopher J. Collins, Dublin, OH, affidavit, 11/2/04
"I served as a volunteer for the Ohio Voter Protection Coalition outside the polling place for Precinct 6C, City of Columbus, from 6:50 am to 12:30 pm and from 3:00 p.m. until the time of this affidavit (4:00 pm). During this period of time, the waiting time to vote as reported to me, by at least 10 voters was one and one-half to two hours. At least 12 voters told me that they were leaving without voting because the line was so long."

Kris Usselman, Columbus, affidavit, 11/2/04
"It took me two and one-half hours to get through the line. I saw many people leave because of the long lines. I also saw people stand in the wrong lines for long periods of time and then have to get in other lines."

Vincent Bomar, Columbus, affidavit, 11/2/04
"I had to wait in line for approximately four hours before I could actually vote."

Terry Lewis, Columbus, affidavit, 11/2/04
"There were three voting machines for two precincts at my voting place, Presbyterian Church (Broad Street) which resulted in long waiting periods. I personally didn't get to vote until 15:46 (3:46 pm) after arriving at 11:00 am."

Stacey G. Hunt, Columbus, affidavit, 11/2/04
"There are only three voting booths!!! I have been here for hours, standing in the rain, waiting to vote. People are leaving without voting due to work policies. My husband (age 77) fell from fatigue while waiting. It is now 2:07 and I have not been able to vote! This is wrong!

Ernest Clyburn, Columbus, affidavit, 11/2/04
"I arrived at the polls and saw several long lines. There were no signs visible from where I parked, so I stood in line for an hour and then realized I was in the line for the wrong precinct. There was no one telling me to go inside and get my slip. Then I had to stand in the right line for two more hours, more than three total."

Jason D. Kimble, Columbus, affidavit, 11/2/04
"I arrived at my polling place (17B) ay 11:30 am. I voted at 3:25 pm. The polling place was very disorganized, not enough machines. The poll workers were rude and inefficient.

Jeff Szczygiel, Columbus, affidavit, 11/2/04
"I cannot wait three hours to vote. I have to pick up my children. This is the third time today I have been here – I cannot wait in excess of one hour. I would be willing to return after 7:30 pm. I am legally handicapped and [that] makes it difficult to stand for long periods of time."

Heather Shannon, Columbus, affidavit, 11/2/04
"At 3:45 pm I went to vote at Franklin Heights Recreation Center. I waited for one and one-half hours but heard that it was a three-hour wait. I had to leave because I didn't have anyone else to watch my child. At the time I was there, only two machines were working. I was not able to go back to the polls because of child care needs and was not able to vote."

Donald D. Germany, Columbus, affidavit, 11/2/04
"When I arrived to vote at Livingston School at 6:30 am, the polls were not open. The machines were not up. The election officials who sign you in had not arrived. I left without voting, as did a number of other people. This is precinct 4-B."

(These next two statements show the impact of moving established precincts without updating voter rolls)

Margaret Downs, Cincinnati, affidavit 11/2/04
"Told I was not registered and unable to vote. Was not told there was another precinct around corner where I could vote."

Steven Mason, Columbus, affidavit, 11/2/04
"My name was on voter list at precinct 26B but I was sent to precinct 56 and waited two hours, then called and got correct info and came back to vote."

Marcia Woods, Columbus, affidavit, 11/2/04
"I arrived at 1:45 and left at 4:20 pm in order to vote. Most time when I vote there were six booths. Today the most important election in 75 years there were only three booths in my voting area. That is unfair to the people."

Document 2.7—Continued

Margaret L. Thomas, Columbus, affidavit, 11/2/04
We were busy all day. Voters waiting 2-3 hours. We had an overflow all day. No breakfast. No lunch snack. I called several times to get more machines. The lines were always busy. I then called 462-4100. No luck. No answer. They refused to send any more machines."

John Saler, Columbus, affidavit, 11/2/04
"I have to work!"

Mary Taylor, Columbus, affidavit, 11/2/04
"I requested curb-side voting at Wards 17A and B. A chair would single me out as disabled. This is an unacceptable accommodation. No curbside voting was provided... My disability is unable to stand for long periods of time. The wait is over three hours."

Bertha Boatley, Columbus, affidavit, 11/2/04
"I came to vote around 2 pm. I had to wait approximately two hours to cast my vote. I completed voting around 4 pm. I am 90 years old."

Toi Crimley, Columbus, affidavit, 11/2/04
"I had to wait a long time to vote. I was unable to vote until 3:15 pm. There were a lot of people waiting. There was a handicapped woman and they told her there was no one to help her."

Loretta Ingram, Columbus, affidavit, 11/2/04
"Long line, a wait of two and one-half to three hours. That's too long. Help. Recalled in the past there was five voting machines."

Daniel G. Johnson, Mt. Gilead, affidavit, 11/2/04
"I was transporting voters to polling place at 2355 Middlehurst Ave. and South Mifflin School. I found that the polling place had no provisional ballot booklets – resulting in that no one has been allowed to vote provisionally the whole day."

Ted Dyrdek, Jr., Columbus, affidavit, 11/2/04
"I waited in line for 1 hour 45 minutes. A friend of mine left after voting. At this time I was standing where he was when I came in. I have a 1 hour 45 minute wait until I get to vote. Total three and one-half hours. My voting place had three voting machines and appears to be 90 percent black voters."

Carlos Pace, Columbus, affidavit, 11/2/04
"Standing in line – then I was asked to get out of one line and get into another line. In the process of doing this – instead of moving up the line I was put almost in back of the line, because I didn't have a authority to vote ticket. I took 3 hr. vacation time to vote. Now I have to try and get 3 hours more of vacation."

C. Joyce Sharp, Columbus, affidavit, 11/2/04
"My signature was challenged. I showed two pieces of I.D."

(The following is excerpted testimony and affidavits from field hearings, sponsored by the Columbus League of Pissed-Off Voters and other local voting rights activists and held on Nov. 13th and 15th, 2004, in Columbus. Some of the people who testified were not from Columbus, but drove to the state capital to tell what happened in their communities. Subsequent hearings were held in Cleveland, Cincinnati, and Toledo. In contrast to statements gathered on Election Day, people generally gave more detailed reports at the hearings.)

Werner Lange, testimony, a pastor from Youngstown, Ohio, 11-13-04:
"In precincts 1 A and 5 G, voting as Hillman Elementary School, which is a predominantly African American community, there were a woefully insufficient number of voting machines in three precincts. I was told that the standard was to have one voting machine per 100 registered voters. Precinct A had 750 registered voters. Precinct G had 690. There should have been 14 voting machines at this site. There were only 6, three per precinct, less than 50 percent of the standard. This caused an enormous bottleneck among voters who had to wait a very, very long time, many of them giving up in frustration and leaving. . . . I estimate, by the way, that an estimated loss of over 8,000 votes from the African American community in the City of Youngstown alone, with its 84 precincts, were lost due to insufficient voting machines, and that would translate to some 7,000 votes lost for John Kerry for President in Youngstown alone. . . ."

"Just yesterday I went to the Trumbull Board of Elections in northeast Ohio, I wanted to review their precinct logs so I could continue my investigation. This was denied. I was told by the Board of Elections official that I could not see them until after the official vote was given."

Boyd Mitchell, testimony, Columbus, 11-13-04:
"What I saw was voter intimidation in the form of city employees that were sent in to stop illegal parking. Now, in Driving Park Rec Center there are less than 50 legal parking spots, and there were literally hundreds and hundreds of voters there, and I estimated at least 70 percent of the people were illegally parked in the grass around the perimeter of the Driving Park Rec Center, and two city employees drove up in a city truck and said that they had been sent there to stop

Document 2.7—Continued

illegal parking, and they went so far as to harass at least a couple of voters that I saw..."

"I calculated that I maybe saw about 20 percent of the people that left Driving Park (precincts) D and C, I personally saw and talked to about 20 percent of them as they left the poll between 12:30 and 8 p.m. And I saw 15 people who left because the line was too long. The lines inside were anywhere from 2 1/2 to 5 hours. Most everybody said 4 hours, and I saw at least 15 people who did not vote."

Carol Shelton, testimony, presiding judge, precinct 25 B, Columbus, 11-13-04:
"The precinct is 95 to 99 percent black. . . . There were 1,500 persons on the precinct rolls. We received three machines. In my own precinct in Clintonville, 19E, we always received three machines for 700 to 730 voters. Voter turnout in my own precinct has reached as high as 70 percent while I worked there. I interviewed many voters in 25 B and asked how many machines they had had in the past. Everyone who had a recollection said five or six. I called to get more machines and ended up being connected with Matt Damschroder, the Director of the Board of Elections. After a real hassle -- and someone here has it on videotape, he sent me a fourth machine which did not dent the length of the line. Fewer than 700 voted, although the turnout at the beginning of the day would cause anyone to predict a turnout of over 80 percent. This was a clear case of voter suppression by making voting an impossibility for anyone who had to go to work or anyone who was stuck at home caring for children or the elderly while another family member voted."

Allesondra Hernandez, Toledo, testimony, 11-13-04:
"What I witnessed when I had gotten there about 9 A.M. was a young African American woman who had come out nearly in tears. She was a new voter, very first registered, very excited to vote, and she had said that she had been bounced around to three different polling places, and this one had just turned her down again. People were there to help her out, and I was concerned. I started asking around to everyone else, and they had informed me earlier that day that she was not the only one, but there were at least three others who had been bounced around.

Also earlier that day the polls had opened an hour late, did not open until about 7:30 A.M. The polling machines were locked in the principal's office. Hundreds of people were turned away, were forced to leave the line because they needed to be at school, they needed to be at work, or they needed to take their children to school. The people there who were assisting did the best they could to take down numbers and take down names, but I am assuming that a majority of those people could not come back because of work and/or because of school, because they had shown up to vote, and that was the time that they could vote, and that is why they were there. Also along the same lines, they ran out of pencils for those ballots."

Matthew Segal, Gambier, testimony, 11-13-04:
"In this past election, Kenyon College students and the residents of Gambier, Ohio, had to endure some of the most extenuating voting circumstances in the entire country. As many of you may already know, because they had it on national media attention, Kenyon students and the residents of Gambier had to stand in line up to 10 to 12 hours in the rain, through a hot gym, and crowded narrow lines, making it extremely uncomfortable. As a result of this, voters were disenfranchised, having class to attend to, sports commitments, and midterms for the next day, which they had to study for. Obviously, it is a disgrace that kids who are being perpetually told the importance of voting, could not vote because they had other commitments and had to be put up with a 12-hour line."

Robin Smith, Upper Arlington, testimony, 11-15-04:
"Back home at 8:00 p.m., I watched on TV how some areas of Franklin County still had long lines of people that were going to have to wait hours to vote. This could not have been an accident. In my affluent predominantly Republican community where 62 percent of the people voted for George Bush in the 2000 election, lines were not a problem...

"Yet late on election night, the news programs continued to show people in Franklin County and other parts of the state waiting in line to vote hours after the polls had closed. It appeared that these lines were primarily in low income, student or minority communities, areas that consisted predominantly of Democrat voters...

"The only conclusion I can draw from this is there was an intentional effort to usher Republican voters through relatively short lines while creating excessively long lines in Democratic areas to suppress their right to vote by ensuring some people would leave without voting, because they were incapable of standing in lines for three or four hours or they had to get to work."

Arthur Liebert, Columbus, testimony, 11-15-04:
"I voted at Marburn Academy on Walden Road. Let me just frame this first. The first week of August, my neighbor and I, his name is Randy Walker, we visited the Franklin County Board of Elections and after being vetted by a couple of mid-level staffers, we ended up talking to Matt Damschroder, and we questioned him on the voting machine and he gave us answers. He told us they were calibrated, they were tested, they were sealed, they were stored and they would be ready to go on Election Day. And at the end, I asked him about are you going to be able to handle the flow of voters that we're going to have, because everybody knows that this is going to be a mass turnout. And he assured me in no uncertain terms that they would be able to handle it...

Document 2.7—Continued

"Just to put this in perspective, my daughter voted in southern Delaware County [an affluent Republican enclave just north of Franklin County]. They had 14 voting machines. They were in and out in about 10 minutes. We [in Columbus] had six [machines], two of them weren't working."

(Under a 1950s Ohio court ruling known as the Reynolds case, each precinct is supposed to have one voting for every 100 voters.)

Jay Wamsley, Athens, testimony, 11/15 hearing
"I'm an attorney in Athens, Ohio, who volunteered as an attorney observer in Franklin County on Election Day... I, like so many people, saw extremely long lines all day... In the middle part of the day, we decided – I and the other member of our team - drove to some other precincts [in predominantly white suburbs], two in Upper Arlington, one at Upper Arlington High School, a firehouse on Coach Road, and then the Whetstone Recreation Center, which is partly in upper Arlington and partly Clintonville. And in each of those, they had at least four machines per precinct, and one of the four precincts at Whetstone Recreation Center had five machines. And so the disparity was pretty stark."

Pat Johnson, testimony, Columbus, 11/15 hearing
"I was a poll observer at the Parsons Ave branch library. There are 1,215 people registered to vote in that precinct. We had approximately 800 people show up who did vote. There were four machines.

"I called downtown to the Board of Elections and I spoke to a young man named... Jeff Gressel and I asked how many – how they allocated their voting machines. And he said you get approximately one to one and one-half machines for every 300 people... So I said, at 1,200, how many should you have? He said, "Well, you should have six, possibly, seven, maybe eight. There were four in this precinct. This is a highly Democratic precinct and there were four machines."

Michael Greenman, Westerville, testimony, 11/15 hearing
"I live in Westerville, voted in Precinct 3B. I voted there in elections for the last five years. When I came to this precinct this last election, I came in and looked at the list and my name was not on the list. It was a computerized list. My wife's name was on the list. I asked them how could this be? They had no explanation. They were very cooperative, gave me a provisional ballot. I was in and out quickly. They were very efficient. It was a good precinct. But I cannot imagine my name could have been removed from the list without some active action."

(Toledo and Lucas County experienced many problems, from voter roll purges before the election to problems with processing registration and counting the vote that were so severe even Blackwell had to demand the entire BOE step down after the election. These two statements highlight indirect and direct forms of voter intimidation.)

Michael Hayes, Toledo, testimony, 11/13 hearing
"I am with the Toledo League of Pissed Off voters... Imagine the sight, in a Black neighborhood where a lot of young black voters are showing up for the first time, you have full police presence, even though they are sitting in cars. Black neighborhood on Door St, you have six cars in the parking lot, and you have a well-known Republican businessman in the community asking people, 'please disperse, please get into your cars."

Susan Husami, Toledo, testimony, 11/13 hearing
"I received a letter from the Lucas County Board of Elections containing both the challenge of (my) right to vote and correction of registration list, as well as a notice of hearing. The challenge of my right to vote was filed by Daphne Sims, with an address included here. I never met Ms. Sims, and I have reason to believe Ms. Sims does not know who I am. The challenge form stated that Ms. Sims had reason to believe that I, Susan Husami, was not eligible to vote based on the following reason, and I quote, the person is challenged as unqualified on the ground that the person is not a resident of the precinct where the person offers to vote, unquote... The form I received is a form of intimidation and its authors should be held accountable and should be punished to the fullest extent of the law."

Victoria Lovegren, Columbus, testimony, 11/13 hearing
"I was concerned when I was registering students at the university where I work. I had voter registration cards. The voter registration cards had nothing in the way of a mailing address. You can give these to people, but it was not easy for them to mail them back, because there was no address. So I found that odd...

"I was also concerned about the directive or whatever you want to call the rules or the laws that Blackwell comes up with... The date of birth has to be on the envelope of the provisional ballot for it to be acceptable, and this is a change in the rules, and this change came down on Tuesday, and I saw that coming with my own eyes....

"The other thing that I have seen is they are not letting us look at the records. They are not letting us go to the Board of Elections and look at the records. Blackwell, again, made phone calls to counties, telling them that we are not to see those records, and this is public information. The Ohio Open Records Act says so."

Document 2.7—Continued

Mike Swinford, testimony, 11/13 hearing, Columbus
"You had a previous person talk about [long lines and delays past midnight at] Kenyon College…. Knox County has two colleges. The one that has been profiled is Democratic, had long lines, that has already been testified to. The other one, Mt. Vernon Nazarene University, that has been profiled as a Republican. That one did not have any problem as to waiting lines."

Eliza Jane Synder, testimony, 11/13 hearing, Columbus
"What I witnessed was at Columbia Alternative High School, during the hours of 6:30 am to 8:30 am. Everyone was turned away due to broken machines. That is what I watched… They started turning people away because they did not have any working machines."

Fiona Mitchell, Athens, testimony, 11/13 hearing
"I am from Athens, Ohio…. The night before the election, just after midnight we received a call… that there had been fliers posted on South Green stating that due to an unprecedented voter registration turnout, voting dates had been changed by the bi-partisan voting authority. Republicans and undecided will vote November 2nd. Democrats and undecideds will vote November 3rd. It went on to say make sure you bring proper ID…"

Gorman Paul Gregory, Westerville, affidavit, 11/13/04
"My friend, Kathy Janoksi, attempted to vote in our precinct 73F (Columbus, Westerville School District), but she was not on the rolls. I saw her being given the punch card to vote provisionally at approximately 1.30 pm. Ms. Janoski and I have resided together at the above address since 2001. Between 2001 and 2004, I personally saw communications from the Board of Elections to her address at the 4978 Smoketalk Lane address, bearing this address and assigning her to precinct 73F."

Sherri Suarez, Reynoldsburg, affidavit, 11/15/04
I was told that I was being challenged. Asked for ID and told "Sorry I would be unable to vote today." I refused to take this and then I was asked for a utility bill. I looked in my car – nothing. I called and had a bill faxed to my polling location. Walked in with a bill, ID, and registration from Internet, again told no. I demanded representation from Democratic Party and attorney and I was told no. Then offered provisional ballot – I refused. Then offered challenge form after being told to leave three times…

"First to use form at 2:30 pm ! Polling workers had to find forms!

Kay Kranz, Columbus, affidavit, 11/15/04
"As a poll worker, I experienced that our lines were over an hour long until noon. Our register went from 300 odd voters to 825 and we still had only three machines to process our votes. Our presiding judge Charles, explained that he would challenge votes based on signatures (going against our training). When setting up for voters, we asked for paperwork to deal with provisional voters. In training, we were told to go out of our way to get voters to the correct precinct and would be provided extra paperwork to guide these voters to help them to get to vote.

"At the end of voting, while closing up the Presiding judge mysteriously found the information needed to guide provisional voters. We were not able to guide voters to the correct precinct and they were made to vote provisionally."

Donna Adassa, Columbus, affidavit, 11/13/04
"Later in the day, after hearing from a friend that there were long lines at the poll at New Salem Baptist Church and people needed food and water – I went there with food and water and trash bags (for rain protection).

"It was pandemonium there. People were getting into lines – but didn't know why. I went into the building and spoke to the poll workers. There were two precincts operating there, A and C. There was no line to get to poll workers. They checked people in, handed out the voting ticket authorization and told people to go outside to the staircase up (and in the rain). It was unclear what to do there. People were in that line without authorizations. I told them how to get one and they returned with them. At the top of the stairs, these folks went into an anteroom, then a larger very hot room. Eventually a church volunteer would go upstairs and bring 10-20 people to stand in another line for the polls."

Angela Greene, Columbus, affidavit, 11/13/04
"I went to Whitehall Yearling High School to vote. Usually, we have five-to-six voting booths, but there were only three on this day. One of the three machines was not working and had not been since 6:30 am. There were 40 to 50 people ahead of us. I finished voting about 10 am. At 9:45 am people arrived to fix the machine. The repairmen reported that the machine had been sent without a cartridge. Whitehall is a racially diverse with a significant youth and African-American voting population."

Document 2.7—Continued

Catherine Chaney, Columbus, affidavit, 11/13/05
"My precinct, Perry Township Precinct A at Worthington Hills Elementary School, had four voting machines. However, the poll workers told us that only two were working. The others were broken. I saw someone come in and fix the machines. By 7 a.m., all four machines were working. I votes shortly after 7 a.m. The voters I observed that day and in the past at my precinct are almost all white. There are very few minorities that live or vote in my precinct."

Sandra L. Francesconi, Akron, affidavit, 11/13/04
"A larger than normal turnout – out the door! Which is great except there were too few voting machines (tho plenty of booths) and one of them broken. The poll director said she called election bureau the night before – got a recording – requesting more voting machines. By Tuesday morning, when she had to borrow a voter's cell phone, no one at election bureau had returned her call. I'd estimate we were four-five machines short (for amount of booths, since there were two precincts voting there. The director tried to alleviate my precinct's wait by "borrowing" from the other precinct (where the line was much shorter). When I asked if this switching back and forth might damage the vote count, she assured me not."

Catherine Buchanan, Toledo, affidavit, 11/12/04
I met numerous ex-felons who absolutely believed they had no right to vote. The ones I had approached prior to Oct. 4th I was able to convince to register. The ones I had encountered after Oct. 4th still honestly believed they had no right to vote.

I had also met elderly people and infirm people one week before the election who had not received their absentee ballot yet. Several of them told me the BOE told them they had the wrong address. How can they be at the wrong address when they had been living in heir homes for years and had voted in prior elections?'

Richard M. Smith, Sr., Columbus, affidavit, 11/15/04
"My wife received a notice on Nov. 2 challenging her right to vote. She was to appear before the Franklin County Board of Elections for a hearing (Oct. 28th, 9 am). The challenge was in Ward 68 (2003). Her current address is Ward 55 (2004). Her voting record is current. 40+ years."

(The following two statements suggest how some voters were targeted before the vote, as people who were designated recipients of provisional ballots, which would have to verified before being counted.)

Mary L. Harmon, Lebanon, affidavit, 11-13-05
I was a Democratic poll worker at Pct. 107 (ADX-TC-T-M)… which is located at Turtlecreek Fire Department, 1433 W. main St., Lebanon, Ohio. This is in Warren County.

My first concern is with provisional ballots. There are several voters whose names appeared in our book with the notation "I.D. required" beneath their names. According to the training I received at the Warren County Board of Elections, these voters were to be treated as "provisionals…" After the election, I asked about the Board's decision to place these voters in the provisional category and I was told that the Board was instructed to do so by the Secretary of State's office."

Martha S. Parge, Lebanon, affidavit, 11/13/04
"Precinct 16, City of Lebanon, Warren County. Two voters – not related, had "I.D. Required" next to their names on the voter roll. They presented valid I.D., then were told they needed to fill out a "HAVA Provisional Voter Statement of Affirmation." They voted and their ballots were put in a "provisional" envelope. I questioned why were the ballots being put in these envelopes?

"The presiding judge informed me that the BOE informed her to do this. Subsequently these ballots were treated as "provisional ballots." The name of the voter was scratched out on the vote roster and added to the "provisional ballot" voters list. The ballots were tallied as provisional on the ballot count tally sheet."

Penny Maroldo, Oberlin, written statement submitted, 11/15/04
"I live in Russia township. My mailing address is Oberlin. I have voted at the Russia Township Hall for the past four years (just moved from New Jersey in 2000). There has never been any lines for voting in the town hall and there are usually only a few voters at any one time. This year was no exception. I asked the folks running the polling place and they reported that at no time were there any lines from 6:30 am until I was there at 11:30 am. Apparently it continued to be steady, but light all day long.

"This year I and others noted a huge increase in voting booths there. Where we usually have eight or 10, this year there were twice that many! When I was there only three of them were being used! And there are not enough folks in all of Russia Twp to warrant such an increase for any reason! Those booths were desperately needed in other parts of Lorain County!

Document 2.7—Continued

"Right next door in Oberlin, where the Board of Election knew well that there was a huge increase in voter registration at Oberlin College (up from about 600-700 students to over 2,100 this year!), the two polling places where students voted had lines that snaked around blocks for hours and the students were forced to stand in the rain for up to five-six hours!

"Those two places, Oberline Public Library and First Church had fewer booths than Russia Twp – for a much larger voting population. That is just ridiculous. I think that this was done on purpose to make it difficult for students to vote."

Barry McPeek, Reynoldsburg, affidavit, 11/15/04
"I was sent a provisional ballot card forwarded by the post office due to a permanent change of address. I have been a resident at this address since 1980 - January to be exact."

Renee Smith, Columbus, affidavit, 11/13/04
"(1) Ward 48, Precinct D – excessive long line. (2) Ward 48, Precinct D – inadequate no. voting machine. (3) Witnessed a young black youth – first time voter – who was initially told he was not allowed to vote because he had a felony. When they made a call and determined he had no record, he was allowed to vote. (4) Problems of undetermined origin at 26 D - Lutheran Village – with elderly voting."

Joseph Kuspan, Bexley, affidavit, 11/15/04
"No problems. I was a runner in Bexley precincts 1A, 1B, 1C. There were no lines in my visits to these precincts three times. I will point out that 1B is perhaps the wealthiest precinct in Franklin County – including the Governor, OSU (Ohio State University) President, etc."

Thom Pintello, Columbus, affidavit, 11/15/04
"A problem with the voting machine. It would negate my vote for John Kerry by returning to "no-vote" status."

Esther Hampton, Columbus, affidavit, 11/13/04
"The electronic voting machine would not take my vote although I tried repeatedly by pressing the "vote" button. Election officials tried to help, then finally the screen (front of machine) went black and I was told I had voted." I felt that I had been blocked from voting. Multiple calls resulted in no help."

Jeanne Smith White, Youngstown, affidavit, 11/15/04
"I was voting for John Kerry and Edwards. I pushed the button besides John Kerry's name and my vote jumped up to George Bush. I began complaining about them cheating again this year. The attendant ran over to my booth and announced "just push the button again, that's been happening a lot." I then pushed the button again. It remained on John Kerry. Many others in different precincts experienced the same problem."

John Wooden, Sr., Columbus, affidavit, 11/14/04
"I arrived at Northtown Elem. I stood in the rain, then once in the building it took three and one-half before I could place my vote. The process was slow and relentless. It was like playing musical chairs. Once a vote was cast, we would move to the next chair. I was amazed to see only three voting booths - and all the people that were inside and outside waiting to place their vote. I thought with all the media attention predicting the voter turnout that there would be more voting booths."

Natalie Dobie, Cincinnati, affidavit, 11/13/04
"I was a poll worker at a precinct, at an apartment building, precinct 8C., on the west side of Cincinnati. I and my group witnessed numerous people who received absentee ballots but had not mailed them in. When these voters tried to vote in their precincts, they were not allowed to cast regular ballots or their absentee ballots at their precincts. Instead they were told that in order to vote they had to bring their absentee ballots downtown and cast them at the Board of Election office."

Jason Parry, testimony, 11/15 hearing, Columbus
"My name is Jason Perry. I live in Franklin County and was a poll monitor at Columbus 12A the whole day... My concern is that they knew – then Franklin County Board of Election knew the voter registration was double what it was in previous elections and they made absolutely no efforts to account or make any availability of (machines for) these people to vote.

"The question I have is where are these voting machines that have been there for the last decade? I realize they're probably waiting to buy new machines so they haven't replaced any, but I think it's completely irresponsible when the number of new voters is so large, especially in this precinct...

"By allowing four-hour waits in line and unreasonable expectations upon voters... They knew ahead of time that X number of people were registered to vote. They only provided the ability for about 50 percent of those, at least in my precinct, to actually be able to vote."

Document 2.7—Continued

(Public hearings convened by activists were also held in Cleveland, Cincinnati and Toledo. The following are sworn statements submitted and testimony from those hearings.)

Micheal Sowiski, sworn statement (Cuyohoga County, 11-20)

"I volunteered on Election Day for the Election Protection headquarters and worked one of the support hotlines for volunteers to document reports and send volunteers where they were needed. The following stories were all ones I heard on Election Day from other volunteers for Election Protection...

- Five visually impaired people told they could not vote.
- ID requirements only for Latino people at one polling location.
- Ballots with holes already punched in them when voters received them.
- Broken machines/not enough machines at polling places leading to long waits.
- Lots of problems with provisional ballots: People not getting the right signatures on them. Many reports and miscommunications about provisional ballot process. One volunteer had heard from the Cuyahoga County Board of Elections that "green stickers" required by HAVA were needed for all ballots, and that polling locations needed to make these provisionals official. Later we found that the stickers needed were white. Several polling locations did not start putting stickers on provisionals until noon or even later that day. Polling locations did not have the stickers – and needed them to certify the ballots. There seemed to be not enough communication with poll workers about the whole process, and definitely not enough education and information for voters about the process.
- Too many provisional ballots were cast as opposed to real ballots. Voters who had been voting for years at the same location weren't on lists, and so had to cast provisionals ballots.
- There were no bilingual translators at some polling stations.
- One report of a police car with lights on in front of a polling location, because they were dealing with a double-parked car. A volunteer approached the officer, suggested that the lights could intimidate voters. The officer replied, stating that, "If they are intimidated, then they shouldn't be voting."
- Reports of overly aggressive Republican challengers.
- One report of a ballot box with a broken seal.

These were all reports I heard as an Election Protection volunteer in Cuyahoga County.

Josephine Hulett, Youngstown, affidavit, 11/10/04

"When I press Kerry I get Bush. I press it three times, then I get Kerry. I speak to the presiding judge. I had them call the Board of Election."

Cyrus Taylor, testimony, 11/20 hearing, Cleveland

"It was quite a day... I was in some sense heartened by the long lines; figuring this meant that we'd had an incredible turnout. So when the next day –when the first canvass report was posted, I was astounded to see that in my precinct, that according to the official numbers, we actually had fewer people vote than voted in 2000. When there was essentially no campaign at all..."

Sarah Taylor, testimony, 11/20 hearing, Cleveland

"I was a Democratic Challenger in Ward 16... If you go to the Board of Elections website and you look at the number of ballots cast in each precinct, the total number of ballots. Then you look at the ballots cast for president, in practically all cases, there's a discrepancy...

"In the case of my precinct, where I was at, 16A, you'll see there's a discrepancy of about 18 people. That means 18 people voted but are not reported as voting for president. That means 5 percent of the people who voted did not have their votes counted for president. It's unlikely that 5 percent of the people who showed up on Election Day and stood in line for an hour or so, actually didn't want to vote for president. So one could assume they did vote but somehow the ballot got spoiled at some point."

Daniel Lotz, testimony, 11/20 hearing, Cleveland

"I was a Democratic Party poll challenger at Election Day Ward 13, precinct K... My main concerns were about the lack of competence and training of the poll staff throughout the day. I noticed early on that they were very disorganized as far as procedures for provisional ballots and a few of the staff really did not have any information at all on what to do with the provisional ballots, and so most of the handling was left to the poll judge and also the special inspector...

"Nearly 50 percent of the provisional ballots were not completely properly filled out, and I wanted to make sure for the counting of the provisional ballots that this can be brought to the Board of Elections. I'm concerned that the counting might not be a standard inclusive approach to counting these ballots."

Document 2.7—Continued

Patricia Blochowiak, testimony, 11/20 hearing, Cleveland
"I was a Democratic challenger, with people having to leave to go to work because they couldn't wait in line. We had a machine malfunction. It was off-set. We don't know if those votes were counted accurately or not. We had people who came in with cards from the Board of Election, who were not on the list, and were given provisional ballots.

"None of the election officials at the polls knew how to deal with the provisional ballot issue, and we were forever trying to go back to the rules and clarify them. But no-one seemed to have received training about how to deal with provisional ballots. When we had problems, we were unable in many cases to reach either of the two phone numbers we had for the board of elections."

Patricia Jackson, testimony, 11/20 hearing, Cleveland
"I do want to see the recount. What I want you to understand is that as a poll worker we're not the enemy. We're trained well and if we follow those things it goes well. I had a lot of people in my precinct who vote religiously and some of them, their names were not in the poll books.

"I had a shortage of equipment. I called them about seven in the morning – I needed another booth. I had another apparatus to accommodate another poll booth, but I did get one at six in the evening."

(After the hearings, which were covered on FreePress.org, more statements were sent to Bob Fitrakis. This one concerns the layout of ballot, which was confusing and could lead to mistaken votes.)

James R. Hanson, Columbus, statement, 11/26/04
"I'm sending you this sample ballot copy for my precinct because both my wife and I were slowed down in our voting because the layout of the presidential race confused us. This must have happened to others. She and I "drill" on the races, especially the judicial ones, so that we can vote expeditiously, then at the voting place (Jones Middle School gymnasium) we always study the sample ballot.

"This time we didn't study the sample ballot because the gym was full of people in several lines waiting to vote and even if that wall had been open, we were principally concerned about finding the right line…

"The problem was caused by the joining of presidential candidates with three county offices. One's eye first goes to Nader, then to the right to see a choice between Arlene Shoemaker and Paula Brooks. At the instant, one wonders what happened to the presidential candidates, and turning back sees the names of Peroutka, Baldwin, Badnarik and Campagna, which even though one is aware that there would be third party candidates on the ballot, glancing to the right one embraces the names of Mary Jo Kilroy and David Goodman as familiar ground.

"I think at that point , I started again at the top left, then went to the bottom where I saw Kerry running for prosecuting attorney—some other Kerry? Checking back at the top of the column, I confirmed that this was the presidential ballot, to which for some reason, apparently in error, the ad for Ron O'Brien had been attached…

"I couldn't get over the feeling that I was looking at a botched ballot, where senatorial candidates got a lesser position, out of sequence. The feeling I got was that I was being tricked, but passed the test."

Lisa Casini, affidavit, 12/28/04, (Independence, Cuyohoga County)
"When it was my turn to vote, I was handed a ballot in the usual sleeve. I took it out of the sleeve and was ready to put it in the voting apparatus, when I noticed that the bottom third of the ballot had already been punched out. My 11-year-old daughter and I quickly walked back to the voting table and showed them the ballot.

"A poll worker said "That's fine. It supposed to look like that." I replied, "No. The ballot was not supposed to be pre-punched at all" and asked for another ballot. Another worker took the punched ballot from me a new one, without any pre-punched chads.

"Then I asked a woman who had been standing in line behind me to look at her ballot before going into the voting booth. She took it out of the sleeve and we saw that her entire ballot had been punched.

"I asked the workers if there was a Checker present. A man introduced himself as the Checker and seemed very dismayed and said he would note the incident. I made a quick announcement to everyone waiting in line to check their ballot before they vote. I voted and left."

Document 2.8

County	Polling Place	Incident Time	Reported On	Type	Decription
Cuyahoga	Spring Hill Apartments 4300 Jennings Road	11/2/2004 7:00	2004-11-02 04:28:34 PST	Machine problem; Long lines	6 Boothes all close together. SOme lights do not work in boothes can't see the ballot. Long lines. PUnch card ballots.
Cuyahoga	11/2/2004 7:56	2A	2004-11-02 17:42:53 PST	Long lines	she didn't know she could vote if she is in line by 7:30 pm, so we told her she could.
Cuyahoga	12510 Maple Avenue	11-02-04, 7:50 a.m.	2004-11-02 08:21:07 PST	Machine problem; Long lines	2 voting machines have no light. Can't see. Complaints of long lines and some people are leaving.
Cuyahoga	12730 Shaker Blvd.	7:39am	2004-11-02 09:13:44 PST	Long lines	Too few voting machines, lines out the door.
Cuyahoga	15600 Terrace Rd., East Cleveland	11/2/04 10:00 a.m.	2004-11-02 07:16:47 PST	Other ballot-related problem; Long lines; Other polling place problem	Long lines (excess of 30 min.). Voting location is too small, very hot inside. Poll workers not well trained, slow. Voters report that if they make a mistake or have a ballot problem, the poll workers are reluctant to provide a replacement ballot.
Cuyahoga	1701 Caspte Ave,	11/2/04 5:35 (multiple times during day)	2004-11-02 19:09:11 PST	Identification-related problem; Long lines	Only Latinos required to show ID
Cuyahoga	17608 Euclid	11/2/2004	2004-11-02 13:28:10 PST	Long lines	Waits are 50-60 minutes. Traffic is a disaster. Soon to spill outside.
Cuyahoga	17608 Euclid		2004-11-02 08:28:52 PST	Long lines; Other	OVPC 10, long lines 35 to 50 minutes, and traffic problems
CUYAHOGA	1865 GARFIELD ST.,	8:25 AM	2004-11-02 07:04:15 PST	Long lines	2 PRECINCTS, CONFUSION AT POLLING PLACE, LONG LINES
Cuyahoga	24800 Broadway, Oakwood Village, 44146	11/2, 10:30 am	2004-11-02 09:51:15 PST	Long lines	OVPC 10, 3 precints in polling place, precint with largest population does not have more booths, short wait at 1 a and 3b, i long wait at 2a, which seems to be partisan motivated

Raw data thanks to the Election Incident Reporting System

Calls made to the EIR Helpline - Category: Long Lines

114   WHAT HAPPENED IN OHIO?

Document 2.8—Continued

Cuyahoga	Alexander Graham Bell	11/2/2004 8:30	2004-11-02 05:34:31 PST	Long lines	Poll workers requiring ID from everyone. Tried to prevent a man from voting whose middle initial was different. Taking over an hour to vote. Election protection volunteer berated and asked to leave by poll workers.
Cuyahoga	Alexander Graham Bell	11/2/04 9:00 a.m.	2004-11-02 15:14:35 PST	Long lines	Broken machines. 4 out of 7 broken and line is 1 1/2 hours long.
cuyahoga	Alexander Graham Bell	8:54am	2004-11-02 19:11:47 PST	Voter intimidation; Long lines; Other	
cuyahoga	alexander graham bell school	11/2/2004	2004-11-02 19:43:28 PST	Machine problem; Long lines; Other	workers to old. inspectors are rude
cuyahoga	alexander graham bell school	11/02/04 8:09am	2004-11-02 19:45:10 PST	Long lines	the student had to go to school and the line was too long to wait
cuyahoga	alexander graham bell school	11/2/04 9:21am	2004-11-02 19:23:35 PST	Machine problem; Long lines	not all the ballot areas are being used
cuyahoga	alexander graham bell school	9:01am, 11/02/04	2004-11-02 19:28:45 PST	Machine problem; Long lines	out of 7 machines, 2 are not working, people are leaving
Cuyahoga	Alexander Graham School	111/2/2004 l7:00	2004-11-02 04:40:16 PST	Long lines	Long lines. People leaving.
Cuyohoga	all precincts in Ward 6	11-2-04 2:30pm	2004-11-02 11:46:00 PST	Long lines; Other polling place problem	voters are being required to sign two books (poll book and "audit book of elections)—process is slowing down voting, is this proper procedure?
cuyahoga	almira elementary school		2004-11-10 11:13:52 PST	Long lines	many people complained of waiting for a long time in a line only to be told they were in the wrong line (4 precints in this same location) so they had to wait all over again, also when some lines were short the poll workers wouldn't let pepie with long lines switch to shorter lines.
Cuyahoga	Almira School	morning	2004-11-02 12:12:38 PST	Long lines	Some precincts much slower than others in same polling place - 30-35 minute waits.

Document 2.8—Continued

Cuyoga	2533 West 150th Street (VFW hall)	2-Nov	2004-11-02 08:20:10 PST	Machine problem; Long lines; Other polling place problem	{lquote}State inspectors" are taking names of people at the door. Then they go inside and have to be checked off another 2 times. Really slowing down the lines.
Cuyahoga	3484 Martin Luther King Dr.	11/2/2004 9:30	2004-11-02 06:33:28 PST	Long lines	Long lines (45 to 1 hr wait) due to insufficient poll workers and elderly slow poll workers
Cuyahoga	4747 E. 176th Street, Emile Day Sauze	7:15 a.m. 11/2/2004	2004-11-02 15:03:33 PST	Long lines	Short 1 poll worker. Long Lines. Presiding officer can't locate additional help.
Cuyahoga	5521 Warrensville Ctr Rd/ Ft Warren		2004-11-02 08:30:42 PST	Long lines	45 minute to 1.5 hr wait times
CUYAHOGA	5801 MEMPHIS AVE, CLEVELAND	11/2/2004	2004-11-02 13:33:43 PST	Long lines	OVPC#10-ONLYONE CHECXK-IN WORKER-LARGEST NUMBER OF VOTERS. nEW MACHINES CAME. LONG LINES.
Cuyahoga	79 Canaan Missionary Baptist Church	11/2/04 11:15am	2004-11-10 07:04:38 PST	Machine problem; Long lines; Other polling place problem	Election officials were not putting people in right precinct lines. Also polling places had broken machines.
CUYAHOGA	9113 PARMALEE RD, CLEVELAND	111/02/04, 8:10 AM	2004-11-02 07:12:24 PST	Long lines	LONG LINES, 45 MINUTE WAIT, NO STICKERS FOR PROVISIONAL BALLOTS, BALLOTS ARE UNSEALED.
Cuyahoga	9719 Ramona Blvd, Cleveland	7:30 a.m., 11/2/2004	2004-11-02 15:20:48 PST	Long lines; Other polling place problem	No enough polls-machines not working properly, long lines. People are leaving
Cuyahoga	Addison	12:10	2004-11-03 12:46:16 PST	Long lines	Waited in line 3 hours (9:30 -12). Lots of people left frustrated w/o votin. Out of 17 machines, 10 were working. 2 precincts and too few people
Cuyahoga	Addison Branch Library	8:00 AM	2004-11-02 06:24:20 PST	Long lines	ovpc 10, wait of 1.5 - 2 hours, not; enough parking
Cuyahoga	Addison Branch Public Library, 6901 Superior Ave.	11/2/2004	2004-11-03 12:53:35 PST	Machine problem; Long lines	secondhand report of problems with too few voting machines. OVPC 10
Cuyahoga	Alexander Graham Bell	11/2/2004	2004-11-02 06:36:51 PST	Long lines	Scrutinizing every voter. Checking all ID's. Taking over an hour to vote.

Document 2.9

Ohio County by Vendor by Election Incident Report

COUNTY Map Key#	Declared Winner		Registered voters Nov.04	No. of Voters Nov.04	04 Turnout	04 Vendor & Technology	05-06 Vendor & Technology	Category of 04 EIR (partial listing)
ADAMS 31	BUSH		17,696	12,373	70%	ES&S PUNCH CARD	Diebold DRE*	Vote switch
ALLEN 16	BUSH		68,151	49,929	73%	ES&S Optical Scan	ES&S PCOS	Vote switch
ASHLAND 49	BUSH		34,850	25,739	74%	Triad & ES&S OPTICAL SCAN	Diebold DRE	
ASHTABULA 88	KERRY		62,926	46,438	74%	Triad Punch Card	ES&S PCOS	
ATHENS 61	KERRY		45,103	30,586	68%	ES&S PUNCH CARD	ES&S PCOS	
AUGLAIZE 15	BUSH	WB	33,094	23,297	70%	ES&S DRE	ES&S PCOS	Security; Vote switch; Tamper
BELMONT 78	KERRY		44,231	34,095	77%	ES&S DRE	Diebold DRE	Tamper - recount
BROWN 30	BUSH		28,922	20,281	70%	Triad Punch Card	ES&S PCOS	Vote switch
BUTLER 8	BUSH		238,022	168,983	71%	ES&S PUNCH CARD	Diebold DRE	Unusual results; Vote switch
CARROLL 81	BUSH		20,076	14,416	72%	Triad Punch Card	Diebold DRE	

County	Winner			%			Issue
CHAMPAIGN 25	BUSH	25,376	19,081	75%	Triad Punch Card	ES&S PCOS	Vote switch
CLARK 26	BUSH	89,721	70,124	78%	Triad Punch Card	ES&S PCOS	Tamper - recount
CLERMONT 10	BUSH	125,832	89,812	71%	ES&S Optical Scan	ES&S PCOS	Vote switch
CLINTON 28	BUSH	25,092	18,674	74%	Triad Punch Card	ES&S PCOS	Vote switch
COLUMBIANA 82	BUSH	78,536	50,357	64%	Triad Punch Card	ES&S PCOS	
COSHOCTON 65	BUSH	22,679	17,636	78%	Triad & ES&S Optical Scan	Diebold DRE	Security
CRAWFORD 43	BUSH	29,591	22,289	75%	ES&S Optical Scan	Diebold DRE	Vote switch
CUYAHOGA 70	KERRY	1,005,807	687,255	68%	ES&S PUNCH CARD	Diebold DRE	Unusual results; Ballot misdesign; Targeted misinformation; Provisionals & Registrations tossed
DARKE 6	BUSH	38,290	27,022	71%	Triad Punch Card	Diebold DRE	Vote switch
DEFIANCE 2	BUSH	25,849	18,853	73%	Triad Punch Card	Diebold DRE	Vote switch
DELAWARE 40	BUSH	100,676	81,175	81%	ES&S PUNCH CARD	ES&S DRE	Vote switch
ERIE 17	KERRY	55,517	40,546	73%	ES&S Optical Scan	ES&S PCOS	
FAIRFIELD 54	BUSH	91,498	68,766	75%	ES&S PUNCH CARD	Diebold DRE	Vote switch; Tamper-recount
FAYETTE 35	BUSH	16,094	11,954	74%	ES&S PUNCH CARD	ES&S PCOS	

Document 2.9—Continued

COUNTY Map Key#	Declared Winner	Registered voters Nov.04	No. of Voters Nov.04	04 Turnout	04 Vendor & Technology	05-06 Vendor & Technology	Category of 04 EIR (partial listing)
FRANKLIN 38	KERRY	845,720	533,575	63%	DANAHER CONTROLS DRE	ES&S DRE	Vote switch; Security; Ballot misdesign; Machine shortages; Malfunction; Absentees rejected; Registrations tossed; Targeted misinformation
FULTON 19	BUSH	28,561	22,231	78%	Triad Punch Card	Diebold DRE	
GALLIA 59	BUSH	23,568	14,395	61%	Triad & Add'l unknown vendor Punch Card	Diebold DRE	
GEAUGA 86	BUSH	65,396	51,059	78%	ES&S Optical Scan	ES&S PCOS	Vote switch
GREENE 27	BUSH	105,079	80,602	77%	Triad Punch Card	Diebold DRE	Vote switch; Security-recount; §149.43 denied
GUERNSEY 74	BUSH	26,889	18,179	68%	Triad Punch Card	Diebold DRE	Recount-tamper
HAMILTON 9	BUSH	573,612	433,058	75%	ES&S PUNCH CARD	Hart InterCivic PCOS	Vote switch; Malfunction; Shortages; Ballot misdesign; Provisionals tossed; Registrations tossed; Misinformation felons; Intimidation

County	Candidate				%	ES&S Optical Scan	Diebold DRE	
HANCOCK 22	BUSH		49,617	35,926	72%	ES&S Optical Scan	Diebold DRE	Vote switch
HARDIN 23	BUSH		18,921	13,572	72%	Triad & Diebold LEVER and/or OPTICAL SCAN	Diebold DRE	
HARRISON 79	BUSH		11,475	8,312	72%	Triad Punch Card	Diebold DRE	Recount-tamper
HENRY 18	BUSH		19,685	15,405	78%	Triad Punch Card	Diebold DRE	
HIGHLAND 29	BUSH		28,243	18,864	67%	Triad Punch Card	Diebold DRE*	Vote switch
HOCKING 55	BUSH	WB	18,209	13,484	74%	Triad Punch Card	Diebold DRE	Recount-tamper
HOLMES 66	BUSH		17,870	11,788	66%	Triad Punch Card	Diebold DRE	Vote switch
HURON 48	BUSH		39,352	26,094	66%	unknown vendor PUNCH CARD	Diebold DRE	
JACKSON 57	BUSH		23,998	14,732	61%	PUNCH CARD	Diebold DRE	
JEFFERSON 80	KERRY		49,656	37,176	75%	ES&S PUNCH CARD	Diebold DRE	Registrations tossed
KNOX 52	BUSH		36,972	27,302	74%	Triad & MicroVote DRE	ES&S DRE	Security; machine shortages; unlikely registrations
LAKE 87	BUSH		160,196	122,862	77%	Triad & Sequoia DRE	ES&S DRE	Security; Targeted misinformation
LAWRENCE 58	BUSH		41,524	28,419	68%	ES&S PUNCH CARD	ES&S PCOS	Vote switch
LICKING 53	BUSH		111,387	80,539	72%	ES&S PUNCH CARD	Diebold DRE	Vote switch; Undervotes
LOGAN 24	BUSH		29,406	21,715	74%	Triad Punch Card	ES&S PCOS	Vote switch
LORAIN 69	KERRY		198,601	143,043	73%	Triad Punch Card	Diebold DRE	Recount-tamper

Document 2.9—Continued

COUNTY Map Key#	Declared Winner		Registered voters Nov.04	No. of Voters Nov.04	04 Turnout	04 Vendor & Technology	05-06 Vendor & Technology	Category of 04 EIR (partial listing)
LUCAS 20	KERRY	WB	300,137	221,980	74%	Diebold OPTICAL SCAN	Diebold DRE	Burglary; Machine shortages & malfunctions; Recount-tamper
MADISON 37	BUSH		23,183	17,784	77%	Triad Punch Card	ES&S PCOS	Vote switch
MAHONING 83	KERRY		194,903	134,290	69%	ES&S DRE	ES&S DRE	Software malfunction; machines jammed; Security; vote switch
MARION 41	BUSH		43,323	29,656	68%	Triad Punch Card	Diebold DRE	
MEDINA 68	BUSH		118,268	86,016	73%	Fidlar PUNCH CARD	Diebold DRE	Vote switch
MEIGS 60	BUSH		15,205	11,037	73%	Triad Punch Card	ES&S PCOS	
MERCER 5	BUSH		31,306	21,333	68%	Triad Punch Card	Diebold DRE	Vote switch; Undervotes
MIAMI 13	BUSH		72,169	52,104	72%	Triad & ES&S Optical Scan	Diebold DRE	Overvotes; Vote switch; Unlikely turnout
MONROE 77	KERRY	WB	10,350	7,989	77%	Triad Punch Card	ES&S PCOS	Recount-tamper
MONTGOMERY 12	KERRY	WB	391,914	287,646	73%	Triad Punch Card	Diebold DRE	Undervotes
MORGAN 62	BUSH		9,358	6,904	74%	Triad Punch Card	Diebold DRE	

County	Winner				%	Fidlar PUNCH CARD	Diebold DRE	Vote switch
MORROW 51	BUSH		24,248	16,694	69%		Diebold DRE	Vote switch
MUSKINGUM 64	BUSH		51,552	39,565	77%	Triad Punch Card	Diebold DRE	Recount-tamper
NOBLE 75	BUSH		8,879	6,794	77%	Triad Punch Card	ES&S PCOS	
OTTAWA 46	BUSH		30,334	23,468	77%	ES&S Optical Scan	ES&S PCOS	
PAULDING 3	BUSH		14,226	10,085	71%	Triad Punch Card	Diebold DRE	
PERRY 63	BUSH		23,480	15,472	66%	Triad Punch Card	Diebold DRE	Overvotes; unusual registrations
PICKAWAY 36	BUSH		30,045	23,079	77%	Triad & MicroVote DRE	DRE	Vote switch; Security; Recount-tamper $149.43 denied
PIKE 33	BUSH		19,655	12,970	66%	Triad Punch Card	Diebold DRE	
PORTAGE 84	KERRY	1	109,565	77,634	71%	Triad Punch Card	Diebold DRE	
PREBLE 7	BUSH		28,137	21,559	77%	Triad Punch Card	ES&S PCOS	Vote switch
PUTNAM 17	BUSH		24,579	19,169	78%	Triad Punch Card	ES&S DRE	Vote switch
RICHLAND 50	BUSH		91,311	63,154	69%	ES&S PUNCH CARD	Diebold DRE	
ROSS 34	BUSH		43,463	31,981	74%	Triad & MicroVote DRE	ES&S DRE	Security
SANDUSKY 45	BUSH		39,407	29,458	75%	ES&S Optical Scan	ES&S PCOS	Overvotes
SCIOTO 32	BUSH		48,005	36,043	75%	ES&S PUNCH CARD	Diebold DRE	
SENECA 44	BUSH		37,974	27,607	73%	Triad Punch Card	ES&S PCOS	

Document 2.9—Continued

COUNTY Map Key#	Declared Winner	Registered voters Nov.04	No. of Voters Nov.04	04 Turnout	04 Vendor & Technology	05-06 Vendor & Technology	Category of EIR (partial listing)
SHELBY 14	BUSH	28,460	23,286	82%	ES&S PUNCH CARD	ES&S PCOS	Vote Switch; Records discarded before recount
STARK 72	KERRY	267,939	191,781	72%	ES&S PUNCH CARD	Diebold DRE	Provisionals tossed
SUMMIT 71	KERRY	368,858	281,735	76%	Triad & Voting Technologies PUNCH CARD	ES&S PCOS	Undervotes
TRUMBULL 85	KERRY	142,436	110,747	78%	ES&S PUNCH CARD	Diebold DRE	Overvotes
TUSCARAWAS 73	BUSH	55,656	43,760	79%	ES&S PUNCH CARD	Diebold DRE	
UNION 39	BUSH	30,200	22,911	76%	Triad Punch Card	ES&S DRE	Vote switch; Recount tamper
VAN WERT 4	BUSH	21,100	15,525	74%	Triad Punch Card	Diebold DRE	Vote switch
VINTON 56	BUSH	8,527	6,158	72%	ES&S PUNCH CARD	ES&S PCOS	
WARREN 11	BUSH	125,165	95,512	76%	Triad & Add'l unknown vendor Punch Card	ES&S PCOS	Secret vote count; Vote switch
WASHINGTON 76	BUSH	40,889	30,494	75%	ES&S Optical Scan	ES&S PCOS	
WAYNE 67	BUSH	69,810	52,695	75%	ES&S Punch CARD	Diebold DRE	

WAYNE 67	BUSH	69,810	52,695	75%	ES&S Punch CARD	Diebold DRE	
WILLIAMS 1	BUSH	26,722	18,991	71%	ES&S Punch CARD	Hart InterCivic PCOS	Vote switch
WOOD 21	BUSH	90,688	64,103	71%	Triad Punch Card	Diebold DRE	
WYANDOT 42	BUSH	15,834	11,257	71%	Triad & Add'l unknown vendor Punch Card	ES&S PCOS	
Ohio 04 Totals:		7,972,826	5,722,439				

Compiled by Rady Ananda, BS Natural Resources, from public records; rev. Jan. 21, 2006.

Vendors: InterCivic, MicroVote General Corp., Sequoia Voting Systems, Inc., Triad Governmental Systems, or Triad GSI, and Voting Technologies International

Key No. Each county is numbered to aid in locating the county on a map. Numbering started at top left (NW) corner of the state, with Williams County, moved straight down, then right (east), then up (north), then east again, etc., ending at the top right (NE) corner of the state, with Ashtabula County.

Document 2.9—Continued

WB - whistleblower;   VPM - voters per machine;   FP - Free Press;   PCOS - Precinct Control Optical Scan.

*05-06 Vendor & Technology. Astericked counties used the new voting system in 05.

Sources:

Moss v Bush ("Moss v Bush") Ohio Supreme Court Case No. 04-2088; Cobb 12-23-04 motion in Federal court; Paul Harmon vs. Licking County (2005); John Conyers 1-5-05, Preserving Democracy: What Went Wrong in Ohio..., 6-10-05 "current" production of contracts, technology, 04 and 05 vendor selection, and other Public Records responses by county BOEs and the Secretary of State.

Document 2.10

PRECINCT	2000 VOTER REGISTRATION N	2000 VOTING MACHINE	2000 OFFICIAL TURNOUT	2000 VOTERS PER MACHINE	2004 VOTER REGISTRATION N	2004 ACTIVE VOTERS	2004 VOTING MACHINE	2004 UNOFFICIAL TURNOUT	2004 VOTERS PER MACHINE	VOTER REG % CHANGE	MACHINE CHANGE	TURNOUT % CHANGE	VOTERS PER MACHINE %
COLS 01-A	1096	4	493	123	1412	1018	4	692	173	22%	0	29%	29%
COLS 01-B	1175	5	387	77	1620	1079	3	560	187	27%	-2	31%	59%
COLS 01-C	1145	4	556	139	1446	1048	4	735	184	21%	0	24%	24%
COLS 02-A	976	4	362	91	1319	933	3	502	167	26%	-1	28%	46%
COLS 02-B	1019	4	534	134	1237	881	3	659	220	18%	-1	19%	39%
COLS 02-C	1049	4	585	146	1267	892	4	692	173	17%	0	15%	15%
COLS 02-D	834	3	480	160	1178	879	3	677	226	29%	0	29%	29%
COLS 02-E	979	4	546	137	1216	872	4	681	170	19%	0	20%	20%
COLS 02-F	746	3	444	148	925	685	3	543	181	19%	0	18%	18%
COLS 03-A	1056	4	387	97	1383	1030	3	513	171	24%	-1	25%	43%
COLS 03-B	911	4	463	116	1116	833	3	562	187	18%	-1	18%	38%
COLS 03-C	1206	5	557	111	1670	1254	5	767	153	28%	0	27%	27%
COLS 03-D	1070	4	455	114	1387	982	3	641	214	23%	-1	29%	47%
COLS 04-A	1100	4	426	107	1332	953	4	507	127	17%	0	16%	16%
COLS 04-B	971	4	407	102	1274	953	4	506	127	24%	0	20%	20%
COLS 04-C	728	3	245	82	1270	933	3	412	137	43%	0	41%	41%
COLS 04-D	1054	4	444	111	1353	1037	4	546	137	22%	0	19%	19%
COLS 05-A	853	4	410	103	1070	817	3	494	165	20%	-1	17%	38%
COLS 05-B	932	4	506	127	1123	857	4	571	143	17%	0	11%	11%
COLS 05-C	925	4	460	115	1070	799	4	519	130	14%	0	11%	11%
COLS 05-D	942	3	386	129	1281	934	4	517	129	26%	1	25%	0%
COLS 06-A	774	3	389	130	1045	832	3	461	154	26%	0	16%	16%
COLS 06-B	1066	4	579	145	1256	990	4	617	154	15%	0	6%	6%
COLS 06-C	959	4	486	122	1198	937	4	562	141	20%	0	14%	14%
COLS 06-D	970	4	442	111	1129	818	4	473	118	14%	0	7%	7%
COLS 06-E	828	3	444	148	1016	795	4	513	128	19%	1	13%	-15%
COLS 06-F	690	3	414	138	800	632	3	431	144	14%	0	4%	4%

Document 2.10—Continued

COLS 07-A	728	3	325	108	1015	742	3	449	150	28%	0	28%	28%
COLS 07-B	1074	4	517	129	1100	730	3	466	155	2%	-1	-11%	17%
COLS 07-C	833	3	360	120	1049	810	3	450	150	21%	0	20%	20%
COLS 07-D	874	4	375	94	1071	800	4	469	117	18%	0	20%	20%
COLS 07-E	1238	5	587	117	1809	1436	6	840	140	32%	1	30%	16%
COLS 08-A	1301	5	341	68	2058	1246	5	637	127	37%	0	46%	45%
COLS 08-B	1121	4	493	123	1650	1214	5	740	148	32%	0	33%	17%
COLS 08-C	976	4	387	97	1141	665	3	510	170	14%	-1	24%	43%
COLS 08-D	1109	4	524	131	1259	827	3	649	216	12%	-1	19%	39%
COLS 09-A	1213	4	426	107	1975	1451	6	802	134	39%	2	47%	20%
COLS 09-B	1213	4	342	86	1759	1151	4	507	127	31%	-1	33%	33%
COLS 10-A	1646	4	888	222	1201	741	3	477	159	-37%	-4	-86%	-40%
COLS 10-B	1617	6	849	142	564	389	2	162	81	-187%	-1	-424%	-75%
COLS 10-C	1012	4	379	95	1293	916	3	513	171	22%	0	26%	45%
COLS 10-D	655	3	219	73	941	687	3	357	119	30%	0	39%	39%
COLS 10-E	1343	5	981	196	1193	1051	5	808	162	-13%	0	-21%	-21%
COLS 10-F	1081	4	716	179	1500	1181	5	951	190	28%	1	25%	6%
COLS 10-G	801	3	530	177	940	753	3	628	209	15%	0	16%	16%
COLS 10-H	656	3	373	124	732	548	3	469	156	10%	0	20%	20%

COLS 10-I	598	3	221	74	695	431	2	321	161	14%	-1	31%	54%
COLS 10-J	980	5	548	110	1208	865	4	682	171	19%	-1	20%	36%
COLS 10-K	770	4	465	116	863	625	3	480	160	11%	-1	3%	27%
COLS 10-L	1042	4	610	153	1164	868	4	741	185	10%	0	18%	18%
COLS 10-M	851	3	514	171	949	701	3	593	198	10%	1	13%	13%
COLS 10-N	478	2	300	150	892	759	3	619	206	46%	0	52%	27%
COLS 10-O	1361	5	758	152	1614	1158	5	962	192	16%	1	21%	21%
COLS 10-P	891	4	588	147	1026	792	4	670	168	13%	0	12%	12%
COLS 10-Q	601	2	365	183	855	660	3	500	167	30%	1	27%	-10%
COLS 10-R	841	4	440	110	1017	716	3	551	184	17%	-1	20%	40%
COLS 10-S	177	2	58	29	556	435	2	335	168	68%	0	83%	83%
COLS 10-T	0	0	0	0	1079	884	4	719	180	100%	4	100%	100%
COLS 10-U	0	0	0	0	2275	1750	5	1183	237	100%	5	100%	100%
COLS 10-V	0	0	0	0	808	767	3	640	213	100%	3	100%	100%
COLS 11-A	900	3	309	103	1430	1043	3	504	168	37%	0	39%	39%
COLS 11-B	805	4	442	111	905	679	3	510	170	11%	-1	13%	35%
COLS 11-C	1023	4	604	151	1172	896	4	674	169	13%	0	10%	10%
COLS 11-D	1007	4	485	121	1305	982	3	617	206	23%	-1	21%	41%
COLS 11-E	926	4	553	138	1035	816	3	568	189	11%	-1	3%	27%
COLS 12-A	1171	4	339	85	1655	1096	3	571	190	29%	-1	41%	55%
COLS 12-B	893	3	297	99	1360	1017	3	525	175	34%	0	43%	43%
COLS 12-C	650	3	274	91	909	646	3	436	145	28%	0	37%	37%
COLS 12-D	920	4	478	120	1163	823	3	595	198	21%	-1	20%	40%
COLS 13-A	397	2	182	91	691	558	2	279	140	43%	0	35%	35%
COLS 13-B	871	4	368	92	1172	894	3	494	165	26%	-1	26%	44%
COLS 13-C	707	3	285	95	1095	891	4	498	125	35%	1	43%	24%
COLS 13-D	1048	4	525	131	1444	1156	4	706	177	27%	0	26%	26%
COLS 14-A	1597	5	719	144	2041	1430	6	930	155	22%	1	23%	7%

Document 2.10—Continued

COLS 14-B	1083	3	483	161	1720	1167	5	754	151	37%	2	36%	-7%
COLS 14-C	1687	4	882	221	2158	1554	6	1182	197	22%	2	25%	-12%
COLS 14-D	603	4	322	81	749	543	3	426	142	19%	-1	24%	43%
COLS 15-A	967	3	392	131	1497	997	4	674	169	35%	1	42%	22%
COLS 15-B	867	4	546	137	970	763	4	606	152	11%	0	10%	10%
COLS 16-A	1031	4	392	98	1400	927	4	670	168	26%	0	41%	41%
COLS 16-B	888	3	423	141	1166	758	4	601	150	24%	1	30%	6%
COLS 16-C	1258	4	425	106	2135	1501	5	860	172	41%	1	51%	38%
COLS 16-D	986	4	320	80	1379	890	4	616	154	28%	0	48%	48%
COLS 16-E	928	3	310	103	1310	779	3	550	183	29%	0	44%	44%
COLS 17-A	624	3	282	94	811	602	3	371	124	23%	1	24%	24%
COLS 17-B	1107	4	591	148	1465	1183	5	735	147	24%	0	20%	-1%
COLS 17-C	1062	4	588	147	1539	1226	4	786	197	31%	0	25%	25%
COLS 17-D	863	4	469	117	1191	966	3	569	190	28%	-1	18%	38%
COLS 17-E	710	3	329	110	944	727	3	435	145	25%	0	24%	24%
COLS 18-A	1120	4	524	131	1425	962	3	695	232	21%	-1	25%	43%
COLS 18-B	919	4	549	137	1065	795	4	663	166	14%	0	17%	17%
COLS 18-C	1201	4	585	146	1469	1027	4	746	187	18%	0	22%	22%
COLS 18-D	681	3	448	149	740	583	3	503	168	8%	0	11%	11%
COLS 18-E	848	4	538	135	954	742	3	600	200	11%	-1	10%	33%
COLS 18-F	958	4	476	119	1194	816	3	569	190	20%	-1	16%	37%

Document 2.11

Columbus	4	D	11507	Columbus	6	C	11523
Columbus	4	D	11508	Columbus	6	C	11524
Columbus	4	D	14208	Columbus	6	C	11535
Columbus	4	D	~~14660~~	Columbus	6	C	~~12800~~
			4				4
Columbus	5	A	11539	Columbus	6	D	11525
Columbus	5	A	11540	Columbus	6	D	11526
Columbus	5	A	~~14485~~	Columbus	6	D	11531
Columbus	5	A	14221	Columbus	6	D	~~14909~~
			4				4
Columbus	5	B	11769	Columbus	6	E	11527
Columbus	5	B	12666	Columbus	6	E	11528
Columbus	5	B	12667	Columbus	6	E	11537
Columbus	5	B	~~11496~~	Columbus	6	E	~~12874~~
			4				4
Columbus	5	C	11543	Columbus	6	F	11530
Columbus	5	C	11556	Columbus	6	F	11706
Columbus	5	C	11559	Columbus	6	F	11770
Columbus	5	C	~~14056~~	Columbus	6	F	~~11908~~
			4				4
Columbus	5	D	11541	Columbus	7	A	11544
Columbus	5	D	11542	Columbus	7	A	11545
Columbus	5	D	14298	Columbus	7	A	11865
Columbus	5	D	~~14933~~	Columbus	7	A	~~13542~~
			4				4
Columbus	6	A	11519	Columbus	7	B	11546
Columbus	6	A	11520	Columbus	7	B	~~13976~~
Columbus	6	A	14276	Columbus	7	B	14614
Columbus	6	A	~~14877~~	Columbus	7	B	15053
			4				4
Columbus	6	B	11521	Columbus	7	C	11549
Columbus	6	B	11522	Columbus	7	C	~~12970~~
Columbus	6	B	11533	Columbus	7	C	15042
Columbus	6	B	11534	Columbus	7	C	15045
Columbus	6	B	~~11887~~				4
			5				

Document 2.11—Continued

Columbus	40	A	14288		Columbus	41	E	14305
Columbus	40	A	14289		Columbus	41	E	14341
Columbus	40	A	14292		Columbus	41	E	1437?
			3		Columbus	41	E	14378
Columbus	40	B	13803		Columbus	41	E	15520
Columbus	40	B	14293					**5**
Columbus	40	B	14294		Columbus	42	A	14306
Columbus	40	B	14295		Columbus	42	A	14307
Columbus	40	B	15529		Columbus	42	A	15465
			5					**3**
Columbus	40	C	1389?		Columbus	42	B	14308
Columbus	40	C	14291		Columbus	42	B	14309
Columbus	40	C	15470		Columbus	42	B	14322
Columbus	40	C	15528					**3**
Columbus	40	C	15591		Columbus	42	C	14310
			5		Columbus	42	C	14311
Columbus	41	A	14296		Columbus	42	C	14315
Columbus	41	A	14297					**3**
Columbus	41	A	18261		Columbus	42	D	14312
			3		Columbus	42	D	14313
Columbus	41	B	1389?		Columbus	42	D	14321
Columbus	41	B	1389?					**3**
Columbus	41	B	13967		Columbus	42	E	14316
Columbus	41	B	14299		Columbus	42	E	14317
Columbus	41	B	15055		Columbus	42	E	14318
Columbus	41	B	15471					**3**
Columbus	41	B	15524		Columbus	43	A	11787
			7		Columbus	43	A	11788
Columbus	41	C	14300		Columbus	43	A	11803
Columbus	41	C	14301					**3**
Columbus	41	C	15522		Columbus	43	B	11789
			3		Columbus	43	B	11790
Columbus	41	D	14302		Columbus	43	B	11797
Columbus	41	D	14303					**3**
Columbus	41	D	15521		Columbus	43	C	11801
			3		Columbus	43	C	11802
					Columbus	43	C	11805
								3

Document 2.12

E E Ward Moving & Storage Co., LLC

1177 Joyce Avenue, Suite A
Columbus, OH 43219

Invoice

Date	Invoice #
11/16/2004	3078

Bill To

Franklin County Board of Elections
Attn: Ed King
280 E. Broad St.
Columbus, Ohio 43215

PAID

Description	Amount
Local Delivery of 2,741 Voting Machines	16,966.79
Local Pick-up of 2,787 Voting Machines	17,251.53
Sales Tax	0.00

Thank you for your business.

Total $34,218.32

Document 2.13

Document 2.13—Continued

Document 2.14

J. Kenneth Blackwell

J. KENNETH BLACKWELL
Ohio Secretary of State

180 E. BROAD STREET / 16TH FLOOR / COLUMBUS, OH 43215
614.466.2655 / TOLL FREE: 877.767.6446 / FAX: 614.644.0649
e-mail: blackwell@sos.state.oh.us   www.state.oh.us/sos/

MEMORANDUM

TO: J. Kenneth Blackwell, Ohio Secretary of State

FROM: Richard Weghorst, Director of Campaign Finance
            Faith Lyon, Board of Elections Liaison

CC: Members and Director, Lucas County Board of Elections

DATE: April 5, 2005

RE: Lucas County Board of Elections – Results of Investigation Following
            November 2004 General Election

This document represents a compilation of the investigation performed at your direction into the administrative activities and functions performed by the Lucas County Board of Elections leading up to and culminating with the general election in November 2004. The report begins with background facts regarding the history of the administrative oversight status by which this Board is currently operating. We continue by identifying thirteen (13) areas of major concern and present them in order of severity. Finally, we conclude by summarizing the investigation and by outlining suggested areas of focus for this Board as it moves forward.

Document 2.14—Continued

2005 INVESTIGATION REPORT
LUCAS COUNTY BOARD OF ELECTIONS

Background

In May 2002, an investigative team from the Office of the Ohio Secretary of State was dispatched to the Lucas County Board of Elections to look into allegations of verbal and physical abuse by an office supervisor. The investigation revealed the Board to be deficient in the training of its employees, lacking in communication between its members and its day-to-day management team, inconsistent in its application of discipline and replete with mismanagement in its administration of elections. As a result of that investigation, on May 28, 2002, the Lucas County Board of Elections was placed on administrative oversight. (Exhibit A)

In May 2004, the administration of election procedures in the primary election required an investigation by Patricia Wolfe, Director of Elections, and Richard Weghorst, then, Assistant Director of Elections. After reviewing the results of that investigation, on September 16, 2004, it was decided to not only leave the Lucas County Board of Elections on administrative oversight, but to impose additional terms to the original oversight status. (Exhibit B) A collective public reprimand to all four Board members was also issued at that time. (Exhibit C)

Most recently, following the general election in November 2004, another investigation into the administration of this Board was required. As with the previous two investigations, the Board's operation was thoroughly researched. The Board members, the Director, the Deputy Director and all fulltime employees of the Lucas County Board of Elections were interviewed, with the exception of one person who resigned prior to the commencement of this investigation. Miscellaneous board minutes, e-mails, memoranda, reports and notes were also reviewed as part of the investigation

Since the November 2004 election, several personnel changes have occurred at the Lucas County Board of Elections. Paula Hicks-Hudson, who was the Director, announced her resignation on December 3, 2004. Her resignation became effective on January 14, 2005. Larry Loutzenhiser, who was the Manager of Voting Services, resigned on December 6, 2004. On January 24, 2005, the Board met and promoted Jill Kelly, previously the Deputy Director, to the position of Director. Due to a procedural mistake, the Board had to reconvene on January 26, 2005, to elect Diane Brown its chairperson. On February 11, 2005, the Board met and hired Michael Badik as its new Deputy Director. Mr. Badik's first day as a Board employee was February 28, 2005.

Additionally, Board chairperson Bernadette Restivo-Noe, in a letter addressed to the Ohio Secretary of State, dated December 22, 2004, announced her intent to resign as both chairperson of the Lucas County Republican Party and as chairperson of the Lucas County Board of Elections. (Exhibit D) According to her letter, her resignation from the Board of Elections was to be contingent on and concurrent with the selection of a new

Document 2.14—Continued

party chairperson by the Lucas County Republican Party. Sam Thurber, in a letter to the Ohio Secretary of State, also dated December 22, 2004, announced that he, too, would resign as a member of the Lucas County Board of Elections and that his resignation would also be contingent on and concurrent with the selection of a new chairperson by the Lucas County Republican Party. (Exhibit E)   At this time, the Lucas County Republican Party has not selected a permanent chairperson. Therefore, Ms. Noe and Mr. Thurber remain as members of the Lucas County Board of Elections.

Results of Investigation

As a result of the most recent investigation, it is the investigators' determination that the members of the Lucas County Board of Elections, at the time of the November 2004 election, were directly responsible for the inefficient and unorganized management of the election process in their county. Listed below, in order of importance, are areas of grave concern:

- Failure to maintain ballot security;
- Inability to implement and maintain a trackable system for voter ballot reconciliation;
- Failure to prepare and develop a plan for the processing of the voluminous amount of voter registration forms received;
- Issuance and acceptance of incorrect absentee ballot forms;
- Manipulation of the process involving the 3% recount;
- Disjointed implementation of the Directive regarding the removal of Nader and Camejo from the ballot;
- Failure to properly issue hospital ballots in accordance with statutory requirements;
- Failure to maintain the security of poll books during the official canvass;
- Failure to examine campaign finance reports in a timely manner;
- Failure to guard and protect public documents;
- Lack of staff election plan;
- Current administrative operations; and,
- Non-compliant areas of the administrative oversight status mandates.

Document 2.15

STEALING VOTES IN COLUMBUS

Richard Hayes Phillips, Ph.D.
November 23, 2004

The Free Press on Election Day posted a disturbing
story, later confirmed by the Columbus Dispatch.   The
Free Press reported that Franklin County Board of
Elections Director Matt Damschroder deliberately
withheld voting machines from predominantly black
Democratic wards in Columbus, and dispersed some of
the machines to affluent suburbs in Franklin County.

Damschroder is the former Executive Director of the
Franklin County Republican Party. Sources close to
the Board of Elections told the Free Press that
Damschroder and Ohio's Secretary of State Kenneth
Blackwell met with President George W. Bush in
Columbus on Election Day.

The idea was to discourage turnout in Democratic
wards by forcing voters to wait in long lines at the
polling places. Such a strategy would be far more
effective than encouraging turnout in Republican
wards. Elections are all about margins. There are
74 wards in Columbus. George W. Bush won 12 wards,
with a margin of 7.35%. John F. Kerry won 62 wards,
with a margin of 37.62%. Affecting Kerry's turnout
would greatly reduce his margin of victory in
Columbus, giving the Republicans a much better chance
of overtaking Kerry given a strong enough showing in
suburban and small town Republican strongholds.

COLUMBUS POPULAR VOTE (EXCLUDING PROVISIONAL BALLOTS)

Location	Kerry		Bush		Others	
Kerry Wards	141520	68.40%	63693	30.78%	1704	0.82%
Bush Wards	36228	46.01%	42015	53.36%	496	0.63%
Grand Total	177748	62.22%	105708	37.01%	2200	0.77%

In order to investigate this matter, I obtained from
the Franklin County Board of Elections all the data I
needed in order to calculate, ward by ward, and
precinct by precinct: (1) The ratio of registered
voters per voting machine. (2) Percent turnout,
calculated as total ballots cast divided by the
number of registered voters. (3) Percent for Kerry,
calculated as votes cast for Kerry divided by votes
cast for president. (4) Margin of victory or defeat
for Kerry, calculated as the difference between the
vote totals for Kerry and Bush.

The first thing I noticed was the distribution of
turnout. There is a statistically significant
difference between the turnout in the Bush precincts
and the turnout in the Kerry precincts.

Document 2.15—Continued

DISTRIBUTION OF TURNOUT

Percent Turnout	Bush Precincts	Kerry Precincts
> 60	68	57
55-60	32	55
50-55	17	73
45-50	7	78
40-45	1	49
< 40	0	34
Total	125	346

Median Bush Precinct: 60.56%
Median Kerry Precinct: 50.78%

Best Bush Precinct: Ward 57, Precinct F
Bush 64.97% Kerry 34.82% Margin 30.05%

Best Kerry Precinct: Ward 17, Precinct D
Kerry 97.66% Bush 1.98% Margin 95.68%

Note: Ward 22, Precinct H was a tie.

As the above table shows, turnout was over 60% in 68 of 125 Bush precincts (54.4%), and over 50% in 117 of 125 Bush precincts (93.6%). By contrast, turnout was over 60% in only 57 of 346 Kerry precincts (16.5%), over 50% in only 185 of 346 Kerry precincts (53.5%), and under 40% in 34 of 346 Kerry precincts (9.8%).

Was the uneven distribution of turnout due to a lack of enthusiasm for the Democratic candidate? Or was it due to an uneven distribution of voting machines? To answer this question, I arranged the data, ward by ward, according to the ratio of registered voters per voting machine.

DISTRIBUTION OF VOTING MACHINES, TOP OF THE LIST

Ward	Voters/ Machine	Percent Turnout	Kerry Percent	Kerry Margin
WARD 19	261.2	67.99	63.33	+ 1491
WARD 65	265.1	60.10	44.33	− 496
WARD 30	266.4	56.25	52.50	+ 147
WARD 72	267.4	62.33	39.42	− 774
WARD 22	274.1	60.21	54.89	+ 465
WARD 28	276.2	58.48	82.04	+ 2371
WARD 63	278.7	56.10	47.37	− 242
WARD 48	278.9	52.84	82.37	+ 1909
WARD 46	279.8	58.22	55.19	+ 981
WARD 70	285.5	61.17	50.95	+ 79
WARD 06	292.9	47.44	91.29	+ 2494
WARD 21	293.9	57.92	58.45	+ 719

Document 2.15—Continued

WARD 34	295.8	55.85	65.05	+ 1051
WARD 69	296.4	57.97	41.98	- 1030
WARD 60	296.7	55.97	44.27	- 478
WARD 66	300.0	53.01	52.32	+ 203
WARD 05	302.9	46.24	94.34	+ 1854
WARD 62	303.2	57.96	55.68	+ 760
WARD 45	303.8	57.89	55.47	+ 1208
WARD 47	304.8	52.85	73.83	+ 1534
WARD 20	306.2	61.96	71.46	+ 1077
WARD 53	307.2	53.66	55.01	+ 499
WARD 15	308.4	51.88	60.71	+ 291
WARD 27	308.4	53.06	68.63	+ 1283
WARD 56	308.6	55.71	82.75	+ 4065
WARD 52	308.7	53.68	68.52	+ 1610
WARD 10	311.5	57.18	47.58	- 560
WARD 67	313.1	54.17	48.03	- 221
WARD 64	313.6	52.73	47.88	- 153
WARD 57	314.2	56.81	48.74	- 155
WARD 50	316.4	59.54	77.14	+ 1447
WARD 58	317.6	55.04	49.82	+ 41
WARD 07	318.1	44.24	94.21	+ 2332
WARD 36	318.7	53.31	50.57	+ 91
WARD 43	319.9	56.27	58.53	+ 475
WARD 73	320.6	58.23	44.18	- 1032
WARD 71	322.2	53.93	47.58	- 307
WARD 74	322.8	55.02	46.19	- 339

As the above table shows, the 38 wards in which the number of registered voters per voting machine was the lowest enjoyed high voter turnout. All but 3 of the 38 wards at the top of Damschroder's list had a turnout above 50%, and 6 of the 38 wards at the top of the list had a turnout above 60%. All 12 of the Bush wards are included in the top of the list. The 26 Kerry wards in the top of the list are not his biggest strongholds. In only 13 of the 26 wards did Kerry exceed his city wide share of 62.22% of the vote, which makes 13 of 38 wards altogether. However, these Kerry wards did enjoy a high voter turnout. In 23 of the 26 wards, Kerry's turnout exceeded that of his median precinct, 50.78%. Turnout exceeded 55% in 14 Kerry wards, and exceeded 60% in 3 Kerry wards. Clearly, Kerry enjoyed a higher turnout where the polling places had enough voting machines. What about the bottom of the list?

DISTRIBUTION OF VOTING MACHINES, BOTTOM OF THE LIST

Ward	Voters/ Machine	Percent Turnout	Kerry Percent	Kerry Margin
WARD 38	324.4	48.15	67.32	+ 546
WARD 35	327.5	50.90	92.36	+ 2104
WARD 17	330.6	48.67	93.12	+ 2465
WARD 42	330.6	46.34	70.77	+ 966

Document 2.15—Continued

WARD 14	333.4	49.37	81.31	+ 2068
WARD 13	338.6	44.91	93.36	+ 1702
WARD 44	340.7	48.87	72.98	+ 3212
WARD 18	342.4	55.15	76.84	+ 2043
WARD 51	343.6	46.93	88.59	+ 1857
WARD 61	345.6	49.28	62.35	+ 594
WARD 68	347.3	44.61	75.43	+ 950
WARD 04	348.6	37.69	91.75	+ 1643
WARD 32	348.7	55.11	58.82	+ 456
WARD 26	349.3	41.34	89.69	+ 1692
WARD 33	350.1	52.64	69.19	+ 1803
WARD 54	350.6	52.77	59.82	+ 668
WARD 49	353.9	50.76	54.45	+ 370
WARD 25	354.6	52.90	91.57	+ 3872
WARD 24	356.9	48.99	68.47	+ 991
WARD 37	356.9	44.37	58.99	+ 441
WARD 02	357.1	52.56	69.94	+ 1517
WARD 11	365.4	49.14	58.80	+ 531
WARD 31	367.0	45.05	69.86	+ 1000
WARD 29	369.2	45.65	61.09	+ 417
WARD 16	369.5	44.61	75.98	+ 1732
WARD 09	373.4	35.06	68.71	+ 497
WARD 39	374.4	46.29	70.06	+ 711
WARD 55	377.3	43.55	88.64	+ 1644
WARD 59	381.2	48.32	54.16	+ 288
WARD 08	381.8	41.52	68.99	+ 974
WARD 40	381.8	42.41	78.15	+ 1205
WARD 03	396.9	44.69	84.66	+ 1728
WARD 41	400.5	40.22	65.95	+ 1110
WARD 23	400.9	47.57	73.47	+ 1252
WARD 01	407.1	44.37	68.50	+ 744
WARD 12	423.9	41.81	86.47	+ 1557

As the above table shows, the 36 wards in which the number of registered voters per voting machine was the highest suffered low voter turnout. All but 8 of the 36 wards at the bottom of Damschroder's list had a turnout below 50%, and 2 of the 36 wards at the bottom of the list had a turnout below 40%. All 36 of the wards at the bottom of the list were won by Kerry, and they include most of his strongholds. In 29 of the 36 wards, Kerry exceeded his city wide share of 62.22% of the vote. However, these wards suffered a low voter turnout. In only 7 of the 36 wards did Kerry's turnout exceed that of his median precinct, 50.78%. Turnout was below 45% in 14 of the 36 wards, and was below 40% in 2 Kerry wards. Clearly, Kerry suffered a lower turnout where the polling places did not have enough voting machines.

A similar pattern is evident when examining the data for individual precincts. I have arranged the data in the same manner as above, precinct by precinct, according to the ratio of registered voters per voting machine. The 61 precincts with the lowest ratio of registered voters per voting machine are shown below:

Document 2.15—Continued

PRECINCTS WITH THE MOST VOTING MACHINES

Ward & Precinct	Voters/ Machine	Percent Turnout	Kerry Percent	Kerry Margin	
60-G	166.0	65.06	40.99	−	56
22-H	176.3	63.52	49.23		0
63-I	180.0	53.52	52.10	+	14
28-G	185.7	57.99	76.34	+	170
69-G	190.0	53.16	48.33	−	10
63-E	192.3	62.05	43.75	−	41
52-H	192.7	52.08	70.76	+	133
70-C	199.5	63.73	50.47	+	12
67-K	212.7	64.58	42.16	−	61
65-G	213.8	61.57	40.15	−	153
46-F	215.7	65.84	39.71	−	85
30-C	216.7	66.00	50.95	+	10
65-D	219.3	65.65	44.08	−	50
33-H	221.7	52.48	78.03	+	195
72-D	228.0	67.21	38.30	−	136
46-I	228.2	64.68	54.96	+	76
69-D	228.6	64.48	47.81	−	29
28-E	229.0	69.98	88.23	+	488
21-E	231.0	68.57	58.93	+	142
19-D	232.0	66.55	58.87	+	142
64-D	235.3	58.50	47.33	−	20
46-A	235.7	61.53	48.85	−	10
71-A	236.3	67.14	42.19	−	69
10-E	238.6	67.73	36.63	−	211
56-C	239.3	63.51	74.67	+	224
57-D	240.0	67.33	43.50	−	102
19-G	241.0	68.36	58.66	+	117
21-F	242.0	66.63	57.98	+	105
57-H	242.3	63.82	50.22	+	6
15-B	242.5	62.47	54.62	+	68
34-E	242.7	63.32	59.04	+	90
60-F	242.8	64.37	37.18	−	155
10-H	244.0	64.07	49.46	−	2
66-F	244.3	66.85	46.42	−	32
57-K	245.0	68.42	46.31	−	75
18-D	246.7	67.97	71.49	+	217
72-A	247.0	64.68	40.13	−	122
18-E	247.3	62.89	75.84	+	308
65-H	247.3	50.27	54.86	+	40
48-D	247.5	56.67	83.70	+	380
14-D	249.7	56.88	79.48	+	252
19-C	250.0	72.00	60.55		130
70-E	250.0	51.11	65.83	+	167
46-B	250.8	58.13	51.94	+	27
60-D	251.5	63.62	45.02	−	61
45-I	251.6	52.31	56.31	+	85
64-H	252.8	54.70	52.28	+	26
48-E	253.0	58.50	62.33	+	78
73-E	253.1	60.78	49.67	−	1
06-E	254.0	50.49	94.43	+	453

Document 2.15—Continued

70-D	255.3	66.41	50.30	+	11
66-D	255.6	55.79	48.52	-	18
69-C	255.8	54.50	36.10	-	186
42-C	256.0	61.98	57.14	+	74
46-L	256.0	66.54	57.84	+	162
10-P	256.5	65.30	35.33	-	190
47-F	257.7	50.84	76.96	+	211
45-H	259.8	60.59	44.03	-	183
19-B	261.0	70.11	60.80	+	164
52-B	261.5	62.43	62.21	+	159
69-I	261.5	68.36	37.80	-	169

As the table above shows, of the 61 precincts with
the most voting machines per registered voter, 26
were won by Bush, 34 were won by Kerry, and one was a
tie. Again, Bush enjoys disproportional favoritism.
Bush won 125 precincts and 26 of them (20.80%) are
represented here. Kerry won 346 precincts, only 34
(9.8%) are represented here, and they are not his
major strongholds. In only 12 of the 34 Kerry
precincts did he exceed his city wide share of 62.22%
of the vote, which makes 12 of 61 precincts
altogether. Most of these precincts enjoyed high
voter turnout. In all 61 precincts, turnout was
above 50%. In 42 of the 61 precincts, turnout was
above that of Bush's median precinct, 60.56%. Of
these 42 precincts, 22 were won by Bush, and 20 were
won by Kerry. This proves once and for all that the
Kerry precincts could have enjoyed a voter turnout
similar to that of the Bush precincts, if only they
had been supplied with enough voting machines.

And what of the precincts with not enough voting
machines? The 60 precincts with the highest ratio of
registered voters per voting machine are shown below:

PRECINCTS WITH THE FEWEST VOTING MACHINES

Ward & Precinct	Voters/ Machine	Percent Turnout	Kerry Percent	Kerry Margin	
12-A	551.7	34.50	84.96	+	407
01-B	540.0	34.57	68.41	+	211
25-B	507.7	41.56	91.33	+	522
23-B	501.0	41.38	79.13	+	363
41-C	490.0	38.91	60.53	+	127
60-E	481.0	40.47	51.05	+	15
11-A	476.7	35.24	74.80	+	252
18-A	475.0	48.77	80.46	+	430
59-D	464.3	45.51	59.46	+	123
03-D	462.3	46.21	79.15	+	374

Document 2.15—Continued

03-A	461.0	37.09	92.37	+	442
54-C	459.7	40.54	63.82	+	159
40-A	458.0	40.90	77.10	+	312
10-U	455.0	52.00	53.15	+	85
12-B	453.3	38.60	92.31	+	445
61-C	449.7	43.66	70.31	+	234
49-E	447.3	38.75	52.70	+	30
55-B	446.0	42.38	91.80	+	473
23-A	444.0	45.12	81.76	+	381
09-B	439.8	28.82	68.66	+	195
02-A	439.7	38.06	80.32	+	308
57-A	437.3	42.91	65.41	+	176
31-C	437.0	39.97	65.07	+	160
16-E	436.7	41.98	68.50	+	205
32-C	436.3	43.54	60.99	+	128
74-F	436.3	45.23	51.86	+	25
54-A	435.7	46.82	67.77	+	218
11-D	435.0	47.28	55.67	+	81
69-H	433.8	54.76	40.93	-	167
53-G	432.7	45.30	68.49	+	219
10-C	431.0	39.68	81.80	+	321
69-J	428.8	47.00	47.44	-	38
67-A	427.3	54.37	41.99	-	108
16-C	427.0	40.28	77.13	+	475
29-A	426.0	36.85	70.81	+	196
04-C	423.3	32.44	89.46	+	332
41-D	423.0	42.47	64.75	+	165
36-G	421.0	37.29	66.52	+	156
08-D	419.7	51.55	69.47	+	253
42-A	417.7	40.30	81.64	+	321
57-B	417.0	48.28	57.87	+	97
73-B	415.0	41.69	46.41	-	29
26-A	413.0	41.81	89.88	+	403
02-B	412.3	53.27	69.54	+	263
52-E	412.0	46.60	87.39	+	431
08-A	411.6	30.95	79.75	+	381
73-J	411.6	63.56	42.62	-	189
44-A	409.7	48.90	86.36	+	434
57-G	409.0	43.60	50.00	+	7
33-C	407.0	47.42	64.11	+	170
46-J	405.7	47.99	66.38	+	197
44-B	405.3	45.97	81.37	+	348
44-G	405.0	37.22	79.02	+	348
71-B	404.3	42.04	49.80	+	1
49-D	403.7	45.33	51.58	+	22
24-B	402.7	45.45	65.50	+	174
39-A	401.0	46.05	67.51	+	398
55-D	400.7	42.43	87.38	+	382
10-A	400.3	39.72	55.91	+	60
45-J	398.8	57.30	58.77	+	165

Document 2.15—Continued

As the table above shows, of the 60 precincts with the fewest voting machines per registered voter, only 5 were won by Bush, and 55 were won by Kerry. Again, Bush enjoys disproportional favoritism. Bush won 125 precincts, and only 5 of them (4.00%) are represented here. Kerry won 346 precincts, 55 (15.9%) are represented here, and they include his major strongholds. In 41 of the 55 Kerry precincts, he exceeded his city wide share of 62.22% of the vote. None of these precincts enjoyed high voter turnout. In only 7 of the precincts was turnout was above 50%. Of these, 4 were won by Kerry, and 3 were won by Bush. Turnout was below 45% in 34 precincts, below 40% in 16 precincts, below 35% in 5 precincts, and below 30% in one precinct.

It is important to understand what these numbers mean. The polls in Ohio were open from 6:30 A.M. to 7:30 P.M. That is 13 hours, or 780 minutes. If there are 400 registered voters per voting machine, and turnout is 60%, each voter has less than 3.5 minutes to vote, and that is assuming a steady stream of voters, with no rushes at certain hours. It also assumes no challenges to voters at the polls. If there are 550 registered voters per voting machine, and the turnout is 60%, each voter has 2.4 minutes.

All of this amounts to theft of votes. It has been shown above that the Kerry precincts enjoyed a voter turnout similar to that of the Bush precincts when supplied with enough voting machines.

It is an easy matter to calculate, assuming the same vote percentages for each ward, how many more votes John Kerry would have gotten with a 60% voter turnout. This is not an unreasonable number. The median Bush precinct enjoyed a turnout of 60.56%. The turnout was 66.31% for Cincinnati, city wide.

I am aware that because the Franklin County Board of Elections did not purge its voter rolls, there are more registered voters than adults listed as living in Franklin County by the United States Census. There are many "registered" voters who are dead or have moved away. One might expect, therefore, a lower percentage of voter turnout in Columbus than in Cincinnati. However, 60% of the voting age population is a reasonable figure. Presidential elections have surpassed this figure four times in my lifetime: 1952 (61.6%), 1960 (62.8%), 1964 (61.9%), and 1968 (60.9%). In 1992 the figure was 55.9%, and the 2004 election was probably more hotly contested.

Document 2.15—Continued

PROJECTED COLUMBUS RETURNS WITH 60% TURNOUT

Ward or Precinct	Percent Turnout	Kerry Margin	With 60% Turnout	Gain or Loss
WARD 01	44.37	+ 744	+ 1006	+ 262
WARD 02	52.56	+ 1517	+ 1732	+ 215
WARD 03	44.69	+ 1728	+ 2320	+ 592
WARD 04	37.69	+ 1643	+ 2616	+ 973
WARD 05	46.24	+ 1854	+ 2406	+ 552
WARD 06	47.44	+ 2494	+ 3154	+ 660
WARD 07	44.24	+ 2332	+ 3163	+ 831
WARD 08	41.52	+ 974	+ 1408	+ 434
WARD 09	35.06	+ 497	+ 851	+ 354
WARD 10	57.18	− 560	− 588	− 28
WARD 11	49.14	+ 531	+ 648	+ 117
WARD 12	41.81	+ 1557	+ 2234	+ 677
WARD 13	44.91	+ 1702	+ 2274	+ 572
WARD 14	49.37	+ 2068	+ 2513	+ 445
WARD 15	51.88	+ 291	+ 337	+ 46
WARD 16	44.61	+ 1732	+ 2330	+ 598
WARD 17	48.67	+ 2465	+ 3039	+ 574
WARD 18	55.15	+ 2043	+ 2223	+ 180
WARD 19	67.99	+ 1491		
WARD 20	61.96	+ 1077		
WARD 21	57.92	+ 719	+ 745	+ 26
WARD 22	60.21	+ 465		
WARD 23	47.57	+ 1252	+ 1579	+ 327
WARD 24	48.99	+ 991	+ 1214	+ 223
WARD 25	52.90	+ 3872	+ 4392	+ 520
WARD 26	41.34	+ 1692	+ 2456	+ 764
WARD 27	53.06	+ 1283	+ 1451	+ 168
WARD 28	58.48	+ 2371	+ 2433	+ 62
WARD 29	45.65	+ 417	+ 548	+ 131
WARD 30	56.25	+ 147	+ 157	+ 10
WARD 31	45.05	+ 1000	+ 1332	+ 332
WARD 32	55.11	+ 456	+ 496	+ 40
WARD 33	52.64	+ 1803	+ 2055	+ 252
WARD 34	55.85	+ 1051	+ 1129	+ 78
WARD 35	50.90	+ 2104	+ 2480	+ 376
WARD 36	53.31	+ 91	+ 102	+ 11
WARD 37	44.37	+ 441	+ 596	+ 155
WARD 38	48.15	+ 546	+ 680	+ 134
WARD 39	46.29	+ 711	+ 922	+ 211
WARD 40	42.41	+ 1205	+ 1705	+ 500
WARD 41	40.22	+ 1110	+ 1656	+ 546
WARD 42	46.34	+ 966	+ 1251	+ 285
WARD 43	56.27	+ 475	+ 506	+ 31
WARD 44	48.87	+ 3212	+ 3944	+ 732
WARD 45	57.89	+ 1208	+ 1252	+ 44
WARD 46	58.22	+ 981	+ 1011	+ 30
WARD 47	52.85	+ 1534	+ 1742	+ 208
WARD 48	52.84	+ 1909	+ 2168	+ 259
WARD 49	50.76	+ 370	+ 437	+ 67
WARD 50	59.54	+ 1447	+ 1458	+ 11
WARD 51	46.93	+ 1857	+ 2374	+ 517
WARD 52	53.68	+ 1610	+ 1800	+ 190
WARD 53	53.66	+ 499	+ 558	+ 59

Document 2.15—Continued

WARD 54	52.77	+	668	+	760	+	92
WARD 55	43.55	+	1644	+	2265	+	621
WARD 56	55.71	+	4065	+	4378	+	313
WARD 57	56.81	–	155	–	164	–	9
WARD 58	55.04	+	41	+	45	+	4
WARD 59	48.32	+	288	+	358	+	70
WARD 60	55.97	–	478	–	512	–	34
WARD 61	49.28	+	594	+	723	+	129
WARD 62	57.96	+	760	+	787	+	27
WARD 63	56.10	–	242	–	259	–	17
WARD 64	52.73	–	153	–	174	–	21
WARD 65	60.10	–	496				
WARD 66	53.01	+	203	+	230	+	27
WARD 67	54.17	–	221	–	245	–	24
WARD 68	44.61	+	950	+	1278	+	328
WARD 69	57.97	–	1030	–	1066	–	36
WARD 70	61.17	+	79				
WARD 71	53.93	–	307	–	342	–	35
WARD 72	62.33	–	774				
WARD 73	58.23	–	1032	–	1063	–	31
WARD 74	55.02	–	339	–	370	–	31
GRAND TOTAL						+16788	

Thus I conclude that the withholding of voting machines from predominantly Democratic wards in the City of Columbus cost John Kerry upwards of 17,000 votes. A more detailed calculation could be done on a precinct by precinct basis, but that is not necessary here. The purpose is to illustrate the magnitude of the conspiracy.

Matt Damschroder did not act alone. There are 74 wards and 472 precincts in Columbus, Ohio. It is not possible for one person to have delivered all the voting machines, and it is unlikely that nobody else was involved in planning where to deliver them. Anyone who associated with Mr. Damschroder on or shortly before Election Day should be investigated for possible complicity.

Richard Hayes Phillips, Ph.D.
4 Fisher Street
Canton, New York 13617
(315) 379-0820
richardhayesphillips@yahoo.com

Document 2.16

The Washington Times
November 17, 2004 Wednesday

How Ohio pulled it off
By J. Kenneth Blackwell, SPECIAL TO THE WASHINGTON TIMES

The electoral system in Ohio worked well on Nov. 2. Every eligible voter who wanted to vote had the opportunity to vote. There was no widespread fraud, and there was no disenfranchisement. A half-million more Ohioans voted than ever before with fewer errors than four years ago, a sure sign of success by any measure.

Despite 27 separate lawsuits, hordes of special-interest group "swat teams" descending on polling places and a circus of Michael Moore-inspired camera crews, our bipartisan election system - and the order, integrity and transparency integral to it - prevailed.

Voter enthusiasm was higher than I have ever witnessed. Problems and complaints were minimal. In some polling places, the record-high turnout resulted in long lines. Yet both poll workers and voters were patient, and the civility that has marked the Ohio election process for as long as I can remember reigned once again. There is no question that the long wait times that plagued some precincts must be analyzed and addressed for future elections - a seven-hour wait is clearly unacceptable. I have personally proposed unrestricted use of absentee ballots and consideration of multi-day voting to make the process more convenient and accessible. Yet when the chief problem on Election Day is long lines, that's a great day for democracy in my book.

Elections are a human endeavor and, as such, can never be totally error-free. Yet every eligible voter had the opportunity to vote, using regular or provisional ballots. Was the process perfect? No. But it was perfectly inspiring - a testament to the strength and power of our democratic system, the commitment of American voters to have their voices heard and the integrity of the process that encouraged participation and demanded fairness.

More than 5.5 million Ohioans voted on Election Day. Three key steps paved the way for our successful election:

* We took out the guesswork that plagued Florida's administration of the 2000 election with clear standards, policies and procedures.

* We created an inviting atmosphere by training poll workers and restraining outsiders from interfering with voters and compromising the sanctity of the secret ballot.

* We prepared Ohioans on when to vote, where to vote and how to vote with the most comprehensive voter education program ever undertaken in Ohio.

Because we set clear standards, the lawsuit frenzy that followed Florida's 2000 election was dealt with this year in Ohio in advance. By having litigation decided before the election, the confusion these lawsuits can wreak on poll workers and the voting public was minimized.

Because we trained our poll workers and enforced the "100-foot rule," which requires non-voters to stay at least 100 feet away from each polling place, we were able to create a welcoming, completely non-threatening atmosphere for voters.

Perhaps most importantly, through "Your Vote Counts Ohio," an unprecedented statewide voter education program, Ohio's voters were well informed about when to vote, where to vote and how to vote using the equipment at their polling places.

* At www.YourVoteCountsOhio.org, voters could learn what type of voting equipment would be used in their county, and then watch a video demonstrating how to use it.

* Through television, radio, newspaper and Internet advertisements and public service announcements, voters using punch-card machines were shown how to vote properly, check their ballots before turning them in and make sure "hanging chads" were eliminated. A second wave of advertising emphasized the importance of voting at the correct precinct, in accordance with Ohio law, and informed voters how to find their voting location.

* Posters and how-to pocket guides for voters were available free of charge to third-party groups involved in voter registration and turnout activities. (Our office worked with more than 60 voter-registration campaigns over the past year, helping register more than 1 million new Ohio voters.)

* More than 1 million "intelligent" automated telephone calls were placed to households in Ohio's urban centers, where past error rates have been highest, to remind voters to vote and make sure they knew their polling location.

Since 2000, election reform has become an important issue in America, and rightfully so. But as we continue to address it, let us not aggrandize the problems with our election system. In Ohio, it's a good one, as we demonstrated on Nov. 2. As our nation moves forward, adopting more modern tools to manage voter lists, register voters, and cast and count votes, let's remember that at the center of the system are people - not software and hardware. It was this recognition, and the action we took in Ohio to ensure the people were prepared, that played pivotal roles in our tremendously successful election on Nov. 2.

3

The Exit Poll Discrepancy

Despite frustrations facing many Democratic voters, as the polls closed in Ohio many political observers predicted John Kerry would soon win a tight presidential race. Their conclusions were based on various independent polls conducted that day, including the most sophisticated and thorough survey in American politics, network television's national exit poll of people who had just voted in fifty states across the country.

Network television's national exit poll found Kerry was beating George W. Bush 50.8 percent to 48.2 percent, according to the exit poll results posted on CNN.com at 12:23 A.M. on November 3. Polling organizations typically adjust or fine-tune raw results to ensure those questioned reflect the population at large. The exit pollsters interviewed more than 114,000 people nationally on November 2, 2004. CNN's 12:23 A.M. posting showed the raw results from a subsample of 13,047 people, placing Kerry's lead beyond both the range of expected adjustments and the 1 percent margin of error for a poll of this size. But a little more than an hour later, at 1:41 A.M., the networks drastically revised their earlier projection. Suddenly, a new set of numbers showed George W. Bush was in the lead, with 50.9 percent of the vote, compared to 48.1 percent for Kerry: the networks had substituted voting tallies (actual vote counts) for exit poll results (projections based on interviews with voters). As the documents in this chapter make clear, the swing in numbers from the exit polls to the vote tallies, a total 5.4 percent spread, represented not a giant political turnaround, but a huge statistical discrepancy.

Several academics and voting-rights activists noticed this gap right away. Jonathan Simon, a lawyer, former political survey analyst, and more recently a voting rights activist, captured CNN screen shots through the evening and shared them. Steven F. Freeman, who is on the faculty of the University of Pennsylvania's Center for Organizational Dynamics, where he teaches research methods and survey design (which includes polling), called attention to this gap in his November 2004 article, "The Unexplained Exit Poll Discrepancy." Freeman, first relying on Simon's screen shots and then others, said the gap between the raw poll data from people who had just voted and the official reported results could result from only two causes: flawed exit polling or vote count fraud. Ron Baiman, a policy analyst at Loyola University Chicago's Center for Urban Research and Learning, likewise cited this gap in expert testimony he gave for a presidential election challenge lawsuit filed in Ohio in December 2004. (That suit was withdrawn after Congress ratified the 2004 Electoral College vote in January 2005.) He also co-authored a paper with Simon explaining the problem.

By spring 2005, Freeman, Simon, Baiman, and other statisticians and research methodologists who had investigated this discrepancy had created a group, U.S. Count Votes, and updated their analysis as more complete exit poll data became available. Their findings increasingly pointed to vote count fraud. U.S. Count Votes refuted the primary explanation given by the firms that conducted the national exit poll, which claimed that more Kerry voters had spoken to pollsters, thereby erroneously skewing the exit polls in Kerry's favor. In late January 2005, U.S. Count Votes issued a paper showing that in fact *more Bush voters* had spoken to exit poll questioners in precincts where Bush won, compared to Kerry voters in the precincts where Kerry won. The analysis relied on partial data that was released by the exit poll firms to affirm their work before Bush's second inauguration. While the explanation given by the pollsters of the six major networks forming the National Election Pool (NEP) was covered nationally, the academics' analysis was limited to a few political websites.

But this was not the last word on the exit poll discrepancy. Freeman, speaking at the fall 2005 meeting of the Philadelphia chapter of the American Statistical Association, took the U.S. Count Votes analysis even further. By then, he was working on a book about the exit poll discrepancy. Using the available data, Freeman found that the largest gaps between how people said they voted and the official results were not in Democratic strongholds, but rather in Republican-majority precincts. Reading from his paper in Philadelphia, Freeman said:

> Consider the [national] numbers. . . . In those precincts where the official vote count was 80% or higher for Bush, average PLD [precinct level disparity]—the difference between who people said they voted for as they walked out of the voting booth, and the way those votes were officially recorded—was an astounding 10 percentage points. For example, in those precincts where Bush received 90% and Kerry 10% of the vote, [there were] average exit poll margins 85% to 15%. In other words, in these Bush strongholds across the country, Kerry, on average, only received two-thirds of the votes that exit polls predicted he should have received.
>
> If fraud were afoot, it would make sense that the president's men would steal votes in GOP strongholds, where they control the machinery of government and there's little danger of independent oversight, let alone prosecution.

Freeman does not attempt to explain how fraudulent results were recorded. He simply looks at the official numbers that reelected the president and compares them to the available exit poll data, asking, as he did when opening his October 14, 2005, presentation, "How much doubt must we have before we demand answers?"

The 2004 exit poll discrepancy has never been resolved. It was the first sign—with more evidence unearthed in the weeks after the 2004 election—that the reported and subsequently certified vote count was not credible. The presidential exit poll could serve as a check and balance to ensure the integrity of American elections, as national exit polls have in other countries. But it did not in 2004. And because the 2004 national exit poll data remains in private hands, as does the software used to tally countywide votes in Ohio, the American public may never fully know who was truly elected president in 2004.

Leading up to Election Day, neither the public, the national media, nor the Democratic Party were anticipating a corrupted vote count. Many independent national polling firms saw momentum for Kerry building. Voter turnout would be high, and historically that favored the challenger and his party's candidates.

The Harris Poll, in its final pre-election poll, predicted Kerry would win a "narrow" victory, perhaps by 3 percentage points. Late in the afternoon on Election Day, John Zogby of Zogby International, which has been polling since 1984, said Ohio and Florida were heading toward Kerry victories and predicted Kerry would be elected president. Other polling organizations were more circumspect, seeing numbers too close to call. Indeed, many pollsters and pundits were looking to that day's biggest survey apart from the vote itself, the television network's national exit poll.

The survey was conducted for six of the biggest networks—ABC, AP, CBS, CNN, FOX, and NBC—known on election night as the National Election Pool (NEP). The polling was done by two firms, Edison Media Research and Mitofsky International, whose co-founder, Warren Mitofsky, was known for inventing the exit poll. Mitofsky has done three thousand of these surveys over the decades.

Unlike polls done by leading news organizations before the election, the NEP poll was far more extensive. It relied on many thousands of additional interviews, which lowers the margin of error. The NEP had good reason to be careful in 2004. Election night 2000 was a major blot on the national media. The race came down to several hundred votes in Florida, and the networks, relying on exit polls and just-reported results, went back and forth between predicting George W. Bush and Al Gore as the winner. Moreover, computer glitches marred Mitofsky's polling in the November 2002 election, as well. Therefore, unusual steps were taken in 2004 to avoid errors.

The Mitofsky-Edison team had been preparing for months. On Election Day 2004, they interviewed 114,559 people nationwide who had just voted at 1,480 precincts across the country. They created a sub-sample of 11,719 voters and 500 absentee ballot voters, who were chosen as reflecting the nation as a whole. When compared to typical pre-election polls involving 2,000 or so respondents, the margin of error—the statistical measure of how accurate the poll will be compared to the vote count—drops from about plus or minus 3 percent to plus or minus 1 percent.

Unlike the voting machinery in local precincts, where a variety of systems are used, each with quirks and potential problems (punchcard machines have "hanging chads," optical-scan machines may or may not read votes, electronic touch-screen machines may or may not register votes for the intended candidate, etc.) the national exit poll was done with a uniform methodology. That uniformity improves accuracy. (Even the Edison-Mitofsky post-election report found no problems with the methodology on November 2.)

The national exit poll also differs from interviewing "likely voters" in telephone surveys, as is usually the case in pre-election polls, because the Election Day exit polls interview actual voters after they have cast their actual ballots. People leaving precincts are more likely to report exactly how they voted than people saying how they might vote in the future. For these reasons, exit polls are have been used to validate—or invalidate—national elections in other countries, notably in the Ukraine in late November 2004 and in Mexico in 2000, when the Institutional Revolutionary Party (PRI) lost its first presidential election in seventy-five years. In both cases, the exit polls were used to verify the vote count. In the Ukraine, the polls were used to show the count had been manipulated, with the exit polls more accurately reflecting the way the populace had voted. The official election result was overturned as a result. In Mexico's 2000 presidential election, the exit poll showed the PRI had indeed lost the election.

On Election Night in 2004, the National Election Pool (NEP) exit poll results showed John Kerry winning in the nationwide results and in Ohio, where nearly 2,000 people were in the NEP sample. In Ohio alone, the NEP sample showed Kerry with 52.1 percent of the vote, compared to 47.9 percent for Bush, according to a CNN.com screen shot, taken at 12:21 A.M. EST on Wednesday, November 3. A screen shot of the national NEP totals taken at 12:23 A.M. showed the presidential election result, with Kerry taking 50.8 percent of the vote and Bush taking 48.2 percent of the vote.

Steven Freeman and Joel Bleifuss address the CNN anomaly in their 2006 book, *Was the 2004 Presidential Election Stolen? Exit Polls, Election Fraud, and the Official Count*. According to Freeman and Bleifuss, editor of *In These Times*, CNN contends that it erred in posting the raw exit poll data—because of a computer glitch. They note that CNN said the data was "early," larger than the final sub-sample that the NEP would cite, and that the unadjusted data was never intended for public consumption. But Freeman and Blieffiss's analysis show that, even if all that is true, the shift from projections favoring Kerry to results favoring Bush in Ohio and nine other battleground states (Colorado, Florida, Iowa, Michigan, Minnesota, Nevada, New Hampshire,

New Mexico and Pennsylvania) reflects a discrepancy so large as to be statistically impossible.

Not surprisingly, after the election, the networks that had commissioned the exit poll circled their wagons. The NEP refused to release its "unblurred," precinct-specific raw data and polling assumptions, prompting Representative John Conyers, D-MI, the ranking Democrat on the House Judiciary Committee, to ask Warren Mitofsky in December 2004 to release the data. Mitofsky declined, saying "the data are proprietary information gathered and held for the benefit of those news organizations, and I am not at liberty to release them." Jack Stokes, a spokesman for the Associated Press, told Conyers's staff that the pollsters were evaluating their data. With an apparent popular vote margin for Bush (despite exit polls suggesting otherwise) and John Kerry conceding quickly, the NEP news organizations did not want to challenge the results, even though most seasoned political editors fully know election results often are adjusted for days or even weeks after the vote before they are "certified" as final.

Thus it was left for a handful of academics with statistical expertise to counter the explanations offered to account for Bush's "victory." They began by noting that CNN posted the raw data from the NEP pool of 13,047 selected voters and that data was later "adjusted" or "calibrated" to conform to vote tallies from state officials. As Ron Baiman of the University of Illinois wrote in a spring 2005 article:

> A national exit poll of over 12,000 respondents predicted that John Kerry would also win the national popular vote by a 2.6 percent margin. This is a more than a 100 percent swing from the reported Bush 2.8 percent popular vote margin. As this is a very large sample with a corresponding very small margin of error, this represents a swing of over 4.7 standard deviations with less than a one in 959,000 probability.

The academics and U.S. Count Votes parse the explanations given by the GOP for why this one-time-in-a-million shift might have occurred. First, Republican defenders said the NEP poll was flawed because too many women were polled. But when these analysts adjust Bush's exit poll numbers to correspond to the U.S. population—52 percent female, not 54 percent as in the NEP poll—Kerry still wins. Next, Republican defenders say that Bush supporters were more reluctant to be polled after voting and therefore were under-represented in the NEP results. In particular, they assert that Bush's female voters in Republican counties near the close of voting suddenly refused to answer exit poll questions—the "reluctant responder hypothesis."

A spring 2005 analysis by the National Election Data Project of U.S. Count Votes found *exactly the opposite* to be true. Using data from the Mitofsky-Edison report, they debunk the GOP's reluctant responder theory, stating, "In precincts with higher numbers of Bush voters, [exit poll] response rates were slightly higher than in precincts with higher numbers of Kerry voters." They also say there was no indication that the same "reluctant responder" orientation would not also affect Kerry supporters. Freeman's presentation in October 2005 to the Philadelphia chapter of American Statistical Association took the analysis further, saying the NEP's data showed that not only did more Republicans speak to exit poll questioners, but the greatest discrepancy between the presidential vote of people polled and official results *were in the Republican districts* where George Bush had won with 80 percent of the vote or more. That finding suggests it was in the GOP-majority locales where the president's supporters padded their results.

The exit poll discrepancy raises strong suspicions—and only a limited number of explanations—about the reported results of the 2004 presidential election. While the media organizations and polling firms that conducted the national survey resist admitting the possibility or plausibility of vote fraud, the independent analyses done by Steven Freeman, Jonathan Simon, Ron Baiman, the National Election Data Project, and others have ruled out all the explanations given except for vote-counting fraud.

Even using the incomplete data set from NEP (which still declines to release complete data), Freeman points out that the greatest discrepancy between how people said they voted, and the subsequent official results, were not in Democratic strongholds: they were in Republican districts, where few Democrats or political independents were present to verify the vote.

This book's analysis reaches the same conclusion, explained in Chapter 4, "Counting the Vote," using an entirely different data set and analysis—examining the precinct-by-precinct vote count in Ohio's Republican strongholds. In other words, two independent analyses of primary source data, the raw exit poll results and precinct-level voting records, conclude that the GOP fraudulently padded their vote in the 2004 presidential election.

Chapter 3 Documents: The Exit Poll Discrepancy

3.1 Final Harris Poll
(http://www.harrisinteractive.com/harris_poll/index.asp?PID
=515), pp. 158–160

The final Harris poll conducted in the three days before the election, with results released on election morning, predicted that "Kerry will win the White House today in a narrow victory." The poll also showed Kerry with a "modest" lead in Florida, Pennsylvania, and Ohio. The poll noted an axiom of undecided voters that "frequently split 2:1 to 4:1 for the challenger." In this case, however, if we are to believe the certified results for Ohio, the undecided voters split overwhelmingly for the incumbent, Bush.

3.2 CNN Website Screen Shots at 12:21 A.M.,12:23 A.M.,
and 1.41 A.M., pp. 161–163

The six major television networks agreed to broadcast exit poll results before the actual results became available as a way of covering the presidential election. These screen shots from CNN.com were taken on Election Night 2004, by Jonathan Simon. The first two were based on raw exit poll data and show clear Kerry victories in Ohio and nationally, at 12:21 A.M. and 12:23 A.M., respectively. The third screen shot, taken at 1:41 A.M., shows the "adjusted" results, which simply "recalibrate" or change poll results to conform to actual vote counts. These place Bush in the lead in Ohio. These screen shots are discussed in detail in Steven Freeman's paper, "The Unexplained Exit Poll Discrepancy," in document 3.3.

3.3 Research Report, "The Unexplained Exit Poll
Discrepancy" by Steven F. Freeman, December 29,
2004, pp. 164–169

In November 2004, the University of Pennsylvania's Steven Freeman, a graduate school business professor who was not an active political partisan, provided the first major analysis sounding the alarm over the discrepancies between the exit polls and the final tally. Drawing on the available exit poll data at that time, he pointed out how the actual national election results were highly statistically improbable. This paper, an update of his initial work released on December 29, 2004, examines the national exit polls and reported election results, looks at how the polls are used abroad to verify or invalidate national elections, and examines eleven of 2004's battleground states: Colorado, Florida, Iowa, Michigan, Minnesota, Nevada, New Hampshire, New Mexico, Ohio, Pennsylvania, and Wisconsin. Freeman subsequently updated and expanded on this report in the book, co-authored with Joel Bleifuss, *Was the 2004 Presidential Election Stolen?*

3.4 Representative John Conyers Jr., D-MI, Letter to Exit Pollster Warren Mitofsky, December 3, 2004, pp. 170–171

In early December, the statistically implausible nature of Bush's victory margin, given the historically accurate exit polls, caught the attention of U.S. Representative John Conyers Jr., the ranking member of the House Judiciary Committee. Conyers sent a letter to Warren Mitofsky, who had overseen the exit polls, requesting that the "actual raw exit poll data" be released. Mitofsky, in a letter dated December 7, 2004, said he could not release the data because it was proprietary and owned by the news networks. Mitofsky's reply was noted in the House Judiciary Committee Democratic staff report, "Preserving Democracy: What Went Wrong in Ohio."

3.5 Exit Pollsters Respond: Evaluation of Edison/Mitofsky Election System 2004, Prepared by Edison Media Research and Mitofsky International for the National Election Pool (NEP), pp. 172–175

On January 19, 2005, on the eve of George W. Bush's second inauguration, the two firms that conducted the November 2 national exit poll for the television networks released their report explaining why their poll incorrectly projected John Kerry winning—which was not reflected in the official results announced on Election Night. This is the executive summary of that report, which points to a handful of technical factors that incorrectly skewed the exit poll in Kerry's favor, as well as the assertion that more Kerry voters responded to exit poll questioners. That assertion was later found to be inaccurate, especially in early 2005, when analysts like Steven Freeman, Jonathan Simon, Ron Baiman, and other academics were able to scrutinize more of the raw exit poll data (though not the complete record) and in fact found more Republicans than Democrats had actually responded.

3.6 US Count Votes' Report Showing Exit Poll Discrepancies
Increase with Concentration of Bush Voters, April 12,
2005, Pages 9–11, pp. 176–179

Steven Freeman was not the only analyst who examined the exit poll
discrepancy. His work is highlighted in this anthology because it is the
least technical explanation of complex polling statistics. U.S. Count
Votes is a consortium of academics and analysts, including Jonathan
Simon, Ron Baiman, Kathy Dopp, and others, who did pioneering
work on the 2004 presidential exit poll discrepancy. This is an excerpt
from a detailed paper, "Analysis of the 2004 Presidential Election Exit
Poll Discrepancies," from April 2005, authored and endorsed by twelve
statisticians, mathematicians, and pollsters. This analysis also finds
that the largest gaps between the raw exit poll results and official tallies were in Republican strongholds. That finding will take on added
significance in the vote-counting chapter, which follows, as it matches
the precinct-by-precinct analysis from Ohio's rural Republican counties where the results find thousands of voters apparently voted for
Democratic positions and candidates lower down on the ballot at the
same time that they voted for Bush for president—if the results are to
be believed.

Document 3.1

The Harris Poll® #87, November 2, 2004

Final Pre-election Harris Polls: Still Too Close to Call but Kerry Makes Modest Gains

The final Harris Polls show Senator John Kerry making modest gains at the very end of the campaign in an election that is still too close to call using telephone methods of polling.. At the same time, the final Harris Internet-based poll suggests that Kerry will win the White House today in a narrow victory.

Harris Interactive's final online survey of 5,508 likely voters shows a three-point lead for Senator Kerry. The final Harris Interactive telephone survey of 1,509 likely voters shows a one-point lead for President Bush. Both surveys are based on interviews conducted between October 29, 2004 and November 1, 2004. The telephone survey is consistent with most of the other telephone polls, which show the race virtually tied.

Both surveys suggest that Kerry has been making some gains over the course of the past few days (see Harris Polls #83 http://www.harrisinteractive.com/harris_poll/index.asp?PID=512, and #78 http://www.harrisinteractive.com/harris_poll/index.asp?PID=507). If this trend is real, then Kerry may actually do better than these numbers suggest. In the past, presidential challengers tend to do better against an incumbent President among the undecided voters during the last three days of the elections, and that appears to be the case here. The reason: undecided voters are more often voters who dislike the President but do not know the challenger well enough to make a decision. When they decide, they frequently split 2:1 to 4:1 for the challenger.

About one percentage point of the current difference probably reflects the inclusion in the online sample of people with cell phones but no landline (and therefore not included in the telephone survey) who favor Kerry by a wide margin (see The Harris Poll #86 released yesterday at www.harrisinteractive.com/harris_poll).

The surveys both suggest an increase of a few percentage points above the 51.3% turnout (of all adults) in 2000, but not as big an increase as some reports have suggested.

Three Key States (Florida, Pennsylvania, and Ohio)

Another piece of evidence pointing to a likely Kerry victory is that online Harris Polls in these large, key states, which may well determine the Electoral College result, all show modest Kerry leads. However, all these leads are within the possible sampling error for these surveys. Assuming the forecast is correct, Kerry is likely to win all three large

Document 3.1—Continued

states, and almost certainly the White House along with it. The sample sizes were well over 1,000 likely voters in Florida (1,433), Pennsylvania (1,204), and Ohio (1,218).

TABLE 1

BUSH VS. KERRY (ONLINE SURVEY)

Q: "If the presidential election were held today, for whom would you most likely vote?"

If respondent said "not sure/refused":

Q: "Well, if you had to say would you lean toward. . . ?"

Base: Likely Voters who express a preference (5,508)

	Likely Voters
	%
George W. Bush	47
John Kerry	50
Ralph Nader	1
Michael Badnarik	1
Other	1
Kerry Lead	**3**

TABLE 2

BUSH VS. KERRY (TELEPHONE SURVEY)

Q: "If the presidential election were held today between George W. Bush for the Republicans, John Kerry for the Democrats and Ralph Nader as an Independent, for whom would you most likely vote?"

If respondent said "not sure/refused":

Q: "Well, if you had to say would you lean toward George W. Bush, John Kerry, or Ralph Nader?"

Base: Likely Voters who express a preference (1,509)

	Likely Voters
	%
George W. Bush	49

Document 3.1—Continued

John Kerry	48
Ralph Nader	2
Other (including Michael Badnarik)	1
Bush Lead	**1**

TABLE 3

BUSH VS. KERRY IN THREE KEY STATES (ONLINE SURVEYS)

Q: "If the presidential election were held today, for whom would you most likely vote?"

If respondent said "not sure/refused":

Q: "Well, if you had to say would you lean toward . . . ?"

Base: Likely Voters who express a preference

	Florida (n=1,433)	Pennsylvania (1,204)	Ohio (1,218)
	%	%	%
George W. Bush	47	48	47
John Kerry	51	50	51
Ralph Nader	1	1	1
Michael Badnarik	1	1	1
Other	*	1	*
Kerry Lead	**4**	**2**	**4**

* = Less than 0.5 percent.

Note: Percentages may not add up exactly to 100% due to rounding.

Notes for Tables 1, 2, and 3:

1. These numbers were calculated after allocating "not sure" and refusals.
2. Likely voters in the tables are defined as registered voters who:
   a. Have already voted; OR
   b. Were too young to vote in 2000 and are "absolutely certain" to vote; OR
   c. Voted in 2000 and are "absolutely certain" to vote; OR
   d. Were old enough to vote in 2000 but did not do so, but are "absolutely certain" to vote and are "extremely interested" in the election.

Document 3.2

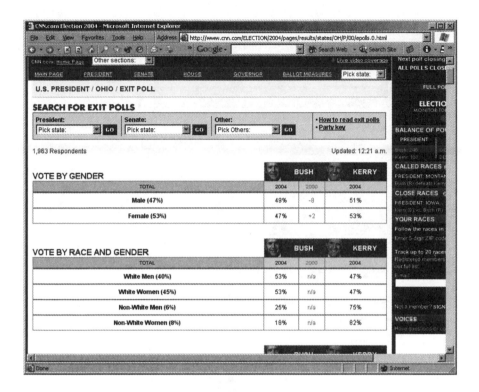

Document 3.2—Continued

CNN.com Election 2004

.com ELECTION RESULTS

Posted 1:25 a.m. ET, November 3
CNN projects the Republican party will retain control of the U.S. Senate.

Other sections:

U.S. PRESIDENT / NATIONAL / EXIT POLL

SEARCH FOR EXIT POLLS

President: Pick state: Senate: Pick state: Other: Pick Others: • How to read exit polls
• Party key

13,047 Respondents   Updated: 12:23 a.m.

VOTE BY GENDER

	BUSH		KERRY	NADER
TOTAL	2004	2000	2004	2004
Male (46%)	52%	n/a	47%	1%
Female (54%)	45%	+2	54%	1%

VOTE BY RACE AND GENDER

	BUSH		KERRY	NADER
TOTAL	2004	20%%	2004	2004
White Men (36%)	56%	n/a	40%	1%
White Women (41%)	51%	n/a	47%	1%
Non-White Men (11%)	28%	n/a	68%	2%
Non-White Women (13%)	22%	n/a	77%	1%

VOTE BY RACE

	BUSH		KERRY	NADER
TOTAL	2004	2000	2004	2004
White (77%)	55%	+1	44%	1%
African-American (11%)	10%	+1	90%	1%
Latino (9%)	41%	+6	56%	3%
Asian (2%)	39%	-2	61%	•
Other (2%)	38%	n/a	56%	2%

VOTE BY AGE

	BUSH		KERRY	NADER
TOTAL	2004	2000	2004	2004
18-29 (17%)	42%	-4	56%	1%
30-44 (29%)	49%	+0	48%	2%
45-59 (30%)	47%	-2	51%	1%
60 and Older (24%)	51%	+4	48%	0%

VOTE BY AGE

	BUSH		KERRY	NADER
TOTAL	2004	2000	2004	2004
18-64 (84%)	48%	+0	51%	1%
65 and Older (16%)	50%	+3	50%	0%

VOTE BY INCOME

	BUSH		KERRY	NADER
TOTAL	2004	2004	2004	2004
Under $15,000 (8%)	34%	n/a	65%	1%
$15-30,000 (15%)	38%	n/a	60%	1%
$30-50,000 (22%)	46%	n/a	53%	1%
$50-75,000 (23%)	53%	n/a	46%	1%
$75-100,000 (14%)	51%	n/a	40%	0%
$100-150,000 (11%)	53%	n/a	44%	2%
$150-200,000 (4%)	55%	n/a	45%	•
$200,000 or More (3%)	50%	n/a	39%	2%

VOTE BY INCOME

	BUSH		KERRY	NADER
TOTAL	2004	2004	2004	2004
Less Than $50,000 (45%)	41%	n/a	58%	1%
$50,000 or More (55%)	53%	n/a	46%	1%

VOTE BY INCOME

	BUSH		KERRY	NADER
TOTAL	2004	2000	2004	2004
Less Than $100,000 (82%)	46%	n/a	53%	1%
$100,000 or More (18%)	55%	n/a	43%	2%

Document 3.2—Continued

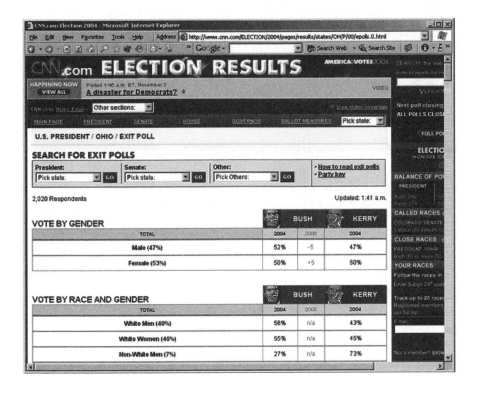

Document 3.3

UNIVERSITY *of* PENNSYLVANIA

Penn Arts & Sciences
Organizational
Dynamics

A Research Report from the University of Pennsylvania Graduate Division, School of Arts & Sciences Center for Organizational Dynamics

The Unexplained Exit Poll Discrepancy

Steven F. Freeman[1]
stfreema@sas.upenn.edu

December 29, 2004[2]

Most Americans who listened to radio or surfed the internet on election day this year sat down to watch the evening television coverage thinking John Kerry won the election. Exit polls showed him ahead in nearly every battleground state, in many cases by sizable margins. Although pre-election day polls indicated the race dead even or Bush slightly ahead, two factors seemed to explain Kerry's edge: turnout was very high, good news for Democrats,[3] and, as in every US

---

1 I would like to thank Jonathan Baron, Bernard B. Beard, Michael Bein, Mark Blumenthal, James Brown, Elaine Calabrese, Becky Collins, Gregory Eck, Jeremy Firestone, Lilian Friedberg, Robert Giambatista, Kurt Gloos, Gwen Hughes, Clyde Hull, Carolyn Julye, John Kessel, Mark Kind, Joe Libertelli, Warren Mitofsky, Michael Morrissey, John Morrison, Barry Negrin, Elinor Pape, David Parks, Kaja Rebane, Sandra Rothenberg, Cynthia Royce, Joseph Shipman, Jonathon Simon, Daniela Starr, Larry Starr, Barry Stennett, Roy Streit, Leanne Tobias, Andrei Villarroel, Lars Vinx, Ken Warren, Andreas Wuest, Elaine Zanutto, John Zogby, and Dan Zoutis for helpful comments or other help in preparing this report. I would also like to thank the many others who wrote to me expressing support, and apologize for not having had time to answer. I also apologize to those who may have sent helpful suggestions that I did not have time to read. I was overwhelmed with the response to the initial drafts of the paper.

2 This report was originally published on November 12, 2004 as Center for Organizational Dynamics Working Paper #04-10 (University of Pennsylvania, School or Arts & Sciences, Graduate Division). It was revised on November 21, 2004; the most important change was to use more conservative assumptions on the statistical accuracy of the exit polls. I made only minor clarifications since.

3 Nonvoters are generally more Democratic than voters. Democratic Party candidates generally benefit from higher turnout because the increase comes disproportionately from voters in socio-economic groups that traditionally vote Democratic. (Jack Citrin, Eric Schickler & John Sides (2003) "What If everyone voted? Simulating the impact of increased turnout in senate elections," *American Journal of Political Science*, 47(1):75-90)

Document 3.3—Continued

presidential election with an incumbent over the past quarter-century, undecided voters broke

heavily toward the challenger.[4]

But then, in key state after key state, counts showed very different numbers than the polls

predicted; and the differentials were all in the same direction. The first shaded column in Table

1.1 shows the differential between the major candidates' predicted (exit poll) percentages of the

vote; the next shaded column shows the differential between their *tallied* percentages of the vote.

The final shaded column reveals the "shift." In ten of the eleven consensus battleground states,[5]

the tallied margin differs from the predicted margin, and in every one, the shift favors Bush.

Table 1.1[6]: Predicted vs. tallied percentages in battleground states

	Bush predicted	Kerry predicted	Predicted differential	Bush tallied	Kerry tallied	Tallied differential	Tallied vs. predicted
Colorado	49.9%	48.1%	Bush 1.8	52.0%	46.8%	Bush 5.2	Bush 3.4
Florida	49.8%	49.7%	Bush 0.1	52.1%	47.1%	Bush 5.0	Bush 4.9
Iowa	48.4%	49.7%	Kerry 1.3	50.1%	49.2%	Bush 0.9	Bush 2.2
Michigan	46.5%	51.5%	Kerry 5.0	47.8%	51.2%	Kerry 3.4	Bush 1.6
Minnesota	44.5%	53.5%	Kerry 9.0	47.6%	51.1%	Kerry 3.5	Bush 5.5
Nevada	47.9%	49.2%	Kerry 1.3	50.5%	47.9%	Bush 2.6	Bush 3.9
New Hampshire	44.1%	54.9%	Kerry 10.8	49.0%	50.3%	Kerry 1.3	Bush 9.5
New Mexico	47.5%	50.1%	Kerry 2.6	50.0%	48.9%	Bush 1.1	Bush 3.7
Ohio	47.9%	52.1%	Kerry 4.2	51.0%	48.5%	Bush 2.5	Bush 6.7
Pennsylvania	45.4%	54.1%	Kerry 8.7	48.0%	50.0%	Kerry 2.2	Bush 6.5
Wisconsin	48.8%	49.2%	Kerry 0.4	49.4%	49.8%	Kerry 0.4	No dif

The media have largely ignored this discrepancy (although the blogosphere has been abuzz),

suggesting either that the polls were flawed, or that the differential was within normal sampling

error, a statistical anomaly, or could otherwise be easily explained away. In this report, I examine

the validity of exit poll data, sampling error, the likelihood of statistical anomaly, and other

explanations thus far offered to explain this discrepancy.

---

4 There have been four incumbent presidential elections in the past quarter-century. On average, the incumbent comes in half a point below his final poll result; challengers exceed their final poll result by an average of 4 points. (Guy Molyneux, "The Big Five-Oh," *The American Prospect Online*, October 1, 2004)   Exit poll data from the CNN website indicate that those who decided in the last three days chose Kerry over Bush 55% - 40%.

5 These eleven are classified as battleground states based on being on at least two or three prominent lists. Zogby, MSNBC, and the *Washington Post*. Another sometimes-mentioned state, Oregon, did not have a comparable exit poll because voting in the state is by mail. (These twelve states did in fact turn out to be the most competitive in the election; in no other state was the winning margin within 7%.)

6 Source: *CNN* website, November 3, 2004 12:21 a.m.

Document 3.3—Continued

Exit Poll Data

The data I use for this report are those posted on the CNN website election night. CNN had the data by virtue of membership in the National Election Pool (NEP), a consortium of news organizations that pooled resources to conduct a large-scale exit poll, as was done in the 2000 and 2002 elections. NEP, in turn, had contracted two respected firms, Edison Media Research and Mitofsky International,[7] to conduct the polls.

Calibrated and Uncalibrated Exit Poll Data

Part of the reason the issue went away for the media – and simultaneously raised suspicion on the web – is secrecy and confusion about the data and what exactly is being characterized as the exit poll. If you go to the CNN website or any other website on which 2004 exit poll data are available, you'll see numbers very different from those released on election day. This is because the survey results originally collected and presented to subscribers were subsequently "corrected" to conform to official tallies.

The pollsters explain this as a natural procedure: the "uncalibrated" data were preliminary; once the counts come in, they recalibrate their original data on the assumptions that the count is correct, and that any discrepancies must have been due to imbalanced representation in their samples or some other polling error. The pollsters have taken great pains to argue that their polls were not designed to verify election results,[8] but rather to provide election coverage support to subscribers – as one set of data that the networks could use to project winners and to explain voting patterns, i.e., who voted for whom, and why people voted as they did.

Whatever the merits of calibrating exit poll data, it obscures the issue of *why* the uncalibrated polls were so far off and mostly in the same direction. Although this calibration process may seem perfectly natural to NEP, it confuses nearly everyone else, even sophisticated analysts intimately involved in voting issues. The MIT-Caltech Voting Project, for example, issued a

---

7 Warren Mitofsky, the founder of Mitofsky International, is credited with having invented the exit poll. (David W.
   Moore, Senior Gallup Poll Editor, "New Exit Poll Consortium Vindication for Exit Poll Inventor," *Gallup News
   Service*, October 11, 2003)
8 Martin Plissner, "In Defense of Exit Polls: You just don't know how to use them," *Slate,* November 4, 2004

Document 3.3—Continued

report concluding that exit poll data were consistent with state tallies and that there were no discrepancies based on voting method, including electronic voting systems. But they used these adjusted data to validate the process. In other words, they used data in which the count is assumed correct to prove that the count *is* correct! Sadly, this report is being used to dismiss allegations that anything might be awry.[9]

It's an awful mistake, but entirely understandable – few of us realized that these data were corrected. Neither the CNN website, nor any other site of which I am aware, gives any indication that the data were anything other than what nearly all of us imagine exit poll data to be – data based solely on subjects surveyed leaving the polling place.

Data Used in This Report

For this report, I use data that apparently are based solely on subjects surveyed leaving the polling place. These data were reportedly not intended for public release,[10] and were available to late evening election night viewers only because a computer glitch prevented NEP from making updates sometime around 8:30 p.m. that evening.[11] They were collected by Jonathon Simon, a former political survey research analyst, and are corroborated by saved screen shots (see Figure 1.1). I happened to have sixteen CNN exit poll pages stored in my computer memory from viewing the evening before, and in each case, his figures are identical to mine. The numbers are also roughly consistent with those released elsewhere (Appendix B shows *Slate* numbers at 7:28 EST).

To derive the "predicted values" used in Tables 1.1 and 1.5, I combine the male and female vote, weighted for their percentage of the electorate. Ohio exit poll data (Figure 1.1) indicate that 51% of men and 53% of women voted for Kerry. Since the electorate is 47% male/53% female, Kerry's overall share of the exit poll was calculated as (51% x 47%) + (53% x 53%) or 52.1%.[12]

---

9 Tom Zeller, Jr., "Vote Fraud Theories, Spread by Blogs, Are Quickly Buried," *New York Times* (Front page); John Schwartz, "Mostly Good Reviews for Electronic Voting," *New York Times*; Keith Olbermann, *MSNBC Countdown*. All three on November 12, 2004

10 Martin Plissner, "In Defense of Exit Polls: You just don't know how to use them. *Slate*, Thursday, Nov. 4, 2004

11 Richard Morin, "New Woes Surface in Use of Estimates." *Washington Post*, November 4, 2004

12 Displaying these numbers out to one decimal point is not meant to imply that the numbers are precise to that level of significance, but rather to provide as much data as accurately as I can. Among the limitations of the CNN exit

Document 3.3—Continued

Doing the same calculations for other battleground states and comparing these numbers with final

tallies (*New York Times*, Nov. 7), I completed the columns in Tables 1.1 and 1.5.

Figure 1.1. CNN web page with apparently "uncorrected" exit poll data
(12:21 am Wed, Nov. 3, 2004)

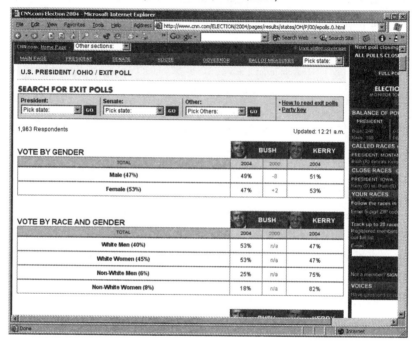

Are the Data Valid?

Some commentators on an early draft of this report rejected these data as unweighted,

meaning that they have not been adjusted to appropriately weight demographic groups pollsters

---

poll data are the lack of significant digits. I did not want to unnecessarily degrade the data further by rounding numbers derived from calculations.

Because CNN data is provided without decimals, underlying percentages for the exit poll numbers may be rounded by as much as .5%. It's unlikely that the derived number would be that far off, because the data come from two groups, male and female, both of which would have to have been maximally rounded in the same direction. Despite this, the extent of the discrepancy is such that even if every number that I use in this report had been rounded the full .5% in an unfavorable direction, the basic findings would all still hold.

Document 3.3—Continued

knowingly under- or over-sampled,[13] but it makes no sense that NEP would *ever* distribute unweighted data to anyone, let alone publish them on the web election night. NEP's predecessor, Voter News Service, warns in bold letters in its 2000 methodology statement never to use unweighted data for any reason (see Appendix A). Pollsters want to get it right. Their customers are depending on it. Broadcasters want to be alerted to probable outcomes, so as to plan their coverage accordingly (e.g., pre-writing stories so they can be completed shortly after poll-closings, assigning top reporters to winners' headquarters, being prepared for when concession or victory speeches might be forthcoming, etc.). In this case, subscribers were taken by surprise. Anchor people were discussing who Kerry would choose for his cabinet, conservative radio hosts were warning how now we're going to see the true John and Teresa Heinz Kerry. Prominent pollster John Zogby trusted the data sufficiently to call the race for Kerry. In the end, network managers had to scramble for coverage; editors and journalists had to rewrite headlines and lead stories.

It is alternatively possible that the data were already partially calibrated to the count by 12:20 a.m., but given the news report of the computer glitch preventing NEP updates and an abrupt change shortly after 12:20 a.m.,[14] that seems unlikely. If, in fact, the data already had been partially calibrated, however, it would mean that the uncorrected exit poll numbers favored Kerry to an even greater extent.

In summary, I'd rather have NEP data; lacking that (and unless NEP has a change of heart, no one is going to see those until well into 2005[15]), these CNN data look good, and can be used to generate some highly suggestive findings.

---

13 Using *unweighted* data, Democrats would almost always outpoll Republicans. Pollsters oversample minorities so that they have a sufficient sample size of important demographic groups – but then they negatively weight respondents in these groups to adjust for their actual percentage of the electorate.

14 An Ohio screen shot taken at 1:41 a.m. shows 2,020 respondents with the following percentages:

Male (47%):	Bush 52%	Kerry 47%
Female (53%):	Bush 50%	Kerry 50%

15 When the data are finally released, they may also be unusable for count verification purposes, because this would require original weighting assumptions rather than those that assume the count correct. First, we would need to know whether precincts were originally chosen randomly or to ensure sufficient subsamples of important demographic groups, i.e., minority precincts. Second, we would need to know the weighting of individual respondents to adjust for exit poll observations, e.g., African-Americans disproportionately participated in the poll, rather than weighting to make the numbers match up with the tallies, e.g., African Americans must have been oversampled because otherwise Kerry's vote total would have been higher.

Document 3.4

F. JAMES SENSENBRENNER, JR., Wisconsin
CHAIRMAN

HENRY J. HYDE, Illinois
HOWARD COBLE, North Carolina
LAMAR S. SMITH, Texas
ELTON GALLEGLY, California
BOB GOODLATTE, Virginia
STEVE CHABOT, Ohio
WILLIAM L. JENKINS, Tennessee
CHRIS CANNON, Utah
SPENCER BACHUS, Alabama
JOHN N. HOSTETTLER, Indiana
MARK GREEN, Wisconsin
RIC KELLER, Florida
MELISSA A. HART, Pennsylvania
JEFF FLAKE, Arizona
MIKE PENCE, Indiana
J. RANDY FORBES, Virginia
STEVE KING, Iowa
JOHN R. CARTER, Texas
TOM FEENEY, Florida
MARSHA BLACKBURN, Tennessee

JOHN CONYERS, JR., Michigan
RANKING MINORITY MEMBER

HOWARD L. BERMAN, California
RICK BOUCHER, Virginia
JERROLD NADLER, New York
ROBERT C. "BOBBY" SCOTT, Virginia
MELVIN L. WATT, North Carolina
ZOE LOFGREN, California
SHEILA JACKSON LEE, Texas
MAXINE WATERS, California
MARTIN T. MEEHAN, Massachusetts
WILLIAM D. DELAHUNT, Massachusetts
ROBERT WEXLER, Florida
TAMMY BALDWIN, Wisconsin
ANTHONY D. WEINER, New York
ADAM B. SCHIFF, California
LINDA T. SANCHEZ, California

ONE HUNDRED EIGHTH CONGRESS

Congress of the United States
House of Representatives
COMMITTEE ON THE JUDICIARY

2138 RAYBURN HOUSE OFFICE BUILDING

WASHINGTON, DC 20515-6216

(202) 225-3951
http://www.house.gov/judiciary

December 3, 2004

Warren Mitofsky
Mitofsky International
1776 Broadway - Suite 1708
New York, NY 10019

Dear Mr. Mitofsky:

I am writing to ask you to help clear up many of the rumors and disputes surrounding the 2004 Presidential election exit polls by releasing the "raw data" from your exit polls and by testifying at a hearing we will be holding next week.

As you are well aware, many questions have been raised regarding the discrepancy between the early exit polls conducted by the National Election Pool and the final result of the election. Specifically, just after noon on November 2, numbers were reportedly released showing that Senator John Kerry was leading in several key states such as Florida and Ohio, by a three percentage point lead late in the day. As we now know, these numbers are at odds with official results.

This discrepancy is objectively problematic and raises serious concerns about voting irregularity. While reasonable minds can differ as to the latter theory, the only way to restore complete legitimacy on this election is to have an independent firm conduct a detailed analysis of the data, including the raw data taken at the polls early in the day.

Indeed, exit poll data is now being used by Administration officials to evaluate the legitimacy of the election in the Ukraine. As Secretary of State Colin Powell stated, "We cannot accept this result as legitimate because it does not meet international standards and because there has not been an investigation of the numerous and credible reports of fraud and abuse." Powell recently called for "a full review of the conduct of the election" and tallying of results. Such an inquiry into the legitimacy of election results should be a priority for our country as well.

I would also like to request your attendance at a forum that I, along with many of my colleagues on the Judiciary Committee will be holding to discuss any issues and concerns regarding the numerous voting irregularities that have been reported in Ohio during the 2004 election. The forum will be held on Wednesday, December 8th, 2004 at 10:00 a.m. in Room

Document 3.4—Continued

Mr. Warren Mitofsky
Page Two
December 3, 2004

2237 of the Rayburn House Office Building. We are sure that you agree with us that regardless of the outcome of the election, it is imperative that we examine and openly discuss any and all factors that may have led to voting irregularities and any failure of votes to be properly counted. This will be a very informative forum for everyone in attendance and any insight or concerns that you may have on this issue will be greatly appreciated.

I sincerely hope that you will be able to attend and look forward to your response. If you have any questions, please contact Perry Apelbaum or Ted Kalo of the House Judiciary Committee Democratic Staff at (202) 225-6504.

Sincerely,

John Conyers, Jr.
Ranking Member
House Committee on Judiciary

Document 3.5

Evaluation of Edison/Mitofsky Election System 2004
prepared by Edison Media Research and Mitofsky International for the National Election Pool (NEP)

Table of Contents

Document 3.5—Continued

Executive Summary

On November 2, 2004, the Election System created by Edison Media Research and Mitofsky International for the National Election Pool (NEP) produced election estimates and exit poll data for analysis in 120 races in all 50 states and the District of Columbia. In addition, between January and March 2004, Edison and Mitofsky conducted exit polls for 23 Democratic Primaries and Caucuses. For every election, the system delivered on its main goals: there were no incorrect NEP winner projections, and the exit poll data produced on election day were used on-air and in print by the six members of the NEP (AP, ABC, CBS, CNN, FOX and NBC) as well as several dozen media organizations who subscribed to that data. However, the estimates produced by the exit poll data on November 2nd were not as accurate as we have produced with previous exit polls.

Our investigation of the differences between the exit poll estimates and the actual vote count point to one primary reason: in a number of precincts a higher than average Within Precinct Error most likely due to Kerry voters participating in the exit polls at a higher rate than Bush voters. There have been partisan overstatements in previous elections, more often overstating the Democrat, but occasionally overstating the Republican. While the size of the average exit poll error has varied, it was higher in 2004 than in previous years for which we have data. This report measures the errors in the exit poll estimates and attempts to identify the factors that contributed to these errors.

The body of this report contains the details of our analysis of the performance of the exit polls and the election system. In addition to the information included in this report, exit poll data from this election is being archived at the Roper Center at the University of Connecticut and at the Institute for Social Research at the University of Michigan and is available there for review and further analysis. This is the procedure that we have followed for all previous exit polls, which are also available at the Roper Center and ISR. The description of the methodology of the exit polls has already been posted on our Web site – www.exit-poll.net - along with all questionnaires used on election day and the completion rates nationally and by state.

Here is a brief summary of our findings:

1. Exit Poll Estimates

The exit poll estimates in the 2004 general election overstated John Kerry's share of the vote nationally and in many states. There were 26 states in which the estimates produced by the exit poll data overstated the vote for John Kerry by more than one standard error, and there were four states in which the exit poll estimates overstated the vote for George W. Bush by more than one standard error. The inaccuracies in the exit poll estimates were not due to the sample selection of the polling locations at which the exit polls were conducted. We have not discovered any systematic problem in how the exit poll data were collected and processed. Exit polls do not support the allegations of fraud due to rigging of voting equipment. Our analysis of the difference between the vote count and

Document 3.5—Continued

the exit poll at each polling location in our sample has found no systematic differences for precincts using touch screen and optical scan voting equipment. We say this because these differences are similar to the differences for punch card voting equipment, and less than the difference for mechanical voting equipment.

Our detailed analysis by polling location and by interviewer has identified several factors that may have contributed to the size of the Within Precinct Error that led to the inaccuracies in the exit poll estimates. Some of these factors are within our control while others are not.

It is difficult to pinpoint precisely the reasons that, in general, Kerry voters were more likely to participate in the exit polls than Bush voters. There were certainly motivational factors that are impossible to quantify, but which led to Kerry voters being less likely than Bush voters to refuse to take the survey. In addition there are interactions between respondents and interviewers that can contribute to differential non-response rates. We can identify some factors that appear to have contributed, even in a small way, to the discrepancy. These include:

- Distance restrictions imposed upon our interviewers by election officials at the state and local level

- Weather conditions which lowered completion rates at certain polling locations

- Multiple precincts voting at the same location as the precinct in our sample

- Polling locations with a large number of total voters where a smaller portion of voters was selected to be asked to fill out questionnaires

- Interviewer characteristics such as age, which were more often related to precinct error this year than in past elections

We plan further analysis on the following factors:

- Interviewer training and election day procedures

- Interviewing rate calculations

- Interviewer characteristics

- Precinct characteristics

- Questionnaire length and design

We also suggest the following changes for future exit polls:

- Working to improve cooperation with state and local election officials

Document 3.5—Continued

- Improvements in interviewing training procedures

- Changes in our procedures for hiring, recruiting and monitoring interviewers

Even with these improvements, differences in response rates between Democratic and Republican voters may still occur in future elections. However, we believe that these steps will help to minimize the discrepancies.

It is also important to note that the exit poll estimates did not lead to a single incorrect NEP winner projection on election night. The Election Night System does not rely solely on exit polls in its computations and estimates. After voting is completed, reported vote totals are entered into the system. Edison/Mitofsky and the NEP members do not project the outcome of close races until a significant number of actual votes are counted.

As in past elections, the final exit poll data used for analysis in 2004 was adjusted to match the actual vote returns by geographic region within each state. Thus, the discrepancy due to differing response rates was minimized and did not significantly affect the analysis of the vote. The exit polls reliably describe the composition of the electorate and how certain demographic subgroups voted.

2. Survey Weighting

Early in the afternoon on November 2nd, preliminary weightings for the national exit poll overstated the proportion of women in the electorate. This problem was caused by a programming error involving the gender composition that was being used for the absentee/early voter portion of the national exit poll. This error was discovered after the first two sets of weighting; subsequent weightings were corrected. This adjustment was made before NEP members and subscribers used exit poll results on-air or in print.

After election day, we adjusted the exit poll analysis data in three states (Tennessee, Texas, and Washington) to more accurately reflect the proportion of absentee ballots that came from each geographic region in those states. We have implemented a change to the survey weighting program to take into account the geographic distribution of the absentee votes in the future.

3. Technical Performance

While the computer system performed well for most of the night, a database server problem led to NEP member and subscriber screens "freezing up" shortly after 10:35 PM ET election night. This problem caused disruptions in the system until shortly after midnight when we switched to a backup server for the rest of the night. There was a second occurrence of this problem at approximately 2:45 AM ET. Details of the data server problems and other technical issues are outlined in the technical performance report being distributed to the NEP Technical Committee. We have isolated the reasons behind the database server problem and list several recommended technical changes in this report to help avoid a repeat of this problem in future elections.

Document 3.6

US Count Votes'
National Election Data Archive Project

Analysis of the 2004 Presidential Election Exit

Poll Discrepancies

http://electionarchive.org/ucvAnalysis/US/Exit_Polls_2004_Mitofsky-Edison.pdf

Response to the *Edison/Mitofsky Election System 2004* Report
http://exit-poll.net/election-night/EvaluationJan192005.pdf

March 31, 2005

Updated April 12, 2005

Authors and Endorsers

Ron Baiman, Ph.D. Institute of Government and Public Affairs, University of Illinois at Chicago
Kathy Dopp, MS mathematics, USCountVotes, President
Steven F. Freeman, Ph.D. Visiting Scholar & Affiliated Faculty, Center for Organizational Dynamics,
     University of Pennsylvania
Brian Joiner, Ph.D. Professor of Statistics and Director of Statistical Consulting (ret), University of Wisconsin
Victoria Lovegren, Ph.D. Lecturer, Department of Mathematics, Case Western Reserve University
Josh Mitteldorf, Ph.D. Temple University Statistics Department
Campbell B. Read, Ph.D. Professor Emeritus, Department of Statistical Science, Southern Methodist
     University
Richard G. Sheehan, Ph.D. Professor, Department of Finance, University of Notre Dame
Jonathan Simon, J.D. Alliance for Democracy
Frank Stenger, Ph.D. Professor of Numerical Analysis, School of Computing, University of Utah
Paul F. Velleman, Ph.D. Associate Professor, Department of Statistical Sciences, Cornell University
Bruce O'Dell, USCountVotes, Vice President

This report has been reviewed via USCountVotes' email discussion list for statisticians, mathematicians and
pollsters.

Press Contact: **Kathy Dopp**, USCountVotes, President kathy@uscountvotes.org

Document 3.6—Continued

Table 1: Partisanship Precinct Data given in the Edison/Mitofsky Report (pp. 36, 37)		Number of Precincts	mean WPE exit poll discrepancy	median WPE exit poll discrepancy	Combined Response Rate	Refusal Rate	Miss Rate
Partisanship of Precinct by Election Results							
80< Kerry <=100%	0< Bush <=20%	90	0.3%	-0.4%	53%	35%	12%
60< Kerry <=80%	20< Bush <=40%	165	-5.9%	-5.5%	55%	33%	12%
40< Kerry <=60%	40< Bush <=60%	540	-8.5%	-8.3%	52%	37%	11%
20< Kerry <=40%	60< Bush <=80%	415	-6.1%	-6.1%	55%	35%	10%
0< Kerry <=20%	80< Bush <=100%	40	-10.0%	-5.8%	56%	33%	11%

The following analysis by US Count Votes is based on the data in the above Table 1 which is provided in the Edison/Mitofsky report. We will use it to show that it is not plausible that the "Reluctant Bush Responder" hypothesis explains the exit poll discrepancy in the November 2004 presidential election.

B. Exit Poll Discrepancies Rise with Concentration of Bush Voters

The reluctant Bush responder hypothesis would lead one to expect a higher non-response rate where there are many more Bush voters, yet Edison/Mitofsky's data shows that, in fact, the response rate is slightly higher in precincts where Bush drew ≥80% of the vote (High Rep) than in those where Kerry drew ≥80% of the vote (High Dem).

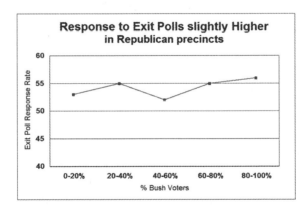

The chart above was constructed from data within the E/M report (p. 37). This data bears directly on the plausibility of the report's central hypothesis, and it goes in the wrong direction. In precincts with higher numbers of Bush voters, response rates were slightly *higher* than in precincts with higher number of Kerry voters.

Document 3.6—Continued

Precincts in which Bush supporters were dominant actually completed the poll questionnaire at a rate higher than precincts in which Kerry dominated. This fact undermines the report's central premise that Kerry supporters were more likely than Bush supporters to participate in the exit poll.

"Reluctant Bush Responder in Mixed Political Company" (rBrmpc) hypothesis

Yet it is not conclusive proof that the E/M hypothesis is wrong, because some have hypothesized that Bush supporters were more diffident about expressing their views in mixed political company than Kerry supporters.

It has been suggested that the Bush supporters participated at high rates in precincts where they were surrounded by other Bush supporters, while Bush supporters in predominantly-Kerry precincts were more reticent than their counterpart Kerry supporters voting in predominantly Bush precincts. This "reluctant Bush exit poll participant in predominantly Kerry precincts" hypothesis is also inconsistent with the E/M data.

If the polls were faulty because Bush voters were shy in the presence of Kerry voters and less likely to cooperate with pollsters, then the polls should be most accurate in those precincts where Bush voters were in the overwhelming majority and where exit poll participation was also at its maximum.

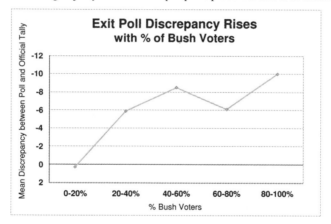

What we find is just the opposite: in fact, *the mean exit poll discrepancy was dramatically higher in Bush strongholds than in Kerry strongholds (-10.0 versus 0.3).* In precincts with 80-100% Bush voters, where exit poll participation reached its highest level (56%), there was a full 10% mean difference between official vote tallies and the exit poll results.

Document 3.6—Continued

Alternate hypothesis: "Bush Strongholds have more Vote-Count Corruption" (Bsvcc)

An alternative hypothesis that is more consistent with the data is that corruption of the official vote count occurred most freely in districts that were overwhelmingly Bush strongholds.

If Edison/Mitofsky would release the detailed results of their poll to the public then much more could be said about this hypothesis, and the suspicious precincts could be identified. If E/M does not release its list of sampled precincts, US Count Votes believes it will still be possible to rigorously test the hypothesis that the vote counts were corrupted by assembling and analyzing a precinct-level nationwide database containing detailed election results, voting equipment information and demographic data.

Higher exit poll response rates and higher exit poll discrepancies occurred in Bush strongholds. E/M's own data contradict both the rBr and the rBrmpc hypotheses and support the Bsvcc hypothesis.

4

Counting the Vote

If the discrepancy between the exit polls and the certified result raised suspicions about the validity of the vote count, investigation into the counting process confirms our worst fears. Vote counting at every level was fraught with problems ranging from misleading ballots, to computers misreading or rejecting ballots, to uneven standards for counting and rejecting provisional ballots, to outright vote-count fraud.

The discussion begins with the anecdotal or publicly visible, and then looks for an underlying or systemic pattern. It is important to note that the affidavits and testimonials gathered from hundreds of people across Ohio after the 2004 election were sworn under oath administered by lawyers and other court officers. (Sworn statements are a higher standard than what most media outlets use when interviewing people.) They were gathered for use in a presidential election challenge lawsuit filed at the Ohio Supreme Court, *Moss v. Bush*.

That lawsuit never stood much chance of being heard, because Ohio Secretary of State J. Kenneth Blackwell and Ohio's Republican Attorney General Jim Petro stonewalled all attempts at evidence gathering before Congress ratified the 2004 Electoral College vote in early January. At that point the election challenge was withdrawn because the court was poised to rule it was moot. Still, the suit began to document what happened using an evidence standard admissible in court, and the testimonials were compelling enough to prompt a historic congressional protest by House and Senate Democrats of Ohio's Electoral College votes, which, after debate, was defeated by the GOP majority.

Still, anecdotal evidence remains just that—impressionistic, unless it can confirm a larger pattern. The next step is to examine Ohio's 2004 public election records at the county level, and then sharpen the focus by analyzing the Election Night precinct-by-precinct returns obtained from the county boards of election (BOEs) or their websites and the certified vote tallies later posted on the BOE and the Ohio secretary of state websites. (These finalized results add in the absentee and provisional ballot counts and the presidential recount.)

As we saw in a previous chapter, by comparing how turnout varied from Kerry-majority precincts to Bush-majority precincts in the same cities, it is possible to project how many votes Kerry lost as a result of voter suppression tactics. In this chapter, analysts use precinct data to show whether known Democratic or Republican neighborhoods experienced higher or lower rates of machine-rejected or uncounted ballots, as well as higher or lower rates of provisional ballot use, both consequences of partisan targeting. Similarly, looking at countywide totals from the precinct level also reveals implausible voter registration trends, voter turnout, and vote counts, all pointing to election fraud. In some cases, where 2004 presidential ballots were made public eighteen months after the election, examining the actual ballots adds to the evidence of vote-count fraud.

The following analyses follow that methodology: looking past the anecdotal to precinct-by-precinct results and then either expanding that analysis or extrapolating the impact based on nearby or county vote totals. This is a fundamentally conservative approach. It is not a case of finding an anomaly in one city and assuming it occurred statewide, which would distort statewide trends. As the analysis below shows, there is ample evidence, based on the most specific public record available by June 2006, that voter suppression tactics, machine-rejected and disqualified ballots, and vote-count fraud in Ohio cost John Kerry tens of thousands of votes and inflated by tens of thousands of votes George W. Bush's total.

Questions that remain about the accuracy of Ohio election results— whether votes were meaningful and counted, or how frauds were committed—would require access to additional 2004 election records and the voting machines, which have been under seal by Ohio Secretary of State J. Kenneth Blackwell since Election Day. In early 2006, county boards of election made some of these records available for the first time, including some voter purge statistics, city-versus-suburbs provisional-ballot rejection rates, and in a few precincts with suspect results, the actual ballots themselves. These public records are by no means the full accounting, but they confirm our conclusion: that George W. Bush did not win Ohio in a "free and fair" election.

Michael Collins of Scripps Howard News Service was one of the first to note a "number of missing votes" in Ohio. "Nearly 97,000 ballots, or 1.7% of those cast across the state, either did not record a preference for president or could not be counted because the voter selected more than one presidential candidate," Collins wrote in a December 22, 2004, article. The Scripps Howard analysis found "that Ohio recorded the second-highest number of missing votes in the country, behind California." Collins stated, "Election experts say a large number of missing votes in a high-profile race like president should raise a red flag that something may be amiss."

In fact, the ballots cited by the Scripps Howard report did not include all the uncounted ballots from the 2004 election, according to the secretary of state's official results. That larger figure is nearly 130,000 votes and includes rejected provisional ballots. During a statewide recount in December (discussed in the next chapter), only Coshocton County conducted a hand count of all of its ballots, which re-enfranchised 1,080 voters after 17,322 votes were tallied. Among the re-enfranchised voters, Bush beat Kerry by a close 50.5 percent to 49.1 percent. (In contrast, the unofficial Election Night returns showed Bush beating Kerry 57.1 percent to 42.3 percent.) The vast majority of Ohio's uncounted 2004 ballots have not been examined or recounted. They remain in storage where, under Ohio law, they can be destroyed on or after September 2, 2006.

Beyond the tens of thousands of ballots with no vote for president, perhaps the most striking vote-counting anomaly occurred in three southwest counties near Cincinnati. This was the part of the state where White House political guru Karl Rove claimed that evangelical Christians had rallied behind the president and voted in droves. Their alleged turnout was cited by pundits to claim the White House had a resulting moral mandate. But as the following analysis will show, for the certified results in these counties to be true, more than 10,500 people in the state's Bible Belt would have to have voted both *for* gay marriage (opposing a proposed state constitutional amendment banning it) and *for* the president's reelection—a highly unlikely and suspect combination that was not seen anywhere else in the country.

As Chapter 2 makes clear, the first pillar of Bush's victory was suppressing the Democratic vote. Nobody can dispute the confusion across Democratic strongholds on Election Day. But the impact of that chaos on the vote count escaped wider notice after the election. On October 29, 2004, Blackwell predicted a 72 percent statewide voter turnout. But once the votes were counted, a stark and partisan disparity emerged. In the precincts won by Bush, the average turnout was far higher than the precincts where Kerry won.

County by county, the disparities were stark. Consider Columbus. In the Democratic precincts, too few voting machines led to delays, long lines, poll worker confusion, and other well-documented complications. In contrast, the city's Republican neighborhoods had enough machines and few problems. The resulting "voter turnout"—which might more accurately be termed "voter accommodation rate," since it reflects voters who were allowed to vote rather than those who "turned out"—averaged 60.56 percent in 125 precincts where Bush won, compared to 50.78 percent in the 346 precincts where Kerry won, according to BOE data available just after Election Day. How many votes did Kerry lose due to this accommodation disparity?

Richard Hayes Phillips, Ph.D., a geomorphologist whose specialty is spotting anomalous, or irregular, data, found Kerry's victory in Columbus "was wrongly reduced by 17,000 votes." Phillips did an exhaustive series of precinct analyses in Ohio's largest counties starting in late 2004 with Bob Fitrakis (a co-author of this book). By July 2006, he had examined and analyzed the results in 9,300 of Ohio's 11,300 precincts. The calculations were laborious, but the principle was simple. To start, Phillips and his research assistants projected how many more votes Kerry would have won if voters in the same city or town (often in neighboring precincts and wards) had faced mostly similar conditions when casting their ballots and having their votes counted.

In the precincts Kerry won with the highest voter accommodation rate, the number of voters per voting machine was on par with the Bush-majority precincts. By extrapolating Kerry's 51 percent reported voter turnout average in Columbus—where the shortage of machines had the greatest impact—to 60 percent, the level in precincts won by Kerry where voters were accommodated (and also Bush's citywide average), Phillips concluded Kerry's victory in Columbus "was wrongly reduced by 17,000 votes."

A shortage of voting machines was not the only problem delaying voters, but it was a key indicator. Though Phillips's projections were attacked by Bush supporters and pundits as conjecture by conspiracy theorists, the *Columbus Dispatch* on January 7, 2005, a day after Democrats in Congress challenged certifying Ohio's Electoral College vote, reported that too few voting machines cost Kerry 15,000 votes. The *Washington Post* similarly projected the loss of 15,000 Kerry votes in Columbus. The larger point is not whether Phillips or the newspapers are off by 2,000 votes, but the extent to which GOP-favoring voter suppression tactics worked and the magnitude of votes lost by Kerry in this way. Other social scientists have put the figure higher than Phillips.

Phillips applied the same voter accommodation analysis to Cleveland, Ohio's largest city and biggest Democratic stronghold. There he found similar disparities with a few other local wrinkles, most notably what he called "incorrect presidential vote tallies." Sixteen precincts reported a total of several hundred votes for obscure third-party presidential candidates with no political base among Cleveland's poorest voters: the Constitution Party's Michael Peroutka and the Libertarian Party's Michael Badnarik. While this raised many eyebrows, Phillips and others concluded that Ohio's practice of rotating, whereby candidate names are placed differently on the ballot from precinct to precinct, was to blame: if someone stood in the wrong line at a multi-precinct polling station and poll workers took his or her ballot without redirecting him or her to the correct precinct, scanners would record an inaccurate vote, since each scanner was calibrated differently to reflect the different ballot layouts.

More significant to Kerry's margin in Cleveland, however, was low voter turnout in neighborhoods that overwhelmingly voted Democratic in 2000, with Al Gore typically receiving 90 percent of the vote. Phillips found at least thirty precincts where the reported turnout was inexplicably low, such as 7.1 percent; 13.05 percent; 19.6 percent; 21.01 percent; 21.80 percent; 24.72 percent; 28.83 percent; 28.97 percent; and 29.25 percent. In 2004, seven wards—one-third of Cleveland—reported voter turnout below 50 percent, and in one case, 39.35 percent. (In 2000, only three wards had turnout below 50 percent.) Moreover, across the city voter turnout fell from 57.43 percent in 2000 to 53.27 percent in 2004. In contrast, in the rest of Cuyahoga County voter turnout jumped from 58.07 percent in 2000 to 68.24 percent in 2004.

Using the same approach as in Columbus, Phillips conservatively calculated that if the actual voter turnout, versus the accommodation rate, were actually only 50 percent in precincts with Democratic-majority histories, Kerry would have gained 6,000 votes. If the turnout—or voter accommodation rate—had been 60 percent, as in other Ohio cities, Kerry would have gained 16,000 more votes against Bush in Cleveland. Local election observers reported record lines at the polls.

How could this be? Unlike Columbus, Cleveland had plenty of voting machines, but local election observers still reported long lines at the polls, denying many citizens the vote outright, and creating unmanageable delays for others. In March 2006, Cuyahoga County's BOE released voter-purge data that offered one clue. Between the 2000 and 2004 presidential races, nearly 20 percent of the voters in Cleveland's core Democratic communities had been removed from voter rolls, the BOE data showed, under a seldom-invoked National Voting Rights Act clause permitting purges of voters who had not voted in the previous two federal elections. (Indeed, in seventeen of Cleveland's twenty one wards, Phillips found 50 percent to 74 percent of voters who did not cast ballots in 2000 were purged before the 2004 election.) Additionally, Cleveland relocated a number of precincts. Taken together, these factors appear to have had as big an impact on suppressing the Democratic vote in Cleveland as shorting voting machines had in Columbus. People turned out in droves expecting to vote, but many were stopped at the polls.

Phillips also applied this methodology to the city of Toledo in Lucas County. There, sixty-three precincts—all overwhelmingly won by Kerry—had less than a 60 percent turnout. When extrapolating the city's turnout numbers to levels equal to the rest of that county, and in keeping with the city's historical record, he projected that Kerry's plurality should have been 6,500 votes larger. Overwhelmingly, Election Protection observers and under-oath witnesses reported massive problems in the heavily Democratic inner-city wards. In spring 2006 when some county records were released, Phillips found 87 percent of the voters whose registrations were challenged by GOP challengers were in Toledo, where Kerry got 68 percent of the vote.

In Columbus, Cleveland, and Toledo alone, Phillips projected that Kerry lost 39,500 votes, and did so because voting was not conducted equally, regardless of race, party, or residence. To be sure, different cities experienced different forms of voter intimidation: in Columbus, machine shortages; in Toledo's Democratic precincts, longtime residents removed from the voting rolls, broken voting machines, polls running out of ballots, incorrect optical-scan markers, and poll workers turning people away or sending them to the wrong line. Some problems can be attributed to poll workers' lack of training and inexperience. But others, such as inadequate election supplies and using voter lists that have been inaccurately purged or lacked new voter registrations, stem from problems in state and county supervision and management of the election. (Recall that all Lucas County's top election officials were forced to resign after the election, and even Blackwell published a report describing their failures on his website the following spring.)

Voter purges further reduced Kerry's margin in Cuyahoga County. A total of 168,169 voters were purged (63,721 in Cleveland and 104,448 in the suburbs). The Voting Rights Act allows purges to clear voter rolls of people who move, die, and to prevent vote-count fraud. To determine the impact on the county's vote totals, the authors used the rate of wrongly purged voters from Florida's 2000 presidential election, as determined by the U.S. Commission on Civil Rights and described in its 2001 report, "Voting Irregularities in Florida During the 2000 Presidential Election." The federal panel found 14.1 percent of the voters purged from Florida's voter rolls were wrongly removed, primarily because of mismatched names. We applied this rate to the county's purged voters (subtracting the provisional ballots that had been rejected as "not registered," as we analyze provisional ballots separately), and then applied the official turnout rates in Cleveland (52.27 percent) and its suburbs (71.95 percent) to predict how many people would have been likely to vote. Finally, we applied the percentages for Kerry and Bush. (In Cleveland, Kerry received 83.36 percent of the vote, compared to 15.78 percent for Bush; in the suburbs, Kerry had 60.38 percent, compared to Bush's 39.18 percent.) Thus, Kerry would have netted an additional 2,450 votes in Cleveland and 1,735 votes in the rest of Cuyahoga County.

In Lucas County, where Toledo is located, 28,000 voters were purged in August 2004. Applying this same methodology (countywide Kerry received 60.02 percent, compared to 39.54 percent for Bush), we found Kerry would have picked up an additional 598 votes. In these two counties, we estimate that Kerry lost more than 4,750 votes to voter purges.

Suppressing the vote alone could not assure George W. Bush's re-election. But in an election where the vote certification and a much-delayed and problematic recount (discussed in the next chapter) lowered Bush's plurality from 136,483 to 118,775 votes, it was a key ingredient in Bush's margin of victory. Indeed, the combined voter suppression tactics and purges cost Kerry an estimated 44,250 votes, more than a third of that margin.

The other part of the voter suppression story involved disqualifying ballots or a failure to count them. Again, the precinct-level analysis shows that Democratic numbers were further eroded as ballots were rejected by voting machines or classified as "invalid."

Statewide, 128,967 ballots—35,094 provisional ballots and 93,873 standard ballots—with votes for president remain uncounted to this day, according to the final official results. Election officials in Ohio told the House Judiciary Committee Democratic investigators that more than 76,000 of the so-called machine rejected ballots were paper punch cards, meaning voters' efforts to poke holes in the actual ballot were not read by the machines, or there was more than one vote for president. (There were also 6,404 paper ballots rejected by optical-scan voting machines, and 11,067 unrecorded electronic votes.)

In some cases, the sensitivity settings of the vote-counting computers could have been set too high and rejected ballots, particularly in the case of the Diebold optical-scan machines used in Lucas County. In a handful of cases, such as that documented in an affidavit on December 28, 2004, by Lisa Casini, a Democratic congressional staffer who votes in Cleveland, punch-card ballots were given out that had been pre-punched for Bush. That meant a vote for Kerry would cause the ballot to be rejected, because the scanner rejects ballots with more than one vote as "over-votes." In Lucas County, where optical-scan ballot readers tally the vote, precincts ran out of the correct optical-scan markers to ensure the ballots would be properly read and counted—and many were rejected as a result. There are also numerous Election Day reports of the optical-scan machines being improperly calibrated and therefore rejecting valid ballots.

To what extent do the machine-rejected ballots contain more Kerry votes than Bush votes? Here, too, there is evidence suggesting

Kerry's margin was compromised by many thousands of votes. The Judiciary Committee Democrats were particularly sensitive to the racial dimensions of disenfranchisement tactics, which they said were likely violations of the federal Voting Rights Act. They looked at Cleveland and found rejected ballots were more than twice as likely to appear in zip codes where 85 percent or more of the population was black. Cleveland's black zip codes recorded one in thirty-one ballots with no vote for president, the committee Democrats report, while the rate in white-majority zip codes was one in seventy-five ballots.

As with voter turnout, a wider pattern betrayed the uncounted ballots. Phillips did a precinct-by-precinct analysis of seven out of the eight Ohio counties with the most uncounted regular ballots and found Democrats lost far more votes this way than Republicans. He looked at Cuyahoga County, where Cleveland is located; Summit County, where Akron is located; Hamilton County, where Cincinnati is located; and also at Montgomery, Stark, Trumbull, and Lorain Counties. Phillips found precincts with the highest percentage of uncounted or rejected ballots had voted overwhelmingly for Kerry, by margins of 12 to 1 in Cleveland; 7 to 1 in Dayton; 5 to 1 in Cincinnati; 4.5 to 1 in Akron; 3 to 1 in Lorain County; 2.7 to 1 in Stark County, and 2.3 to 1 in Trumbull County. Making projections based on the assumption that ballot-rejection rates in Democratic strongholds should be equal to those in the nearby Bush-majority districts, the authors estimate that Kerry lost more than 26,000 votes from the 82,806 paper ballots (punch card and optical scan) not read by voting machines.

These ballots were not spoiled, but rather rejected by voting machines. They represent people who stood in line to vote during one of the most heated recent presidential races. Unlike the rejected electronic ballots with no paper trail, voter intent could have been determined if these paper ballots were examined during a hand recount, which didn't happen. Statewide, 1.68 percent of the ballots cast in 2004 had no vote for president. In 2000, the corresponding figure was 1.97 percent. The authors applied a 2 percent under-vote rate, and then, based on the returns in the counties where most of these ballots came from, projected that Kerry would get 65.1 percent of this vote, compared to 33 percent for Bush. Thus, Kerry would see a net gain of 26,049 votes.

In addition to the machine-rejected ballots, 35,000 provisional ballots were disqualified and remain uncounted. As discussed in prior chapters, in September 2004 Blackwell implemented highly restrictive rules for provisional ballots—which were to be given to voters whose names did not appear on precinct voter rolls. Under HAVA, the federal Help America Vote Act, and prior Ohio law, voters could turn in a provisional ballot anywhere in their county of residence. Under Blackwell's new rules, voters could turn in these ballots only at their precinct, even if that meant a single table in a building that housed several precincts. As the Judiciary Democrats report noted, in one such multi-precinct building in Hamilton County, more than 2,100 provisional ballots were turned in at the wrong table, causing those ballots to be rejected and not counted. Likewise, in Cuyahoga County, 1,200 provisional ballots were turned in at the correct polling place, but at the wrong precinct table, and were disqualified. Further analysis by Phillips of Hamilton County's results found 95 percent of the 3,179 provisional ballots that were rejected came from inside Cincinnati itself, a Democratic stronghold, not the surrounding municipalities.

The Judiciary Democrats report noted that Blackwell had not issued provisional ballot rules until late September 2004, when his administrative order unleashed a flood of litigation and further directives to BOE directors to follow his rules or risk being fired. As a result, counties implemented varying standards for collecting, validating, and disqualifying the ballots. In Cuyahoga County, where Cleveland is located, ballots had to be placed in yellow packets with the voter's birthday written on the outside or they would be disqualified. In Cuyahoga and other counties, longtime voters whose names were not on precinct rolls were refused provisional ballots, according to testimony at hearings held after the election and the Judiciary Democratic report.

Two post-election reports shed some light on what happened in Cleveland. According to an August 2005 report on OhioVigilance.org by Victoria Lovegren, a Ph.D. mathematics lecturer at Case Western Reserve University in Cleveland who investigated Cleveland's vote and interviewed BOE employees, Cuyahoga County's BOE experienced high staff turnover that prevented absentee ballot applications from being processed. Many were just left in the boxes. That situation was compounded by the BOE decision to switch to a new electronic voter-registration system two months before the election. That system, from Diebold, had been designed for another state and omitted hundreds of names of longtime voters from the new rolls. Meanwhile, last-minute use of temporary employees facing deadline pressure resulted in more voter-roll mistakes.

The impact of these pressures on the county's voter rolls and approximately 313,000 newly registered voters was estimated by Norman Robbins of the Greater Cleveland Voter Coalition. That organization's February 26, 2005, report describes following 9,600 valid voter registrations through the BOE process and finding, when extrapolating countywide, that "up to 7,000 Cuyahoga County voters were probably disqualified and another 12,500 voters were put at varying degrees of risk of disqualification." As the study says, the people who are more likely to be subject to registration errors "include youth, those who rent rather than own homes, African Americans and Hispanics, and the poor."

Again, most of the disqualified provisional ballots appear to have affected Democrats disproportionately. In Cuyahoga County, one-third of provisional ballots (8,559) were ruled invalid, the highest number in the state. The county's 16,750 provisional ballots that *were* counted saw Kerry gaining 9,483 votes (71.31 percent of the vote) on Bush. If these percentages were applied to the county's disqualified provisional ballots, Kerry would have gained 3,650 votes. The Greater Cleveland Voter Registration Coalition report estimates "over 41 percent of rejected provisional ballots (or 14 percent of all provisional votes) may have been unnecessarily rejected" because registrations were incorrectly processed. Similarly, in Hamilton County, BOE records show that 95.12 percent of the rejected provisional ballots were from Cincinnati, where only 33.89 percent of the voters were located. If the 1,100 provisional ballots from Cincinnati that were turned in at the right location—but wrong table and were thus disqualified—were counted, then the Democratic nominee would gain an additional 401 votes (according to citywide results where Kerry received 67.98 percent and Bush received 31.54 percent). Together, this would be a net gain of 4,051 votes for Kerry.

These precinct-by-precinct analyses (of voter suppression in Columbus, Cleveland, and Toledo, of voter purges in Cuyahoga and Lucas Counties, and of uncounted machine-rejected paper ballots and uncounted provisional ballots in Cuyahoga and Hamilton Counties) conservatively show partisan barriers increased George W. Bush's lead over

John Kerry by more than 79,000 votes—two-thirds of Bush's 118,775 vote margin of victory in Ohio.

Complementing these efforts to suppress the Democratic vote count, the other pillar of the president's "win" in Ohio was to *inflate* the reported Republican vote counts in selected Republican-majority counties. Here the evidence also is the precinct-level results in tandem with other public files, such as voter registration records, precinct-level voter sign-in logs, absentee ballot records, and actual ballots. Showing that reported votes do not add up—defying logic and political credibility—is easier than explaining exactly how Republicans committed the specific frauds. That is not because the proof does not exist, or did not exist after the 2004 election, but because Blackwell and local officials imposed a gag order that remains largely in place today, sealing most 2004 election records until mid-2006 (just months before the 2004 ballots could be destroyed under Ohio law). Moreover, computer vote-counting machines have been reprogrammed and reused in subsequent elections, thwarting any investigation.

Still, the simplest single explanation of the results discussed in this chapter is that Republicans stuffed ballot boxes—either electronically during the vote count or with paper ballots at the close of voting on November 2—or they shifted votes from Kerry to Bush, while leaving the rest of the results involving other races alone. Indeed, as described next, access gained to some ballots in spring 2006 suggests ways that both could be done.

It is important to distinguish between isolated incidents of vote-counting mistakes and the larger patterns and public record where far larger numbers of votes are at issue and where intentionality seems clear. The anecdotal evidence—from election protection "incident reports," to sworn testimony at hearings after the election, to statements by BOE officials about voting machine contractors trying to cover up programming errors, to partisan statements supporting the president's reelection by top executives at those companies, to computer vote-counting problems on Election Day underscores how problem plagued the vote-counting process is, and how vulnerable the arena is to fraud and partisan manipulation.

There are several paths to follow in the vote-padding evidence trail: the certified precinct results, voter registration records, and, where possible, the actual ballots in a handful of Republican-dominated counties. Sixty-eight of Ohio's eighty-eight counties used punch-card ballots, leaving a paper trail that has barely been opened to public scrutiny.

The most visible vote-counting errors are the touch-screen voting machine errors that surfaced before the polls closed on Election Day. In northeast Ohio's Mahoning County, where the Democratic city of Youngstown is located, the BOE reported that twenty to thirty touch-screen machines were casting votes for the wrong candidate and had to be recalibrated during the day. In some precincts, these machines failed to record Kerry votes or recorded no votes at all. In other precincts, electronic machines switched votes from Kerry to Bush (never the reverse) unless voters repeatedly touched the screen above Kerry's name. These problems were covered in the local press and further described in affidavits after Election Day. Phillips estimates this problem cost Kerry about 2,250 votes in the county. A similar problem emerged in testimony by Franklin County voters where the Kerry vote, once pushed, would simply fade away.

Activists who oppose computer voting without an auditable paper trail say the machines could have been programmed to default to Bush, or to "flip" a Kerry vote to Bush at regular intervals, say every tenth vote. But no one has been able to examine the actual software or components used in 2004 to prove that, because Ohio's Republican secretary of state sealed access to those machines immediately after the election. (See Victoria Parks affidavit about trying to examine Pickaway County's records, taken on November 13, 2004 [document 4.16].)

The more significant concern posed by these new voting machines involves tabulating and reporting the vote at both the precinct and the county levels. Here it is important to distinguish between the machines used by individual voters and machines designed to tabulate totals, because the magnitude of error or fraud increases at the tabulation and compilation stage.

On Election Day, there were two well-known examples, both covered in the Ohio press, of tabulation error and vote-count fraud. On the error side, one machine in Youngstown registered "negative 25 million votes" for Kerry. While this number seems absurd and was corrected, it points to the kind and scope of problems that accompany these machines. On the fraud side, one Columbus precinct located in a right-wing church, Ward 1B in Gahanna, reported 4,258 votes for

Bush and 260 votes for Kerry, though the precinct has only 800 registered voters, 638 of whom cast votes on Election Day, according to
the Judiciary Committee Democrats. Their report states that neither
Blackwell nor other authorities would comment or clarify "whether
the computer glitch was intentional or not." Later, a county election
official blamed it on a "transmission error."

The Gahanna "glitch" was not an isolated example of vote-
padding. In a throwback to "old-school" ballot box stuffing, in northeast Ohio's Trumbull County, Werner Lange, a university professor,
part-time preacher, and voting-rights activist, examined 106 precinct
poll books in five communities—before Blackwell ordered those
records sealed—and found 580 more absentee ballots were cast and
counted than the number of registered absentee voters in those
precincts. (Unlike other Ohio counties, Trumbull handles its absentee
ballots by including them in precinct totals along with other ballots.
Thus, examining precinct records, as Lange did, was the only way to
verify fraud.)

The big numbers that padded the president's vote were electronic
versions of this basic tactic. In west-central Ohio's Miami County, on
Election Night after 100 percent of the vote was reported, almost
19,000 votes inexplicably were added to the totals. The percentage of
the vote for Bush and Kerry remained the same, which increased Bush's
margin by 6,000 votes. Suspiciously, the final margin for Bush was
16,000 votes exactly, and turnout in one precinct—South Concord—
was reported as 98.55 percent. (Just after the election, this book's co-
author Bob Fitrakis sent reporters to South Concord, where 679 out
of 689 registered voters allegedly cast ballots; in the course of several
hours they found twenty-five people who said they were registered but
did *not* vote in November 2004.)

Just these two examples, Youngtown's electronic voting machine
problems and Miami County's suspect final count, would have added
another 8,250 votes to the 79,000 votes lost to voter suppression and
machine-rejected and uncounted ballots, reducing Bush's margin by at
least 87,000 votes.

The House Judiciary Committee Democratic staff report notes
that Miami County election officials did not count votes themselves,
but used a contractor, who dismissed any suggestion of fraud and said
the additional votes were inadvertently missing from the early returns.
But that explanation actually raises more questions than it answers.

First, it highlights one of the most troubling aspects of electronic voting technologies: that public officials are not counting the vote but giving that most public of responsibilities to private firms. That very issue caused Ken Nuss, the ex–deputy director of the Auglaize County BOE, to write a letter to Blackwell on October 21, 2004, noting that an employee of another private voting machine maker, ES&S, accessed and used the county's main vote-counting computers that fall, violating county protocol. Blackwell's response was to suspend Nuss, a Democrat, who then resigned his post.

It remains difficult to parse what happened in Miami County, but a big clue appeared in June 2006 when Fitrakis and Phillips were granted permission to look at actual ballots. They were met by Miami BOE director Steve Quillen, who presented a new summary that restated the 2004 vote totals. Quillen told the researchers that their analysis—concluding turnout rates exceeding 95 percent was inaccurate—was indeed correct. However, the BOE director said Miami County's vote totals, showing exactly 52,000 people voting, were unchanged. Quillen offered the explanation that local youths who had helped to deliver ballots on Election Night had confused and misidentified precincts, creating erroneous totals. He said the BOE was not required to report the final corrected results to the secretary of state's office.

Quillen's explanation was curious. The hand recount of 3 percent of Miami County's vote in December 2004 did not find or correct these problems. When Fitrakis and Phillips examined the county's precinct sign-in books and conducted their own hand count of ballots, which had not been touched since the 2004 election, they found the number of voter signatures, or people who signed in to vote, did not match the certified vote count in six precincts. In July 2006, a subsequent hand count by Ron Baiman found a 5 percent discrepancy between the certified vote and the actual ballots cast in 8 percent of the county's precincts. That discrepancy meant the official vote count was, at best, incorrect, or at worst, fraudulent. This gap is the first strong evidence suggesting the county's computer central vote tabulator was corrupted.

What is important about Miami County is that the problem there was not isolated computer fraud, but computer anomolies in tandem with a very suspect upswing in Republican voter registrations in GOP-dominated counties. In sum, while the national media and Democratic Party were primarily paying attention to the voter suppression in the

Democratic cities, another scenario was unfolding in Republican rural areas. Indeed, if the GOP's tactics in Ohio's cities resurrected Jim Crow voter suppression and disenfranchisement tactics, in the state's rural Republican counties, the ghost of the old, urban machine-style politics emerged to pad the president's vote count.

The evidence trail here continues with the certified vote and voter registration records. In central Ohio's Perry County, one precinct, W Lexington G AB, had 350 registered voters but reported 434 votes cast, creating a 124 percent turnout. After the House Judiciary Committee Democratic staff brought this to their attention, the BOE said the mistake was due to a computer error and that, in reality, 224 people had voted, the Committee Democratic report says. But then the congressional report turns to a much larger fraud in that Republican county—thousands of fraudulent voter registrations:

> In Perry County, there appears to be an extraordinarily high level of 91% voter registration; yet, a substantial number of these voters have never voted and have no signature on file. Of the voters that are registered in Perry County, an extraordinarily large number are listed as having registered in 1977, a year in which there were no federal elections. Of these, an exceptional number are listed as having registered on the exact same day: in total, 3,100 voters apparently registered in Perry County on November 8, 1977.

As was the case with virtually all of the anomalies documented by the House Judiciary Committee Democratic staff and presented to Blackwell and Ohio's other Republican constitutional officers, no Ohio election official would respond or comment.

These twin facets—suspect Republican voter registrations and computer "errors" overreporting actual totals—bring us to the biggest vote-counting mystery of the 2004 Ohio election: what happened in southwestern Ohio, particularly in Butler, Clermont, and Warren Counties. These three counties, north and east of Cincinnati, alone gave Bush his entire margin of victory in Ohio, 132,685 votes. All three counties experienced a huge increase in turnout. In all three counties, Bush received more votes than he did in 2000, and Kerry received fewer votes than Al Gore. Did these three counties really reelect Bush?

The most superficial sign that the vote in these counties would not be a straightforward affair came on Election Night in Warren County, when officials announced the county was the target of a Level 10 Federal Bureau of Investigation (FBI) homeland security terrorism alert and therefore would be counting ballots behind locked doors. The FBI has since said that no such homeland security alert had been issued, and county officials later said they had planned the lockdown more than a week before. Ballots were diverted to an unauthorized warehouse for "safe-keeping." The county was the last in Ohio to report and when it did, it gave Bush a 14,000 vote boost as its final numbers came in.

How did Warren County's vote in 2004 compare to the 2000 election? Since 2000, the county's population had grown by 14.75 percent. The number of registered voters, however, increased by 29.66 percent. Voter turnout increased by 33.55 percent. And Bush's point spread with his opponent increased from 42.24 percent in 2000, to 44.58 percent in 2004. Thus, Bush's margin in the county grew from 29,176 votes in 2000, to 41,124 votes in 2004. These same dynamics— voter registrations and turnout far outpacing population growth— were also seen in Butler and Clermont Counties, where Bush's margin increased by more than 22,000 votes from 2000 to 2004.

Were Bush numbers credible or were they padded? The answer becomes clear by examining two different votes being conducted on the same ballot: the state ballot question on gay marriage, known as Issue One, and the Ohio Supreme Court Chief Justice race. Using precinct-by-precinct results and a little math, it quickly becomes evident that for Bush to have won so convincingly in these counties, many thousands of people would have to have voted for George W. Bush *and* taken the pro-gay rights side on the ballot initiative banning gay marriage. Moreover, many thousands of people would also have had to vote for Bush *and* voted for the Democratic chief justice candidate, an African American, liberal, pro-union, trial lawyer–endorsed, retired municipal judge from Cleveland.

Again, starting with the anecdotal, compared to 2000, Bush faced opposition in the region. Al Gore did not campaign in southwestern Ohio, because it was solidly pro-Bush. Indeed, the Gore campaign pulled out of the state three weeks prior to the election. But John Kerry and "independent" groups aligned with the Democrats did campaign there. This is not to say that the president's supporters did not work hard. But come Election Day, something else happened that cannot be easily explained: Cleveland Judge C. Ellen Connally, the Democratic chief justice candidate, who had virtually no campaign presence in rural southern Ohio and was not at the top of the ballot, received over 5,000 more votes than Kerry in Butler County. She received more votes than Kerry in 12 counties, in a statewide race that drew 1.2 million fewer voters than the presidential contest.

Voting-rights activists who oppose electronic voting machines with no paper trail speculate that shifting Kerry's votes to Bush during the vote-tabulation stage could have produced that result while letting down-ballot votes for Connally stand. Without access to the computers themselves, that hypothesis remains unproven. The precinct-by-precinct analysis, however, casts doubt on the president's vote totals another way. For both Connally and the president's vote count to be true and accurate, Phillips declared that at least 13,500 voters in Warren, Butler, and Clermont Counties would have had to vote for both Connally and Bush. (The analysis is done simply by looking at the total number of voters who did not vote for each of these candidates in the same locales and comparing the figures.)

This apparent political contradiction is not an isolated example. The 2004 Ohio ballot also contained "Issue One," a constitutional amendment prohibiting gay marriage. Readers will recall that Karl Rove and others said the measure would drive conservative Christian turnout in support of the president's reelection. As in the chief justice race, Phillips found in these three counties that at least 10,500 people would have to have voted both for the president *and* in support of gay marriage for the certified results to be true. If that was not the case, the results had to be fraudulent. (And there are other examples of down-ballot Democrats outpolling Kerry, which can be seen in excerpts from Phillip's analysis of the vote in Brown, Butler, Clermont, Darke, and Auglaise Counties in the following documents.)

What really happened in those counties? In spring 2006 a big clue emerged when Phillips and a team of researchers were able to view and photograph ballots from twelve of Warren County's 157 precincts. (They were allowed to view only the fronts of the ballots and not permitted to touch them.) In suspicious precincts, the team discovered single ballots with only one vote punched—always for Bush and none for Kerry—evidence contradicting the idea that voters came to the polls to vote on the constitutional amendment, and suggesting old-fashioned ballot box stuffing. Phillips found similar evidence of apparent ballot box stuffing in Delaware County, where in two separate precincts where Bush won with upward of 70 percent of the vote, every one of the final 359 ballots in one precinct and 210 ballots in the other were cast for Bush. That unbroken streak of Bush votes is statistically implausible and suggests ballot box stuffing. (To complete this fraud, GOP partisans would have to have forged signatures in precinct log books, so the number of voters equaled the votes cast. Phillips and his team photographed signatures that looked suspicious, but they are not handwriting experts.)

More important than ballot box stuffing, however, they found an explanation of how Kerry votes on some ballots could have been shifted to Bush's column, while leaving untouched votes supporting gay marriage or votes for a liberal democratic chief justice candidate. In Ohio, the order of candidates' names is rotated on the ballot and each precinct's vote tabulator is programmed to read that particular precinct's ballot layout. (Ohio does this so no one candidate has an unfair advantage by being listed at the top of the ballot.) Simply put, punch-card ballots with Kerry votes could have been swapped between Warren County's precincts, where computers would read an intended Kerry vote as a vote for Bush.

Unlike ballots in most of Ohio, Warren County's punch-card ballots, Phillips discovered, were not encoded to show which precincts they came from. Thus, Republican partisans, counting sequestered ballots under the guise of a homeland security alert, could have moved ballots between precincts on purpose. If that were the case, a Kerry vote would be read by machines programmed for another precinct as a Bush vote. Meanwhile, the Issue One vote would not change because its position was not rotated on the ballot—it was a constant. As long as the number of ballots traded between precincts remained the same, the vote tabulators would not see an error. Similarly, the numbers of people who signed the voter books would match the official totaled result.

By June 2006, Phillips had examined and analyzed all the ballots in four Warren County precincts this way. In those precincts, he found that 256 people had voted for gay marriage and to reelect the president. If that rate of vote-shifting were applied across the county's 157 precincts, then the loss to Kerry would be as high as 10,000 votes. Phillip's tabulation theory is consistent with all the observable evidence—anomalous official returns showing in those precincts that 50 percent of the people who supported gay marriage *also* voted for Bush, and 57.7 percent who voted for Connally *also* voted for Bush. However, his efforts to examine more ballots in the county, as well as ballots from other southwestern Ohio counties, continues to be met with stiff resistance, in some cases from local law enforcement. In 2006, Blackwell asked county prosecutors, not BOE officials, to respond to public records requests, making it harder to obtain election records.

Before dismissing ballot swapping as an arcane theory, it is worth noting that the same dynamic, but with a different result, occurred in Cleveland, where two right-wing presidential candidates received hundreds of votes in inner-city precincts. There, Phillips deduced ballots were run through voting machines programmed for other precincts. Misreading the order of the candidates scrambled the results. Also, early Election Night returns posted on the Ohio secretary of state's website showed David Cobb, the Green Party candidate, with 39,541 votes in Hamilton County and 4,685 votes in Lucas County. Cobb received only 192 votes in the entire state, according to the official results, also suggesting large-scale problems with vote tabulating and scrambling of the results. (Those screen shots are reproduced in the documents section.)

How would ballot swapping affect Bush's margin? If we make the conservative assumption that the 10,500 people in Warren, Clermont, and Butler Counties who supported gay marriage and the president are a subset of the 13,500 people in those counties who also voted for Ellen Connally and Bush, then we can minimally surmise that at least 13,500 Kerry votes were taken from his column and added to Bush's totals. Because each vote moved subtracts a vote from Kerry and adds a vote for Bush, this would have padded Bush's margin overall by at least 27,000 votes.

Based on ballots he has examined from these and other rural Republican counties with anomalous results in these three races—for president, Issue One, and chief justice—Phillips projects that Kerry could have lost upward of 45,000 votes due to fraudulent voter registration and vote counts. (These ballots come from Delaware City in Delaware County; Shelby County, where the reported voter turnout was the highest in the state, at 81.82 percent; Brown County, where Kerry ran behind down-ballot candidate Ellen Connally in twenty-two of thirty-five precincts; Auglaise County, where Kerry ran behind Connally in thirty-four of thirty-nine precincts; Van Wert County, where the population had decreased since the 2000 election but the county had a 15.25 percent increase in ballots cast; Darke County, where Kerry received 105 more votes than Al Gore but Bush gained 3,489 votes compared to 2000; and Mercer County, where more than 1,200 people voted for Bush and Connally.)

The analyses in this chapter are conservative and are based on the available public record as of June 2006. They are not a complete accounting by any means. They do not include other likely Kerry votes that the authors could not verify or are still under investigation. Chief among these are the Kerry votes lost to vote shifting in the twelve counties where Connally received more votes than the Democratic nominee. Indeed, the final Phillips report in this book, document 4.24, projects that as many as 60,000 Kerry votes could have been shifted to Bush in these counties. That inquiry is ongoing and therefore its estimate is not included in our tallies. Other academics, particularly those basing their work on the available 2004 exit poll data, also project more votes for Kerry. These investigations are continuing during the summer of 2006, as Ohio law permits the 2004 ballots to be destroyed on or after September 2, 2006.

Still, our projections show that: Kerry lost nearly 39,500 votes due to voter suppression in three cities; another 8,750 votes due to voter purges and rejected provisional ballots in two cities; another 26,000 votes from uncounted, machine-rejected paper ballots; another 8,250 votes due to suspect computer vote tabulating and electronic voting machine malfunctions; and another 44,500 votes due to suspected vote count fraud in rural Republican counties. Together, these add up to more than 127,000 likely Kerry votes.

Bush's post-recount plurality was 118,775 votes. If Ohio's 2004 election had been free and fair, John Kerry would be president today.

Chapter 4 Documents: Counting the Vote

4.1. "John Kerry Conceded Too Soon" by Richard Hayes Phillips, Ph.D., pp. 216–219

Dr. Richard Hayes Phillips documented that Kerry conceded with nearly 250,000 uncounted votes, more than 4 percent of all the Ohio ballots cast. While Bush's unofficial 136,483 vote lead over Kerry appeared insurmountable, there were obvious errors in the Bush tally. Gahanna's Ward 1B precinct was perhaps the most famous of these errors, where 638 people cast votes for president and Bush was awarded 4,258 votes to Kerry's 260. Officially, a "computer glitch" gave Bush an additional 3,893 votes. Bush's lead was later reduced to 118,775 votes, the figure certified by Ohio Secretary of State J. Kenneth Blackwell.

4.2 Blackwell Certifies Statewide Election Results, pp. 220–222

During the process of certifying the actual tally, remarkably, Bush's statewide lead fell from 136,483 to 118,775. This adjustment came before a statewide recount, where 3 percent of the ballots were examined by hand, was conducted (only one county out of eighty-eight examined and recounted all of its ballots by hand). Bush lost nearly 18,000 votes between Election Night and the vote certification, suggesting sloppy if not biased counting in GOP-majority counties on Election Night. This is Secretary Blackwell's press release from December 6, 2004, announcing the certified result.

4.3. Ottawa County Prosecutor's Response to Open Public Records Request (document 4.3.1) Compared to Logan County Board of Elections' Response to the Same Request (document 4.3.2), pp. 223–224

Efforts to obtain all detailed local voting records were met with varying responses, and in some cases obstruction. In Ottawa County, the board of elections hired "a private contractor" to provide public records. County prosecutor Mark Mulligan estimated that it would cost between $2,000 and $5,000 to duplicate the election data by precinct. In contrast, Logan County sent the requested precinct breakdown with an attached bill for $3.41, of which $2.21 was for postage.

4.4 E-mail from TRIAD Governmental Systems, Inc., to Madison County Board of Elections, p. 225

When Richard Hayes Phillips and his researchers requested the election results from Madison County, the County BOE officials received the information from a private firm, TRIAD Governmental Systems, a company whose executives are known to have ties to the Republican Party. (TRIAD sold on their website commemorative copies of the notorious "butterfly ballot" from Florida's 2000 election debacle, in which elderly Florida voters were confused by the ballot layout and voted for Pat Buchanan while thinking they had voted for Al Gore.) This letter to the Madison BOE underscores that private firms, not public officials, conducted the vote count. (A letter with identical wording was sent to the BOE in Pike County. This is important, because it suggests that this e-mail was a form letter from Brandlin Sandlin, and that many of the forty-one TRIAD counties may have been serviced in this way.)

4.5 Comparison Chart of Counties Won by Bush Versus Democrats in 2000 and 2004, by Susan Greenhalgh, p. 226

Although little noticed on Election Night, Ohio's rural counties saw dramatic increases for Bush compared to his 2000 returns. Similarly, there were a handful of counties where Kerry lost votes compared to Gore's 2000 totals. This chart documents the increases for Bush in Ohio's *Republican-controlled* counties (a subset of the state's eighty-eight counties) and losses for Kerry in relation to Gore in Darke, Van Wert, Mercer, and Shelby Counties. While critics will say some of Gore's supporters voted to reelect a wartime president, there was no indication before the election that this would be the case. The Democrat's 2004 campaign was more hard-fought than during 2000, when Gore's staff pulled out of Ohio three weeks before the election. Kerry focused on Ohio with the largest Democratic campaign in the state's modern history. Moreover, many purportedly independent groups helped Kerry, breaking Ohio presidential election spending records. No pre-election polls showed a shift from Gore voters to Bush. And raw exit poll results that were released after midnight on November 3 reported a Kerry victory in Ohio. The huge reported Bush vote in the state's rural counties led this book's researchers to examine precinct results for evidence of voter fraud.

4.6 Franklin County Ballot, p. 227

In the state of Ohio, the order in which the candidates' names appear on the ballot rotates from precinct to precinct. The sequence stays the same, but the starting point differs. This is done to prevent any candidate from having a top-of-page advantage. However, if voters stood in the wrong line and placed their punch cards in machines not intended for their precinct, votes could be shifted to candidates not of their choosing. This ballot also has the Green Party candidates, Ralph Nader and Peter Camejo, listed, even though the Nader-Camejo ticket was not supposed to be on the ballot because it did not qualify with the needed signatures. In most states, this error is avoided by printing new ballots, closing off the possibility that voters might select a candidate whose vote will not be counted.

4.7 Franklin County Turnout History, p. 228

After Columbus saw what may have been the longest lines in its history, the actual vote in the county was lower than in 2000, declining from 61.27 percent to 60.95 percent. The Columbus turnout rate was more than 12 percent lower than the state average. Yet the suburban areas of Columbus voted at higher rates than the rest of Ohio, at 76.15 percent. Despite the greatest voter registration drive in Columbus history, only 52.7 percent of the registered voters cast counted ballots. As described previously, the "turnout rate" might better be described as the "accommodation rate," reflecting voters accommodated with the opportunity to vote, a far smaller number than those who "turned out." (These figures do not include absentee ballots, which are counted in Ohio as a separate, countywide category.)

4.8 Chart of Uncounted Provisional Votes in Franklin County by Rady Ananda, p. 229

The nonprofit Columbus Institute of Contemporary Journalism analyzed reasons why provisional ballots were rejected in Franklin County. This chart presents those findings and shows an urban bias among rejected ballots, which is symptomatic of partisan targeting. Of the 2,711 rejected and uncounted provisional ballots, 1,783—or 65.76

percent—were from the city of Columbus, where elected officials are all Democrats and 2004 voter turnout (or voter accommodation rate) was 52.7 percent. In contrast, outside Columbus, voter turnout was 76.15 percent.

The Franklin County provisional ballot rejection chart reveals three items of interest. First is the fact that 68.06 percent of the ballots (623 people) that were rejected because people voted in the right location but at the wrong precinct table were from Columbus. Those 623 people would have had their vote counted in the spring presidential primary and past elections, but Secretary of State Blackwell's new ruling on counting provisional votes only if cast in the correct precinct negated those votes. Second, 356 people *were* in the right precinct but *were forced to vote provisionally* by poll workers. According to Matthew Damschroder, director of the Franklin County Board of Elections, their votes also did not count. Again, 64.61 percent of these uncounted ballots were from Columbus. Third, 1,597 people waited for up to seven hours in the city, only to cast provisional ballots because their names were not on the list of registered voters. Sixty-five percent of these came from the city of Columbus, and some have provided statements to the CICJ specifying details of where and when they registered to vote. This suggests clerical errors or worse at the Franklin County BOE.

4.9 Franklin County Provisional Voter Affidavits, pp. 230–235

FreePress.org obtained the list of all Franklin County provisional voters. A mailing was sent to a cross-section of the 2,338 voters *whose votes were not counted* in the 432 zip code area of Columbus and nearby Franklin County suburbs, where approximately two-thirds of the uncounted voters resided. These responses are a sample of the statements from voters explaining the circumstances on Election Day under which they voted provisionally.

4.10 "Stealing Votes in Cleveland" by Richard Hayes Phillips, Ph.D., pp. 236–238

This is Dr. Phillips's first precinct-by-precinct analysis of where Kerry lost votes in Cleveland, completed soon after the 2004 election and the first of several papers on Cuyahoga County reproduced here. This paper, which was edited by Phillips for inclusion in this book, notes precincts with inexplicably low turnout, and votes that appeared to "migrate" or accrue to Bush or little-known third-party candidates. This paper explains how Kerry's margin of victory in Cleveland was wrongly reduced by 16,000 votes.

4.11 "Uncounted Votes in Cuyahoga County" by Richard Hayes Phillips, Ph.D., pp. 239–242

This is Dr. Phillips's study that found that the pattern of uncounted votes in Cuyahoga County disproportionately came from precincts that heavily favored Kerry over Bush. Phillips describes more than 64 precincts where 4 percent or more of the ballots are uncounted, and where "John Kerry won them all overwhelmingly, by a margin of 12 to 1 in the aggregate." A public hearing was held in Cleveland on November 20, 2004, to gather under oath testimony about voting irregularities, including abnormally low voter turnout rates in the heavily Democratic wards. One explanation came from Irma Olmedo, who noted that while there were long lines in the heavily Hispanic Ward 13, there were no instructions in Spanish and "some people put their punch card ballots in backwards when they voted. . . ."

4.12 Cuyahoga County Provisional Ballot Verification Procedures, pp. 243–248

In Cuyahoga County, 8,559 provisional ballots, or one-third of the ballots issued, were ruled invalid, the most in the state. The county's purge of 168,000 voters between the 2000 and 2004 elections increased the likelihood that voters would show up in 2004 and not be on the voter rolls, and thus be given provisional ballots. The BOE also installed a new voting records system in 2004, which also mistakenly deleted thousands of long-established voters from the new database. Several days after the 2004 election, the BOE issued new rules on how provisional ballots were to be counted. The Provisional Verification Procedure issued on October 28, 2004, was superseded by new instructions, that a voter's date of birth was now mandatory, along with name, address, and signature, on the provisional voting envelope.

In 2004, the number of invalid provisional ballots nearly doubled in Cuyahoga County, going from 17 percent in 2000 to 33 percent in 2004, according to the *Cleveland Plain Dealer*. Seventy percent of the rejected provisional ballots (5,595) were not counted because there was no record of the voter's registration on file. Dr. Norm Robbins, a professor of neuroscience at Case Western University who tracked the county BOE's processing of voter registrations throughout 2004, found that the BOE had committed clerical errors that eliminated at least 7,000 voter registrations (and possibly 12,000). "I find it inconceivable that over 5,000 voters in the county would wait an hour in the pouring rain to vote if they hadn't registered," Robbins told the *Plain Dealer*. Robert Bennett, the chair of both the Cuyahoga County BOE and the Ohio Republican Party, conceded to the *Plain Dealer* that "we like to think it's a perfect system, but it's not."

4.13 Neil Shoenwetter Jr. Affidavit on Summit County (Akron) Provisional Ballots, p. 249

An affidavit from a Democratic Party poll challenger underscores how Blackwell's late ruling on counting provisional votes led to the disenfranchisement of provisional ballot casters in urban areas. The county election supervisors are citing the rule that was in effect in the spring presidential primary—telling people their votes would be counted—when Shoenwetter knew that would not be the case.

4.14 "Purging the Voter Rolls in Cuyahoga County" by Richard Hayes Phillips, Ph.D., pp. 250–254

This analysis by Phillips is from BOE data released in spring 2006. It examines two voter purges in Cuyahoga County between the 2000 and 2004 elections. The first chart described how fully one-quarter of Cleveland's voters—63,721 people—were purged from the voter rolls in Ohio's largest Democratic stronghold. The analysis continues and shows how broad the purges were in precincts that voted overwhelmingly for Al Gore in 2000. Removing a quarter of the voters from the city's voter rolls between the presidential elections created confusion and delays at the polls on November 2, 2004. The impact on the turnout, or voter accommodation rates, can be seen in the final chart, where only two out of twenty-one Cleveland Wards (Ward 16 and 20) had higher voter turnouts in 2004 than in 2000. These massive purges were a factor in voter turnout in Cleveland falling from 57.43 percent in 2000 to 53.27 percent in 2004.

4.15 Dr. Werner Lange Affidavit, December 13, 2004, pp. 255

In an affidavit submitted in the *Moss v. Bush* election suit challenging Ohio's 2004 presidential election results, Dr. Werner Lange, a university professor, did an analysis that found there were 580 more absentee votes certified in Trumbull County than voters listed in the poll books as voting absentee. The *Free Press* received reports that absentee votes were being mailed to homes unsolicited in certain rural Republican areas. This reported illegal practice may account for the Trumbull unexplained absentee votes. Dr. Lange also states that Secretary of State J. Kenneth Blackwell "refused public access to precinct poll books until after certification of the Ohio vote," thus preventing further documentation of possible absentee ballot stuffing.

4.16 Victoria Parks Affidavit (November 13, 2004) on Denied Access to Election Records, p. 256

After the election, a handful of citizen activists tried to examine voting records. In this affidavit by Victoria Parks, we see how J. Kenneth Blackwell imposed a blackout on all presidential voting records—a violation of the state's open records laws. Parks went to the Pickaway County BOE and was told Blackwell ordered local election officials to specifically prohibit her from examining poll signature books—a violation of Ohio's public records law.

4.17 Josh Butler E-mail to Cam Kerry, on Vote Hopping Incident, p. 257

The most visible malfunctioning electronic voting machines were in Youngstown, in Mahoning County. Mark Munroe, chair of the Mahoning County Board of Elections, told the *Youngstown Vindicator* that "We've never seen anything like this before." Sixteen of the precincts in Mahoning County could not be counted at the precinct level due to "human, [or] computer error." Election results were not finalized until 1:30 A.M. Munroe was concerned that one machine posted a negative 25 million votes for Kerry. Munroe also told the *Vindicator* that "20 to 30 machines . . . needed to be recalibrated during the voting process because some votes for a candidate were being counted for the candidate's opponent." This became known as the Mahoning County Hop.

Josh Butler, stationed in Youngstown precinct 6-A, forwarded an e-mail to attorney Cliff Arnebeck (one of four lawyers who filed the 2004 presidential election challenge suit at the Ohio Supreme Court) that had been sent to John Kerry's brother, Cam Kerry, outlining his problems on Election Day and immediately after in Mahoning County. Butler writes that the presiding poll judge had voted for Kerry but the machine indicated a vote for Bush. Typical of the Democratic Party response, there was no real follow-up or further investigation into this complaint.

4.18 Computer Screen Shots of Early Election Results Showing Large Tabulation Errors, pp. 258–259

Election Protection volunteers used their computers to record election results on Election Night. In Lucas County, where Toledo is located, David Cobb, a write-in candidate who officially got 28 votes in the state, appears to be winning with over 70 percent of the vote. In Hamilton County, where Cincinnati is located, Cobb is winning with 35 percent of the vote—39,541 ballots.

The screen shots raise questions that cannot be fully answered, but suggests how massive blocs of votes could be erroneously tallied in countywide counts. One theory is that these were Kerry votes, wrongly attributed to Cobb, that later disappeared. As in Florida in 2000, third-party candidates received unexplained high vote totals in early returns before those votes vanished. Co-author Robert Fitrakis, who was trained as an international election observer and monitored Central American elections in the 1980s, said one of the first things he was taught to look for when detecting election fraud were inexplicably large third-party tallies in early returns. These screen shots raise the possibility that blocs of Kerry votes were initially counted as Green Party votes for Cobb (4,685 votes in Lucas County; 39,541 votes in Hamilton County) but then "corrected" and possibly discarded. Because the vote-tabulation procedure is not transparent, it is all but impossible to account for this vote-counting anomaly.

4.19.1 "Hacking the Vote in Miami County" by Richard Hayes Phillips, Ph.D., pp. 260–262

There were other results that suggested computer vote-count fraud. Dr. Phillips notes, for example, that Miami County merits further scrutiny. Despite a county population increase of only 1.38 percent since 2000, unprecedented voter turnout increases occurred in Bush-majority precincts, such as the reported 194.6 percent increase of voters in Troy precinct 4-F, and 152.8 percent increase in Troy precinct 3-G. In the early hours of the morning, 18,615 new votes came in to Miami County even though 100 percent of the vote had been reported. BOE officials suggest that this is a reporting error. Oddly, the additional votes came in at exactly the same percentage for John Kerry as the earlier total, 33.92 percent. Bush's percentage came in virtually unchanged as well, from 65.80 percent to 65.77 percent of the new votes. Along with these new votes came absurdly high, and in Phillips's opinion "fraudulent" voter turnout reports. Miami County also raised suspicions because its optical-scan machines were not counted at the precinct level, but by a central counting machine provided by ES&S. Thus, ballots were brought to a central location where BOE officials counted them and then the disks were handed off to a private contractor, Roger Kearney, who took them to his home business office to post the results on the county's website.

4.19.2 Roger Kearney of Rhombus Technologies, Criticism of the FreePress.org Analysis of the Miami County Vote, p. 263

Roger Kearney, a Democrat and contractor who manages the county's website, said he observed the Miami County vote tabulation and attempted to explain the vote-count discrepancy in this letter to the editor of the *Free Press*. He noted the county reported not by precinct, but in percentage of the vote quintiles (20 percent, 40 percent, 60 percent, 80 percent, 100 percent). He said there may have been confusion over how absentee ballots were labeled online, leading some people to think the vote count was complete when it was not.

The problem is not with this explanation, but with what Kearney did not see: possible computer manipulation that would have added votes before the final reporting. Computer scientists and other political scientists say that it is statistically improbable that the final results, adding in a fifth quintile, would have resulted in Kerry's total changing by only one-one-hundredth of a percentage point. Thus, they say the jump in Bush and Kerry totals, maintaining their margins (although Bush gained .97 percent), is highly questionable. Co-author Robert Fitrakis says that vote-count fraud typically is seen at the beginning of the count, or at the evening's close, when additional votes need to be manipulated to produce "desired" results.

If Miami County's 2004 reported turnouts were more in line with past elections, perhaps Kearny's explanation could be given more credence. But they are not. Indeed, the combination of the improbable reported turnout and the late-breaking vote count that computer scientists say is improbable point toward election fraud. One of the problems of investigating irregularities in Miami County and other rural Republican strongholds such as Clermont County, where Bush had high vote totals, is that the ballots are not counted on the precinct level. Counting votes by 20 percent blocks masks irregularities at the precinct level. In Miami County, Election Systems & Software optical scanners were used with a centralized voter counter at the BOE.

4.19.3 "Freely Amended Results in Miami County," from Steve Quillen, Miami County BOE Director, June 2006, pp. 264–266

In June 2006, when Richard Hayes Phillips and Bob Fitrakis went to Miami County to count ballots, Steve Quillen, the BOE director and a registered Republican, met the pair and said, "You guys are right," referring to their prior assertions that the 2004 certified vote was inaccurate. There was no 98.55 percent turnout in the Concord South West precinct, he stated, saying instead it was closer to 79 percent. Quillen presented a printout of the new 2004 results for the county's 82 precincts, which he called "freely amended results." It is reproduced here.

Quillen stated the errors in reporting on Election Night 2004 were due to young volunteers confusing and misidentifying ballots that they delivered from various precincts. Overall, the county's vote totals were unchanged, he said, adding that he did not have to file the new 2004 results with the secretary of state's office. If Quillen's new results were true and correct, the number of ballots cast should be on par with the certified vote. However, when analyzing the new precinct-by-precinct results, Phillips found significant gaps—in half the county's precincts—between the registered voters and ballots cast in the official 2004 results, and the newest numbers presented by Quillen in June 2006.

In the Troy 3-E precinct, for example, the official 2004 results show 1,082 registered voters and 675 ballots cast; in the "freely amended" results (from 2006), there are 344 registered voters and 228 ballots cast. In the Concord South East precinct, the official 2004 results show 1,199 registered voters and 678 ballots cast; in the "freely amended" results, there are 1,143 registered voters and 952 ballots cast. Not only do Quillen's new numbers refute Roger Kearny's critique (document 4.19.2), they provide the strongest evidence yet that computer errors, if not electronic vote count fraud, occurred in Miami County. (Moreover, in July 2006, a subsequent hand count by Ron Baiman found a 5 percent discrepancy between the certified vote and the actual ballots cast in 8 percent of the county's precincts.)

4.20 Kenneth Nuss Resignation Letter, p. 267

Another disturbing feature of the 2004 vote was subcontracting of the actual vote counting to private firms. This prompted Kenneth Nuss, the Auglaize County BOE deputy director, to resign. He then wrote a letter to Jack Fashner, the field supervisor for Ohio Secretary of State J. Kenneth Blackwell. Nuss charged that a former ES&S employee was allowed unauthorized access to the Auglaize County BOE computer over the weekend of October 16, 2004. He noted that "Joe McGinnis was allowed to use our election computer that has all our counties current ballots on it and is used to compile our election results." Nuss also complained that the Republican Elections director, Jean Burklo, controlled the election computer and failed to give Nuss "the proper training" to ensure bipartisan checks and balances regarding the vote counting in Auglaize County. Efforts by whistle-blowers like Nuss did not result in a more open vote count process.

4.21 Warren County Hand-drawn Maps Showing the Diversion of Ballots, p. 268

On Election Day, Warren County was under a Level 10 homeland security lockdown, called not by the FBI, but by local county officials. Warren County officials brought in a "bomb sniffing dog," according to the *Cincinnati Enquirer*. A county employee contacted an Election Protection attorney and offered to testify that election officials knew on the Thursday before the election that there would be a homeland security alert on Election Day. The employee and another individual familiar with the lockdown both offered to testify that ballots had been diverted to an unauthorized warehouse under the control of a Republican Party operative. Each individual supplied maps to the *Free Press*, the first of which is reprinted here.

What happened in Warren County on Election Night is significant, not just because of the eyebrow-raising circumstances of the vote count, but because the county total that was reported—the last county in Ohio to do so—gave Bush a 14,000-vote boost in its final returns, signaling to the national media that Bush's lead was growing, which contributed to declaring him the winner.

As the following analyses reveal, the county's reported vote was fraught with anomalies defying political logic, which strongly suggest election fraud through vote shifting. Diverting the ballots to a remote warehouse for counting would be the first step in executing that fraud.

4.22 "Log Cabin Republicans in Ohio" by Richard Hayes Phillips, Ph.D., p. 269–276

Just three counties, all with suspiciously low vote totals for Kerry in southwest Ohio, provided the entire margin for the Bush victory in the state. Initially, Bush won Butler, Clermont, and Warren counties by 130,050 votes. (On Election Night, Bush won Ohio by a 136,483 vote margin over Kerry. After certification, that margin fell to 118,775 votes while Bush's margin in these three counties rose to 132,685 votes— making their massive vote totals even more important.) This detailed analysis calls into question the certified vote in these three counties, as well as Delaware County, where the most striking incongruity found by Phillips was 10,500 people voted for the president *and* in support of gay marriage, if the certified results are true.

The GOP has gay supporters known as Log Cabin Republicans, but conservative, rural Ohio is not a known stronghold. Phillips also notes that in these counties more than 13,500 people voted for Bush and an obscure Democratic chief justice candidate from across the state. That chief justice candidate, C. Ellen Connally, was a retired African American municipal judge from Cleveland with politically liberal endorsements. Phillips concludes that, conservatively, 13,500 votes attributed to Bush belonged to Kerry in those three counties. This would boost Kerry's total by 13,500 votes, and reduce Bush's total by 13,500 votes, affecting Kerry's margin by 27,000 votes. (This statistical analysis confirms just how far-reaching these vote count anomalies are; subsequent analysis and examination of actual ballots, in document 4.25, suggests how this may have happened in Warren County.)

4.23 "The Connally Anomaly: A Political Analysis" by Richard Hayes Phillips, Ph.D. (July 24, 2006), pp. 277–278

All of Phillips's analyses presented in this book have been estimates and projections based on the most locally available precinct data to gauge lost Kerry votes or inflated Bush votes. The authors have used the low end of these projections to explain what happened in Ohio, as that methodology is the most conservative approach. As Phillips and the authors looked at actual ballots and precinct records in the spring of 2006, Phillips concluded that the certified results—especially in high-turnout, GOP-majority counties where Bush derived his margin of victory— were deeply problematic. His hand counts of ballots and subsequent analysis found that for Bush's certified numbers to be true, that even more Connally voters would have had to have voted for the president than what the precinct results had indicated.

This document is Phillips's attempt to estimate an upper range of votes that were shifted from Kerry to Bush. It projects that as many as 60,000 votes could have been switched in twelve counties, which would have increased Bush's margin by 120,000 votes. Other academic analysts, such as Ron Baiman, a Ph.D. economist-statistician with Loyola University Chicago's Center for Urban Researched Learning, who relies on exit poll data, put that figure even higher at 75,000 to 82,000 votes switched, which would have affected Bush's margin by 150,000 to 164,000 votes. This final analysis is included to underscore how conservative our estimates and projections are. Until all the 2004 ballots in Ohio are examined and hand-counted, the final story of what happened in Ohio will not be known.

4.24 "Beyond the Connally Anomaly" by Richard Hayes Phillips, Ph.D., pp. 279–281

Reverend Jesse Jackson Jr. coined the phrase "the Connally anomaly." This Phillips analysis shows that down-ballot Democratic candidates— not just C. Ellen Connally, but obscure local candidates—also outpolled Kerry. In many instances, these were Democratic candidates who were not expected to win. Typically, presidential candidates will outpoll local candidates in the fall general election.

Dr. Phillips prepared many more analyses of Ohio counties than could be printed here. In addition to uncounted regular ballots, he looked at provisional ballots rejection rates, the performance of optical-scan voting machines, and other anomalies county by county. Not all Ohio counties had flawed elections. One Phillips paper presents complete results from what appear to be seven clean counties. They are available at www.FreePress.org.

4.25 Warren County Ballots, Photographed and Analyzed, pp. 282–289

This series of ballots shows how ballots could have been swapped between precincts during the vote count in Warren County on Election Night to produce ballots with votes to reelect Bush *and* in favor of gay marriage. These photographs also suggest evidence of ballot-box stuffing on behalf of the president.

The first series of ballots (document 4.25.1) shows how candidates' names are rotated on Ohio's ballots. These are the five different versions of the Warren County presidential ballot. These differing ballots (and layouts) were distributed among Warren County's 157 precincts. The next photograph (document 4.25.2) shows four ballots (from Precinct 128, Mason City) with only one punch, in the number 10 position, which in this precinct would be a vote for Bush. The ballot to the right, which is pink, was a "duplicate card" that replaces a spoiled ballot. It also has only one punch on it, for Bush. Finding ballots with only one vote on them—always for the same candidate, in this case Bush—suggests ballot-box stuffing. The appearance of the duplicate card leaves open the possibility that a spoiled ballot with a Kerry vote was replaced with a Bush vote.

The next photograph contains four ballots from Warren County Precinct 155, in Lebanon City. From left to right, there are: two ballots with single punches for Bush; then a ballot with votes only for Bush and Ohio's incumbent Republican senator, George Voinovich; and on the far right, a ballot with punches in the numbers 6 and 7 positions, which are two punches in the presidential vote section. Because punch-card ballots are placed in a holder for voters, it was not possible to punch both positions 6 and 7 unless the ballot was outside the voting machine—or punched elsewhere by someone *who was not* the voter. That possibility takes us to the next photographs, where we see ballots that appear to have been cast in precincts where the order of the candidates in the voting booth—as seen by voters—was not the same as the order that was read by the vote-counting machines. In other words, we theorize that under the cloak of a fake homeland security alert and a media gag order on Election Night, Republican partisans swapped ballots between the county's precincts to produce results where votes for Democratic candidates—especially for Kerry—would be read by voting machines in other precincts as a vote for Bush and possibly other Republicans. (This is possible because the punch cards were not read at the precinct level, as required by Ohio law, but were moved to be counted at the county level only. Moreover, individual ballots did not contain precinct identifier codes.)

The evidence for such ballot swapping can been seen in the vote, or punch, at position 125, which would have opposed Issue One, the proposed state constitutional amendment banning gay marriage. Ballot questions do not rotate on Ohio's ballot, creating a control to show why these votes do not make political sense *unless they were counted by voting machines intended for another precinct.* The final panel of ballots, from Precinct 118 in Clear Creek, shows ballots with votes for Republican candidates and a vote in favor of gay marriage. This suggests the political damage was not confined to the presidential race, but affected other contests. In this precinct, there were thirty-six such ballots with this configuration—a strong conservative Republican slate and support of gay marriage.

Document 4.1

JOHN KERRY CONCEDED TOO SOON

Richard Hayes Phillips, Ph.D.
November 16, 2004

These are data from the official website of J. Kenneth Blackwell,
Ohio Secretary of State, at
http://www.sos.state.oh.us/sos//results/index.html?

Not expecting such current data to be archived as "historical,"
it took me a long time to find this. I had been searching the
websites of the Boards of Elections, county by county, trying to
find data for actual votes cast, so that I could find out for
myself how many ballot cast had gone uncounted.

The columns in this table show, from left to right, Total
Registered Voters, Total Votes Cast, Percentage of Votes Cast,
and Provisional Ballots Issued.

Voter Turnout: November 2, 2004
Unofficial Results

County	Registered	Votes Cast	Turnout	Provisional
Adams	17,696	12,094	68.34	184
Allen	68,174	48,121	70.59	1,374
Ashland	34,847	25,171	72.23	629
Ashtabula	62,926	45,474	72.27	1,142
Athens	45,100	27,960	62.00	2,504
Auglaize	33,094	22,528	68.07	647
Belmont	44,452	33,452	75.25	1,067
Brown	28,922	20,030	69.26	326
Butler	238,117	163,668	68.73	5,793
Carroll	20,076	14,172	70.59	304
Champaign	25,376	18,564	73.16	555
Clark	89,683	68,883	76.81	1,279
Clermont	125,823	88,019	69.95	1,818
Clinton	25,092	18,177	72.44	378
Columbiana	78,536	49,249	62.71	1,085
Coshocton	22,679	17,331	76.42	277
Crawford	29,591	21,906	74.03	424
Cuyahoga	1,005,807	665,334	66.15	24,788
Darke	38,290	26,379	68.89	710
Defiance	25,847	18,169	70.29	672
Delaware	100,676	79,691	79.16	1,891
Erie	55,517	39,690	71.49	972
Fairfield	91,498	67,632	73.92	1,306
Fayette	16,093	11,704	72.73	293
Franklin	845,720	515,472	60.95	14,446
Fulton	28,561	21,902	76.69	381
Gallia	23,567	13,944	59.17	574
Geauga	65,393	51,286	78.43	668
Greene	105,079	77,830	74.07	2,127
Guernsey	27,129	16,570	61.08	558
Hamilton	573,612	418,001	72.87	14,386
Hancock	49,607	35,087	70.73	791
Hardin	18,921	13,146	69.48	349
Harrison	11,769	8,410	71.46	89

Document 4.1—Continued

Henry	19,685	15,188	77.16	250
Highland	28,243	18,323	64.88	494
Hocking	18,378	13,258	72.14	251
Holmes	18,089	11,542	63.81	170
Huron	37,436	25,584	68.34	670
Jackson	23,997	14,332	59.72	422
Jefferson	49,655	36,528	73.56	650
Knox	36,971	26,661	72.11	689
Lake	160,165	119,657	74.71	1,975
Lawrence	41,424	27,876	67.29	599
Licking	111,387	78,876	70.81	1,565
Logan	29,406	21,135	71.87	650
Lorain	196,601	139,069	70.74	4,134
Lucas	302,136	216,453	71.64	6,719
Madison	23,477	17,451	74.33	392
Mahoning	194,673	131,938	67.77	2,717
Marion	43,323	28,762	66.39	928
Medina	118,330	84,725	71.60	1,266
Meigs	15,205	10,813	71.11	240
Mercer	31,306	20,478	65.41	931
Miami	72,169	50,562	70.06	1,609
Monroe	10,350	7,857	75.91	132
Montgomery	391,914	279,801	71.39	9,227
Morgan	9,358	6,770	72.34	160
Morrow	24,249	16,403	67.64	314
Muskingum	51,552	38,817	75.30	871
Noble	8,879	6,715	75.63	75
Ottawa	30,251	23,052	76.20	469
Paulding	14,226	9,881	69.46	243
Perry	23,480	15,328	65.28	428
Pickaway	30,045	22,579	75.15	553
Pike	19,661	12,708	64.64	285
Portage	109,565	76,306	69.64	1,445
Preble	28,137	21,226	75.44	493
Putnam	24,572	18,948	77.11	246
Richland	95,359	61,907	64.92	1,357
Ross	43,463	31,402	72.25	563
Sandusky	39,408	32,433	82.30	760
Scioto	48,012	35,317	73.56	867
Seneca	37,974	27,148	71.49	494
Shelby	28,460	22,688	79.72	791
Stark	267,939	186,252	69.51	6,653
Summit	368,858	275,551	74.70	5,932
Trumbull	142,548	108,533	76.14	2,700
Tuscarawas	55,656	42,871	77.03	987
Union	30,200	22,515	74.55	436
Van Wert	21,100	15,252	72.28	297
Vinton	8,527	6,059	71.06	129
Warren	125,919	93,321	74.11	1,465
Washington	40,881	29,707	72.67	643
Wayne	69,672	51,898	74.49	818
Williams	26,772	18,324	68.44	694
Wood	91,492	61,865	67.62	2,655
Wyandot	15,834	10,785	68.11	138
TOTAL	7,979,639	5,574,476	69.86	155,428

The columns in this table show, from left to right:

Total Votes Cast, as reported at
http:/www.sos.state.oh.us/sos//results/index.html?

Total Votes Counted, as reported at
http://election.sos.state.oh.us/results/RaceDetail.aspx?race=PP

Total Votes Uncounted, derived by subtracting column two from
column one

Provisional Ballots Issued, as reported at
http:/www.sos.state.oh.us/sos//results/index.html?

The official Voter Turnout is 5,574,476. This does not include
the 155,428 Provisional Ballots Issued. The true voter turnout
was 5,729,904. This does not include persons who grew weary of
waiting in line, or were turned away at the polls, or were denied
provisional ballots, or were discouraged from going to the polls.
The Total Votes Counted were 5,481,804. This leaves 248,100
votes uncounted. George W. Bush presently holds a lead of
136,483 votes in Ohio. With 100% of the precincts reporting,
only 95.67% of the votes are in. John Kerry conceded too soon.

Voter Turnout: November 2, 2004
Unofficial Results

County	Votes Cast	Counted	Uncounted	Provisional
Adams	12,094	11,735	359	184
Allen	48,121	47,643	478	1,374
Ashland	25,171	24,363	808	629
Ashtabula	45,474	44,465	1,009	1,142
Athens	27,960	27,465	495	2,504
Auglaize	22,528	22,279	249	647
Belmont	33,452	32,684	768	1,067
Brown	20,030	19,641	389	326
Butler	163,668	161,590	2,078	5,793
Carroll	14,172	13,854	318	304
Champaign	18,564	18,268	296	555
Clark	68,883	67,595	1,288	1,279
Clermont	88,019	87,250	769	1,818
Clinton	18,177	17,923	254	378
Columbiana	49,249	48,377	872	1,085
Coshocton	17,331	15,966	1,365	277
Crawford	21,906	21,433	473	424
Cuyahoga	665,334	652,381	12,953	24,788
Darke	26,379	25,687	692	710
Defiance	18,169	17,841	328	672
Delaware	79,691	78,980	711	1,891
Erie	39,690	38,736	954	972
Fairfield	67,632	66,754	878	1,306
Fayette	11,704	11,511	193	293
Franklin	515,472	512,419	3,053	14,446
Fulton	21,902	21,628	274	381
Gallia	13,944	13,559	435	574
Geauga	51,286	49,733	1,553	668
Greene	77,830	76,541	1,289	2,127
Guernsey	16,570	16,261	309	558
Hamilton	418,001	408,238	9,763	14,386

Hancock	35,087	34,411	676	791
Hardin	13,146	12,969	177	349
Harrison	8,410	8,207	203	89
Henry	15,188	14,891	297	250
Highland	18,323	17,955	368	494
Hocking	13,258	12,973	285	251
Holmes	11,542	10,976	566	170
Huron	25,584	25,065	519	670
Jackson	14,332	13,946	386	422
Jefferson	36,528	35,722	806	650
Knox	26,661	26,430	231	689
Lake	119,657	118,643	1,014	1,975
Lawrence	27,876	27,187	689	599
Licking	78,876	77,779	1,097	1,565
Logan	21,135	20,829	306	650
Lorain	139,069	136,810	2,259	4,134
Lucas	216,453	214,800	1,653	6,719
Madison	17,451	17,078	373	392
Mahoning	131,938	130,396	1,542	2,717
Marion	28,762	28,374	388	928
Medina	84,725	83,614	1,111	1,266
Meigs	10,813	10,550	263	240
Mercer	20,478	20,058	420	931
Miami	50,562	50,235	327	1,609
Monroe	7,857	7,594	263	132
Montgomery	279,801	274,147	5,654	9,227
Morgan	6,770	6,574	196	160
Morrow	16,403	16,043	360	314
Muskingum	38,817	38,129	688	871
Noble	6,715	6,461	254	75
Ottawa	23,052	22,802	250	469
Paulding	9,881	9,679	202	243
Perry	15,328	15,047	281	428
Pickaway	22,579	22,364	215	553
Pike	12,708	12,315	393	285
Portage	76,306	75,347	959	1,445
Preble	21,226	20,795	431	493
Putnam	18,948	18,631	317	246
Richland	61,907	60,630	1,277	1,357
Ross	31,402	31,096	306	563
Sandusky	32,433	31,846	587	760
Scioto	35,317	34,498	819	867
Seneca	27,148	26,541	607	494
Shelby	22,688	22,274	414	791
Stark	186,252	183,017	3,235	6,653
Summit	275,551	270,244	5,307	5,932
Trumbull	108,533	106,025	2,508	2,700
Tuscarawas	42,871	42,038	833	987
Union	22,515	22,234	281	436
Van Wert	15,253	14,564	600	007
Vinton	6,059	5,833	226	129
Warren	93,321	92,251	1,070	1,465
Washington	29,707	29,310	397	643
Wayne	51,898	51,067	831	818
Williams	18,324	17,982	342	694
Wood	61,865	61,140	725	2,655
Wyandot	10,785	10,588	197	138
TOTAL	5,574,476	5,481,804	92,672	155,428

Document 4.2

Blackwell Certifies Statewide Election Results

COLUMBUS -- Secretary of State J. Kenneth Blackwell today certified Ohio's statewide election results by signing the 2004 Official Canvass of Votes. Following are the certified vote totals as reported to Secretary Blackwell by the 88 county boards of elections:

President:	Total Votes
Michael Badnarik (Other-party candidate)	14,695
George W. Bush (Republican)	2,858,727
David Keith Cobb (Write-in)	186
Richard A. Duncan (Write-in)	16
James Harris (Write-in)	22
John F. Kerry (Democrat)	2,739,952
John T. Parker (Write-in)	2
Michael Anthony Peroutka (Other-party candidate)	11,907
Joe Schriner (Write-in)	114
Thomas F. Zych (Write-in)	10
U.S Senator:	
Eric D. Fingerhut (Democrat)	1,961,002

Document 4.2—Continued

Helen Meyers (Write-in)	296
George V. Voinovich (Republican)	3,464,044
Chief Justice of the Ohio Supreme Court:	
C. Ellen Connally	2,073,858
Thomas J. Moyer	2,358,088
Justice of the Ohio Supreme Court (unexpired term):	
Terrence O'Donnell	2,560,555
William O'Neill	1,671,760
Justice of the Ohio Supreme Court:	
Nancy A. Fuerst	1,885,930
Judith Ann Lanzinger	2,508,935
Justice of the Ohio Supreme Court:	
Paul E. Pfeifer	3,384,144
State Issue 1	
"Yes"	3,329,250
"No"	2,065,411

Document 4.2—Continued

County boards of elections completed their official canvasses this year sooner than in previous years. In 2000, Secretary Blackwell certified statewide results on December 11 at 5 p.m; in 2002, statewide results were certified on December 20 at 11 a.m.

A by county breakdown of official results is available on line at http://www.sos.state.oh.us/.

Document 4.3.1

MARK E. MULLIGAN
Ottawa County Prosecuting Attorney

Ottawa County Courthouse	(419) 734-6845
315 Madison Street, Suite 205	Within Ottawa County Dial Toll Free:
Port Clinton, Ohio 43452	1-800-788-8803
	Facsimile (419) 734-3862

January 6, 2005

Harvey Wasserman
735 Euclaire Ave.
Columbus, OH 43209-2409

Dear Mr. Wassermàn:

I have been asked to respond to your correspondence of December 1, 2004 directed to the Ottawa County Board of Elections. Within your correspondence you mention that you or someone on your behalf would be calling to coordinate the record inspection and copying process. To our knowledge this has not yet occurred.[1]

Ordinarily Ottawa County responds to records requests with available County resources. Unfortunately your request and others received for recent election materials make it impossible to comply using County resources.[2] Ohio law allows the County to contract with a private contractor to provide the duplication services you request. Thus there have been consultations with a contractor.

My conversations with this contractor lead me to believe that the cost we are allowed to charge you under Ohio law will range between two thousand ($2,000) and five thousand ($5,000) dollars (or more). Much depends on resolving ambiguities in your request. If you are still interested in obtaining Ottawa County election records, please contact me to resolve these ambiguities. We stand ready to start processing your request as soon as you give the approval.

Yours truly,

Mark E. Mulligan
Ottawa County Prosecutor

Cc: Jo Friar, Director
Ottawa County Board of Elections

---

[1] I qualify this statement because someone did inquire in person about public records; however, this person did not identify themselves and did not disclose any agency. Of course, such conduct is entirely lawful.
[2] Your request coupled with the other requests demand over one hundred thousand (100,000) documents and computer data outside the expertise of the Board of Elections to provide.

Document 4.3.2

LOGAN COUNTY BOARD OF ELECTIONS
COURT HOUSE
101 SOUTH MAIN ST., ROOM 1
BELLEFONTAINE, OHIO 43311

PHONE: (937) 599-7255   FAX: (937) 599-7270

December 2, 2004

Harvey Wasserman
735 Euclaire Avenue
Columbus, Ohio 43209-2409

Dear Sir:

Enclosed are the Logan County 2004 unofficial and official abstracts that you requested. Costs for these abstracts are as follow:

Copied abstracts	$ 1.20
Postage	2.21
TOTAL	$ 3.41

Mail check to the Logan Co. Board of Elections as soon as possible.

Respectfully,

Naoma Gauder

Naoma Gauder, director

YOUR VOTE IS YOUR VOICE IN AMERICA

Document 4.4

----- Original Message -----
From: "Brandon Sandlin" <brandon@triadgsi.com>
To: <madison@sos.state.oh.us>
Sent: Monday, November 29, 2004 2:40 PM
Subject: Election Reports

> Hello to all in Madison County!
>
> Attached, you will find the cumulative report (oh49unov.pdf) with
over and
> under votes reported as well as the official abstract (oh49abs.pdf).
These
> reports may be printed for your records and then mailed to the state
along
> with your other certification reports.
>
> You will also find the electronic abstract (the two TXT files)
contained
in
> the email. You may forward this email to the state so that they
receive
all
> information in an electronic format. Let me know if you have any
questions.
>
> Brandon Sandlin
> TRIAD Governmental Systems, Inc.
> brandon@triadgsi.com
> 800-666-5446
>
>
>
>

Document 4.5

County	Bush			Democrats		
	Bush 2000	2004	% Change	Gore 2000	Kerry 2004	% Change
Auglaize	13,770	16,437	19.37	5,564	5,729	2.88
Brown	10,027	12,480	24.46	5,972	7,058	15.39
Butler	86,587	106,735	23.27	46,390	54,185	14.39
Champaign	9,220	11,432	23.99	5,955	6,752	11.80
Clark	27,660	34,444	24.53	27,984	32,824	14.75
Clermont	47,129	61,694	30.9	20,927	25,318	17.34
Clinton	9,824	12,625	28.51	4,791	5,244	8.64
Columbiana	21,804	25,212	15.63	20,657	22,884	9.73
Coshocton	8,243	9,121	10.65	5,594	6,763	17.29
Crawford	11,666	13,667	17.15	6,721	7,626	11.87
Darke	14,817	17,869	20.6	7,741	7,663	-1.02
Defiance	9,540	11,018	15.49	6,175	6,683	7.60
Fairfield	33,523	42,057	25.46	19,065	24,321	21.61
Fayette	5,685	7,221	27.02	3,363	4,244	20.76
Fulton	11,546	13,442	16.42	6,805	8,098	15.97
Geauga	25,417	29,957	17.86	15,327	19,571	21.69
Greene	37,946	46,841	23.44	25,059	29,349	14.62
Hamilton	204,175	215,639	5.61	161,578	190,956	15.38
Hancock	20,985	24,345	16.01	8,798	9,930	11.40
Harrison	3,417	4,318	26.37	3,351	3,824	12.37
Highland	9,728	11,871	22.03	5,328	6,012	11.38
Hocking	5,702	6,821	19.62	4,474	6,065	26.23
Holmes	6,754	8,299	22.88	2,066	2,622	21.21
Jackson	6,958	8,382	20.47	5,131	5,519	7.03
Knox	13,393	16,677	24.52	7,133	9,613	25.80
Lake	51,747	60,615	17.14	46,497	57,471	19.09
Lawrence	12,531	15,178	21.12	11,307	11,874	4.78
Licking	37,180	48,092	29.35	23,196	29,350	20.97
Logan	11,849	14,084	18.86	5,945	6,644	10.52
Madison	8,892	10,931	22.93	5,287	6,080	13.04
Marion	13,617	16,729	22.85	10,370	11,492	9.76
Medina	37,349	47,499	27.18	26,635	35,725	25.44
Mercer	12,485	15,022	20.32	5,212	4,924	-5.85
Miami	26,037	33,039	26.89	15,584	17,039	8.54
Morrow	7,842	10,313	31.51	4,529	5,651	19.85
Muskingum	17,995	21,901	21.71	13,415	16,050	16.42
Pickaway	10,717	13,864	29.36	6,598	8,388	21.34
Putnum	12,837	14,196	10.59	4,063	4,348	6.55
Richland	30,138	36,253	20.29	20,572	24,056	14.48
Ross	13,706	16,940	23.6	11,662	13,701	14.88
Sandusky	13,699	17,824	30.11	11,146	13,909	19.86
Scioto	15,022	17,938	19.41	13,997	16,438	14.85
Seneca	13,863	15,624	12.7	9,512	10,770	11.68
Shelby	12,476	15,825	26.84	6,593	6,337	-4.04
Tuscarawas	19,549	23,359	19.49	15,879	18,460	13.98
Union	11,502	15,593	35.57	5,040	6,546	23.01
Van Wert	8,679	10,484	20.8	4,209	4,026	-4.55
Warren	48,318	66,523	37.68	19,142	25,399	24.63
Washington	15,342	17,029	11	10,383	12,137	14.45
Wayne	25,901	31,433	21.36	14,779	19,455	24.03
Wood	27,504	32,574	18.43	22,687	28,216	19.60

Document 4.6

OFFICIAL PRESIDENTIAL BALLOT
GENERAL ELECTION – NOVEMBER 2, 2004
FRANKLIN COUNTY, OHIO

For President and Vice-President		
To vote for President and Vice-President, punch the hole beside the number for the set of candidates of your choice. Your vote will be counted for each of the candidates for presidential elector whose names have been certified to the Secretary of State. (Vote not more than ONCE)	**For President:** **MICHAEL ANTHONY PEROUTKA** other-party candidate	**For Vice-President:** **CHUCK** and **BALDWIN** **6**
	For President: **MICHAEL BADNARIK** other-party candidate	**For Vice-President:** **RICHARD V.** and **CAMPAGNA** **2**
	For President: **GEORGE W. BUSH** Republican	**For Vice-President:** **DICK** and **CHENEY** **3**
	For President: **JOHN F. KERRY** Democrat	**For Vice-President:** **JOHN** and **EDWARDS** **4**
	For President: **RALPH NADER**	**For Vice-President:** **PETER MIGUEL** and **CAMEJO** **5**

Document 4.7

	Franklin County	The rest of Ohio	Difference
1992	75.03%	75.62%	0.60%
1996	64.81%	68.14%	3.33%
2000	61.27%	63.88%	2.62%
2004	60.95%	70.91%	9.96%

Document 4.8

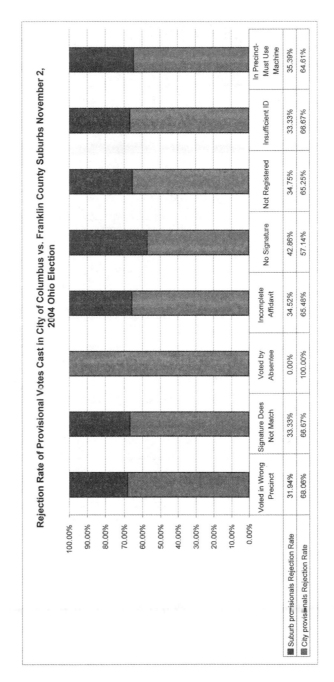

Rejection Rate of Provisional Votes Cast in City of Columbus vs. Franklin County Suburbs November 2, 2004 Ohio Election

	Voted in Wrong Precinct	Signature Does Not Match	Voted by Absentee	Incomplete Affidavit	No Signature	Not Registered	Insufficient ID	In Precinct-Must Use Machine
Suburb provisionals Rejection Rate	31.94%	33.33%	0.00%	34.52%	42.86%	34.75%	33.33%	35.39%
City provisionals Rejection Rate	68.06%	66.67%	100.00%	65.48%	57.14%	65.25%	66.67%	64.61%

Document 4.9

Provisional Voter
VOTE NOT COUNTED

Name _Bonita Jamison_

Address _2471 Abbotsford Way_

City _Dublin_ State _OH_ Zip _43016_

Did you fill out a provisional ballot on 11/2/2004? _X_ YES ____ NO

What polling place? _____

Address_____

Reason given to you as to why you had to fill out a provisional ballot: _They had me registered at an address we lived at 3yrs ago._
(use back side of paper if necessary)

*Optional: Are your registered: ____ Republican _X_ Democrat ____ Independent

When did you register to vote? Approximate date or year: _not sure_

Who registered you to vote? _I registered myself_

Have you ever voted before? _X_ YES ____ NO

If you voted before, did you have to fill out a provisional ballot? ____ YES _X_ NO

If you voted before, was it at the same polling place as you listed above? _X_ YES _X_ NO

Was your polling place changed for the Nov. 2, 2004 election? ____ YES ____ NO ____ DON'T KNOW

Did you move since you registered to vote in this last election? _X_ YES ____ NO

Any additional comments: _Yes, I beleive all votes should have been counted, no matter what the outcome would have been. After all the talk of voting + how important_

Thank you for your time and consideration. Email:_____
If you DO NOT want to be contacted, check here ____
Please return to: Bob Fitrakis, The Free Press, 1240 Bryden Rd., Columbus, OH 43205

It is to vote, when you think your vote will make a difference, its not counted. So whats the point in voting again?

Document 4.9—Continued

Provisional Voter
VOTE NOT COUNTED

Name _Dallas j. Kincar jr._

Address _931 Filock rd._ pre add. _70 Amsterdam rd_

City _Columbus_   State _OH_   Zip _43207_

Did you fill out a provisional ballot on 11/2/2004? _✓_ YES ____ NO

What polling place? _South expo_

Address _S. High st._

Reason given to you as to why you had to fill out a provisional ballot: _They_
told me the wrong place
to vote. (wrong voters card)
(use back side of paper if necessary)

*Optional: Are your registered: ____ Republican ____ Democrat _X_ Independent

When did you register to vote? Approximate date or year: _5-16-04_

Who registered you to vote? _people outside Columbus court house_

Have you ever voted before? ____ YES _X_ NO

If you voted before, did you have to fill out a provisional ballot? ____ YES ____ NO

If you voted before, was it at the same polling place as you listed above? ____ YES ____NO

Was your polling place changed for the Nov. 2, 2004 election? ____ YES _X_ NO
____ DON'T KNOW

Did you move since you registered to vote in this last election? _X_ YES ~~NO~~

Any additional comments: _I canot belive my vote_
was not counted I lost! my job to vote!!
(PJ's pizza)

Thank you for your time and consideration. Email: _N/A_
If you DO NOT want to be contacted, check here ____
Please return to: Bob Fitrakis, The Free Press, 1240 Bryden Rd., Columbus, OH 43205

Document 4.9—Continued

Provisional Voter
VOTE NOT COUNTED

Name John P. Goff

Address 2279 Arlington Ave

City Columbus   State Ohio   Zip 43221

Did you fill out a provisional ballot on 11/2/2004? ✔ YES ____ NO

What polling place? Jones Middle School, Upper Arlington

Address _____

Reason given to you as to why you had to fill out a provisional ballot: not a registered voter.

_____

(use back side of paper if necessary)

*Optional: Are your registered: ✔ Republican ____ Democrat ____ Independent

When did you register to vote? Approximate date or year: 1959

Who registered you to vote? myself

Have you ever voted before? ✔ YES ____ NO

If you voted before, did you have to fill out a provisional ballot? ____ YES ✔ NO

If you voted before, was it at the same polling place as you listed above? ✔ YES ____ NO

Was your polling place changed for the Nov. 2, 2004 election? ____ YES ✔ NO
____ DON'T KNOW

Did you move since you registered to vote in this last election? ____ YES ✔ NO

Any additional comments: I have voted in almost every election since 1959! primaries included! Cannot remember if started at 18 or 21.

Thank you for your time and consideration. Email: jgoff@columbus.rr.com
If you DO NOT want to be contacted, check here ____
Please return to: Bob Fitrakis, The Free Press, 1240 Bryden Rd., Columbus, OH 43205

Document 4.9—Continued

Provisional Voter
VOTE NOT COUNTED

Name _RONA MOORE_

Address _1800 GAULT STREET #E_

City _COLUMBUS_   State _OHIO_   Zip _43205_

Did you fill out a provisional ballot on 11/2/2004? _✓_ YES ____ NO

What polling place? _EASTMOOR MIDDLE SCHOOL_

Address_____

Reason given to you as to why you had to fill out a provisional ballot: _BECAUSE TO_

MAKE SURE MY VOTE WOULD BE IN THE CORRECT PRECINT I NEEDED TO

VOTE WHERE I CURRENTLY RESIDED. I WAS PLANNING ON VOTING IN MY
(use back side of paper if necessary)

*Optional: Are your registered: _____ Republican _____ Democrat _____ Independent

When did you register to vote? Approximate date or year: _1986_

Who registered you to vote? _SELF_

Have you ever voted before? _✓_ YES _____ NO

If you voted before, did you have to fill out a provisional ballot? _✓_ YES _____ NO

If you voted before, was it at the same polling place as you listed above? _____ YES _✓_ NO

Was your polling place changed for the Nov. 2, 2004 election? _✓_ YES _____ NO
_____ DON'T KNOW

Did you move since you registered to vote in this last election? _✓_ YES _____ NO

Any additional comments: _ON THE BACK_

_____

Thank you for your time and consideration. Email: _M1340F@AOL.COM_
If you DO NOT want to be contacted, check here ____
Please return to: Bob Fitrakis, The Free Press, 1240 Bryden Rd., Columbus, OH 43205

Document 4.9—Continued

PREVIOUS PRECINT WHICH WAS FRANKLIN ALTERNATIVE.
I SUBMITTED A NEW VOTER REGISTRATION AND NEVER
RECEIVED MY VOTING LOCATION. BY WORD OF MOUTH
I WAS TOLD TO GO TO EASTMOOR MIDDLE SCHOOL.
I STOOD IN A LONG LINE FOR A COUPLE OF HOURS TO
VOICE MY CHOICE AND TO BE TOLD MY VOTE WOULDNT
COUNT HURT AND DISAPPOINTED; TO THE POINT I WAS
GOING TO STOP VOTING ALL TOGETHER. WHAT'S THE
USE! I AM GRADUALLY PUTTING FAITH BACK INTO
THE SYSTEM AND TRY AGAIN. I FEEL IF VOTERS
KNEW THE PROCEDURES ON HOW THE VOTES
ARE TALLIED ~~WOULD~~ THERE WOULD BE MORE
SUPPORT. I MYSELF ENCOURAGED NON-VOTERS
TO VOTE; IT DOES MAKE A DIFFERENCE.

Document 4.9—Continued

Provisional Voter
VOTE NOT COUNTED

Name __WILLIAM J. Kyle__

Address __6138 Ambleside DR.__

City __Columbus__ State __Ohio__ Zip __43229__

Did you fill out a provisional ballot on 11/2/2004? __✓__ YES ____ NO

What polling place? __Devonshire School__

Address __Ambleside. DR.__

Reason given to you as to why you had to fill out a provisional ballot: _____

____ moved across the street and

address changed

(use back side of paper if necessary)

*Optional: Are your registered: ____ Republican __✓__ Democrat ____ Independent

When did you register to vote? Approximate date or year: __1972__

Who registered you to vote?_____

Have you ever voted before? __✓__ YES ____ NO

If you voted before, did you have to fill out a provisional ballot? ____ YES __✓__ NO

If you voted before, was it at the same polling place as you listed above? __✓__ YES ____ NO

Was your polling place changed for the Nov. 2, 2004 election? ____ YES __✓__ NO
____ DON'T KNOW

Did you move since you registered to vote in this last election? ____ YES __✓__ NO

Any additional comments: __the people working the polls were unprepared for the situation__

Thank you for your time and consideration. Email: __wkyle @: insight, RR. com__
If you DO NOT want to be contacted, check here ____
Please return to: Bob Fitrakis, The Free Press, 1240 Bryden Rd., Columbus, OH 43205

Document 4.10

STEALING VOTES IN CLEVELAND

Richard Hayes Phillips, Ph.D.
November 18, 2004

The following is a precinct by precinct analysis of the reported vote totals for the presidential candidates in the City of Cleveland, Cuyahoga County, Ohio, in the 2004 presidential election. These are data readily available online at the official website of the Cuyahoga county Board of Elections. What you see is copied directly from the unofficial precinct canvass records.

In order to conduct this analysis I set up separate Microsoft windows for: (1) registered voters, 2004; (2) voter turnout, by percentage, 2004; (3) vote totals for president, 2004; and (4) vote totals for president, 2000. By clicking back and forth I was able to compare these data easily, if tediously.

I have discovered wholesale "irregularities" in the reported votes, some of them highly suspicious, others obviously fraudulent. For every precinct I believe to be untrue I have written a brief one-line explanation immediately afterward. The following write-up is the most conservative estimate I can make as to how many votes were stolen from John F. Kerry in Cleveland, Ohio. In some cases there have been wholesale shifts of votes from the Kerry column to the Bush column or to third-party candidates; to estimate the number of votes taken from Kerry, I have assumed that the proportions of the vote allotted elsewhere in the ward are correct; in fact, any underreported votes could all have come from Kerry. In other cases the reported voter turnout was astonishingly low for a presidential election. For purposes of this analysis, I adopted 50% as an arbitrary estimate of the true voter turnout for the underreported precincts, and assumed that the proportions of the vote allotted for these precincts are correct. Later, when writing my Affidavit to the Ohio Supreme Court, I adopted a turnout of 60%, which seems much more reasonable given the reported voter turnout in other major cities in Ohio.

These estimates are just that. Fortunately, Ohio has a paper trail. Unfortunately, the Ohio recount was a sham, and the true numbers did not emerge. Very few of the unreported votes turned up as provisional ballots, and none of the uncounted punch cards were examined. I had expected that the Ohio recount would expose the election fraud once and for all, but the seven Cleveland precincts were selected not at random, but because there was little evidence of voter suppression.

LINE 1604	50% TURNOUT WOULD BE 129 VOTES, KERRY LOSES 25 VOTES.
LINE 1614	50% TURNOUT WOULD BE 166 VOTES, KERRY LOSES 38 VOTES.
LINE 1702	41 VOTES APPEAR IN BADNARIK COLUMN, KERRY LOSES 41 VOTES.
LINE 1709	70 VOTES APPEAR IN PETROUKA COLUMN, KERRY LOSES 70 VOTES.
LINE 1806	215 VOTES APPEAR IN PETROUKA COLUMN, KERRY LOSES 213 VOTES.
LINE 1814	163 VOTES APPEAR IN BADNARIK COLUMN, KERRY LOSES 162 VOTES.
LINE 1902	16 VOTES APPEAR IN PETROUKA COLUMN, KERRY LOSES 15 VOTES.
LINE 1903	50% TURNOUT WOULD BE 390 VOTES, KERRY LOSES 142 VOTES.
LINE 1909	50% TURNOUT WOULD BE 362 VOTES, KERRY LOSES 119 VOTES.

Document 4.10—Continued

CLEVELAND 5J	50% TURNOUT WOULD BE 228 VOTES, KERRY LOSES 66 VOTES.
CLEVELAND 5L	50% TURNOUT WOULD BE 324 VOTES, KERRY LOSES 93 VOTES.
CLEVELAND 5O	50% TURNOUT WOULD BE 157 VOTES, KERRY LOSES 25 VOTES.
CLEVELAND 5P	50% TURNOUT WOULD BE 49 VOTES, KERRY LOSES 11 VOTES.
CLEVELAND 6B	50% TURNOUT WOULD BE 197 VOTES, KERRY LOSES 106 VOTES.
CLEVELAND 6C	50% TURNOUT WOULD BE 324 VOTES, KERRY LOSES 272 VOTES.
CLEVELAND 6D	50% TURNOUT WOULD BE 229 VOTES, KERRY LOSES 93 VOTES.
CLEVELAND 6F	NOT AN IRREGULARITY; BUSH DID WELL IN CLEVELAND 6F IN 2000.
CLEVELAND 6K	50% TURNOUT WOULD BE 283 VOTES, KERRY LOSES 81 VOTES.
CLEVELAND 6L	81 VOTES APPEAR IN BUSH COLUMN, KERRY LOSES 36 VOTES.
CLEVELAND 6W	50% TURNOUT WOULD BE 144 VOTES, KERRY LOSES 20 VOTES.
CLEVELAND 7C	50% TURNOUT WOULD BE 276 VOTES, KERRY LOSES 74 VOTES.
CLEVELAND 7K	50% TURNOUT WOULD BE 120 VOTES, KERRY LOSES 35 VOTES.
CLEVELAND 7V	50% TURNOUT WOULD BE 482 VOTES, KERRY LOSES 177 VOTES.
CLEVELAND 8G	51 VOTES APPEAR IN BADNARIK COLUMN, KERRY LOSES 51 VOTES.
CLEVELAND 8H	45 VOTES APPEAR IN BUSH COLUMN, KERRY LOSES 32 VOTES.
CLEVELAND 8I	27 VOTES APPEAR IN PETROUKA COLUMN, KERRY LOSES 26 VOTES.
CLEVELAND 9A	41 VOTES APPEAR IN BUSH COLUMN, KERRY LOSES 33 VOTES.
CLEVELAND 9P	87 VOTES APPEAR IN BUSH COLUMN, KERRY LOSES 68 VOTES.
CLEVELAND 9S	39 VOTES APPEAR IN BUSH COLUMN, KERRY LOSES 31 VOTES.
CLEVELAND 10L	50% TURNOUT WOULD BE 433 VOTES, KERRY LOSES 212 VOTES.
CLEVELAND 11M	35 VOTES APPEAR IN THIRD PARTY COLUMNS, KERRY LOSES 33 VOTES.
CLEVELAND 11U	50% TURNOUT WOULD BE 377 VOTES, KERRY LOSES 104 VOTES.
WARD 12	50% TURNOUT WOULD BE 6095 VOTES, KERRY LOSES 475 VOTES.
CLEVELAND 13D	50% TURNOUT WOULD BE 962 VOTES, KERRY LOSES 586 VOTES.
CLEVELAND 13F	50% TURNOUT WOULD BE 411 VOTES, KERRY LOSES 242 VOTES.
CLEVELAND 13H	50% TURNOUT WOULD BE 134 VOTES, KERRY LOSES 41 VOTES.
CLEVELAND 13O	50% TURNOUT WOULD BE 117 VOTES, KERRY LOSES 61 VOTES.
CLEVELAND 13Q	17 VOTES APPEAR IN THIRD PARTY COLUMNS, KERRY LOSES 15 VOTES.
CLEVELAND 13W	50% TURNOUT WOULD BE 481 VOTES, KERRY LOSES 133 VOTES.
CLEVELAND 13X	37 VOTES APPEAR IN BADNARIK COLUMN, KERRY LOSES 36 VOTES.
CLEVELAND 13Y	50% TURNOUT WOULD BE 28 VOTES, KERRY LOSES 7 VOTES.
WARD 14	50% TURNOUT WOULD BE 6878 VOTES, KERRY LOSES 1106 VOTES.
CLEVELAND 15B	50% TURNOUT WOULD BE 132 VOTES, KERRY LOSES 36 VOTES.
CLEVELAND 15H	22 VOTES APPEAR IN THIRD PARTY COLUMNS, KERRY LOSES 20 VOTES.
CLEVELAND 15S	50% TURNOUT WOULD BE 138 VOTES, KERRY LOSES 20 VOTES.
WARD 17	50% TURNOUT WOULD BE 6394 VOTES, KERRY LOSES 706 VOTES.
CLEVELAND 19O	50% TURNOUT WOULD BE 239 VOTES, KERRY LOSES 44 VOTES.

CLEVELAND   KERRY LOSES 6032 VOTES

Thus, a not unreasonable conclusion is that tampering with the numbers cost John Kerry 6,000 votes (assuming 50% turnout), or 22,000 votes (assuming 60% turnout).

I am not claiming that the final results, when all the votes have been counted and recounted, will come close to matching the estimates I have given above. I have made these estimates only to give the reader some idea of the magnitude of the problem. Not all of these irregularities will turn out to be fraud. But some of them will. Wholesale shifting of scores of votes to the columns of third party candidates who received less than one half of one percent of the statewide vote between them, voter turnout of 7.10%, 13.05%, 19.60%, 21.01%, 21.80%, 24.72%, 28.83%, 28.97%, 29.25% in certain precincts, and voter turnout of 39.35% for an entire ward, are simply not credible.

Document 4.10—Continued

There may be some correlation between the precincts with astonishingly low voter turnout, and the reports of long lines at the polling places. People on the ground in Ohio should look at the precinct maps, check the news reports, talk with local residents, and figure this out.

NOTE: These calculations were redone in March 2006 based on official results, after provisional ballots and late-arriving absentee ballots had been counted, as part of my summary table entitled "Estimated Vote Count in Ohio." The official results gave to Kerry a net gain of 4,486 votes in Cleveland (5324 for Kerry, 838 for Bush) and increased the reported turnout from 51.23% to 53.27%. Assuming 60% turnout, as seems likely based upon turnout in other major cities of Ohio (see table below), Kerry's margin of victory in Cleveland was wrongly reduced by 16,000 votes.

PERCENT TURNOUT IN MAJOR CITIES OF OHIO

City	Registered Voters	Ballots Cast	Percent Turnout
Akron	127,427	76,191	59.79%
Cincinnati	215,454	142,867	66.31%
Cleveland	323,202	172,160	53.27%
Dayton	104,740	64,298	61.39%
Toledo	195,171	133,977	68.65%

Data for Cincinnati and Toledo are from unofficial results. The true percentage would be higher.

Voter turnout in Cleveland was 57.43% in 2000, but only 53.27% in 2004, both according to official results. This is completely contrary to the statewide trend. In 2000, Ohio was not contested. Al Gore pulled out of Ohio one month before the 2000 election in order to concentrate on Florida. In 2000, voter turnout was only 63.65% statewide. In 2004, Ohio was the major battleground state, and voter turnout was 71.76% statewide. Thus, according to official results, voter turnout in Cleveland was only 6.22% below the statewide percentage in 2000, but 18.49% below the statewide percentage in 2004. This is despite the fact that, between the 2000 and 2004 elections, 63,721 registered voters were purged from the voter rolls in Cleveland.

Document 4.11

UNCOUNTED VOTES IN CUYAHOGA COUNTY

Richard Hayes Phillips, Ph.D.
December 24, 2004

I give my heartfelt thanks to Brian Julin for
producing the spreadsheets and the tables of data
that made it possible for me to write this report in
a timely manner.

This is the fourth in a series of reports on
uncounted votes in urban counties of Ohio. These are
ballots cast but not counted because they were
regarded as "undervotes" and "overvotes," or "blank"
and "void," as they are known in New York State. The
true number of such votes can be easily determined by
subtracting votes counted from total ballots cast.

Shortly after the election I obtained from the
website of the Ohio Secretary of State the data I
needed to make a statewide compilation on a county by
county basis of the uncounted votes, exclusive of
provisional ballots. These data have since been
taken down from said website. I present them here.

Cuyahoga County

Registered Voters	1,005,807
Ballots Cast	665,334
Votes Counted	652,381
Votes Uncounted	12,953
Provisional Ballots	24,788
John F. Kerry	433,262
George W. Bush	215,624
Other candidates	3,495

Thus, according to the Ohio Secretary of State's own
data, the countywide percentage of uncounted votes,
exclusive of provisional ballots, was 1.95%.

The Cuyahoga County Board of Elections has posted its
official precinct canvass records dated November 30,
2004. The official results are presented here:

Cuyahoga County

Registered Voters	1,005,807
Ballots Cast	687,260
Votes Counted	673,729
Votes Uncounted	13,531
John F. Kerry	448,486
George W. Bush	221,606
Other candidates	3,637

Document 4.11—Continued

There are still 13,531 uncounted votes in Cuyahoga
County. Presumably 578 are provisional ballots, and
the other 12,953 are the regular ballots that went
uncounted on Election Day.

From the Cuyahoga County canvass records I have
compiled the following table, presenting separate
data for the vote totals, counted and uncounted, for
Cleveland, the suburbs, regular ballots, and absentee
ballots:

Cuyahoga County

Breakdown	Ballots Cast	Uncounted		Bush	Kerry
CLEVELAND	172,160	4,708	2.73%	26,435	139,580
SUBURBS	515,100	8,823	1.71%	195,171	308,906
REGULAR	602,048	10,701	1.78%	192,518	395,543
ABSENTEE	85,212	2,830	3.32%	29,088	52,943
TOTAL	687,260	13,531	1.97%	221,606	448,486

As shown in the table above, 34.79% of the uncounted
votes are in Cleveland, which Kerry won with 83.36%
of the vote to 15.79% for Bush. The percentage of
uncounted votes in Cleveland, 2.73%, is much higher
than the county wide percentage of 1.97%, but lower
than the surprisingly high percentage of uncounted
absentee ballots, 3.32%.

I had Brian Julin prepare a table of precincts sorted
according to their percentage of uncounted ballots.
Here are the results for the City of Cleveland:

PRECINCTS WITH 4.0% OR MORE UNCOUNTED BALLOTS

Precinct	Ballots Cast	Uncounted		Bush	Kerry
CLEVELAND 6-M	467	90	19.27%	9	367
CLEVELAND 8-I	328	41	12.50%	8	251
CLEVELAND 13-H	95	10	10.52%	10	71
CLEVELAND 5-F	464	45	9.70%	4	415
CLEVELAND 6-J	313	28	8.95%	9	276
CLEVELAND 15-I	303	24	7.92%	85	188
CLEVELAND 1-D	439	33	7.52%	14	391
CLEVELAND 6-D	145	10	6.90%	5	130
CLEVELAND 13-X	406	27	6.65%	8	333
CLEVELAND 11-R	373	23	6.17%	44	304
CLEVELAND 9-M	504	31	6.15%	15	458
CLEVELAND 14-F	299	18	6.02%	69	211
CLEVELAND 7-A	511	30	5.87%	20	460
CLEVELAND 9-R	430	25	5.81%	12	392
CLEVELAND 13-A	417	24	5.75%	44	347
CLEVELAND 7-U	472	27	5.72%	22	421
CLEVELAND 12-L	404	23	5.69%	56	323

Document 4.11—Continued

CLEVELAND 17-N	311	17	5.47%	53	238
CLEVELAND 4-Q	484	26	5.37%	13	439
CLEVELAND 6-U	354	19	5.37%	11	324
CLEVELAND 2-K	396	21	5.30%	10	365
CLEVELAND 14-J	379	20	5.28%	92	266
CLEVELAND 8-L	213	11	5.16%	19	182
CLEVELAND 4-F	563	29	5.15%	20	299
CLEVELAND 5-A	626	32	5.11%	28	556
CLEVELAND 4-G	431	22	5.10%	12	395
CLEVELAND 7-F	299	15	5.02%	10	274
CLEVELAND 5-K	419	21	5.01%	15	382
CLEVELAND 5-U	20	1	5.00%	0	19
CLEVELAND 3-K	397	19	4.79%	8	370
CLEVELAND 16-A	379	18	4.75%	95	266
CLEVELAND 6-W	128	6	4.69%	8	113
CLEVELAND 7-J	432	20	4.63%	13	397
CLEVELAND 4-B	326	15	4.60%	21	389
CLEVELAND 3-D	567	26	4.59%	20	521
CLEVELAND 14-E	330	15	4.55%	75	239
CLEVELAND 2-P	441	20	4.54%	11	407
CLEVELAND 10-Q	441	20	4.54%	10	398
CLEVELAND 1-S	443	20	4.51%	17	401
CLEVELAND 6-K	201	9	4.48%	27	165
CLEVELAND 2-F	380	17	4.47%	21	342
CLEVELAND 8-Q	562	25	4.45%	15	521
CLEVELAND 11-B	540	24	4.44%	52	463
CLEVELAND 6-G	451	20	4.43%	15	415
CLEVELAND 5-L	249	11	4.42%	9	229
CLEVELAND 8-B	569	25	4.39%	23	520
CLEVELAND 10-J	388	17	4.38%	44	327
CLEVELAND 7-I	343	15	4.37%	11	317
CLEVELAND 5-G	482	21	4.36%	14	447
CLEVELAND 5-E	392	17	4.34%	6	369
CLEVELAND 2-A	324	14	4.32%	18	292
CLEVELAND 14-O	304	13	4.28%	54	233
CLEVELAND 11-O	400	17	4.25%	42	329
CLEVELAND 2-O	546	23	4.21%	19	500
CLEVELAND 11-U	285	12	4.21%	25	247
CLEVELAND 17-B	409	17	4.16%	89	302
CLEVELAND 8-R	434	18	4.15%	6	409
CLEVELAND 17-L	316	13	4.11%	46	256
CLEVELAND 8-D	439	18	4.10%	25	394
CLEVELAND 10-N	415	17	4.10%	16	382
CLEVELAND 7-T	415	17	4.10%	19	377
CLEVELAND 9-N	464	19	4.09%	16	427
CLEVELAND 8-E	320	13	4.06%	8	299
CLEVELAND 6-L	425	17	4.00%	82	325
CLEVELAND 14-T	375	15	4.00%	71	286

In Cleveland there are 12 precincts with more than
6% of the ballots uncounted. These account for 380
uncounted votes, 8.07% of the city wide total, and
9.19% of the total ballots cast in these 12
precincts. John Kerry won them all overwhelmingly,

Document 4.11—Continued

by a margin of 12 to 1 in the aggregate.   There are
29 precincts with 5% or more of the ballots
uncounted.   These account for 743 uncounted votes,
15.78% of the city wide total, and 6.84% of the total
ballots cast in these 29 precincts.   John Kerry won
them all overwhelmingly, by a margin of 12 to 1 in
the aggregate.   There are 65 precincts with 4% or
more of the ballots uncounted.   These account for
1,366 uncounted votes, 29.01% of the city wide total,
and 5.43% of the total ballots cast in these 65
precincts.   John Kerry won them all overwhelmingly,
by a margin of 12 to 1 in the aggregate.

Elsewhere in Cuyahoga County there are 19 precincts
with more than 4% of the ballots uncounted.   These
account for 383 uncounted votes, or 5.63% of the
total ballots cast in these precincts.   John Kerry
won 17 of these precincts, 16 of them by overwhelming
margins, 8 to 1 in the aggregate, and he ran nearly
even with Bush, 585 to 589, in the other three.

PRECINCTS WITH 4.0% OR MORE UNCOUNTED BALLOTS

Precinct	Ballots Cast	Uncounted		Bush	Kerry
BEACHWOOD J	309	34	11.00%	53	222
EUCLID 3-C	448	45	10.04%	98	211
STRONGSVILLE 1-J	31	3	9.68%	13	15
EUCLID 4-D	595	41	6.89%	29	523
NORTH ROYALTON 3-A	524	34	6.49%	246	200
NORTH ROYALTON 5-B	444	25	5.63%	213	205
EAST CLEVELAND 2-D	273	15	5.49%	9	248
EUCLID 3-A	76	4	5.26%	22	37
EAST CLEVELAND 2-F	423	21	4.96%	23	379
GARFIELD HTS 1-B	61	3	4.92%	3	54
EAST CLEVELAND 4-D	469	23	4.90%	60	384
SOUTH EUCLID 1-D	535	24	4.49%	48	462
EAST CLEVELAND 3-A	388	17	4.38%	13	358
EAST CLEVELAND 2-C	368	16	4.35%	14	337
LAKEWOOD 3-E	351	15	4.27%	88	246
PARMA 9-J	328	14	4.27%	130	181
EAST CLEVELAND 3-F	379	16	4.22%	9	354
BEDFORD HTS 2-C	436	18	4.13%	28	389
EAST CLEVELAND 2-B	364	15	4.12%	9	339

Document 4.12

Provisional Verification Procedure
rev July 8, 2002, July 28, 2004, August 10, 2004,October 28, 2004.

NOTE: ALL PROVISIONAL BALLOTS MUST BE VERIFIED INTO TWO
CATEGORIES (REGISTERED & REJECTED) FOR THE OFFICIAL COUNT
PROCESS. Be sure to write the city ward and precinct on the back of each envelope before
removing from a precinct.

Prior to verification, Senior Clerks are to examine each envelope and put aside the
following envelopes:
  a.   No Signature

This will ensure that envelopes with the above mentioned are not counted as "OK" and get sent
to the ballot department for counting.

The initial verification process of the Provisional Ballots will be done in teams of one Democrat
and one Republican. The initial verification will consist of stamping each envelope across the
top, in red ink, as follows:

Provisionals that are ok are only checked one time. Rejected provisionals are checked twice.

OK #	INIT	dem / rep
REJ #	INIT	dem / rep

Yellow Provisional Envelopes that are stamped "OK" will be counted in the official count
process.

VERIFICATION PROCESS FOR "OK" PROVISIONALS:
NOTE: to verify a provisional envelope as "OK", all necessary information must be in place on
the envelope - NAME, ADDRESS & SIGNATURE (as long as the signature matches the one in
the data base). Date of birth is not mandatory and should not reject a provisional ballot.

The initial check involves only the verification of registration.
  •   Query the voter as you would a regular registration status card by last name, first name,
       birth date and what ever other information is available on the envelope.
  •   Check the signature if the signature matches the data base signature and the status of the
       voter is either "A" or "I" (Active or Inactive) the voter is registered and the envelope
       should be stamped "OK".
  •   Place your initials on the envelope.
  •   Write in the Old city, ward and precinct directly above the "OLD RESIDENCE
       ADDRESS" please write legibly.
  •   Write the New city, ward and precinct directly above the NEW/CURRENT RESIDENCE
       ADDRESS" please write legibly.

(SEE SAMPLE "A" COMPLETED VERIFIED "OK" ENVELOPE)

Document 4.12—Continued

VERIFICATION PROCESS FOR "REJ" PROVISIONALS:
NOTE: verifying a provisional envelope as "REJ" includes checking every possible means of registration. When a provisional is marked "REJ" you could be disenfranchising a voter if not checked properly. "REJ" Provisionals Do Not receive voter history.
Yellow Provisional Envelopes that are stamped "REJ" DO NOT get counted. Only actual NOT REGISTERED provisional envelopes are sent a registration card through the registration " NR LETTER PROCESS".

- Query the voter as you would a regular registration status card, last name, first name and whatever other information is available on the envelope.
- If you are unable to find the voter and you have exhausted all means of locating the name on the envelope, stamp the envelope "REJ" and initial.
- Write the New city, ward and precinct directly above the NEW/CURRENT RESIDENCE ADDRESS" please write legibly.

(SEE SAMPLE "B" COMPLETED "REJ" VERIFIED ENVELOPE)

NOTE: All rejected provisional must have a rejection letter stapled to the envelope identifying reason for rejection. Follow the steps below:

PROVISIONAL BALLOT (lemon-envelope) REJECTION FORM"
　　a) name of voter.
　　b) city ward and precinct.
　　c) party politics (if a party primary election is held).
　　d) reason for rejection .
　　e) sign your name under proper politics.
　　f) have a person of the opposite party double check the envelope and sign the form.

(SEE SAMPLE "C" COMPLETED REJECTION FORM)

PLEASE NOTE:
ONE (1) YELLOW ENVELOPE TO A REJECTION LETTER!!
EXCEPTION; Multiple empty envelopes can be attached to a rejection form if they are from the same city and ward.

Once completed the Manager, Director and Deputy Director must sign off on all rejected provisionals.

As the verification process is completed, the PROVISIONAL BALLOT STATUS REPORT must be completed. The file is located on the Manager's computer in Microsoft Excel.
As provisionals are completed break them down into NEW city and ward order. Count and transfer the numbers to the report. Rejected provisional are broken down on the report by reason.

Ballots are now ready to transfer to the Ballot Department and the following procedure must be followed: YELLOW ENVELOPES MARKED "REJ" DO NOT GET COUNTED AND NEVER GET SENT TO BALLOT COUNT WITH "OK" PROVISIONALS)

Document 4.12—Continued

Complete a Transfer form (SAMPLE" D"). Count the number of envelopes to be transferred under the appropriate type and transfer the number to the form. One Democrat and one Republican must deliver to the Ballot Department. Once delivered to the Ballot Department, one Democrat and one Republican from that department must sign the Transfer form and give a copy back to registration to be filed.

C:\AARegistration\Procedures\Provisional Verification - manual\PROVISIONAL VERIFICATION.wpd

Document 4.12—Continued

OK #123456   init MD/BS.

Cuyahoga County Board of Elections
PROVISIONAL BALLOT
STATEMENT OF VOTER R.C. 3503.16

(A) I, JOHN DOE declare under
(PRINT NAME)
penalty of election falsification that I moved and/o
changed my name on or prior to the ☐General
☐ Primary ☐ Special Election held on the 6 day
NOV 20 01.   PARMA-1-B

NEW/CURRENT RESIDENCE ADDRESS:
1234 DAY DRIVE
(STREET ADDRESS)
PARMA   44134
(CITY)   (Zip)

of Cuyahoga County, Ohio   PARMA-6-F
OLD RESIDENCE ADDRESS:
4231 NIGHT DR
(STREET ADDRESS)
PARMA   44134
(CITY)   (Zip)

of Cuyahoga County, Ohio
- - - - - - - - - - - - - - - - - -
(B) CHANGE OF NAME:

_____
(PRINT FORMER NAME)
_____
(PRINT NEW NAME)

(C) I am voting at: (Check one)
☐ office of the Cuyahoga County Board of
Elections
☐ my new ward and precinct (Ward____, Pct ____

at _____
(NEW VOTING LOCATION)
(D) I will not vote or attempt to vote at any other
location for the election held on this date. I
understand that the statements above are made
under penalty of election falsification. I request
a ballot for the
                            Party (Only if party primary
☞
SIGNATURE OF VOTER
                            DATE 11/6/01
DATE OF BIRTH 1/1/81
                            MONTH/DAY/YEAR

WHOEVER COMMITS ELECTION FALSIFICATION
GUILTY OF A FELONY OF THE FIFTH DEGREE
R.C. 3501.38

Checked for Completeness and Accuracy:

_____
Election Day Official
Form No. 12-1

SAMPLE "A"

Document 4.12—Continued

NR # 187654 Init MD/ BJ

Cuyahoga County Board of Elections
PROVISIONAL BALLOT
STATEMENT OF VOTER R.C. 3503.16

(A) I, Bill Doe _____ declare under
(PRINT NAME)

penalty of election falsification that I moved and/o
changed my name on or prior to the ☐ General
☐ Primary ☐ Special Election held on the __6__ day
NOV __20 01__.   [SEVEN HILLS 1-C

NEW/CURRENT RESIDENCE ADDRESS:

4567   SUN DR
(STREET ADDRESS)
SEVEN HILLS   44130
(CITY)   (Zip)

of Cuyahoga County, Ohio   [SEVEN HILLS ?

OLD RESIDENCE ADDRESS:

7654   MOON DR
(STREET ADDRESS)
SEVEN HILLS   44130
(CITY)   (Zip)

of Cuyahoga County, Ohio
— — — — — — — — — — — — — — — —

(B) CHANGE OF NAME:

_____
(PRINT FORMER NAME)

_____
(PRINT NEW NAME)

(C) I am voting at: (Check one)
☐ office of the Cuyahoga County Board of
Elections
☐ my new ward and precinct (Ward____, Pct____

at_____
(NEW VOTING LOCATION)

(D) I will not vote or attempt to vote at any other
location for the election held on this date. I
understand that the statements above are made
under penalty of election falsification. I request
a ballot for the
_____ Party (Only if party prima

☞ Bill Doe
    SIGNATURE OF VOTER

                    DATE 11/6/01

DATE OF BIRTH 1/1/78
               MONTH/DAY/YEAR

WHOEVER COMMITS ELECTION FALSIFICATIC
GUILTY OF A FELONY OF THE FIFTH DEGRI
R.C. 3501.38

Checked for Completeness and Accuracy:

_____
Election Day Official
Form No. 17

SAMPLE "B"

Document 4.12—Continued

<u>PROVISIONAL BALLOT REJECTION FORM</u>
<u>R.C. 3503.16</u>

ELECTION DATE _____

Name of voter (PLEASE PRINT CLEARLY)			
Municipality		Ward	Precinct

PARTY	✓	REASON FOR REJECTION	✓
DEMOCRAT		NOT REGISTERED	
REPUBLICAN		NO INFORMATION	
ISSUES ONLY		NO SIGNATURE	

_____
REPUBLICAN

_____
DEMOCRAT

_____
MANAGER

_____
DIRECTOR

_____
DEPUTY DIRECTOR

_____
DATE

C:\AARegistration\Provisionals\Reject Form.wpd

Document 4.13

Election officials gave wrong information about provisional ballots - revealed in affidavit.
by *Neil F. Schoenwetter, Jr.*
November 25, 2004

The following is the affidavit by:
Neil F. Schoenwetter, Jr., Summit County, Ohio:

As a "challenger" for the Democratic party, I was at a polling place that contained six precincts. I was there from 630 a.m. to 6: 30 p.m. At at least four of the six precincts, elections judges were telling potential voters that they could cast a provisional ballot at any table/precinct and it would be counted. I tried, unsuccessfully to point out the judges' error, including showing them three or four signs posted on the wall that said specifically that provisional ballots must be cast at the proper precinct. I observed at least two, maybe three, voters being given provisional ballots at/from the wrong precinct -- despite the fact that the correct precinct was only feet away. (We were able to convince these voters to go to the correct precinct (and stand in line again). Since there were six precincts in this one location, I am sure that many, many provisional ballots were given to voters in the wrong precinct. I witnessed one voter who decided to cast a provisional ballot in the incorrect precinct because she wanted to believe the incorrect poll worker instead of trusting me -- who she clearly believed to be partisan (especially since I was legally labeled as a "challenger" (and the fact that it was Republican "challengers" who had been accused in the media as trying to disenfranchise.) Additionally, she would have had to travel a mile to the correct location.

At or about 11:30 a.m., two gentlemen who identified themselves as election supervisors from the board of elections stopped by. (I don't have there names with me at this moment, but I do have them recorded and will be able to provide them.) I informed them of the election judges' errors and asked them to re-instruct the poll workers. They assured me that ANY PROVISIONAL BALLOT THAT WAS CAST IN THE COUNTY WOULD BE COUNTED; THEY DID NOT HAVE TO BE CAST AT ANY PARTICULAR PRECINCT. I was forceful (pointing out the signs). They refused to budge, and demanded to see my credentials --- hoping, I think to eject me from the polling place. They left, saying that they had to visit (and, I assume, incorrectly instruct) 56(?) other precincts.

I am certain, that because of incorrect instructions given by poll workers, election judges, and supervisors, there are many provisional ballots cast by eligible voters, that will not be counted because they were "cast" at the incorrect location.

Document 4.14

PURGING THE VOTER ROLLS IN CUYAHOGA COUNTY

Richard Hayes Phillips, Ph.D.
April 8, 2006, Revised

A cogent question has been raised by a Contributing Editor to Rolling Stone magazine: Could a failure to purge the voter rolls be an explanation for the very low voter turnout percentage in Cleveland?

Purging the voter rolls from time to time is a necessary and desirable thing. People die, or move away, and if their names remain on the list of registered voters, two undesirable consequences ensue: (1) a window of opportunity is left open for those who would engage in election fraud by voting under someone else's name; and (2) the voter turnout percentage (number of ballots cast divided by number of registered voters) will be reduced due to an artificially inflated denominator.

The simplest way to decide who should be purged from the voter rolls is to delete the names of all who have not voted for a certain number of years, and who have no written record of asking to maintain their status as registered voters. In Ohio, most counties purge the rolls every two years, removing the names of registered voters who have been inactive for four years. Some counties purge the rolls more often, while other counties place these names on a list of "inactive voters" and wait another four years before removing the names altogether.

In Cuyahoga County, where Cleveland is located, the voter rolls were purged on July 6, 2001 and January 5, 2002. I have added up the numbers purged in each of 1,436 precincts. Troy Seman prepared a spreadsheet showing that 168,169 voters, or 19.44% of the electorate, were purged from the rolls in Cuyahoga County. By comparison, Bush's official margin of victory over Kerry, statewide, was 118,599 votes.

In Cleveland alone, 63,721 voters, or 24.93% of the electorate, were purged. In 5 of 21 wards, more than 30% of the voters were purged. Subsequent voter registration drives were so successful as to overcome the effect of the purges; there were far more registered voters in every ward in Cleveland in 2004 than there had been in 2000. But the fact remains that 63,721 people were purged from the rolls in 2001 and 2002, and many of these did not reregister in 2004, because they did not know they had to.

VOTERS PURGED FROM THE ROLLS IN CLEVELAND

Ward	Number Purged	Not Purged	Before Purges	Percent Purged	Registered Voters 2004
CLEVELAND 01	2850	12090	14940	19.08%	17072
CLEVELAND 02	2559	10095	12654	20.22%	15352
CLEVELAND 03	3496	9988	13484	25.93%	16258
CLEVELAND 04	3383	9387	12770	26.49%	15218
CLEVELAND 05	3694	8602	12296	30.04%	15762
CLEVELAND 06	4569	9323	13892	32.89%	16117
CLEVELAND 07	4133	9537	13670	30.23%	16705
CLEVELAND 08	3491	9152	12643	27.61%	15602
CLEVELAND 09	3456	8655	12111	28.54%	15192

Document 4.14—Continued

CLEVELAND 10	2595	9572	12167	21.33%	15641
CLEVELAND 11	1884	10220	12104	15.57%	15528
CLEVELAND 12	1876	7773	9649	19.44%	12537
CLEVELAND 13	3566	10493	14059	25.36%	19541
CLEVELAND 14	4352	8251	12603	34.53%	14174
CLEVELAND 15	2934	9141	12075	24.30%	13831
CLEVELAND 16	2912	10123	13035	22.34%	14221
CLEVELAND 17	3524	7147	10671	33.02%	13143
CLEVELAND 18	3533	8645	12178	29.01%	14651
CLEVELAND 19	3158	9024	12182	25.92%	14013
CLEVELAND 20	3021	10286	13307	22.70%	14547
CLEVELAND 21	1893	13352	15245	12.42%	17505
TOTAL	63721	191832	255553	24.93%	323202

The significance of these purges cannot be overstated. Kerry won Cleveland with 83.36% of the vote. His margin of victory was 113,145 votes. For every six persons unable to vote for having been purged from the rolls, four votes were shaved from Kerry's margin of victory.

The percent of voters purged should be inversely related to the percent turnout in preceding elections. The best indicator is the presidential election, because it always draws the highest turnout. Because the number of registered voters in the 2000 general election was not the same as when the purges took place, no direct calculation can be made of what percentage of inactive voters were actually purged. A more meaningful comparison has been devised by Troy Seman. He has divided the percentage of voters purged in 2001 and 2002 by the percentage of registered voters not voting in 2000, resulting in a "purge ratio."

COMPARISON OF PERCENTAGES, CLEVELAND

Ward	Percent Purged	Percent Turnout	Percent Gore	Purge Ratio
CLEVELAND 09	28.54%	61.45%	94.03%	74.04%
CLEVELAND 06	32.89%	54.03%	88.18%	71.55%
CLEVELAND 05	30.04%	57.76%	96.24%	71.12%
CLEVELAND 04	26.49%	61.86%	92.66%	69.45%
CLEVELAND 07	30.23%	54.87%	94.06%	66.98%
CLEVELAND 08	27.61%	58.29%	95.63%	66.19%
CLEVELAND 17	33.02%	48.97%	71.35%	64.71%
CLEVELAND 03	25.93%	59.24%	97.00%	63.61%
CLEVELAND 19	25.92%	59.19%	68.02%	63.52%
CLEVELAND 14	34.53%	44.17%	72.85%	61.85%
CLEVELAND 18	29.01%	52.96%	69.66%	61.68%
CLEVELAND 15	24.30%	57.91%	64.27%	57.73%
CLEVELAND 20	22.70%	60.08%	64.26%	56.86%
CLEVELAND 10	21.33%	61.97%	95.15%	56.09%
CLEVELAND 16	22.34%	59.83%	58.54%	55.61%
CLEVELAND 01	19.08%	62.40%	97.16%	50.75%
CLEVELAND 02	20.00%	60.00%	94.01%	50.09%
CLEVELAND 13	25.36%	46.86%	73.23%	47.72%
CLEVELAND 11	15.57%	60.56%	75.51%	39.47%
CLEVELAND 12	19.44%	50.67%	70.74%	39.41%
CLEVELAND 21	12.42%	64.22%	55.95%	34.71%

Document 4.14—Continued

It may be readily seen that the purge ratio in Cleveland is completely unrelated to the percent turnout in 2000. To the contrary, there is a much stronger relationship between the purge ratio and the percent of the vote won by Al Gore in the 2000 election. This suggests strongly that the most heavily Democratic wards in Cleveland were targeted for selective purging, which would be a violation of the Voting Rights Act.

Simply stated, 7 of the 10 wards in which Gore received his highest percentage of the vote were among the 8 wards with the highest purge ratio. 10 of the 11 wards in which Bush received his highest percentage of the vote were among the 14 wards with the lowest purge ratio. Most telling of all is Ward 21, where Gore received only 55.95% of the vote (64.26% in Ward 20 being his second-worst showing). The purge ratio in Ward 21 was only 34.71%.

By contrast, there were 13 entire towns, and 2 wards in Strongsville, where the percentage of voters purged was less than that of any ward in Cleveland. Bush defeated Gore in most of these places. The purge ratio was less than that of any ward in Cleveland (other than Ward 21) in all of them.

COMPARISON OF PERCENTAGES, OUTSIDE OF CLEVELAND

Ward	Percent Purged	Percent Turnout	Percent Gore	Purge Ratio
BAY VILLAGE	11.82%	68.66%	37.16%	37.71%
INDEPENDENCE	11.79%	67.62%	42.58%	36.41%
LYNDHURST	11.77%	67.51%	51.92%	36.22%
BEACHWOOD	11.62%	62.04%	82.52%	30.61%
BRECKSVILLE	11.19%	68.46%	34.86%	35.48%
WALTON HILLS	10.86%	72.35%	49.37%	39.28%
PEPPER PIKE	10.57%	67.85%	56.14%	32.88%
BROOKLYN HEIGHTS VIL	9.88%	66.52%	51.46%	29.51%
CUYAHOGA HEIGHTS	5.22%	60.76%	55.52%	13.30%
GATES MILLS	7.66%	75.80%	28.67%	31.66%
HIGHLAND HEIGHTS	9.16%	67.98%	43.90%	28.60%
ORANGE	7.01%	70.78%	68.12%	23.99%
STRONGSVILLE 03	6.36%	69.97%	41.48%	21.18%
STRONGSVILLE 04	6.04%	69.88%	41.22%	20.05%
VALLEY VIEW	7.98%	65.89%	47.97%	23.40%

It was not easy to put these numbers together. The numbers of purged voters were listed precinct by precinct, but the names of the precincts were abbreviated, and thus appeared in a different alphabetical order than in the records for the 2000 election. The Cuyahoga County Board of Elections never prepared for public consumption a table showing registered voters, ballots cast, and percent turnout, at the precinct level, for the 2000 election. The number of ballots cast is reported along with the presidential vote totals in the precinct canvass records. The number of registered voters, precinct by precinct, was provided by the Board of Elections after a diligent three-day search by three information specialists. The precinct boundaries have changed since the 2000 election, making comparisons with 2004 data at the precinct level impossible. The percentage of the vote received by Gore was calculated by hand, which proved the simplest method because there were seven candidates on the ballot in 2000, and sum total of votes

Document 4.14—Continued

counted for president were needed for the denominators. After entering these data into a table, we were able to calculate the percent turnout for each ward and town. The task of assembling the data was tedious and time-consuming. But one would expect that Robert T. Bennett, Chairman of the Cuyahoga County Board of Elections, who has been State Chairman of the Republican Party since 1988, would have had access to data on the percentage of the vote received by Gore in each precinct.

Because the data on purged voters are available at the precinct level, in a format readily converted to a spreadsheet, we were able to calculate, precinct by precinct, the percentage of voters purged.

There are 1,436 precincts in Cuyahoga County. In 151 (10.5%) of the precincts, more than 30% of the registered voters were purged from the rolls. Of these 151 precincts, 114 (75.5%) were in Cleveland. Another 8 were in East Cleveland, where Gore received 96.53% of the vote. In Cleveland precinct 6-C, 341 of 605 registered voters, or 56.36%, were purged from the rolls. And yet, in November 2004, this same precinct had an official turnout of only 7.85%, the lowest of any precinct in Cuyahoga County. In the 2000 election, voter turnout was 59.82% for Precinct 6-C, and 54.03% for the entire ward, which makes it almost impossible for this purge to be legitimate.

By contrast, in 133 (9.26%) of the 1,436 precincts in Cuyahoga County, less than 10% of the voters were purged from the rolls. Of these 133 precincts, only 14 were in Cleveland, and 8 of these were in Ward 21, where Gore received only 55.95% of the vote, his worst showing of any ward in Cleveland. In Strongsville Precinct 4-C, where only 19 of 779 registered voters, or 2.44%, were purged from the rolls, the voter turnout was 74.56% in 2000, which works out to a purge ratio of 9.6%.

The upshot of all this would be its effect upon the 2004 election. In most places, the percent turnout increased dramatically compared to the 2000 election. One would expect the percent turnout in Cleveland to have increased, given the deflated denominator caused by the purging of 63,721 voters from the rolls, and given the statewide and countywide trends, which showed increases of 8.11% and 10.17%, respectively, in voter turnout, compared to the 2000 election. And yet, somehow, even with the massive purges of the voter rolls, voter turnout in Cleveland reportedly decreased from 57.43% in 2000 to 53.27% in 2004.

COMPARISON OF PERCENT TURNOUT, 2000 AND 2004

	2000	2004
City of Cleveland	57.43%	53.27%
Cuyahoga County	58.07%	68.24%
State of Ohio	63.65%	71.76%

Presented below are the turnout percentages for each ward in Cleveland, taken from the Official Precinct Canvass Results for Cuyahoga County in 2004, as posted on the Cuyahoga County Board of Elections website at

http://boe.cuyahogacounty.us/results/history/2004/110204 GE Canvass.txt

They are compared with the turnout percentages for 2000 as derived in this paper and listed in the second table.

Document 4.14—Continued

COMPARISON OF TURNOUT, BY WARDS

	2000	2004
CLEVELAND WARD 1	62.40%	62.22%
CLEVELAND WARD 2	59.60%	57.48%
CLEVELAND WARD 3	59.24%	56.53%
CLEVELAND WARD 4	61.86%	55.15%
CLEVELAND WARD 5	57.76%	45.46%
CLEVELAND WARD 6	54.03%	48.74%
CLEVELAND WARD 7	54.87%	47.49%
CLEVELAND WARD 8	58.29%	53.01%
CLEVELAND WARD 9	61.45%	55.31%
CLEVELAND WARD 10	61.97%	54.44%
CLEVELAND WARD 11	60.56%	55.47%
CLEVELAND WARD 12	50.67%	47.67%
CLEVELAND WARD 13	46.86%	41.69%
CLEVELAND WARD 14	44.17%	41.15%
CLEVELAND WARD 15	57.91%	56.73%
CLEVELAND WARD 16	59.83%	62.67%
CLEVELAND WARD 17	48.97%	44.90%
CLEVELAND WARD 18	52.96%	52.52%
CLEVELAND WARD 19	59.19%	56.50%
CLEVELAND WARD 20	60.08%	61.17%
CLEVELAND WARD 21	64.22%	62.34%
CLEVELAND CITY	57.43%	53.27%

We have been suspicious of the reported turnout in Cleveland ever since the unofficial results showed precincts with turnout of 7.10%, 13.05%, 19.60%, 21.01%, 21.80%, 24.72%, 28.83%, 28.97%, and 29.25%. These numbers were reported in my paper "Stealing Votes in Cleveland," presented under oath to the Ohio Supreme Court. These numbers are not credible. Not in the 2004 presidential election, which voters of both parties regarded as the most important election of their lifetimes.

Document 4.15

AFFIDAVIT

I, Werner Lange, resident at 510 Superior Street in Newton Falls, Trumbull County, Ohio, do swear and affirm the following:

1. I hold a PhD in the social sciences as well as a Doctor of Ministry, and am an ordained Minister of Word and Sacrament;

2. that during the week of November 8 and again on November 16, I went to the Trumbull County Board of Elections and requested to inspect the poll books. On both occasions I was refused access to the poll books. On November 16, I was informed that the Ohio Secretary of State, Kenneth Blackwell, ordered all 88 county Boards of Elections to refuse public access to precinct poll books until after certification of the Ohio vote.

3. Upon being refused access to public documents I filed a Complaint in the Trumbull County Court of Common Pleas which charged the Trumbull County Board of Elections with violation of Ohio statutes mandating public access to poll books. The case was assigned to Judge Peter Kontos, who, to date, has not even set a hearing date in this crucial matter.

4. After the Trumbull County vote was certified on or about November 29, I again went to the Trumbull County Board of Elections on November 30 and once again requested permission to view the poll books of select precincts. This time the request was granted, and I was able to discover discrepancies between the certified absentee vote and the number of absentee voters identified in precinct poll books.

5. I returned to the Trumbull County Board of Elections on December 6, and spent most of the office hours inspecting 106 precinct poll books of Trumbull County. The detailed results of that research are being provided the court along with this affidavit.

6. I was informed at the Board of Elections that all absentee voters are identified as such in the signature box of the poll books of the precincts in which they are registered. I was told that the identity of those voting on Saturday or Monday at the Trumbull County Board of Election prior to the General Election was shared with poll workers who then entered "absentee voter" or something similar into the signature box next to the absentee registered voter's name in the precinct poll book. Hence, the precinct poll books are to contain all the names of the absentee voters.

7. There are 580 more absentee votes certified in these 106 precincts than there are absentee voters identified as such in the poll books of these 106 precincts. This discrepancy of an average of more than 5 absentee votes than absentee voters per precinct remains unexplained. If this rate is consistent statewide, then there were some 62,513 absentee votes certified in the State of Ohio than there were absentee voters identified in the precinct poll books.

TO THIS I SWEAR AND AFFIRM,

_____   December 13, 2004
Werner Lange   Date

Notary Public: Kathleen M. Mowrer
My Commission Expires
12-2-09

Document 4.16

Affidavit by Victoria Parks, November 13, 2004.

"On Nov. 12, 2004, I walked into the Pickaway County Ohio Board of Elections without prejudice or preference and requested to look at the polling books of 53 precincts in Pickaway County. I asked for the Deputy Director, who referred me immediately to the Pickaway County BOE Director. She asked my name. I gave her my first name. Initially she seemed agitated and seemed reluctant to give me permission to see these poll books. However, she relented and showed me to a room where she, in a very agitated manner, plunked what I assumed were the 53 Pickaway County precinct poll books down on the table in front of me.

"The Director left the room and I began my task of reading the vote tallies for each precinct. I began with Circleville 1-A. I noticed immediately that these books contained only the printed name and addresses of everyone who voted in the precinct according to the poll book Circleville 1-A. The poll book DID NOT contain the signatures on file OR the signature required to be given before being given the Authority to Vote slip to voters of this precinct. Furthermore, these names appeared to have been transcribed by the poll worker themselves.

"I turned to a younger office worker still in the room with me and mentioned that the poll book in question contained no signatures and asked if she had them available. She replied, and I paraphrase, "I have seen them. They are here somewhere." She then appeared to look for them in a half-hearted manner. I looked for the total in the Circleville 1-A and was about to record Circleville 1-A's 515 votes in my notes, when the Director burst back in the room, snatching the poll books, all of them, off the table before me.

"She declared at that moment that, "I have been on the phone with the Secretary of State and YOU ARE NOT ALLOWED TO SEE THESE BOOKS."

"I then asked her, "Do you know that what you are doing is against the law?"

"She replied tersely, "That is what the Secretary of State said."

"I immediately left the Board of Elections after having spent not more than five minutes at the Pickaway County Ohio Board of Elections.

"I question whether Secretary of State Kenneth Blackwell knows he was breaking the law by demanding the Director of the Pickaway County Board of Elections deny me access to the poll books. She effectively denied me my civil right to examine public record. That Kenneth Blackwell chooses to ignore the Open Book, or Sunshine Laws, is rather incredible."

Document 4.17

From: JoshButler@aol.com
Subject: Vote Switching incident in Mahoning County
To: Arnebeck@aol.com, truth@freepress.org

Dear Sirs:

I recently received an email from Werner Lange regarding a vote switching incident that I witnessed while I was serving as a democratic challenger. Werner Lange stated that he thought I should submit an affidavit to you, however, I am unaware of the format that is needed. I have attached the email that I sent to Cam Kerry regarding this incident. If this is not in the proper format please inform me of the format needed and I will submit it.

Thank you,

Josh Butler

EMAIL TO CAM KERRY -

I was an appointed challenger for the Democrats in Mahoning County (Youngstown) Ohio. I was assigned to precinct 6-A (inner city). All day I was aware of problems with voting machines.

In mid-afternoon of election day, the Presiding Poll Judge for precinct 6-A asked to speak to me. She had minutes earlier voted her own ballot in precinct 6-F which was located at the same polling place as 6-A.

Presiding Poll Judge (Karen M.) stated to me that she cast her personal vote for Kerry but the machine indicated that she voted for Bush.

She asked me to report this. This I did, after conferring with the Democratic Challenger for precinct 6-F. I called the hotline twice: First I left a message, then I spoke to someone, explained the problem and gave him the machine's serial number.

I subsequently (Thursday, two days later) reported this situation to Democratic headquarters. They arranged a conference call (Friday, November 5th) with Democratic attorney (Bob Clyde) in Columbus.

I never heard further from anyone. I am a credible witness. The Presiding Poll Judge is a credible witness, as is the Democratic Challenger for Precinct 6-F.

There were many problems at the poll that day. The situation herein related deserves special note.

I am Joseph G. (Josh) Butler. Joshbutler@aol.com. Cell: 330 506-6400

Document 4.18

Zych, Thomas F.-WI		0	0.00%
Precincts Reporting: 48.08%		**8,014**	
Lorain			
Kerry, John F.	Democratic	29,651	55.16%
Bush, George W.	Republican	23,878	44.42%
Badnarik, Michael		133	0.25%
Peroutka, Michael Anthony		95	0.18%
Cobb, David Keith-WI		0	0.00%
Duncan, Richard A.-WI		0	0.00%
Schriner, Joe -WI		0	0.00%
Parker, John T.-WI		0	0.00%
Harris, James -WI		0	0.00%
Zych, Thomas F.-WI		0	0.00%
Precincts Reporting: 33.89%		**53,757**	
Lucas			
Cobb, David Keith-WI		4,685	70.86%
Bush, George W.	Republican	1,917	28.99%
Badnarik, Michael		5	0.08%
Peroutka, Michael Anthony		5	0.08%
Schriner, Joe -WI		0	0.00%
Parker, John T.-WI		0	0.00%
Kerry, John F.	Democratic	0	0.00%
Duncan, Richard A.-WI		0	0.00%
Harris, James -WI		0	0.00%
Zych, Thomas F.-WI		0	0.00%
Precincts Reporting: 6.06%		**6,612**	
Madison			
Cobb, David Keith-WI		0	0.00%
Schriner, Joe -WI		0	0.00%
Parker, John T.-WI		0	0.00%
Harris, James -WI		0	0.00%
Zych, Thomas F.-WI		0	0.00%
Badnarik, Michael		0	0.00%
Duncan, Richard A.-WI		0	0.00%
Peroutka, Michael Anthony		0	0.00%
Bush, George W.	Republican	0	0.00%
Kerry, John F.	Democratic	0	0.00%
Precincts Reporting: 0.00%		**0**	
Mahoning			
Kerry, John F.	Democratic	69,570	61.79%
Bush, George W.	Republican	42,271	37.54%
Badnarik, Michael		425	0.38%
Peroutka, Michael Anthony		322	0.29%
Cobb, David Keith-WI		0	0.00%
Schriner, Joe -WI		0	0.00%
Zych, Thomas F.-WI		0	0.00%
Precincts Reporting: 48.08%		**8,014**	

Document 4.18—Continued

Guernsey

Bush, George W.	Republican	7,150	55.91%
Kerry, John F.	Democratic	5,561	43.48%
Peroutka, Michael Anthony		44	0.34%
Badnarik, Michael		33	0.26%
Cobb, David Keith-WI		1	0.01%
Schriner, Joe -WI		0	0.00%
Parker, John T.-WI		0	0.00%
Duncan, Richard A.-WI		0	0.00%
Harris, James -WI		0	0.00%
Zych, Thomas F.-WI		0	0.00%
Precincts Reporting: 81.08%		**12,789**	

Hamilton

Cobb, David Keith-WI		39,541	34.62%
Kerry, John F.	Democratic	39,541	34.62%
Bush, George W.	Republican	34,804	30.47%
Badnarik, Michael		186	0.16%
Peroutka, Michael Anthony		138	0.12%
Schriner, Joe -WI		0	0.00%
Parker, John T.-WI		0	0.00%
Duncan, Richard A.-WI		0	0.00%
Harris, James -WI		0	0.00%
Zych, Thomas F.-WI		0	0.00%
Precincts Reporting: 11.25%		**114,210**	

Hancock

Bush, George W.	Republican	22,209	70.94%
Kerry, John F.	Democratic	8,973	28.66%
Peroutka, Michael Anthony		64	0.20%
Badnarik, Michael		61	0.19%
Cobb, David Keith-WI		0	0.00%
Schriner, Joe -WI		0	0.00%
Duncan, Richard A.-WI		0	0.00%
Parker, John T.-WI		0	0.00%
Harris, James -WI		0	0.00%
Zych, Thomas F.-WI		0	0.00%
Precincts Reporting: 90.32%		**31,307**	

Document 4.19.1

HACKING THE VOTE IN MIAMI COUNTY

Richard Hayes Phillips, Ph.D.
December 8, 2004

On Election Night, when 100% of the precincts in Miami County had reported, only 31,620 votes had been counted. George W. Bush was reported to have won Miami County with 20,807 votes (65.80%) to 10,724 votes (33.92%) for John F. Kerry. These numbers did seem low. In 2000 there had been 42,841 ballots cast. Bush had won Miami County with 26,037 votes (60.78%) to 15,584 votes (36.38%) for Al Gore.

Somehow the final total came in later that night at 50,235 votes cast, giving Bush a margin of 16,000 votes, exactly – 33,039 to 17,039. Moreover, as has been widely reported, even with the addition of 18,615 new votes, Bush's percentage was almost unchanged (65.80% to 65.77%), and Kerry's percentage was exactly the same (33.92%). This led some observers to believe that the optical scanner had been programmed to come out that way, to provide the desired 16,000-vote plurality.

Miami County is also noteworthy because of the increase in Bush's point spread. Bush beat Gore by 60.78% to 36.38% in Miami County, a margin of 24.40%, for a plurality 10,453 votes. While Kerry did receive more votes than Gore, his percentage of the vote was much lower. This time, Bush was reported to have won Miami County by a margin of 31.85%. Coupled with an increase in turnout, then reported at 17.26%, Bush increased his margin from 10,453 votes to 16,000, winning 7,002 of 7,394 new voters.

Now the 1,609 provisional ballots have been examined, 1,542 of them have been counted, and the results have been certified. Bush now claims victory in Miami County with 34,005 votes (65.68%) to 17,611 votes (34.01%) for Kerry. Officially there were 51,777 votes counted for president, an increase of 20.86% over the 2000 presidential vote total.

This represents an astonishing increase in voter turnout. The population of Miami County is reported to have grown from 98,868 to 100,230 since the 2000 census, an increase of only 1.38%. The number of registered voters has risen from 66,765 in 2000 to 72,169 in 2004, an increase of 8.09%.

How did the Republicans do it? To answer this question I have compared, on a precinct by precinct basis, the presidential vote totals for 2004 with those of 2000. Since turnout was key to Bush's impressive margin in Miami County, I have organized the data according to voter turnout.

First a disclaimer: When Diane Miley of the Miami County Board of Elections faxed me the election results, she made the following disclaimer on the cover sheet: "Please note that the 11/7/00 turnout report is not included. Our predecessors made a programming error which didn't permit a complete report."

Document 4.19.1—Continued

Therefore, while I can calculate voter turnout for 2004 as total ballots cast divided by the number of registered voters, I cannot do the same for 2000. When comparing turnout in the two elections I can only compare the votes counted for president.

MIAMI COUNTY PRECINCTS WITH HIGHEST TURNOUT, 2004 ELECTION

	Registered Voters	Votes Cast	Percent Turnout	Bush	Kerry	Bush	Gore
CONCORD SOUTH WEST	689	679	98.55	520	157	378	132
CONCORD SOUTH	698	658	94.27	468	182	300	151
TIPP CITY F	622	550	88.42	360	184	249	166
TROY 3-G	848	732	86.32	496	231	184	96
TIPP CITY E	1195	979	81.92	754	221	581	205
TROY 4-F	604	490	81.13	395	94	122	42
MONROE EAST CENTRAL	935	757	80.96	508	247	426	275
TROY 2-D	650	524	80.62	306	216	306	288
PIQUA 5-B	1155	929	80.43	652	273	528	216
MONROE SOUTH EAST	1175	943	80.26	682	252	598	224
MONROE SOUTH	693	555	80.09	379	175	362	167

It is my professional opinion that these numbers are fraudulent, and that this election has been hacked. There simply was not a 98.55% turnout in Concord South West precinct or anywhere else in Ohio. Nor was there a 94.27% turnout in Concord South precinct. I do not believe that Bush won 111 of 129 new voters in Tipp City Precinct F, or 173 of 189 new voters in Tipp City Precinct E, or 273 of 325 new voters in Troy Precinct 4-F, or that voter turnout increased by 194.58% in Troy Precinct 4-F, or that voter turnout increased by 152.78% in Troy Precinct 3-G, or that Bush increased his margin by 110 votes among 54 new voters in Monroe East Central Precinct, or that 72 Democrats who voted in the 2000 election chose not to vote in 2004 in Troy Precinct 2-D while all the Republicans did. To further illustrate my point I have included the other three precincts with 80% turnout, all of which show modest increases for both candidates, as would be expected.

MIAMI COUNTY PRECINCTS WITH LOWEST TURNOUT

	Registered Voters	Votes Cast	Percent Turnout	Bush	Kerry	Bush	Gore
PIQUA 1-B/D	1095	545	49.77	270	270	164	220
PIQUA 3-A	1277	681	53.33	391	282	198	200
PIQUA 1-A	692	387	55.92	193	188	97	126
CONCORD SOUTH EAST	1199	678	56.55	502	171	572	206
TROY 4-A	796	477	59.92	278	194	202	164
TROY 4-B/D	881	520	59.02	256	258	178	211
PIQUA 5-A	757	456	60.24	231	220	175	192
TROY 4-E	711	429	60.34	217	203	148	195

Document 4.19.1—Continued

It is my professional opinion that the reported results for the first four of these precincts are fraudulent also. I do not believe that (excluding third-party candidates in order to make my point clearly), John Kerry ran 7.3% behind Al Gore in Piqua Precinct 1-B/D, 8.35% behind Al Gore in Piqua Precinct 3-A, or 7.2% behind Al Gore in Piqua Precinct 1-A, nor do I believe the reported turnout of 49.77%, 53.33%, and 55.92% in a county said to have averaged 72.23% county wide, nor do I believe that turnout in these precincts, compared to the 2000 election, increased by 34.24%, 66.50%, and 63.25%, respectively, in a county that experienced only a 1.38% increase in population. Nor do I believe the reported turnout of 56.55% in Concord South East Precinct, which is no doubt contiguous to Concord South West and Concord South precincts, with their reported turnouts of 98.55% and 94.27%. I challenge the extremely high reported turnout in the Bush precincts and the very low reported turnout in the Kerry precinct. It is not my experience that Democrats don't like to vote. I am skeptical of the results reported for the next four precincts also, where, in the aggregate, Bush gained 279 votes among 392 new voters, where Kerry ran behind Gore by 3.7%, 4.0%, 3.5%, and 8.5%, respectively.

OTHER MIAMI COUNTY PRECINCTS WITH LARGEST INCREASE IN TURNOUT

	Vote Count 2000	2004	Percent Increase	Bush	Kerry	Bush	Gore
TROY 2-F	192	321	67.19	407	227	282	146
PIQUA 5-C	380	580	52.63	375	205	214	159
TROY 2-E	435	634	45.75	407	227	282	146
BETHEL SOUTH CENTRAL	708	999	41.10	666	327	412	274
TIPP CITY G	536	708	32.09	478	229	332	186
TROY 1-D	538	704	30.86	459	243	344	185
TROY 3-E	515	672	30.49	406	265	296	208
PIQUA 2-B/C	403	523	29.78	278	243	167	219
PIQUA 4-B/C	334	431	29.04	238	193	173	154
WEST MILTON C	557	718	28.90	465	248	351	193
PIQUA 1-C/E	367	472	28.61	261	210	150	197
CONCORD NORTH	283	363	28.27	239	121	197	79
NEWBERRY WEST	478	612	28.03	428	183	337	131
PIQUA 3-D/E	364	464	27.47	273	186	185	166

It is my professional opinion that the reported results for many of these precincts are fraudulent also. I do not believe that voter turnout increased by 67.19% in Troy Precinct 2-F, 52.63% in Piqua Precinct 5-C, 45.75% in Troy Precinct 2-E, and 41.10% in Bethel South Central Precinct, in a county with 1.38% population growth. Nor do I believe that Bush won 254 of 307 new voters in Bethel South Central Precinct, 146 of 189 new voters in Tipp City Precinct G, 111 of 135 new voters in Piqua Precinct 2-B/C, 111 of 124 new voters in Piqua Precinct 1-C/E, or 88 of 108 new voters in Piqua Precinct 3-D/E. The reported results for the other six precincts could well be true, but only if voter turnout really did increase by 28.03% to 30.86%.

Document 4.19.2

None dare call it voter suppression and fraud article correction
by *Roger Kearney*
November 12, 2004

I read your article with considerable interest. I am a Miami County democrat who believes that there was probably considerable fraud in the election. But your article has some incorrect information about the Miami County election results. Your critics will try to use the bad info to repudiate your entire article.

I was in the Miami County Board of Elections most of the evening on November 2. We have a small family company that developed and hosts the website for the Miami County Board of Elections. I always post election results on the website. I was at the Board waiting for the final results. I watched as Steve Quillen, the Board Director, put floppy disks that he had taken from the tabulating computer and put them into the reporting computer. He did this at about 20%, 40%, 60%, 80%, and 100% of the count. Each time he added more votes, he generated a paper report which was duplicated and passed out to reporters waiting in the hall outside. I looked at each of the reports. When the final one came out about midnight, we copied the report file onto my floppy disk. I came home and immediately posted it to the website. The page is still on our website exactly as it was shortly after midnight at http://www.co.miami.oh.us/elections/index.htm . No one has access to this computer but me.

The reason for the confusion is probably due to the fact that absentee ballots were counted during the day on Tuesday and the count was placed in the individual precincts of the absentee voters. As a result each of the reports, even the 20% report said at the top "82 out of 82" (precincts). The report you saw the following morning at 9:00 was probably either the 60% or the 80% report.

If there was fraud in Miami County (and I have no reason to believe that there was any), it had to be in the tabulation, not the reporting. As you can see on the website all of the votes, including the 19,000, were included in the midnight report. They were not reported after 9:00 am the following day.

I'm not sure how clear this is, but feel free to call if you have any additional questions. Keep up the good work!

Roger Kearney
Rhombus Technologies, Ltd.

Document 4.19.3

CERTIFICATE OF EARLY AND ABSENTEE BALLOTING

County: Miami   Election Date: 11/02/2004 Election: PRESIDENTIAL GE

Number by Mail	Reason Given		Number by Personal Appearance	Reason Given
266	1. Outside County		0	1. Emergency Hospital
2,428	2. Student		0	2. Emergency Death
	3. Permanent Absentee		0	3. Emergency Jury Duty
0	Voter Registration		0	4. Nursing Home
0	4. Hospitalized		0	5. Early Voting
0	5. Caretaker		0	6. Other
300	6. Handicapped Voter		0	Total
0	7. Jury Duty			
0	8. Over 65		0	Other Total
0	9. Candidate			
159	10. Election Official			
0	11. Religious Holiday			
7	12. Inmate			
0	13. Military			
2,110	14. Other			
5,270	Total			

TOTAL APPLICATIONS PROCESSED   5,708
TOTAL EARLY/ABSENTEE VOTE   5,071
TOTAL REGISTRATIONS   67,558
OF EARLY/ABSENTEE VOTE:

$$\frac{\text{TOTAL EARLY/ABSENTEE VOTE}}{\text{TOTAL REGISTRATIONS}} \times 100 \quad 7.51\%$$

I, _____, Chairperson of the above election commission
affirm that the information contained on this certificate is true and accurate to
the best of my knowledge.

Date: _____   Signature of Chairperson _____

                               Signature of Registrar-at-Large _____

Precinct	Total Registration	Total Early/ Absentee Vote	Total Election Day	Total Vote
001	628	15	364	379
002	965	28	511	539
003	650	25	434	459
004	813	44	511	555
005	664	50	475	525
006	834	46	590	636
007	1,227	127	606	733
008	787	48	487	535
009	669	29	432	461
010	759	37	531	568
011	595	32	401	433
012	577	32	399	431
013	677	44	418	462
014	1,069	86	831	917
015	739	51	537	588
016	928	143	666	809
017	605	35	399	434
018/ 1	542	22	373	395
018/ 2	2	0	2	2
019	598	56	428	484
020/ 1	742	47	497	544
020/ 2	240	16	151	167
021/ 1	1,045	67	646	713
021/ 2	11	1	10	11
022/ 1	504	55	365	420
022/ 2	41	1	33	34
023	757	50	510	560
024	596	71	447	518
025	752	86	537	623
026	449	58	289	347
027	529	36	334	370
028	844	68	548	616

Document 4.19.3—Continued

Precinct	Total Registration	Total Early/ Absentee Vote	Total Election Day	Total Vote
029	749	56	452	508
030	344	22	206	228
031	818	73	501	574
032	968	82	642	724
033	674	41	433	474
034	759	28	478	506
035	1,264	64	825	889
036	644	23	408	431
037	705	43	533	576
038	792	50	550	600
039	727	44	497	541
040	1,213	86	910	996
041	558	40	391	431
042	1,019	92	636	728
043	915	115	586	701
044	1,323	139	951	1,090
045/ 1	943	79	699	778
045/ 2	11	2	9	11
046/ 1	960	61	680	741
046/ 2	400	17	258	275
047/ 1	884	66	626	692
047/ 2	106	3	83	86
048/ 1	681	62	478	540
048/ 2	7	0	3	3
049/ 1	298	12	200	212
049/ 2	765	47	544	591
050/ 1	437	74	275	349
050/ 2	2	0	2	2
051	584	44	434	478
052	653	55	464	519
053	576	64	416	480
054	1,143	140	812	952
055	666	87	460	547
056	1,188	92	884	976
057/ 1	187	16	115	131
057/ 2	1,017	63	760	823
058	898	55	690	745
059/ 1	401	46	301	347
059/ 2	510	23	351	374
060	1,126	109	837	946
061	648	51	492	543
062/ 1	896	54	675	729
062/ 2	44	7	32	39
062/ 3	42	3	30	33
063	658	24	422	446
064	702	50	492	542
065	907	89	601	690
066	951	41	753	794
067/ 1	370	30	270	300
067/ 2	396	31	288	319
068	777	63	576	639
069/ 1	727	57	531	588
069/ 2	51	0	44	44
069/ 3	19	1	14	15
069/ 4	47	3	33	36
070/ 1	567	44	444	488
070/ 2	24	3	18	21
070/ 3	19	2	14	16
070/ 4	8	0	7	7
071/ 1	1,277	113	874	987
071/ 2	80	2	64	66
072	786	60	579	639
073/ 1	608	55	447	502
073/ 2	40	6	25	31
074/ 1	306	17	224	241
074/ 2	15	0	10	10
074/ 3	501	32	364	396

Document 4.19.3—Continued

Precinct	Total Registration	Total Early/ Absentee Vote	Total Election Day	Total Vote
075/ 1	130	5	92	97
075/ 2	29	1	19	20
075/ 3	558	38	420	458
076/ 1	175	11	124	135
076/ 2	70	5	55	60
076/ 3	430	40	335	375
077	992	52	707	759
078	1,113	97	825	922
079	926	60	651	711
080/ 1	1,031	76	770	846
080/ 2	47	6	39	45
080/ 3	6	1	3	4
081/ 1	627	36	510	546
081/ 2	29	3	21	24
082/ 1	1,149	80	872	952
082/ 2	27	1	21	22
Total	67,558	5,071	46,929	52,000

Document 4.20

Kenneth Nuss
Auglaize County Deputy Director
10601 St. Rt. 219
New Knoxville, Ohio 45871
October 19, 2004

Jake Fashner
Field Representative Supervisor
For Secretary of State J. Kenneth Blackwell

Dear Jake Fashner:

Subject: Formal Complaint: I would like to know why the following inadequacies are allowed in our county.

Specifically, last weekend 10/16/2004 Joe McGinnis was allowed to use our election computer that has all of our counties current ballets on it and is used to compile our election results. He no longer has any connection with the Auglaize county election process since he left ES&S.

Another complaint is that Jean Burklo on December 12th 2003 pulled one of the five part petitions that Judge Frederick D. Pepple filed with us earlier that day. She gave the part petition back to him. Jean Burklo retrieved the candidate's copy of the receipt for the five part petitions, and changed the receipt to read four part petitions filed. She also changed the number of signatures, and returned his copy to him. See attached copy of receipt.

I was hired for the transition to computerized voting. My complaint concerns not getting the proper training for the job in which I was hired. The reason Jean Burklo denies me the training that I was hired for is that the information is proprietary and not released until we sign a contract with ES&S. However, ES&S will work with the Director, Jean Burklo, to Set up and Program each election. I am always given tasks away from the election computer. This fall when ES&S and Jean Burklo programmed the election I was told that I was not needed.

I have asked the Director and the Board repeatedly when I'm going to be trained on Power Profile and the election computer with no results. Power Profile is our voter registration software supplied by ES&S.

I also would like to know why our director would mail out absentee ballots for the November 2nd 2004 election that had the party affiliation of the judge's race on them. Also in the primary why the Marion Local schools levy was left off the ballet this past March. Luckily ES&S was able to reprogram the election and get it to the polls before 8:00 AM election day.

There is also a major lack of communication between the Director and the Deputy Director. I am given assignments with little or no Direction. I have heard the comment just wing it to many times or you should know. When I do get direction from Jean it is quick and incomplete. I feel that I should be given adequate instruction since she is a veteran to the election business. All I want is to be able to accomplish my job efficiently and effectively. I have felt for a long time that Jean Burklo doesn't want me to learn the election Business.

Sincerely,

Kenneth Nuss
Deputy Director Auglaize County

Document 4.21

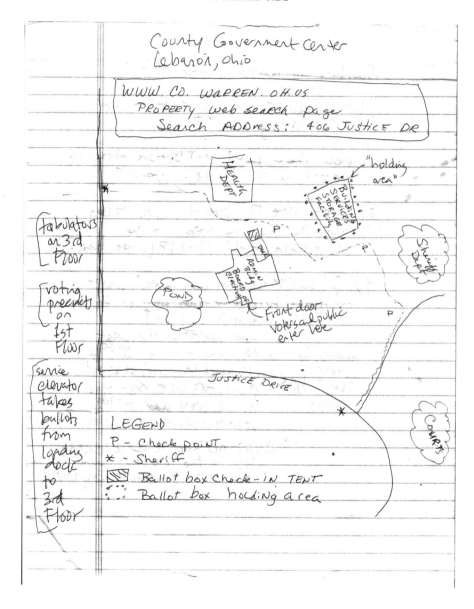

County Government Center
Lebanon, Ohio

WWW. CO. WARREN. OH. US
PROPERTY web search page
Search ADDress: 406 JUSTICE DR

HEALTH DEPT

Building Services Storage Facility

"holding area"

tabulators on 3rd Floor

voting precincts on 1st Floor

service elevator takes ballots from loading dock to 3rd Floor

Sheriff Dept

POND

DMV
Admin Bldg
Board of Elections

Front door
Voters and public
enter here

P

P

JUSTICE DRIVE

COURTS

LEGEND
P - Check point
* - Sheriff
▨ Ballot box check-in TENT
⋯ Ballot box holding area

Document 4.22

LOG CABIN REPUBLICANS IN OHIO

Richard Hayes Phillips, Ph.D.
June 29, 2005, Rewritten

In the 2004 general election, Ohio was one of several states in which
A Constitutional amendment prohibiting gay marriage appeared on the
ballot. This is widely believed to have resulted in an unprecedented
turnout among rural white evangelical Christians, which helped George
W. Bush win the presidential election. In Ohio, the proposition was
known as "Issue One."

To investigate the matter, I prepared a table comparing the vote for
President with the vote on Issue One, county by county. State wide,
Issue One received 61.71% of the vote, whereas Bush, officially, is
reputed to have received 50.81% of the vote, a differential of 10.90%.
Bush ran 469,567 votes (14.10%) behind the "Yes" votes on Issue One,
Kerry ran 675,705 votes (32.71%) ahead of the "No" votes on Issue One.

ISSUE ONE, STATE WIDE TOTALS

Bush	2,859,768	50.81%	Kerry	2,741,167	48.71%
Yes on 1	3,329,335	61.71%	No on 1	2,065,462	38.29%
Differential	-469,567	14.10%	Differential	675,705	32.71%

However, when I looked at the county totals, I discovered that there
were eleven counties in which Bush actually received more votes than
Issue One. In three of these counties (Clermont, Delaware and Warren),
more people actually voted against Issue One than are reported to have
voted for Kerry. That is to say, some people must have voted for gay
marriage and for George W. Bush, in some of the most conservative
counties of Ohio, or else the official results are not true and
correct.

COMPARISON OF VOTE, PRESIDENTIAL AND ISSUE ONE

County	Bush	Yes on 1	Diff.	Kerry	No on 1	Diff.
Clermont	62,949	58,172	4,777	25,887	27,108	-1,221
Delaware	53,143	48,844	4,299	27,048	29,696	-2,648
Warren	68,037	63,431	4,606	26,044	27,960	-1,916

These counties had come to my attention before. Together with Butler
County, they provided Bush with his largest margins of victory in Ohio
and, with it, the presidency.

PRESIDENTIAL RESULTS, BUSH'S BEST COUNTIES

County	Bush	Kerry	Margin
Butler	109,872	56,243	53,629
Warren	68,037	26,044	41,993
Clermont	62,949	25,887	37,062
Delaware	53,143	27,048	26,095
Subtotal	294,001	135,222	158,779
State Wide	2,859,768	2,741,167	118,601

Document 4.22—Continued

Bush outpolled Issue One in Butler County as well. The proposition carried by 109,779 votes to 51,462.

To investigate the matter further, I prepared tables comparing the vote totals for President and for Issue One, for every city, village and township in each of the four counties. Those in which Bush ran far ahead of the "Yes" vote on Issue One, and Kerry ran far behind the "No" vote on Issue One, were singled out for closer examination at the precinct level.

To calculate the number of gay marriage supporters who must have voted for Bush, I subtracted the "No" votes on Issue One from Kerry's total in each precinct where the result was negative. This is an extremely conservative assumption, because it assumes that Bush received the votes of all voters who supported Issue One, and of all who did not vote on Issue One. For each of these who voted for Kerry, and there must have been some, there would have to be yet another gay marriage supporter who voted for Bush.

DELAWARE COUNTY

In at least seven cities and townships in Delaware County, one cannot account for Bush's vote totals unless hundreds of gay marriage supporters also voted for Bush. In these seven cities and townships combined, at least 2960 (18.04%) of 16,411 gay marriage supporters also voted for Bush, or else the official results are not true and correct. The percentage is highest in Dublin City, where at least 373 (35.06%) of 1064 gay marriage supporters also voted for Bush, or else the official results are not true and correct:

DELAWARE COUNTY, COMPARISON OF VOTE, PRESIDENTIAL AND ISSUE ONE

	Bush	Yes	Diff.	Kerry	No	Diff.
Dublin City	2143	1701	442	691	1064	-373
Powell City	3496	2939	557	1530	1968	-438
Westerville City	2754	2451	303	1382	1631	-249
Concord Township	2922	2558	364	1261	1540	-279
Genoa Township	7842	7099	743	3403	3991	-588
Liberty Township	5202	4428	774	2117	2675	-558
Orange Township	6454	5698	756	3067	3542	-475

CLERMONT COUNTY

In Clermont County there are several cities and towns where Bush received far more votes than Issue One. By far the largest of these are Miami Township, Union Township, and Pierce Township.

In Miami Township, Bush ran ahead of the "Yes" votes in all 38 precincts, and Kerry ran behind the "No" votes in 33 of 38 precincts. In seven precincts, at least 600 (25.9% of 2,317) gay marriage supporters voted for Bush, ranging as high as 101 of 306 (33.0%) in Precinct Y, and 122 of 324 (37.7%) in Precinct Z. In the entire

Document 4.22—Continued

township, at least 1,172 gay marriage supporters voted for Bush. Issue One got 67.2% of the vote, while Bush got 73.7% of the vote.

MIAMI TOWNSHIP	BUSH	KERRY	YES	NO		DIFFERENCE
MIAMI TOWNSHIP A	717	281	615	342	102	-61
MIAMI TOWNSHIP B	622	273	508	314	114	-41
MIAMI TOWNSHIP C	942	230	796	335	146	-105
MIAMI TOWNSHIP J	729	229	623	302	106	-73
MIAMI TOWNSHIP X	954	297	792	394	162	-97
MIAMI TOWNSHIP Y	654	205	518	306	136	-101
MIAMI TOWNSHIP Z	734	202	585	324	149	-122

In Union Township, Bush ran ahead of the "Yes" votes in all 40 precincts, and Kerry ran behind the "No" votes in 27 of 40 precincts. In five precincts, at least 329 (23.3% of 1,413) of gay marriage supporters voted for Bush, ranging as high as 76 of 273 (27.8%) in Precinct B1B. In the entire township, at least 609 gay marriage supporters voted for Bush. Issue One got 66.0% of the vote, while Bush got 70.3% of the vote.

UNION TOWNSHIP	BUSH	KERRY	YES	NO		DIFFERENCE
UNION TOWNSHIP A	889	260	771	348	118	-88
UNION TOWNSHIP E	878	305	746	373	132	-68
UNION TOWNSHIP B1B	541	197	421	273	120	-76
UNION TOWNSHIP F1F	527	151	430	193	97	-42
UNION TOWNSHIP P1P	501	171	421	226	80	-55

In Pierce Township, Bush ran ahead of the "Yes" votes and Kerry ran behind the "No" votes in 11 of 12 precincts. In the entire township, at least 278 (14.3% of 1,944) voted for Bush. Issue One got 66.56% of the vote, while Bush got 72.16% of the vote.

BUTLER COUNTY

In Butler County, Bush ran only 93 votes (0.085%) ahead of the "Yes" votes on Issue One, while Kerry ran 4,781 votes (9.3%) ahead of the "No" Votes on Issue One. But even this is inconsistent with the statewide trend, in which Kerry ran 32.71% ahead of the "No" votes, and Bush ran 14.10% behind the "Yes" votes. Some jurisdictions in Butler County show a vote distribution similar to the state wide pattern, for example: Hamilton City, where Kerry ran 30.46% ahead of the "No" votes, and Bush ran 7.88% behind the "Yes" votes; and Middletown City, where Kerry ran 46.51% ahead of the "No" votes, and Bush ran 17.87% behind the "Yes" votes. However, the reverse is true in Liberty Township, West Chester Township, and Oxford City.

In West Chester Township, Bush ran ahead of the "Yes" votes in 41 of 45 precincts, and Kerry ran behind the "No" votes in 38 of 45 precincts. In the entire township, out of 29,926 ballots cast, at least 1,213 (10.00% of 9,000) gay marriage supporters voted for Bush, ranging as high as 68 (28.5% of 239) in Precinct 5LR. Issue One got 67.4% of the vote, while Bush got 71.7% of the vote.

Document 4.22—Continued

In Liberty Township, Bush ran ahead of the "Yes" votes in all 20 precincts, and Kerry ran behind the "No" votes in all 20 precincts. In the entire township, at least 713 (16.8% of 4,232) gay marriage supporters voted for Bush, ranging as high as 33.5% (82 of 245) in Precinct 4DF, and 29.1% (121 of 416) in Precinct 4DI. Issue One got 71.9% of the vote, while Bush got 77.3% of the vote. The numbers from West Chester Township and Liberty Township illustrate perfectly why election investigators must examine the results at the town and precinct levels. At the county level, these numbers are offset by the normal vote distributions in Hamilton City and Middletown City.

Oxford City is home to Miami University. While Bush ran ahead of the "Yes" votes in all 15 precincts, Kerry still won the city, handily. Issue One was defeated with 63.7% of the vote, while Kerry won 56.3% of the vote. In 2000, Al Gore received only 41.2% of the vote in Oxford City. It stands to reason that a proposal to outlaw gay marriage would encounter strong opposition on the campus of a state college, where many young Republicans might be more tolerant on the matter.

WARREN COUNTY

In Warren County, six cities and townships stand out as highly suspect: Clear Creek Township, Deerfield Township, Hamilton Township, Lebanon City, Mason City, and Springboro City. These are the same six cities and townships I singled out in my previous paper, entitled "Election Results in Southwestern Ohio," submitted to the Ohio Supreme Court. I noted that Bush's inflated margin of victory in Warren County came primarily from these six cities and townships (Bush won a plurality of 28,869 votes in 2004, compared to 19,822 votes in 2000), and that all of them reported extraordinary increases in voter registration (from 59,336 in 2000 to 81,355 in 2004, an increase of 37.1%).

WARREN COUNTY, COMPARISON OF VOTE, PRESIDENTIAL AND ISSUE ONE

	Bush	Yes	Diff.	Kerry	No	Diff.
Clear Creek Township	4997	4550	447	1574	1855	-281
Deerfield Township	11319	10059	1260	4529	5343	-814
Hamilton Township	6226	5585	641	2097	2523	-426
Lebanon City	5956	5584	372	2278	2476	-198
Mason City	10858	9742	1116	3805	4462	-657
Springboro City	5985	5278	707	2189	2571	-382

In each of these six jurisdictions, Bush ran well ahead of the "Yes" votes on Issue One, and Kerry ran far behind the "No" votes on Issue One, which is the opposite of the state wide trend exemplified, even in Warren County, in Carlisle City, Franklin City, and Franklin Township.

WARREN COUNTY, COMPARISON OF VOTE, PRESIDENTIAL AND ISSUE ONE

	Bush	Yes	Diff.	Kerry	No	Diff.
Carlisle City	1341	1455	-114	694	503	191
Franklin City	3124	3414	-290	1832	1406	426
Franklin Township	4562	4971	-409	2557	2006	551

Document 4.22—Continued

In Lebanon City, the presidential vote closely resembled the vote on Issue One in 8 of 14 precincts, where only 17 gay marriage supporters are needed in order to explain the vote totals for Bush. And yet, in other precincts in the same city, 58 of 196 (29.6%) of gay marriage supporters voted for Bush in Precinct LEB C SEB AFY, and 79 of 282 (28.0%) voted for Bush in Precinct LEB C SW AAT. City wide, out of 8,372 ballots cast, at least 232 gay marriage supporters voted for Bush. Issue One got 69.3% of the vote, while Bush got 72.3% of the vote.

LEBANON CITY	BUSH	KERRY	YES	NO	DIFFERENCE	
LEB C EA AAJ	313	150	299	151	14	-1
LEB C EB AAK	276	124	255	127	21	-3
LEB C M AAL	347	234	377	185	-30	49
LEB C N AAN	497	164	492	170	5	-6
LEB C NM AAM	460	173	449	180	11	-7
LEB C NWA AAO	479	146	440	159	39	-13
LEB C NWB AAP	544	202	497	233	47	-31
LEB C SE AAR	392	163	384	160	8	3
LEB C SM AAS	289	137	248	165	41	-28
LEB C SW AAT	623	203	538	282	85	-79
LEB C NWC AAQ	443	160	423	160	20	0
LEB C SEA AFG	441	155	400	181	41	-26
LEB C SEB AFY	510	138	444	196	66	-58
LEB C W AFZ	342	129	338	127	4	2

In Springboro City, Bush ran ahead of the "Yes" votes in 12 of 15 precincts, and Kerry ran behind the "No" votes in 11 of 15 precincts. Among these 11 precincts, 67 of 287 (23.3%) of gay marriage supporters voted for Bush in Precinct SPG C SE AFB, 62 of 213 (29.1%) voted for Bush in Precinct SPG C EM AEV, 65 of 224 (29.0%) in Precinct SPG NEA AFN, and 65 of 219 (29.7%) in Precinct SPG C NE AEX. City wide, out of 8,250 ballots cast, at least 441 gay marriage supporters voted for Bush. Issue One got 67.2% of the vote, while Bush got 73.2% of the vote.

SPRINGBORO CITY	BUSH	KERRY	YES	NO	DIFFERENCE	
SPG C EA AES	323	131	290	144	33	-13
SPG C M AEW	236	131	240	110	-4	21
SPG C NWA AEY	286	104	258	123	28	-19
SPG C SW AFC	312	152	323	123	-11	29
SPG C W AFD	290	109	291	101	-1	8
SPG C EB AET	504	151	422	202	82	-51
SPG C NWB AEZ	290	112	259	134	31	-22
SPG C SE AFB	606	220	507	287	99	-67
SPG C EC AEU	298	144	280	143	18	1
SPG C NWC AFA	373	132	327	153	46	-21
SPG C EM AEV	507	151	413	213	94	-62
SPG C NE AEX	516	159	430	224	86	-65
SPG C NEA AFN	537	154	438	219	99	-65
SPG C SEA AFO	470	185	419	208	51	-23
SPG C NEB AFX	437	154	381	187	56	-33

Document 4.22—Continued

In Mason City, Bush ran ahead of the "Yes" votes in all 23 precincts, and Kerry ran behind the "No" votes in all but one precinct. The most egregious example is Precinct MAS C NEA AAY, where 76 of 219 (34.7%) of gay marriage supporters voted for Bush. Issue One got 63.7% of the vote, while Bush got 76.7% of the vote, excluding third parties. City wide, at least 672 (15.1% of 4,462) gay marriage supporters voted for Bush. Issue One got 68.6% of the vote, while Bush got 74.1% of the vote.

MASON CITY	BUSH	KERRY	YES	NO	DIFFERENCE	
MAS C EA AAU	631	211	579	232	52	-21
MAS C EB AAV	368	184	336	193	32	-9
MAS C M AAX	306	133	293	142	13	-9
MAS C NE AAZ	361	107	323	128	38	-21
MAS C SE ABB	585	193	524	234	61	-41
MAS C SM ABC	265	122	251	125	14	-3
MAS C SWA ABE	443	165	418	175	25	-10
MAS C W ABI	621	233	571	258	50	-25
MAS C SWB ABF	363	125	335	137	28	-12
MAS C EC AAW	363	114	335	128	28	-14
MAS C SWC ABG	477	163	445	180	32	-17
MAS C S ABD	490	252	465	237	25	15
MAS C NEA AAY	471	143	385	219	86	-76
MAS C SA ABA	490	196	411	248	79	-52
MAS C WA ABH	499	192	451	221	48	-29
MAS C NW AFE	385	154	345	183	40	-29
MAS C SB AFF	456	162	426	164	30	-2
MAS C WB AFL	754	187	645	260	91	-73
MAS C NWA AFP	591	161	524	211	67	-50
MAS C WC AFS	574	196	483	257	91	-61
MAS C NEB AFU	484	169	437	203	57	-34
MAS C NEC AFV	547	152	471	209	76	-57
MAS C SC AFW	334	91	289	118	45	-27

In Clear Creek Township, Bush ran ahead of the "Yes" votes in 8 of 9 precincts, and Kerry ran behind the "No" votes in the same 8 precincts. In the entire township, at least 313 (16.9% of 1,855) gay marriage supporters voted for Bush, ranging as high as 68 (35.6% of 191) in Precinct CLC T WA ABP, and 93 (33.2% of 280) in Precinct CLC T NM ABM. Issue One got 71.0% of the vote, while Bush got 76.0% of the vote.

CLEAR CREEK TOWNSHIP	BUSH	KERRY	YES	NO	DIFFERENCE	
CLC T EA ABJ	744	237	676	276	68	-39
CLC T EB ABK	633	175	589	210	44	-35
CLC T SA ABN	472	141	435	164	37	-23
CLC T SB ABO	482	178	460	184	22	-6
CLC T WA ABP	447	123	361	191	86	-68
CLC T WB ABQ	507	207	516	175	-9	32
CLC T M ABL	656	194	602	228	54	-34
CLC T NM ABM	650	187	533	280	117	-93
CLC T EC AFK	406	132	378	147	28	-15

Document 4.22—Continued

In Deerfield Township, Bush ran ahead of the "Yes" votes in all 25 precincts, and Kerry ran behind the "No" votes in all but one precinct. In the entire township, at least 818 (15.3% of 5,343) gay marriage supporters voted for Bush, ranging as high as 57 (22.2% of 257) in Precinct DEF T SEC ABZ, 54 (24.0% of 225) in DEF T M ABU, and 68 (28.1% of 242) in DEF T SWC ACG. Issue One got 65.3% of the vote, while Bush got 71.4% of the vote.

DEERFIELD TOWNSHIP	BUSH	KERRY	YES	NO		DIFFERENCE
DEF T KM ABS	488	150	430	199	58	-49
DEF T LP ABT	446	219	412	241	34	-22
DEF T N ABW	738	198	638	267	100	-69
DEF T SEA ABX	426	185	378	218	48	-33
DEF T SM ACD	464	218	416	245	48	-27
DEF T SW ACH	523	200	461	238	62	-38
DEF T SEB ABY	376	175	326	206	50	-31
DEF T SEC ABZ	475	200	400	257	75	-57
DEF T W ACK	482	137	416	182	66	-45
DEF T M ABU	450	171	389	225	61	-54
DEF T NM ABV	345	165	291	197	54	-32
DEF T WM ACJ	555	270	522	274	33	-4
DEF T ZM ABR	345	132	290	171	55	-39
DEF T SMA ACA	319	87	276	123	43	-36
DEF T SWA ACE	484	209	459	219	25	-10
DEF T WMA ACI	420	178	387	201	33	-23
DEF T SMB ACB	448	231	402	266	46	-35
DEF T SWB ACF	377	122	340	147	37	-25
DEF T SMC ACC	285	139	260	152	25	-13
DEF T SWC ACG	612	174	514	242	98	-68
DEF T WMB AFH	466	231	429	237	37	-6
DEF T NMA AFI	348	133	299	169	49	-36
DEF T S AFJ	430	157	402	180	28	-23
DEF T WMC AFM	564	259	489	302	75	-43
DEF T WA AFT	453	189	433	185	20	4

In Hamilton Township, Bush ran ahead of the "Yes" votes in all 10 precincts, and Kerry ran behind the "No" votes in all but one precinct. In the entire township, at least 428 (17.0% of 2,523) gay marriage supporters voted for Bush, ranging as high as 70 of (26.2% of 267) in HAM T S ADI, 69 (27.5% of 251) in HAM T NW ADH, and 82 (33.3% of 246) in Precinct HAM T WB ADK. Issue One got 68.9% of the vote, while Bush got 74.8% of the vote.

HAMILTON TOWNSHIP	BUSH	KERRY	YES	NO		DIFFERENCE
HAM T E ADD	485	188	453	201	32	-13
HAM T NM ADG	578	158	536	194	42	-36
HAM T NW ADH	747	182	676	251	71	-69
HAM T S ADI	662	197	573	267	89	-70
HAM T M ADF	551	193	507	216	44	-23
HAM T WA ADJ	752	302	634	384	118	-82
HAM T WB ADK	665	164	551	246	114	-82
HAM T NMA AFU	774	260	721	293	53	-33
HAM T WC AFR	474	220	442	218	32	2
HAM T MA AGA	538	233	492	253	46	-20

Document 4.22—Continued

CONCLUSION

Actually, I do not really believe that thousands of voters in four Ohio counties, all of them Republican strongholds, went to the polls last November to cast their votes in favor of both gay marriage and George W. Bush.   There may have been some voters who did this, but surely not 3500 voters in Delaware County, 2000 in Clermont County, 2000 in Butler County, and 3000 in Warren County.   There is a small organization of loyal Republicans, known as the "Log Cabin Republicans," who happen to be gay, but they declined to endorse George W. Bush for president in 2004 because of his opposition to civil unions.   And yet, statistically, there is no way to account for the official election results in these four counties without a minimum of 10,500 voters opposing Issue One while supporting George W. Bush, just as there is no way to account for the official election results in three of these same counties without a minimum of 13,500 voters supporting both Ellen Connally and George W. Bush, or without 65% to 80% of new voters choosing Bush over John F. Kerry.   No matter how I look at these election results, the numbers do not add up.   The official, certified results cannot be true and correct.   It is my professional opinion, having exhaustively studied the election results in these counties, that the true vote counts were altered, and that tens of thousands of votes were shifted from Kerry to Bush.

Document 4.23

THE CONNALLY ANOMALY: A POLITICAL ANALYSIS

Richard Hayes Phillips, Ph.D.
July 24, 2006

In several previous papers on the "Connally Anomaly," I have analyzed precinct data, and some of the actual ballots, in order to calculate the absolute minimum number of votes that appear to have been shifted from Kerry to Bush. Now, for the first time, I have analyzed the data for the entire State of Ohio, at the county level, to arrive at a more realistic estimate of the magnitude of the vote shift.

COMPARISON OF PRESIDENTIAL AND CHIEF JUSTICE RACES, 2004

COUNTY	Bush	Kerry	Moyer	Connally
Ashtabula	21,038	24,060	18,240	18,985
Athens	10,847	18,998	9,001	13,150
Belmont	15,589	17,576	13,181	14,169
Cuyahoga	221,600	448,503	205,075	303,995
Erie	18,597	21,421	22,719	11,867
Franklin	237,253	285,801	206,697	179,640
Jefferson	17,185	19,024	15,555	15,147
Lorain	61,203	78,970	55,814	54,863
Lucas	87,160	132,715	80,261	95,157
Mahoning	48,761	83,194	54,217	56,373
Montgomery	138,371	142,997	115,413	108,260
Portage	35,583	40,675	30,691	30,274
Stark	92,215	95,337	94,259	67,183
Summit	118,558	156,587	111,262	103,787
Trumbull	40,977	66,573	44,797	43,614
Statewide	2,859,768	2,741,167	2,358,135	2,073,886
Democratic	1,164,937	1,632,531	1,077,182	1,116,464
Republican	1,694,831	1,108,636	1,280,953	957,422
12 Counties	391,932	173,002	260,707	192,624
61 Counties	1,302,899	935,634	1,020,246	764,798
Ratio	1.277	1.223	.783	.817
C.J. x Ratio	332,934	235,651		
Vote Shift	59,000	62,650		

The 15 counties won by John Kerry are listed in the table above. The other 73 counties were won by George W. Bush. Of these 73 counties, 12 are suspect because Kerry received fewer votes than C. Ellen Connally, as well as some other down-ticket Democratic candidates. In the 12 suspect counties, Connally got 42.49% of the vote, to 57.51% for Chief Justice Thomas J. Moyer. In the other 61 Republican counties, Connally got 42.84% of the vote, to 57.16% for Moyer. There is no significant difference between these two pairs of percentages. The performance of the presidential candidates, however, was strikingly different in the 12 suspect counties where, excluding third-party candidates, Kerry got only 30.62% of the vote, to 69.38%

Document 4.23—Continued

for Bush. In the other 61 Republican counties, excluding third-party candidates, Kerry got 41.80% of the vote, to 58.20% for Bush. Why would Kerry perform so poorly in these 12 counties, when Connally's percentage was comparable to the other 61 Republican counties?

In the 12 suspect counties, the ratio of Bush votes to Moyer votes was 1.503, and the ratio of Kerry votes to Connally votes was only 0.898. In the other 61 Republican counties, the Bush to Moyer ratio was 1.277, and the Kerry to Connally ratio was 1.223. If one multiplies Moyer's totals in the 12 suspect counties by 1.277, and multiplies Connally's totals in the 12 suspect counties by 1.223, the results are 332,934 votes for Bush, about 59,000 fewer than the official results, and 235,651 votes for Kerry, about 62,650 more than the official results. This suggests a vote shift on the order of 60,000 votes from Kerry to Bush, thus affecting the margin by 120,000 votes.

Listed below are the 12 suspect counties where Kerry received fewer votes than Connally. Below these are listed the statewide vote totals and percentages for President and Chief Justice.

COMPARISON OF PRESIDENTIAL AND CHIEF JUSTICE RACES, 2004

County	Bush	Kerry	Moyer	Connally
Auglaize	17,016	5,903	11,795	7,545
Brown	12,647	7,140	8,562	7,498
Butler	109,872	56,243	68,407	61,559
Clermont	62,949	25,887	43,598	30,068
Darke	18,306	7,846	12,762	9,021
Highland	12,211	6,194	8,625	6,298
Mercer	15,650	5,118	9,954	6,919
Miami	33,992	17,606	24,970	17,770
Putnam	14,370	4,392	9,397	4,846
Shelby	16,204	6,534	10,006	8,043
Van Wert	10,678	4,095	7,670	4,587
Warren	68,037	26,044	44,961	28,470
Subtotal	391,932	173,002	260,707	192,624
Statewide	2,859,768	2,741,167	2,358,135	2,073,886
Percentage	50.81%	48.71%	53.21%	46.79%

Document 4.24

BEYOND THE CONNALLY ANOMALY
Excerpted from "Through a Glass Darkly"

Richard Hayes Phillips, Ph.D.
March 16, 2006

A serious question has been raised as to how C. Ellen Connally, a little-known, underfunded, African-American municipal judge from Cleveland, running for Chief Justice of the Ohio Supreme Court against a well-financed incumbent, could have received more votes than John Kerry in 12 counties in Ohio. Not just a larger percentage of the vote. She drew more votes than John Kerry in these counties, in a race for Chief Justice that drew 1,195,882 fewer votes, statewide, than did the presidential race. The matter will be forever known, in the words of Reverend Jesse Jackson, as "The Connally Anomaly."

The 12 counties are: Auglaize, Brown, Butler, Clermont, Darke, Highland, Mercer, Miami, Putnam, Shelby, Van Wert, and Warren.

COMPARISON OF PRESIDENTIAL AND CHIEF JUSTICE RACES, 2004

County	Bush	Kerry	Moyer	Connally
Auglaize	17,016	5,903	11,795	7,545
Brown	12,647	7,140	8,562	7,498
Butler	109,872	56,243	68,407	61,559
Clermont	62,949	25,887	43,598	30,068
Darke	18,306	7,846	12,762	9,021
Highland	12,211	6,194	8,625	6,298
Mercer	15,650	5,118	9,954	6,919
Miami	33,992	17,606	24,970	17,770
Putnam	14,370	4,392	9,397	4,846
Shelby	16,204	6,534	10,006	8,043
Van Wert	10,678	4,095	7,670	4,587
Warren	68,037	26,044	44,961	28,470

By far the largest of these counties are Butler, Clermont, and Warren, all in southwestern Ohio. According to the amended election results, these three counties combined gave to George W. Bush a plurality of 132,684 votes, which is 14,085 votes more than his statewide plurality of 118,599 votes. In other words, these three counties provided to Bush his margin of victory in Ohio. I analyzed these counties on a precinct by precinct basis in my previous paper, "One More Look at Southwestern Ohio," submitted to the Ohio Supreme Court.

http://web.northnet.org/minstrel/connally.htm

The irregularities in the 2004 election reach far beyond the "Connally Anomaly." For example, in Brown County, John Kerry was outpolled not only by Ellen Connally, but by four other Democrats as well:

Document 4.24—Continued

COMPARISON OF BROWN COUNTY RACES, 2004

Office	Republican	Democrat
President of the United States	12,647	7,140
Ohio State Representative	11,675	7,284
County Commissioner	10,922	8,119
County Commissioner	9,548	7,992
Clerk of Courts of Common Pleas	10,248	8,907

These were not locally popular Democrats who might have been expected to run ahead of the Democratic candidate for president. Some of them were sacrificial lambs. Cy Richardson, the Democratic candidate for Ohio State Representative, District 88, lost to Danny Bubp with 37.61% of the vote. Kathy Cooper Gast and Margery Paeltz lost their races for County Commissioner with 42.64% and 42.19% of the vote, respectively.

In Butler County, Dale Richter received only 39.04% of the vote for County Sheriff, in a race that drew 13,115 fewer votes than the presidential race, and still he managed to outpoll John Kerry:

COMPARISON OF BUTLER COUNTY RESULTS, 2004

Office	Republican	Democrat	Others
President of the United States	109,872	56,243	704
County Sheriff	93,694	60,010	0

In Clermont County, the races for County Commissioner and Judge of Common Pleas drew 5,318 fewer votes and 19,508 fewer votes, respectively, than the presidential race, and still the losing Democrats, Peter Strasser and Ronald Mason, outpolled John Kerry:

COMPARISON OF CLERMONT COUNTY RESULTS, 2004

Office	Republican	Democrat	Others
President of the United States	62,946	25,885	243
County Commissioner	54,972	28,789	0
Judge of Common Pleas, Domestic	40,628	28,943	0

In Darke County, David Niley received only 36.98% of the vote for County Commissioner, and still he managed to outpoll John Kerry:

COMPARISON OF DARKE COUNTY RESULTS, 2004

Office	Republican	Democrat	Others
President of the United States	18,302	7,848	161
County Commissioner	12,615	9,337	3,294

Document 4.24—Continued

In Auglaize County, John Kerry ran behind Ellen Connally in 34 of 39 precincts. Connally lost the county with 39.01% of the vote. Kerry ran behind Ben Konop, the Democratic candidate for Congress, in all 39 precincts. Konop lost the district with 41.40% of the vote, winning only 38.80% of the vote in Auglaize County. Kerry also ran behind Kenneth Ludwig, the Democratic candidate for Ohio State Representative, in 12 of 14 precincts. Ludwig lost the district with 32.01% of the vote. Kerry ran behind Theodore Voorhees, Democratic candidate for County Commissioner, in 31 of 39 precincts. Voorhees lost the county with 34.90% of the vote.

COMPARISON OF AUGLAIZE COUNTY RESULTS, 2004

Office	Republican	Democrat	Others
President of the United States	17,016	5,903	115
United States Congress	13,850	8,783	0
County Commissioner	14,224	7,624	0

In Auglaize, Putnam, and Van Wert counties, John Kerry was outpolled not only by Ellen Connally, candidate for Chief Justice, but by the losing candidates in two Associate Justice races as well:

COMPARISON OF PRESIDENTIAL AND ASSOCIATE JUSTICE RESULTS, 2004

County	Bush	Kerry	O'Donnell	O'Neill	Lanzinger	Fuerst
Auglaize	17,016	5,903	11,689	6,602	11,952	6,497
Putnam	14,370	4,392	9,592	4,566	9,406	4,854
Van Wert	10,678	4,095	7,026	4,788	6,333	5,854

This did not happen in any other counties in Ohio. Statewide, these races were competitive, but not as close as the presidential election. And they attracted far fewer voters. There is no credible reason for John Kerry to have received fewer votes than these candidates in any county in the State of Ohio.

Document 4.25.1

**OFFICIAL PRESIDENTIAL BALLOT
GENERAL ELECTION - NOVEMBER 2, 2004
WARREN COUNTY**

	For President: **CANDIDATE REMOVED**	For Vice-President: **CANDIDATE REMOVED** and

For President and Vice-President

To vote for President and Vice-President, punch the hole beside the number for the set of candidates of your choice. Your vote will be counted for each of the candidates for presidential elector whose names have been certified to the Secretary of State.

(Vote not more than ONCE)

For President: **MICHAEL ANTHONY PEROUTKA**	For Vice-President: and **CHUCK BALDWIN** other-party candidate	4➡
For President: **MICHAEL BADNARIK**	For Vice-President: and **RICHARD V. CAMPAGNA** other-party candidate	6➡
For President: **GEORGE W. BUSH**	For Vice-President: and **DICK CHENEY** Republican	8➡
For President: **JOHN F. KERRY**	For Vice-President: and **JOHN EDWARDS** Democratic	10➡

TURN PAGE TO CONTINUE VOTING ➡

Document 4.25.1—Continued

OFFICIAL PRESIDENTIAL BALLOT
GENERAL ELECTION - NOVEMBER 2, 2004
WARREN COUNTY

For President and Vice-President To vote for President and Vice-President, punch the hole beside the number for the set of candidates of your choice. Your vote will be counted for each of the candidates for presidential elector whose names have been certified to the Secretary of State. (Vote not more than ONCE)	For President: **JOHN F. KERRY** and For Vice-President: **JOHN EDWARDS** 2➡ Democratic
	For President: **CANDIDATE REMOVED** and For Vice-President: **CANDIDATE REMOVED**
	For President: **MICHAEL ANTHONY PEROUTKA** and For Vice-President: **CHUCK BALDWIN** 6➡ other-party candidate
	For President: **MICHAEL BADNARIK** and For Vice-President: **RICHARD V. CAMPAGNA** 8➡ other-party candidate
	For President: **GEORGE W. BUSH** and For Vice-President: **DICK CHENEY** 10➡ Republican

A003   **TURN PAGE TO CONTINUE VOTING** ➡

Document 4.25.1—Continued

OFFICIAL PRESIDENTIAL BALLOT
GENERAL ELECTION - NOVEMBER 2, 2004
WARREN COUNTY

	For President: **For Vice-President:** **GEORGE W.** and **DICK** **BUSH** **CHENEY** 2➡ <center>Republican</center>
For President and Vice-President To vote for President and Vice-President, punch the hole beside the number for the set of candidates of your choice. Your vote will be counted for each of the candidates for presidential elector whose names have been certified to the Secretary of State. (Vote not more than ONCE)	**For President:** **For Vice-President:** **JOHN F.** and **JOHN** **KERRY** **EDWARDS** 4➡ <center>Democratic</center>
	For President: For Vice-President: **CANDIDATE** **CANDIDATE** **REMOVED** and **REMOVED** ▸
	For President: For Vice-President: **MICHAEL** and **CHUCK** **ANTHONY** **BALDWIN** 8➡ **PEROUTKA** other-party candidate
	For President: For Vice-President: **MICHAEL** and **RICHARD V.** **BADNARIK** **CAMPAGNA** 10➡ <center>other-party candidate</center>

Document 4.25.1—Continued

OFFICIAL PRESIDENTIAL BALLOT
GENERAL ELECTION - NOVEMBER 2, 2004
WARREN COUNTY

For President and Vice-President

To vote for President and Vice-President, punch the hole beside the number for the set of candidates of your choice. Your vote will be counted for each of the candidates for presidential elector whose names have been certified to the Secretary of State.

(Vote not more than ONCE)

For President:
MICHAEL BADNARIK and For Vice-President: **RICHARD V. CAMPAGNA**   2➡
other-party candidate

For President:
GEORGE W. BUSH and For Vice-President: **DICK CHENEY**   4➡
Republican

For President:
JOHN F. KERRY and For Vice-President: **JOHN EDWARDS**   6➡
Democratic

For President:
CANDIDATE REMOVED and For Vice-President: **CANDIDATE REMOVED**   ▸

For President:
MICHAEL ANTHONY PEROUTKA and For Vice-President: **CHUCK BALDWIN**   10➡
other-party candidate

A001   **TURN PAGE TO CONTINUE VOTING** ➡

Document 4.25.1—Continued

OFFICIAL PRESIDENTIAL BALLOT
GENERAL ELECTION - NOVEMBER 2, 2004
WARREN COUNTY

	For President: MICHAEL ANTHONY PEROUTKA and For Vice-President: CHUCK BALDWIN other-party candidate 2➡
For President and Vice-President	For President: MICHAEL BADNARIK and For Vice-President: RICHARD V. CAMPAGNA other-party candidate 4➡
To vote for President and Vice-President, punch the hole beside the number for the set of candidates of your choice. Your vote will be counted for each of the candidates for presidential elector whose names have been certified to the Secretary of State.	For President: GEORGE W. BUSH and For Vice-President: DICK CHENEY Republican 6➡
(Vote not more than ONCE)	For President: JOHN F. KERRY and For Vice-President: JOHN EDWARDS Democratic 8➡
	For President: CANDIDATE REMOVED and For Vice-President: CANDIDATE REMOVED ▸

TURN PAGE TO CONTINUE VOTING ⟶

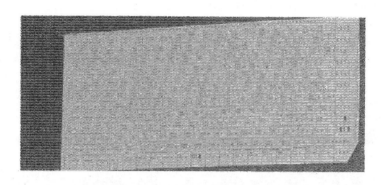

Document 4.25.2

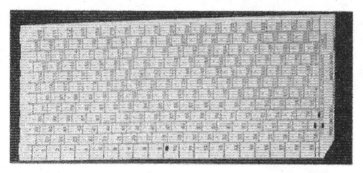

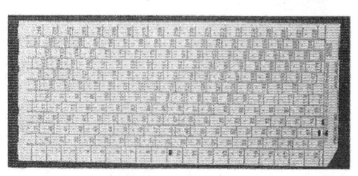

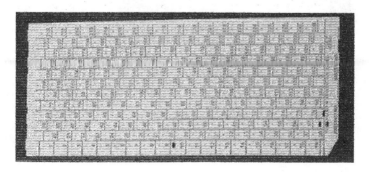

Document 4.25.2—Continued

STUFFING THE BALLOT BOX
WARREN COUNTY   PRECINCT   155
LEBANON CITY, OHIO   (LEB C SEB AFY)

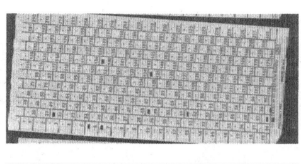

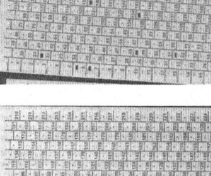

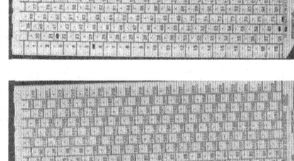

THIS BALLOT CONTAINS NO PUNCHES FOR ANY OFFICE OR BALLOT ISSUE. WHO WOULD STAND IN LINE TO VOTE FOR NOTHING?

THIS BALLOT IS PUNCHED FOR NUMBER 6 ONLY. IN THIS PRECINCT, BUSH WAS IN POSITION NUMBER 6.

THIS BALLOT IS PUNCHED FOR PRESIDENT BUSH AND SENATOR VOINOVICH ONLY. THERE WERE THREE SUCH BALLOTS IN PRECINCT 149.

THIS BALLOT IS PUNCHED FOR NUMBER 7. IT WAS NOT POSSIBLE TO PUNCH THIS NUMBER UNLESS THE BALLOT WAS OUTSIDE THE VOTING MACHINE.

Document 4.25.2—Continued

COLLATERAL DAMAGE TO DEMOCRATIC TICKET
WARREN COUNTY PRECINCT 118
CLEAR CREEK, OHIO (CLC T NM ABM)

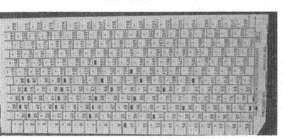

THESE BALLOTS ARE PUNCHED FOR REPUBLICAN CANDIDATES IN EVERY CONTESTED RACE, AND AGAINST ISSUE ONE (#125). THERE ARE 36 SUCH BALLOTS IN THIS PRECINCT.

#10 IS GEORGE W. BUSH FOR PRESIDENT. #21 IS GEORGE VOINOVICH FOR U.S. SENATOR. #26 IS MIKE TURNER FOR U.S. CONGRESS.

#78 IS THOMAS J. MOYER FOR CHIEF JUSTICE. #81 IS JUDITH LANZINGER FOR ASSOCIATE JUSTICE. #89 IS TERRENCE O'DONNELL FOR ASSOCIATE JUSTICE.

IF THESE CARDS WERE SHIFTED FROM AN ODD-NUMBERED PRECINCT, THEN THESE VOTERS WERE GAY-FRIENDLY DEMOCRATS, NOT GAY-FRIENDLY REPUBLICANS.

5

The Recount

Ohio's 2004 presidential recount began December 13, the very day Secretary of State J. Kenneth Blackwell convened and presided over a statehouse session of Republican Electoral College members to cast Ohio's twenty votes and deliver the presidency to George W. Bush. As John Bonifaz, the lead attorney for the minor party candidates and Ohio voters who filed for the recount, said in a Boston speech on January 3, 2005, that juxtaposition was neither ironic nor coincidental.

"We witnessed a crime—a crime against democracy, a crime against the right to vote, a crime against our Constitution," Bonifaz said. "On that day, Ohio Secretary of State J. Kenneth Blackwell presided over a meeting of a group of individuals who claimed to have won the right to serve as presidential electors for the state of Ohio in the Electoral College."

While a recount might or might not have tipped the balance for Kerry, more is at stake than rechecking the accuracy of the vote count. A recount is the accepted mechanism for investigating election results. The actual process of recounting, and the extra scrutiny it demands, is the best tool, short of filing a lawsuit alleging election fraud, for unmasking specific problems with voting results. (Indeed, it is difficult to meet legal standards for alleging fraud without first accessing the ballots, checks of tallies, checks of voter rolls, etc.) The recount is the window that safeguards our democracy and confers legitimacy on those who govern.

Ohio law says election results are not final until after a recount is concluded. But as Bonifaz and others seeking an explanation for what happened in Ohio were to learn, the recount was essentially over before the verification process began. And there would be no clear or full accounting when it was finished, particularly in Republican counties where the certified results suggested Bush backers padded his totals— most visibly evidenced by the thousands of people who ostensibly voted in favor of gay marriage and other down-ballot Democrats, and also for George W. Bush. If anything, the secretary cited the recount and an election challenge filed at Ohio's Supreme Court as reason to lock down 2004's election records except for the publicly announced vote totals. (Those records, for the most part, remain sealed today.)

Blackwell created Ohio's recount rules. The process requires 3 percent of a county's ballots from randomly selected precinct to be hand-counted. If there is no discrepancy with the Election Night results, the remaining 97 percent are counted automatically by the same vote-tabulating machines used in the election. But if the early results do not match the hand count and electronic recalculation, then all county ballots must be hand-counted.

Ohio's 2004 presidential recount did not meet the spirit or letter of the law. Numerous counties did not select precincts randomly. Only one county out of eighty-eight examined all of its ballots, despite discrepancies between the Election Night results and initial hand count. The recount did not examine Ohio's 93,873 uncounted ballots, 77,000 of which were punch cards where voting machines did not detect a presidential vote, according to the *New York Times* on December 14, 2005. Nor did it address ballot security issues, such as ballots found in unlocked warehouses in Greene County days before the recount; or in Lucas County, where observers testified to seeing participants alter ballots so the initial returns would match the 3 percent hand count. Nor did it clarify what happened on Election Night in Warren County, where a homeland security alert was declared—and police barred press from witnessing the vote count. That county's BOE refused requests by recount observers to review absentee and provisional ballots. These and other incidents are described in court filings from the Green and Libertarian Parties and the report by the House Judiciary Committee Democrat staff. (See the December 30, 2004, National Voting Rights Institute memo at http://www.nvri.org/about/ohio_recount.shtml.)

Still, even with these shortcomings, the recount that concluded on December 28 (and only looked at less than 4 percent of Ohio's ballots) had a surprising outcome: it gave John Kerry 17,708 new votes, reducing George W. Bush's Ohio margin of victory from 136,775 votes after November 2 to 118,775 votes. To those seeking the recount and observing its less-than-perfect execution, Kerry's gain suggested a fuller and fairer count would have further reduced Bush's margin.

The recount that did occur was long in coming. Blackwell delayed its start, by taking thirty-four days, until December 6, 2004, to declare the initial results of the November 2 vote. Under Ohio law, any statutorily mandated recount cannot occur until the secretary makes this declaration. By delaying this stage of the process, Blackwell effectively narrowed the window for a meaningful recount. The Democrats, remarkably, strengthened the secretary's hand. The party, despite a promise by Kerry to count every vote, initially did not file for a recount, even though it had the statutory right to do so. Going into Election Day, only the two major parties had legal teams poised for a post-election court fight. When Kerry did not pursue an Ohio recount, Green and Libertarian Party activists convinced their presidential candidates, David Cobb and Michael Badnarik, respectively, to file for a recount and raised the $113,000 filing fee ($10 per precinct) from Internet donations. The activists were more than troubled by the administration of the election and wanted an accounting. Under the state's election law, minor party presidential candidates were entitled to that recount.

As Blackwell ran out the clock before the counting could begin, Bonifaz and the other public-interest lawyers working for the Green and Libertarian Parties sued in federal court in Toledo to expedite the process. But U.S. District Judge James Carr, a Clinton appointee, ruled their candidates were not harmed by Blackwell's timing, because they stood no chance of winning the presidency. Ironically, after Judge Carr's ruling, Kerry's Ohio campaign joined the recount litigation.

Blackwell's decision to convene the Republican presidential electors on the day the actual count began did not occur in a vacuum. On the morning of December 13, Representative John Conyers, D-MI, the House Judiciary Committee's top-ranking Democrat, flew to Ohio with other Democratic committee members to conduct a hearing on the 2004 election's problems. Conyers and eleven other members of Congress asked Blackwell and Republican Governor Robert Taft to postpone Ohio's Electoral College vote—long slated for that day—until after the recount. Taft and Blackwell ignored them. Meanwhile, Republican legislators, Ohio's majority party, would not allow the House Democrats to convene a public hearing on their state's 2004 presidential vote at their statehouse. Instead, the congressional field hearing was hastily convened at Columbus City Hall. This snub was a raw display of power politics and underscored just how partisan Ohio's election was—before, during, and after the 2004 vote.

As Ohio's Republican electors cast their votes for Bush and mingled with the media, and as Conyers convened his hearing, county BOEs began the actual recounting. In perhaps two dozen counties across Ohio—a quarter of the state—the actual recounting was also conducted with little respect for the spirit or letter of the law.

Only Coshocton County conducted a full countywide hand count, even though it was not the only county with a disparity between the November 2 vote and the 3 percent hand count. In several counties, technicians from electronic and punch-card voting machine companies were allowed by BOE officials to pre-select the recounted precincts and reprogram the vote-tabulating software, or in one case, replace a hard drive in a central tabulator, before the recount was conducted, court documents said.

In Coshocton County, more than 1,000 additional votes were "found" between December 6, when Blackwell declared the initial statewide results, and the recount's completion during the last week in December. Curiously, this county's initial vote showed Bush beating Kerry, 9,277 to 6,878, or 57.1 percent to 42.4 percent. But among the 1,080 votes "found" in the recount, Bush received 549 votes, or 50.8 percent, compared to 534 votes, or 49.4 percent, for Kerry—a dramatic tightening of the vote spread, suggesting a full hand count in other Ohio counties would have undercut Bush's margin of victory.

Observers monitoring the recount, mostly from the Green and Democratic Party, said the recount process was often arbitrary. First, many counties did not appear to randomly pick precincts representing 3 percent of the vote, as required. According to court documents, election chiefs in Allen, Clermont, Cuyahoga, Morrow, Hocking, Medina, Vinson, and Summit Counties selected precincts where the total number of voters was closest to 3 percent of the countywide tally or chose precincts where they said there should be the fewest problems. That meant a narrower selection of the county's electorate would be verified.

In Allen County, for example, BOE Director Keith Cunningham said the recount would take far longer if precincts were randomly chosen, so the BOE picked four big precincts, court documents said. In Clermont County, the BOE selected several smaller precincts, according to the Judiciary Democratic Report, because the BOE thought they would see "fewer problems." When Green Party observers protested, they were ignored.

Random means that 3 percent of all voters would have an equal and identical chance of inclusion. But in Hocking County, BOE Director Lisa Schwartze pre-selected the Good Hope precinct because "they had 405 voters" and "3% equates to 404 votes."

In several counties, the full hand count did not ensue, even when the 3 percent recount did not match the prior machine counts, court documents said. In Monroe County, the initial hand count twice failed to match the earlier machine count and hand count. The BOE summoned a repairman from the TRIAD Company, which makes the vote-tabulating computer, and suspended the recount until a new machine could be installed on the next day. When the recount was resumed, the results matched and BOE conducted the rest of the recount by machine, according to court documents.

In Miami County, when this book's authors looked at actual ballots in mid-June 2006, the BOE director, Steve Quillen, presented a new handout acknowledging that the 2004 certified results were wrong, including one precinct that reported a 98.55 percent turnout. Quillen said that local youths helping deliver ballots had given out the wrong ballots to various precincts, creating the inaccuracy. But he said the errors had not affected the overall county result, which implausibly showed that exactly 52,000 people had voted and that Bush's margin was exactly 16,000 votes. Quillen said he was not required by law to resubmit the final counting to the secretary of state. The December 2004 recount did not identify or correct these errors.

In other counties, the recount was essentially privatized. Employees of the computer companies whose proprietary software tabulated the countywide vote totals had access to these computers before the recount. In contrast, observers from the parties that filed for the recount were often not allowed to monitor the hand counts. In Harrison County, a TRIAD Company worker reprogrammed the central tabulator and software prior to the recount, and then ran the numbers for the BOE. In rural Hocking County, Sherole Eaton, deputy director of elections, said in an affidavit that a TRIAD employee replaced a hard drive in the county's central vote tabulator before the recount was conducted. The TRIAD employee showed up unscheduled and did not charge the BOE for his services. Eaton's disclosure and other complaints she made about how that county handled the 2004 vote, including allegations that BOE members destroyed ballots, led to her dismissal in the summer of 2005 by Blackwell. In Fulton and Henry Counties, BOE directors told the judiciary democratic staff that TRIAD reprogrammed their computers by remote dial-up to count only the presidential votes before the recount. These incidents are recited in court filings and the judiciary democratic staff report.

Compromised ballot security and failure to follow vote-counting law and procedure is troubling enough, because it prevents the public from verifying the accuracy of the vote in a presidential election. But privatizing the management and oversight of elections, with concomitant failure to provide audit trails of electronic voting machines or verify vote-counting fraud, threatens the very basis of democratic government. Indeed, when this book's authors examined actual ballots in the spring of 2006—ballots that were not scrutinized during the December 2004 recount—strong evidence of vote-count fraud emerged. But then again, the entire 2004 cycle in Ohio did not approach the standard of a free, fair, or honest election.

Chapter 5 Documents: The Recount

5.1 Why Recount Ohio? Map of Irregularities in Ohio's 2004 Election by VotersUnite.org, p. 299

Immediately following the 2004 presidential election in Ohio, demands arose from various groups for a recount. One of the first to post a demand and the reasons why a recount was necessary was VotersUnite.org. This map points out the most obvious irregularities and targets counties where a recount might easily reveal discrepancies between the recorded vote and the actual tally.

5.2 Affidavit by Sherole Eaton, Former Hocking County BOE Deputy Director, p. 300

Hocking County Board of Elections Deputy Director Sherole Eaton signed an explosive affidavit claiming that a technician from TRIAD Governmental Systems, Inc., showed up unscheduled just prior to the recount and switched out and installed a new hard drive into the BOE's main computer that served as the central tabulator for the election as well as the recount. This is the first page of that affidavit. In the summer of 2005, Eaton was dismissed by Secretary Blackwell after raising more complaints about the 2004 vote.

5.3 Memo by Lisa Schwartze, Hocking County BOE Director, p. 301

The Columbus Institute for Contemporary Journalism obtained an internal memo from Hocking County Board of Elections director Lisa Schwartze to BOE members regarding the recount in her county. The internal memo is revealing since it shows that, for convenience purposes, only one precinct, Good Hope 1, was selected, non-randomly, for recount, instead of a random cross-section of the county. (Ohio law requires a hand count of 3 percent of the county voters, which in the case of Hocking County came out to 404 voters; the Good Hope precinct contained 405 voters.) The memo confirms that a Triad technician had "programmed the computer (for free), and is giving us another run through." Schwartze's primary motivation appears to be avoiding "additional expense" associated with a full hand count of all the county's ballots. She equates a successful recount with avoiding a countywide hand count, not ensuring an accurate record of the vote. The memo also confirms no media will be present.

5.4 Affidavit by Gwen Glowaski, Witness at the Greene County Recount, pp. 302–303

Gwen Glowaski, a witness present at the recount in Greene County, Ohio, swore in an affidavit that she saw the president of TRIAD Governmental Systems, Brett Rapp, feeding the "ballots into the tabulating machine for the first three percent machine count." Glowaski also claimed that Rapp had heard the "hand recount numbers before he put the ballots into the tabulating machine."

Recount critics charge that private companies, including ones like TRIAD whose executives support the Republican Party through political donations, should not be involved with the recount. Rather, election officials should conduct the recount in the presence of witnesses representing interested candidates and parties. Recount critics also say their confidence is undermined when BOE officials and contractors discuss the results they are seeking before conducting the actual recount.

5.5 Kerry Campaign Attorney Donald McTigue Letter, December 10, 2004, pp. 304–305

Don McTigue, an attorney for the Kerry-Edwards campaign in Ohio, faxed a letter to Ohio Board of Elections directors requesting, among other things, a "scientifically valid random sampling method" for the hand recount of 3 percent of the ballots. McTigue's letter also requested that "the programming and calibration of the tabulating system, scanners and electronic voting machines [be] verified by independent experts." Though Kerry's campaign joined the recount effort late, the letter clearly indicates eleven areas of concern regarding the counting and recounting of votes in Ohio, which contrasts with standards used by BOE officials in many Ohio counties.

5.6 Estimated Vote Count in Ohio, pp. 306–313

The following table contains conservative estimates of the shifts in the vote margins between George W. Bush and John F. Kerry due to error, neglect, voter suppression, or vote-count fraud. These estimates show at least 127,000 votes taken from John Kerry, a sum that would have changed the outcome of the 2004 presidential election. Our analysis details what happened across Ohio, and describes our methodology and sources. The final page of this document describes why these calculations are very conservative, and notes areas of inquiry—affecting vote totals—that are ongoing and not included in our totals.

Most are based upon precinct-by-precinct analysis by Richard Hayes Phillips, Ph.D., of the unofficial and/or official election results in every Ohio county for which precinct canvass records were made available (9,300 out of 11,300 precincts) as of June 2006. (Phillips's analyses can be found at www.FreePress.org.) Other sources include "Preserving Democracy: What Went Wrong in Ohio," the January 2005 report by the Democratic staff of the House Judiciary Committee, and investigations by FreePress.org, the Columbus Institute of Contemporary Journalism (CICJ), and the authors' analysis, based on the available public record up to eighteen months after the 2004 election.

5.7 Ballots to Be Destroyed on September 3, 2006, p. 314

This photograph, taken by Ron Baiman in late July 2006 in Darke County, shows 2004 ballots that are to be destroyed on or after September 3, 2006. Whether the ballots will be destroyed is an open question as legal efforts to preserve the ballots were still under way in late summer 2006.

Document 5.1

Why Recount Ohio?

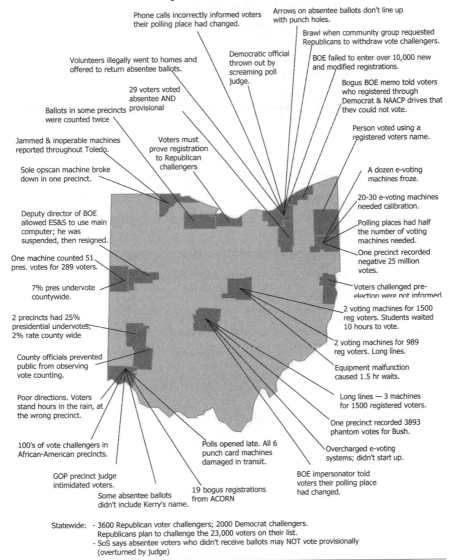

Phone calls incorrectly informed voters their polling place had changed.

Arrows on absentee ballots don't line up with punch holes.

Brawl when community group requested Republicans to withdraw vote challengers.

Volunteers illegally went to homes and offered to return absentee ballots.

Democratic official thrown out by screaming poll judge.

BOE failed to enter over 10,000 new and modified registrations.

29 voters voted absentee AND provisional

Bogus BOE memo told voters who registered through Democrat & NAACP drives that they could not vote.

Ballots in some precincts were counted twice

Person voted using a registered voters name.

Jammed & inoperable machines reported throughout Toledo.

Voters must prove registration to Republican challengers

Sole opscan machine broke down in one precinct.

A dozen e-voting machines froze.

20-30 e-voting machines needed calibration.

Deputy director of BOE allowed ES&S to use main computer; he was suspended, then resigned.

Polling places had half the number of voting machines needed.

One machine counted 51 pres. votes for 289 voters.

One precinct recorded negative 25 million votes.

7% pres undervote countywide.

Voters challenged pre-election were not informed.

2 precincts had 25% presidential undervotes, 2% rate county wide

2 voting machines for 1500 reg voters. Students waited 10 hours to vote.

County officials prevented public from observing vote counting.

2 voting machines for 989 reg voters. Long lines.

Equipment malfunction caused 1.5 hr waits.

Poor directions. Voters stand hours in the rain, at the wrong precinct.

Long lines — 3 machines for 1500 registered voters.

One precinct recorded 3893 phantom votes for Bush.

100's of vote challengers in African-American precincts.

Polls opened late. All 6 punch card machines damaged in transit.

Overcharged e-voting systems; didn't start up.

GOP precinct judge intimidated voters.

19 bogus registrations from ACORN

BOE impersonator told voters their polling place had changed.

Some absentee ballots didn't include Kerry's name.

Statewide: - 3600 Republican voter challengers; 2000 Democrat challengers.
             Republicans plan to challenge the 23,000 voters on their list.
           - SoS says absentee voters who didn't receive ballots may NOT vote provisionally
             (overturned by judge)

www.VotersUnite.Org/electionproblems.asp

Document 5.2

AFFIDAVIT
December 13, 2004
Sherole Eaton
Re: General Election 2004, Hocking County – Tri Ad
Dell Computer about 14 years old – No tower

The undersigned, after first being duly cautioned and sworn, states that the following is true based on her own personal knowledge:

1. I am Sherole Eaton, Deputy Director, Hocking County Board of Elections.
2. On Friday, December 10, 2004, Michael from Tri Ad called in the AM to inform us that he would be in our office in the PM on the same day. I asked him why he was visiting us. He said, "to check out your tabulator, computer and that the attorneys will be asking some tricky questions and he wanted to go over some of the questions they may be ask." He also added there would be no charge for this service.
3. He arrived about 12:30 pm. I hung his coat up and it was very heavy. I made a comment about it being so heavy. Michael, Lisa Schwartze, the director, and I chatted for a few minutes.
4. He proceeded to go to the room where our computer and tabulation machine is kept.
5. I followed him into the room.
6. I had my back to him when he turned the computer on. He stated that the computer was not coming up.
7. I did see some commands at the lower left hand of the screen but no menu.
8. He said that he could put a patch on it and fix it.
9. My main concern was – what if this happened when we were ready to do the recount?
10. He proceeded to take the computer apart and call his office to get information to input into our computer.
11. Our computer is fourteen years old and as far as I know it has always worked in the past.
12. I asked him if the older computer, that is in the same room, could be used for the recount. I don't remember exactly what he said but I did relay to him that the computer was old and a spare.
13. At some point he asked if he could take the spare computer apart and I said, "yes".
14. He took both computers apart.
15. I don't remember seeing any tools and he asked Sue Wallace, Clerk, for a screwdriver. She got it for him.
16. At this point I was frustrated about the computer not performing and feared that it wouldn't work for the recount.
17. I called Gerald Robinette, board chairman, to inform him regarding the computer problem and asked him if we could have Tri Ad come to our office to run the program and tabulator for the recount.
18. Gerald talked on the phone with Michael and Michael assured Gerald that he could fix our computer.
19. He worked on the computer until about 3:00PM and then asked me which precinct and the number of the precinct we were going to count. I told him, Good Hope 1, #17.
20. He went back into the tabulation room. Shortly after that he stated that the computer was ready for the recount and told us not to turn the computer off so it would charge up.
21. Before Lisa ran the tests, Michael said to turn the computer off. Lisa said, "I thought you said we weren't to turn it off." He said, "turn it off and right back on and it should come up." It did come up and Lisa ran the tests.
22. Michael gave us instructions on how to explain the rotation and the purpose of the test.
23. No advice was given by Michael on how to handle the attorneys but to have our prosecuting attorney at the recount to answer any of their legal questions.
24. He said not to turn the computer off until after the recount.
25. He advised Lisa and I on how to post a "cheat sheet" on the wall so that only the board members and staff would know about it and what the codes meant so the count would come out perfect and we wouldn't have to do a full hand recount of the county.
26. He left about 5:00PM.
27. My faith in Tri Ad and the Xenia staff has been nothing but good. The realization that this company and staff would do anything to dishonor or disrupt the voting process is distressing to me and hard to believe. I'm being completely objective about the above statements and the reason I'm bringing this forward is to, hopefully, rule out any wrong doing.

Document 5.3

From Lisa Schwartz to BOE members regarding recount of Nov 2004 General Election recount ... ple

3% EQUATES TO 404 VOTES. I RECOMMEND THAT WE HAND COUNT GOOD HOPE 1 BECAUSE THEY HAD 405 VOTERS.

I HAVE INVITED LARRY BEAL HERE TO REPRESENT US IN CASE WE GET ASKED ANY LEGAL QUESTIONS.

SARA FROM SOS WILL BE HERE

MICHAEL FROM TRIAD HAS PROGRAMMED THE COMPUTER (FOR FREE), AND IS GIVING US ANOTHER RUN THROUGH. I WILL BE RUNNING THE TABULATOR TO AVOID THE ADDITIONAL EXPENSE, AND AM CONFIDENT THAT I CAN SUCCESSFULLY HANDLE THIS TASK.

WE CAN HAVE A TEAM OF 4, WHICH MEANS THAT EACH BOARD MEMBER CAN COUNT THE BALLOTS ONCE BEFORE IT RUNS THROUGH THE TABULATOR, INCREASING OUR CHANCE OF SUCCESS, AVOIDING A HAND COUNT FOR ALL PRECINCTS.

ABC NEWS CALLED, THERE IS A POSSIBILITY THEY WILL BE IN OUR COUNTY. THEY CAN ONLY BE PRESENT FOR THE MEETING PART, NOT THE COUNT.

IF AVAILABLE, WE WELCOME YOU TO COME EARLY TO REVIEW PROCEDURES OR HAVE ANY OF YOUR QUESTIONS ANSWERED.

614-263-7078

Document 5.4

I, Gwen Glowaski, declare as follows:

I live at 1640 Spillan Road, Yellow Springs, Ohio 45387. I was born 5/01/1986.

On Wednesday, December 15th, I was present for the full recounting of the ballots in Greene County, from 9:00 in the morning to perhaps 5:00 in the afternoon. Having heard of the incident involving Triad in Hocking County, I watched suspiciously the Triad technician, who I have since been informed is the president of Triad, Brett Rapp, and who was there for the hand recount. He fed the ballots into the tabulating machine for the first three percent machine count. I heard, and I'm sure he heard, the hand recount numbers before he put the ballots into the tabulating machine. Perhaps it was my imagination, but I thought he spent more time at the computer during the first three precinct counts than the other 97% count—this could also have been because he provided individual printouts for those three precincts. However, in my opinion he could easily have heard the hand recount numbers and typed them into the computer as the ballots went through, and affected those numbers so that they matched the hand recount numbers. He could also have initiated a program after those three precincts went through that would affect the recount of the rest of the precincts. Nobody seemed to be watching him carefully who fully understood what he was doing.

On Friday, December 17th, I went to the Greene County Board of Elections to copy down the names and voter registration numbers of voters in the poll books. I was let into the building at 1:45, when the Board Members came back to the building from a Christmas party. I was preparing to sit in the Break Room with the poll books, but the Assistant Director, Llyne McCoy, told me that since they were very busy I should sit in

Document 5.4—Continued

the main room at a computer desk with the books and they could keep an eye on me there. While I was working on the books that they gave me, I sat with my back to the doorways of two offices. I overheard one worker (I didn't catch her name) say that her computer wouldn't start properly—perhaps it wouldn't start. Another worker (I don't know her name either) suggested that if it continued to be a problem, that she should call Triad and get it fixed—either that or someone called "Greg." However, shortly after she restarted her computer again and it started working, and there was no further discussion of the problem. I find this significant because it is evidence that Triad may have regular and casual access to the upstairs computers, which work with voter information. I don't know if that specific computer was linked into the voter information database.

I declare the above to be true under penalty of perjury.

Date: _____   _____

                        Gwen Glowaski

Document 5.5

LAW OFFICES OF DONALD J.
ATTORNEYS AT LAW

3886 NORTH HIGH STREET • COLUMBUS, OHIO 43214
TEL: (614) 263-7000 • FAX: (614) 263-7078 • mctiguelaw@rrohio.com

December 10, 2004

VIA FACSIMILE
(216) 443-6633

Michael Vu, Director
Gwendolyn Dillingham, Deputy Director
Cuyahoga County Board of Elections
2925 Euclid Ave.
Cleveland, OH 44115-2497

Re: Presidential Recount

Dear Director and Deputy Director:

Enclosed please find a copy of a letter personally signed by John Kerry appointing me as his legal counsel with respect to the recount for President and Vice President of the United States, with full authority to act on behalf of him and John Edwards, including appointing witnesses to attend the recount. Also enclosed is a letter personally signed by John Kerry designating witnesses to attend the recount in your county.

On behalf of John Kerry and John Edwards I am making the following requests regarding the conduct of the recount:

1. The selection of precincts for the three percent hand count should be according to a scientifically valid random sampling method. I am aware that you have received a letter from Votewatch regarding this issue with an offer by that organization to provide resources to ensure that the sampling method is valid. We urge you to accept this offer of assistance or otherwise be able to demonstrate that the method employed by the Board to select the precincts for the three percent hand count is scientifically valid.

2. We request that each candidate be given the opportunity to select at least one precinct for a hand count, either as part of or in addition to the three percent hand count.

3. For those counties that use touch screen voting systems, we request that the three percent hand count include a hand count of three percent of the ballot images stored in the each of the redundant memories of the machines selected for the recount and on any paper trail for the machines.

—*Practice Limited to*—
ELECTION, CAMPAIGN FINANCE, & POLITICAL LAW • FIRST AMENDMENT • INITIATIVE & REFERENDUM • GOVERNMENT ETHICS • OPEN MEETINGS & PUBLIC RECORDS

Document 5.5—Continued

4. We request that the Board provide the opportunity for candidates participating in the recount to have the programming and calibration of the tabulating system, scanners, and electronic voting machines verified by independent experts.

5. We request that the test used by the Board to verify the logic and accuracy of the computer tabulating program be performed for each precinct, including any separate absentee precinct. Further, the test should include testing for under and over voted ballots.

6. We request that computer printouts of the recount results include the under and over votes recorded in each precinct.

7. John Kerry and John Edwards hereby request to have their witnesses visually inspect all ballots for which your voting system has not recorded a vote for President and Vice President, i.e. the undervote and overvote ballots. If the Board does not agree to a visual inspection of these ballots, then we hereby request to visually inspect all ballots pursuant to R.C. § 3515.04 and OAG 74-103.

8. We request to inspect envelopes and related paperwork for all uncounted provisional and absentee ballots. This includes documents stating the reason or reasons that a ballot was not counted and the documentation to support the same.

9. In order to verify candidate rotation, we request to inspect the ballot page assemblies of all punch card voting devices and the ballot faces of all touch screen voting machines used at the polls or at the Board's office.

10. For those counties where the names of Nader and Camejo were visible to voters on the ballots, ballot pages or faces of voting machines, i.e. where the names were not covered over with a sticker or blacked out or the ballots were not reprinted without their names, we request to know whether any votes were cast for Nader and Camejo for President and Vice President.

11. We request that absentee ballots which were postmarked by election day, November 2, 2004, and were received by the board no later than November 12, 2004, be counted if the voter did not vote at the polls.

The above requests are in addition to any other requests that may be made by our witnesses.

If you should have any questions, please do not hesitate to contact me.

Very truly yours,

Donald J. McTigue

cc: Daniel J. Hofheimer
    Kerry-Edwards State Counsel, Ohio

Document 5.6

Doc 5.6. SUMMARY OF UNDERCOUNTED KERRY VOTE IN OHIO'S 2004 PRESIDENTIAL ELECTION

Without winning Ohio in 2004, George W. Bush would not have been re-elected as president. Bush was deemed to have won Ohio by 118,775 votes. The following table contains conservative estimates of the net number of votes shifted away from John F. Kerry in Ohio through voter suppression, error, and vote-count fraud – more than enough to have changed the outcome of the national election. As our analysis indicates, Republicans in Ohio, led by Secretary of State J. Kenneth Blackwell, targeted all stages of the election process to create obstacles that hurt, discouraged, discounted, or disqualified Democratic votes while also taking steps to pad the president's totals in GOP strongholds. Different things happened in different counties. The estimates detail what happened in specific Democratic and Republican locales and come from several sources. Most are based upon precinct-by-precinct analysis of the unofficial and/or official election results in every county where such records were made available as of June 2006. Many analyses were commissioned by the authors from statistician Richard Hayes Phillips, Ph.D., and can be found at www.FreePress.org. Other sources include "Preserving Democracy: What Went Wrong in Ohio," the January 2005 report by the Democratic staff of the House Judiciary Committee, and investigations by FreePress.org, the Columbus Institute of Contemporary Journalism (CICJ), and the authors' own analysis as of June 2006.

VOTER SUPPRESSION

Net Kerry Votes Lost: 26,049
Reason: Uncounted regular paper ballots in Ohio
Source: Authors' analysis, "Uncounted votes in Cuyahoga County," "Uncounted Votes in Summit County," Uncounted Votes in Hamilton County,"
"Uncounted Votes in Montgomery County," Richard Hayes Phillips reports, and "Preserving Democracy: What Went Wrong in Ohio," House Judiciary Committee Democratic staff report.

Explanation: According to official results, there are still 128,967 uncounted votes in Ohio. These include 93,873 regular ballots – almost all from Democratic strongholds – that were machine-rejected (76,404 punch-card ballots, 6,402 optical-scan ballots, and 11,067 electronic votes), as well as 35,094 provisional ballots that were disqualified. These all represent people who turned out to vote, stood in line, and cast ballots – only to have voting machines not record their vote. These are not spoiled ballots, but rather ballots that could not be read by the voting machines. With nearly 85 percent of these ballots. Ohio voting on paper ballots (punch cards or optical-scan), voter intent could almost always have been ascertained via a hand count of these ballots. However, Ohio's "recount" examined only 3 percent of the state's ballots by hand, often from precincts pre-selected for an expedient rather than a thorough accounting. Thus, no serious effort was made to understand why 82,806 paper ballots (punch cards and optical scans) were rejected. Indeed, we assume these ballots had votes for president and for other public offices. Statewide, however, there were a small percentage of ballots that did not contain votes for president. In 2004, 1.68 percent of the ballots cast in 2004 had no presidential vote. In 2000, the corresponding figure was 1.97 percent. Using a conservative undervote rate of 2 percent (i.e., assuming that 2 percent of the 82,806 paper ballots really don't have a vote for president on them), the remaining 81,150 could be expected to have a presidential preference. By averaging the returns in the counties where most of these ballots came from, we projected that Kerry would receive 65.1 percent of this vote, compared to 33 percent for Bush. Were Ohio's uncounted ballots examined by hand to determine voter preference, Kerry would see a net gain of at least 26,049 votes.

Net Kerry Votes Lost: 16,778
Reason: Intentional shortage of voting machines in Columbus
Source: "Stealing Votes in Columbus" and "Favoritism in the Suburbs," Richard Hayes Phillips reports

Explanation: In Franklin County, official records of the 2004 election show that the Republican dominated Board of Elections delivered only 2,741 voting machines to precincts by the start of Election Day. Even "by the close of the polls" only 2,798 machines were in use. In order to meet Ohio Law, which mandates one machine per 100-to-125 voters, the county would have required more than 4,300 machines to accommodate Columbus's 548,267 registered voters in 2004, a number the BOE was aware of long before Election Day. The official 2004 records indicate that an additional 68 machines were available in the county, but were not provided to any polling station. A list of yet another 76 voting machines, identified by serial number, indicates clearly that these were intentionally withheld from polling places in inner-city, Democratic-majority precincts in Columbus. Insufficient voting machines was the principal reason for the very long lines at the polls, which caused many people to leave without voting. Citywide precinct results clearly indicate that the shortage of voting machines depressed the turnout (almost no Republican precincts suffered a shortage of machines). In Kerry-majority precincts with ample voting machines, recorded voter turnout was 60 percent or more. However, in Columbus, where Democratic communities suffered a severe shortage of machines, the median Kerry precinct reported 50.78% turnout. Conservatively assuming the actual turnout in Kerry-majority precincts was 60 percent (as it was in comparable Democratic precincts, and as it has traditionally been in Columbus when enough voting machines have been provided to accommodate all voters) the discriminatory allocation of voting machines resulted in a net loss of at least 16,778 votes for Kerry.

Net Kerry Votes Lost: 16,064
Reason: Implausibly low turnout reported in Cleveland
Source: "Stealing Votes in Cleveland," Richard Hayes Phillips report

Explanation: According to the unofficial precinct canvass records for Cuyahoga County, at least 30 precincts in Cleveland experienced inexplicably low voter turnout, including 7.10%, 13.05%, 19.60%, 21.01%, 21.80%, 24.72%, 28.83%, 28.97%, and 29.25%. Seven entire wards reported voter turnout below 50%, even as low as 39.35%. According to the official certified results, voter turnout was only 53.27% city wide. These turnout numbers are not credible and would be historic lows in a year when all observers saw unprecedented lines at the polls. Cleveland is Ohio's largest city. Kerry won all 21 of its wards, with 83.34% of the vote. Thus, a supposed 53.27% voter turnout hurt him immensely. By comparison, voter turnout was 68.65% in Toledo, 66.31% in Cincinnati, 61.39% in Dayton, and 59.79% in Akron. If voter turnout was actually 60% of registered voters – a conservative estimate based upon Cleveland's past turnout rates and on turnout in other major cities of Ohio, Kerry's margin in Cleveland was wrongly reduced by at least 16,064 votes.

Net Kerry Votes Lost: 6,459
Reason: Burglary and targeting of Democratic precincts in Toledo
Source: "Rigging the Vote in Lucas County," Richard Hayes Phillips report

Explanation: The 2004 election in Lucas County was tainted by professional incompetence at the Board of Election and criminal activity. Three weeks before Election Day, the Toledo Blade reported that thieves had broken into the Lucas County Democratic headquarters in Toledo and stolen computers containing e-mails discussing campaign strategy, candidates' schedules, financial information, and phone numbers of party members, candidates, donors, and volunteers, thus affecting the entire get-out-the-vote operation. This information could have been used by Republicans to target Democratic voters. Phillips examined the election incident reports for Toledo, and compared them to the Lucas County precinct canvass records. The 88 precincts with the lowest reported turnout were all Kerry strongholds in Toledo. Thirty-one of these precincts are cited in the incident reports, which describe voting machine shortage, malfunctioning machines, outdated voter registration records, and marking pens that could not be read by optical-scan vote-counting machines –

Document 5.6—Continued

a level of problems that indicates targeted suppression efforts possibly based on the stolen information. If voting in these 10 wards had been free and fair, and a level of turnout was comparable to other wards in Toledo during the 2004 election and historically, Kerry's would have received at least 6,459 additional votes. (The county's election irregularities were so widespread that the entire Board of Election was fired or forced to resign following the election. Moreover, the BOE was chaired by Bernadette Noe, wife of Tom Noe, a key fundraiser for Bush who pleaded guilty in spring 2006 to three felony federal election law violations and is under indictment for $13 million in missing state funds.)

Net Kerry Votes Lost: 4,783 votes
Reason: Voter Purges in Cuyahoga County (Cleveland) and Lucas County (Toledo)
Source: BOE records, authors' analysis, "Purging the Voter Rolls in Cuyahoga County," Richard Hayes Phillips report.

Explanation: One of the most aggressive and significant voter suppression tactics used by Ohio's Republican election administrators was revoking the right to vote of Ohioans in Democratic locales prior to the election. Between the 2000 and 2004 elections, 168,169 voters were purged from the rolls in Cuyahoga County (63,721 in Cleveland and 104,448 in suburbs) and another 28,000 voters were purged in Lucas County in the summer of 2004. Most Ohio counties do not purge voters. However, these voters were purged under the National Voting Rights Act that allows BOEs to remove people who have not voted in the past two federal elections. The law's provisions are meant to clear voter rolls of people who move or die; not target one party's voters. BOEs can either move the voters from active to inactive status, as was the case with 110,000 voters in Hamilton County (Cincinnati), or remove them completely. In these two counties, BOEs chose the more draconian option (voters listed as inactive can show identification to vote; purged voters cannot – even if they demand a provisional ballot it will not be counted). In Cuyahoga County 5,400 provisional ballots were rejected because the voter was declared "not registered" and 2,000 were similarly rejected in Lucas County, according to the BOEs. An analysis by Richard Hayes Phillips found that most of the purged Cleveland voters came from precincts that voted overwhelmingly for Al Gore in 2000.

After the 2000 election in Florida, which experienced similar purging, the US Commission on Civil Rights issued a 2001 report, "Voting Irregularities in Florida During the 2000 Presidential Election" (http://usccr.gov/pubs/vote2000/report/main.htm). This report determined that 14.1% of the voters purged from Florida's rolls were wrongly purged, primarily because of mismatched names. We applied this wrongly purged percentage to the voters purged in Ohio in 2004, to determine that at least 27,660 voters should have remained on the voter rolls. We assume that the 5,400 provisional ballots from Cuyahoga counties that were rejected because voters were "not registered" correspond to wrongly purged voters who turned out to vote and were told they were not on the rolls. (We subtracted this number from the wrongly purged number, so as not to duplicate the Cuyahoga County provisional ballot analysis below). For the remaining 22,260 voters who were wrongly purged, we applied the official reported voter turnout rates in Cleveland (52.27 percent), its suburbs (71.95 percent), and in Lucas County (73.96 percent) to estimate the number of voters who could have been expected to vote in the 2004 election – had they not been wrongly purged. Using the vote splits between the candidates for these regions (in Cleveland, Kerry won 83.36 percent of the vote, compared to 15.78 percent for Bush; in the rest of Cuyahoga County, Kerry had 60.38 percent, compared to 39.18 percent for Bush; and in Lucas County, Kerry had 60.02 percent of the vote, compared to 39.54 percent for Bush, we determined that voter purges in these two counties resulted in a loss to John Kerry of at least 4,783 votes.

Net Kerry Votes Lost: 4,051
Reason: Rejected provisional ballots in Cuyahoga County and Cincinnati
Source: Authors' analysis; House Judiciary Committee Democratic staff report, Greater Cleveland Voter Coalition

Explanation: Provisional ballots were created to help voters whose registration status on Election Day is in question for any reason. Following the election, if a voter is deemed eligible to have voted, his or her provisional vote is to be counted. However in Ohio, the Secretary of State created new rules – barrier – to validating these ballots, and different Ohio counties interpreted these rules differently. (The fact that GOP-majority suburbs did not have large numbers of provisional ballots discounted and Democratic inner-city neighborhoods did, is evidence of partisan targeting.) Perhaps the most egregious rule contrary to the intent of the federal "Help America Vote Act" was the requirement that ballots be rejected if they were not submitted in the voter's correct precinct. (Before Blackwell created this rule, these ballots could be turned in anywhere in the county.) Because some Republican-dominated Boards of Election consolidated Democratic precincts for the fall 2004 election into multi-precinct locations, there were numerous reports of ballots being turned in at the right building but at the *wrong* table – where poll workers accepted the ballots but later disqualified them. In Cuyahoga County, where Cleveland is located and where there were redrawn precinct lines, voter purges and an error-prone, new election-records database, 8,559 provisional ballots were ruled invalid. This includes 2,164 provisional ballots that were turned in at the right precinct location, but wrong table. Kerry won 71.1 percent of the county's valid ballots. If this percentage is applied to the rejected provisional ballots, Kerry would gain 3,650 votes. Likewise, in Hamilton County, where Cincinnati is located, BOE records show that 95.12% of the rejected provisional ballots were from Cincinnati (where only 33.89% of the voters were located, again indicating partisan targeting), and where Kerry received 67.98% of the vote. The House Judiciary Committee Democratic staff reported that 1,100 provisional ballots were turned in at the right precinct location but wrong table in Hamilton County. If the city's results – 67.98% for Kerry and 31.54% for Bush were applied to these ballots – every one of these people turned out and voted; they simply submitted their ballot at the wrong table – Kerry would gain 401 votes. Together, this is a net gain of 4,051 votes for Kerry.

VOTER SUPPRESSION SUBTOTAL: 74,194 votes

VOTE COUNT ERRORS AND FRAUD

Net Swing in Vote Differential: 27,000 Votes Lost
Reason: Improbable voting patterns in southwest Ohio
Source: "Log Cabin Republicans in Ohio," "Beyond the Connally Anomaly," "Stacking the Deck in Warren County," "Warren County Revisited," and "Pick A Card Any Card," Richard Hayes Phillips reports

Explanation: Among indications of vote-count fraud are certified results that defy common sense. In three southwestern counties in Ohio's Bible belt – Warren, Butler, and Clermont Counties – over 10,000 ballots were counted as having votes both *for* gay marriage *and* to re-elect Bush. Additionally, 13,500 ballots were counted as having votes for Ellen Connally – a Democratic, pro-choice, pro-union, liberal African-American state Supreme Court Chief Justice candidate – *and* for Bush (what the Reverend Jesse Jackson calls "the Connally anomaly.") These votes are not credible. The simplest explanation for these results is that, during the counting phase, votes for Kerry were switched to Bush, while the rest of the ballot was left alone (see following paragraph for the logistics of how this might have been accomplished) – creating this apparent contradiction in the certified results. If we conservatively assume the 10,500 votes for gay marriage and Bush were a subset of the 13,500 votes cast for Connally and Bush, these instances of vote-count fraud cost Kerry a minimum of 27,000 votes, as each vote switched to Bush at the counting phase also subtracted a vote from Kerry's total.

Examination of the ballots from these counties in the spring of 2006 (after 18 months of being denied permission to do so) suggested explanations for how these anomalous vote counts might have occurred. In Warren County, the county's ballots were taken to a "secure, non-public" location because of an ostensible "Homeland Security Alert," that the FBI has denied knowledge of and that evidence indicates was pre-planned by local election officials the week before the election. Reporters and election monitors were denied access to the counting process in Warren County on "national security grounds."

Document 5.6—Continued

Also in Warren County, the punch-card ballots did not have precinct identifier codes on them. Because Ohio rotates the order of candidates' names, ballots from one precinct could have been run through counters programmed for another precinct. Thus a vote cast in one precinct for Kerry would be read by vote-scanning machines programmed for a different precinct as a vote for Bush, while other pro-Democratic votes lower down on the ballot - where the order of candidates did not rotate - would remain the same. Examination of ballots in these three counties also found anomalies that indicate ballot-box stuffing: In several precincts, for instance, every one of the final 100-plus votes was for Bush – a statistical impossibility that was nowhere seen on behalf of John Kerry. A suspiciously high proportion of ballots in these counties also registered only one vote – always for Bush, never for Kerry – with no votes for candidates or issues beyond the presidency. (Election monitors are trained to look for this pattern as classic evidence of tampering and vote fraud.)

Net Swing in Vote Differential: 17,560 Votes Lost
Reason: Improbable voting patterns in seven other rural Republican counties
Source: "Election Results in Southwestern Ohio," "One More Look at Southwestern Ohio," "Log Cabin Republicans in Ohio," "Anomalous Precincts in Delaware County," "Through a Glass Darkely," Richard Hayes Phillips reports.

Seven other Republican-majority counties saw improbable results that raise questions of ballot padding or vote-count fraud. In Delaware County, where county officials went to court to try to block a recount, 46 percent more ballots were cast in 2004 than 2000, including 2,864 people who voted for gay marriage and Bush. These 2,864 votes indicate vote shifting and would have cost Kerry 5,728 votes, a doubling effect, as each vote shifted subtracts one vote from Kerry's total while adding one vote to Bush's total. When examining ballots in the county on June 2006, co-author Fitrakis and Phillips also found several precincts where the final 100 or more votes cast on Election Day were all for Bush, a statistically implausible outcome and indication of ballot box stuffing. (Those ballots are not included in this estimate as that investigation is ongoing.) Shelby County reported 81.82 percent voter turnout, the highest in Ohio. According to precinct results, Bush got 3,092 of 3,155 new voters – which is statistical improbable -- and Kerry ran 1,509 votes behind down-ballot candidate Ellen Connally – a highly suspect tally. We believe these votes are fraudulent and reflect the shifting of at least 1,509 votes from Kerry to Bush. This amounts to a swing of the difference between the candidates of 3,018 votes. In Brown County, Kerry ran behind Connally in 22 of 35 precincts, by 643 votes, and 411 people ostensibly voted for Bush and Connally, suggesting at least 411 votes had been shifted from Bush to Kerry, impacting the vote differential by at least 822 votes. In Auglaise County, Bush got 3,083 of 3,142 the new voters, or the equivalent. Kerry ran behind Connally in 34 of 39 precincts, and one cannot account for Bush's totals unless 1,412 people voted for both Connally and Bush – an indication of vote shifting of 2,824 votes. The former BOE Deputy Director, Ken Nuss, a Democrat, resigned on October 21, 2004, alleging that private contractors had improperly been granted access to the county's central tabulator computer, which compiles election results. In Van Wert County, since 2000 there was a decrease in population and voter registration, but an increase in 2004 ballots cast. Kerry ran behind Ellen Connally by 492 votes. During the recount, BOE officials told Green Party observers that the voting machine manufacturer had serviced the machine via a telephone modem. At minimum, we project the Connally votes were shifted to Bush, costing Kerry 984 votes. In Darke County, Kerry ran behind Connally by 1,175 votes and one cannot account for Bush's totals unless 856 people voted for Connally and Bush. The differential impact is at least 1712 votes. In Mercer County, compared to 2000 there was no change in population but nearly a 25 percent increase in voter registration, and a 13.18% increase in ballots cast – another suspect figure that suggests a combination of fraudulent voter registrations and vote counts. The unreliability of the county's election results was illustrated when the county's website reported 51,818 ballots cast and 47,768 ballots counted, when the County had only 40,933 residents and only 31,306 registered voters. And, once more, one cannot account for Bush's results unless 1,236 people voted for the president and Ellen Connally, evidence of vote shifting at the counting stage that cost Kerry 2,472 votes. The total number of votes taken from Kerry by fraudulent vote shifting during the counting stage in these seven counties was at least 17,560 votes.

(Author's note: All of our analyses and estimates have suggested the low end of the spectrum of vote shifting from Kerry to Bush. In a July 2006 report, Phillips looked at the high end of the spectrum in the 12 counties where Kerry received fewer votes than Connally, even though the Ohio chief justice race drew nearly 1.2 million fewer votes statewide than the race for president. (Those 12 counties were: Auglaize; Brown; Butler; Clermont; Darke; Highland; Mercer; Miami; Putnam; Shelby; Van Wert; and Warren.) Phillips projects that as many as 60,000 votes could have been shifted from Kerry to Bush, thus affecting Bush's margin by 120,000 votes. That analysis is included as document 4.24, but is not included in this estimate.)

Net Kerry Votes Lost: 6,000
Reason: Padding the Vote in Republican Strongholds
Source: "Hacking the Vote in Miami County," Richard Hayes Phillips report; CICJ reports; authors' analysis

Explanation: In traditionally Republican Miami County, after 100% of the precincts had reported, another 18,615 votes were inexplicably added to the totals, increasing Bush's margin by almost 6000 votes. The overall percentage of votes for Bush stayed within three-one-hundredths of a percent of the original result, the percentage for Kerry stayed exactly the same, to one-one-hundredth of a percent, and the final margin for Bush increased from 10,083 votes to the even number of 16,000 votes exactly, a highly suspect set of circumstances. The best explanation for this is that a central tabulator (the computer adding up the county totals) was programmed to turn out specific results. Miami County also reported a 20.86% increase in turnout over the 2000 election, very unlikely for a county that had gained only 1.38% in population. For two precincts in the county town of Concord, voter turnout of 98.55% and 94.27% of registered voters was reported – numbers almost impossible to achieve in a rural farm community. Voter turnout was reported to have increased by 194.58% and 152.78% in two precincts in Troy, another town in the county, compared to the 2000 election, and by 30.49% to 67.19% in 10 other precincts. These numbers indicate vote padding and vote-count fraud that added at least 6,000 extra votes to Bush's total.

When co-author Robert Fitrakis and Phillips were allowed to examine Miami County's ballots in June 2006, the BOE director Steve Quillen actually confirmed that the 2004 certified precinct totals were incorrect, as Phillips' analysis had suggested. In one precinct, Troy 3E, for instance, in the years since the election, Quillen had revised downward the number of ballots cast from 661 votes to 228 votes. In fact, none of the certified 2004 results matched the hand count in precincts conducted by Phillips and Fitrakis in June 2006, the first irrefutable proof that central tabulators had been programmed to produce fraudulent results. When asked, Quillen said he had no intention of submitting corrected vote totals to the Secretary of State's office. (None of these errors were discovered during the December 2004 recount.)

Net Kerry Votes Lost: 2,250
Reason: Computer Fraud in Kerry Strongholds
Source: "Default Settings in Mahoning County" report by Richard Hayes Phillips

Explanation: Ohio experienced numerous problems with electronic voting machines on Election Day. In Mahoning County, according to the Board of Elections, 20-to-30 touch-screen voting machines needed to be recalibrated during the voting process because some votes for a candidate were being counted for that candidate's opponent. In Youngstown precinct 2E, for example, voter testimonials claim and Richard Hayes Phillips' statistical analysis confirms that touch screen machines were programmed to default to Bush – meaning that even if a voter touched the button corresponding to John Kerry's name, a vote would be recorded for George Bush instead. (No testimonials at all claimed that voters intending to select Bush had their votes recorded for Kerry instead.) In Youngstown 5G, a Kerry stronghold, 44 so-called undervotes/overvotes were registered, meaning ballots for which no presidential vote was counted, either because no presidential candidate was selected, or more than one was selected. This was more than three times the rate of any other

Document 5.6—Continued

precinct in the county. Because these were electronic voting machines, there are no ballots to examine. Similarly, no independent examination of these voting machines has ever been conducted. This finding is our only indication of how many Kerry votes were lost on the machines in question. Forty-four votes lost in Youngstown 5G, and 25 machines on which 44 votes each "hopped" from Kerry to Bush, would result in a net loss of about 2,250 votes for Kerry.

VOTE COUNT FRAUD SUBTOTAL   52,810 votes

MOST CONSERVATIVE ESTIMATE OF TOTAL 2004 VOTES TAKEN FROM JOHN KERRY IN OHIO   127,004 votes

CERTIFIED MARGIN BY WHICH GEORGE BUSH WON OHIO   118,775 votes

Author's note: The above calculations are very conservative and do not include other likely Kerry votes that we could not fully investigate or verify, including higher estimates by other respected academics, reporters, authors, and litigators.

Chief among these are the Kerry votes attributed to vote shifting. Cliff Arnebeck, one of the four attorneys to file the 2004 presidential election challenge at the Ohio Supreme Court, who has continued to investigate the vote count, believes the number of votes we attribute to vote switching is understated possibly by a factor of two. He writes, "Phillips' numbers were extraordinarily conservative in bringing Kerry's vote to equal that of Ellen Connally in the suspect counties where she reportedly received more votes than Kerry. To reflect the probabilities of the situation, the Kerry/Bush numbers should be adjusted to reflect the normal ratio of presidential votes to down-ticket races." Indeed, the final Phillips analysis in this book (from July 2006) looks at the high end of the 12 counties where Connally outpolled Kerry, concluding that as many as 60,000 votes could have been shifted – creating a 120,000-vote margin for the president. Ron Baiman, a Ph.D. economist statistician at the University of Illinois Chicago and a co-founder of US Count Votes, believes 75,000–82,000 Kerry votes were lost to vote shifting – creating an even larger margin for Bush - and has been presenting his analysis in speaking engagements during 2006.

Others, such as Norm Robbins, a neurosciences professor at Case Western Reserve University and member of the Greater Cleveland Voter Registration Coalition, have investigated the 2004 election and found statistics that we were not aware of while writing most of this book. For instance, the GCVRC's survey of provisional ballots in 18 counties (representing 60 percent of those 2004 ballots) found 10,500 provisional ballots that were rejected for being cast in the wrong precinct (right location; wrong table). Our above analysis evaluates only 2,300 of those ballots, in Cuyahoga and Hamilton Counties. Until Blackwell changed the rules for validating these ballots in the summer of 2004, they would have been accepted as valid anywhere in their county.

Other big areas of inquiry that we were not able to explore involve the record high vote totals in the rural Republican-majority counties. Our analysis of the certified results indicated vote shifting that could not be explained other than by vote count fraud (the "Connally anomaly" and votes for Bush and for gay marriage.) However, because the actual ballots and poll records were not made available until spring 2006 – and in many counties will not be made public before the 2004 ballots can be destroyed on Sept. 2, 2006 – we could not investigate fraudulent registrations and other components of ballot-box stuffing, whether on paper or electronically. Similarly, because the 2004 election challenge suit was withdrawn, no technician for any voting machine company could be cross-examined under oath to determine how they might have adjusted central vote-count tabulators to alter the reported vote count.

Other probable lost Kerry votes that are difficult to quantify and thus are not in our estimates include: the voting pattern among thousands of ex-felons who were permitted to vote in Ohio but were targeted by GOP disenfranchisement tactics, as well as the thousands of unprocessed 2004 voter registrations (particularly in Cuyahoga and Lucas Counties) that were not entered into BOE databases before the cut-off date one month before the fall election.

Document 5.7